DEMENTED PARTICULARS

The Annotated *Murphy*

C. J. Ackerley

T0386230

Edinburgh University Press

© C. J. Ackerley, 2004, 2010

First published by the Journal of Beckett Studies Books, 2004.

Edinburgh University Press Ltd
22 George Square, Edinburgh

www.euppublishing.com

Book design by Dustin Anderson and Jack Clifford

A CIP record for this book is available from the British Library

ISBN 978 0 7486 4150 5 (paperback)

The right of C. J. Ackerley
to be identified as author of this work
has been asserted in accordance with
the Copyright, Designs and Patents Act 1988.

Printed and bound in Great Britain by
CPI Antony Rowe, Chippenham and Eastbourne

For Katja

and for
Ian Jamieson,
Scholar and Gentleman

"But all things excellent are as difficult as they are rare."
—Spinoza, *Ethica* [V.xlii, Note]

"The danger is in the neatness of identifications."
—Beckett, *Exagmination* [3]

The sheep in Hyde Park

The sheep were a miserable-looking lot, dingy, close-cropped, undersized, and misshapen. They were not cropping, they were not ruminating, they did not even seem to be taking their ease. They simply stood, in an attitude of profound dejection, their heads bowed, swaying slightly as though dazed. Murphy had never seen stranger sheep, they seemed one and all on the point of collapse. They made the exposition of Wordsworth's lovely "fields of sleep" as a compositor's error for "fields of sheep" seem no longer a jibe at that most excellent man.

— *Murphy* pp. 99-100

Table of Contents

Acknowledgements

This work has tapped many sources, and I thank the many individuals who made it possible. Above all, Stan Gontarski, without whose generosity it could not have seen the light of day: I owe him much. Next, John Pilling, who welcomed me to Reading, let me consult the manuscript of *Beckett before Godot*, and shared his knowledge of esoteric references (*A Trip to Scarborough*) and bad jokes (the Gestalt zebra), but whose advice to cut back on the latter I did not always follow. In Reading, the staff at the Beckett International Foundation were courteous and helpful; my thanks to Mike Bott, Julian Garforth, Mary Bryden, Brian Ryder, and Frances Miller. And, as ever, to Jim and Elizabeth Knowlson for their hospitality, and many significant details.

I rely heavily on archival material, and I thank the BIF for permission to cite the *Whoroscope* and Dream Notebooks, the German diaries, 'Lightning Calculation,' Leslie Daiken's course notes, Beckett's copy of Proust, and other items. To the Board of Trinity College Dublin and Bernard Meehan, Keeper of Manuscripts, my thanks for permission to cite the MacGreevy correspondence and notes of Rachel Dobbin; also to Canon Dobbin for the latter. I am grateful to Cathy Henderson and the Harry Ransom Humanities Research Center, Austin, for access to the *Murphy* typescript and Beckett's letters to Mary Manning Howe and George Reavey. Above all, my gratitude to Edward Beckett for his gracious permission to let me use these unpublished materials.

The commentary celebrates small esoteric details as much as the big ones. My thanks to: Mrs J. Adams, Ranger's Lodge, Hyde Park; Pat Allderidge, Archivist at the Bethlem Royal Hospital; Brian Boydell, retired Professor of Music at Trinity; John Gibson, of the *Irish Times*; Barry McGovern, Dublin; Bridie and John Blackburn, Tipperary; Joy Braun, Reading; Judith Curthous of Christ Church, Oxford; Richard Gravil at Plymouth; Julie Campbell at Southampton; Phil Baker before the Harpy Tomb in the British Museum; Tom Ridgeway, Manager at Battersea Park (the sub-tropical garden and owls); Mairi Turner, personel officer at Pentonville Prison; Pat McCarthy, Miami; Anthony and Jean Byrne in Washington; Rick Asals and Sarah Winters in Toronto; Mary Ann Fieldes and Paul Tiessen in Waterloo; Robin Ramsey, Vancouver; Monsieur Louis Soccola, Adjoint au Maire, Ville de Toulon, for his magnificent letter with details of Puget's caryatids [239]; Louise Towersley, Rio de Janeiro, for her company in Reading and Brazil. I owe particular thanks to Vada Hart of the Islington Library Services for taking a personal interest in the project, for helping me locate establishments on Brewery Road and Gray's Inn Road, and for a wonderful photograph of the tripe shop, so near and dear to Murphy [73]. There were many others, some whose names I never knew, such as the Molloy-like figure in the Market Road gardens who told me of the little shelter in which many of his happiest hours had obviously been spent.

Closer to home, the debts mount. My thanks to the University of Otago for granting me leave; to its Library for holding the exact editions I needed (many dusted off for the first time in decades); and to my colleagues for covering my tracks: Jocelyn Harris for her support; Nick Reid for critiquing chapter 6; Shef Rogers for help with the computer; John Dolan for random insights; and Clare Beach for reading the typescript, checking my translations into American. Irene Sutton kept smiling as she xeroxed countless pages; Chris Ehrhardt rendered my translation of Geulincx less barbarous; Alan Musgrave elucidated Barbara, Baccardi and Baroko, and even Bramantip. The last rites, preparation of the camera copy, were presided over by Peter Scott in Dunedin and Roxane Fletcher in Tallahassee; my thanks to both for the quality of the final production. I have only one regret: that this tribute to a European tradition, literary, classical and philosophical, of which Beckett is perhaps the supreme 20th century embodiment, should have been written in an academic climate where those values are being genustuprated [#86.4] by the Ticklepennies of our times.

Finally, special thanks to John Pilling and the BIF for the chess-playing chimps. Beckett found the remarkable illustrations in the *Daily Sketch* of July 1, 1936, and sent them to his agent, George Reavey, who had no intention of doing anything with them until a contract was signed, the pictures being proof of the author's lack of seriousness. They were not even shown to Routledge, and Beckett commented sadly that he would pass the rest of his life "regretting the monkeys" [Bair, 244]. Beckett's original clipping has been used and its inclusion has given this author such pleasure that pleasure is not the word.

Prefatory Statement

Demented Particulars was first published by Journal of Beckett Studies Books in 1998, with a revised and augmented edition in 2004, which incorporated material (e.g., Beckett's notes from Windelband and on Arnold Geulincx) not earlier available (the *Murphy* notebooks, however, are still locked away). Since 2004, other items have appeared, including Matthew Feldman's *Beckett's Books* (Continuum, 2006) and volume 1 of Beckett's *Letters 1929–1940*, ed. Martha Fehsenfeld and Lois Overbeck (2009), which cover the period of *Murphy*'s composition and thus offer small insights into the process of composition and /or publication not previously available. J. C. C. Mays has edited *Murphy* for Faber and Faber (2009), with an excellent Preface that offers a few details I had neglected to observe; and Laura Lindgren has done likewise for the Grove Press Centenary Edition (2006). These excellent editions have eliminated the few previous textual problems, but the odd surprise may still arise: a letter to Barbara Bray reveals that Black's move 42 in the chess game, . . . K – K2, was changed by John Calder to . . . K – Q2 (an illegal move, into check) at Beckett's suggestion, which confirms my prejudice that authors, unlike annotators, should not rewrite their texts.

Chris Ackerley, February 2010

Preface to the Second Edition

I am grateful, as ever, to Stan Gontarski for the chance to offer a second and revised edition of *Demented Particulars,* and to Stan and Marsha, once again, for their hospitality. My thanks, too, to Paul Shields and Dustin Anderson for their hospitality during my visits to Tallahassee; to Scott Kopel for his assistance with my computer; to Pat and Yolande McCarthy for their further generosity; and to Jack Clifford for setting the final revised text. This study reflects a growing awareness among Beckett's scholars of his "grafting techniques" and of the way that his early reading underlies the later works. The revisions have benefited from the work Stan and I did for the *Grove Press Companion*, and from the availability of John Pilling's edition of the Dream Notebook, which I had consulted but rather hurriedly. I also have read Windelband's remarkable *History of Philosophy*, whence so many of Beckett's ideas and their expression were taken, often verbatim. I have made a number of corrections, of fact and expression, added the odd note here and there, and toned down a few overly-enthusiastic comments. Because I wished to retain the original numbering where possible, partly for scholarly continuity but (more honestly) to avoid redoing the Index, this has meant the occasional oddity such as #94.2a. I have tried to be more orthodox in punctuation and formatting, but have retained square brackets for editorial insertions, cross-references and citations, and cheerfully violated the sacred principles of inclusive punctuation when logic or sense seemed threatened. The Bibliography is slightly expanded, and the Index rather more extensive, but, I hope, more accurate. The overall length is about the same as I have taken the opportunity (honed by having to trim the Grove *Companion* from 1100 pages to about 720, without losing the essentials) to rephrase some sentiments more simply. Finally, I am grateful to have the opportunity of revisiting the unfunniest joke in the previous edition, #275.2, the "infinite jest of one of my ex-students, who thought Murphy was cremated." A bit like Celia and the stout porter, you might think, unamused, but an overly-enthusiastic editorial assistant had "corrected" my original "cremoted" (*Cremota* being, in New Zealand, a world-famous brand of porridge). As Winnie says in *Happy Days*, how better can one magnify the Almighty than by sniggering with him at his little jokes, especially the poorer ones? Hapless as it might be, this was my small tribute to a novel that still, after many years of dementia, leaves me overcome by its toxins.

Chris Ackerley,
April 2004

Preface

Reading Beckett's Reading: The *Demented Particulars*

That much of Samuel Beckett's early writing is intimately, even inextricably, tied to his reading is one of the primary developments of current Beckett scholarship. Much of the direct evidence for such connection emerged only after Beckett's death in 1989 with the discovery of documents whose existence was previously unknown: notebooks and chapbooks from the early years, particularly the German diaries of 1936-37 and what is generally called the *Whoroscope* Notebook (or, as John Pilling prefers, the *Murphy* Notebook) of the same period, for example. As James Knowlson explains in his 1996 biography of Beckett, the more we know about Beckett's reading, matter and method, the more fully we understand his creativity, much of which develops through what Knowlson calls a "grafting technique," and, moreover, the more direct resemblance we find to methods of composition employed by Beckett's fellow Dubliner, James Joyce:

> Certain parallels between Beckett's early methods and those of Joyce are fairly obvious. Joyce took particular care with his research, reading books primarily for what they could offer him for his own writing. (Indeed many people who knew him, including Beckett, have claimed he read almost exclusively for this purpose.) Though he was inspired more by disinterested intellectual and scholarly curiosity than Joyce was, Beckett's notebooks show that he too plundered the books he was reading or studying for material that he would then incorporate into his own writing. Beckett copied out striking, memorable or witty sentences or phrases into his notebooks. Such quotations or near quotations were then woven into the dense fabric of his early prose. It is what could be called a grafting technique, and at times it almost runs wild. He even checked off the quotations in his private notebooks once they had been incorporated into his own work. This technique was not specifically adopted by Joyce, but it was very Joycean in its ambition and its impulse. (109)

We have known for some time how heavily Joyce relied on *The Spiritual Exercises* of Saint Ignatius Loyola for the structure of Chapter III, the retreat at Belvedere, of *A Portrait of the Artist as a Young Man*. James R. Thrane has further demonstrated the scope of Joyce's use of a 1688 text by an Italian Jesuit, Giovanni Pietro Pinamonti, *Hell Opened to Christians, To Caution Them from Entering into It* (English translation, Dublin, 1868) in that same chapter of *Portrait*. James S. Atherton has demonstrated in the notes to his 1964 edition of *A Portrait of the Artist as a Young Man* that all of Stephen Dedalus's quotations from John Henry Newman derive from a single source, *Characteristics from the Writings of John Henry Newman* (London, 1875). Atherton also discovered Joyce's principal sources for the 'Oxen in the Sun' chapter of *Ulysses*: Saintsbury's *History of English Prose Rhythm* (1912) and Peacock's *English Prose: Mandeville to Ruskin* (1903).

In Beckett's case, whole passages of his aborted novel of 1932 (published only in 1992), *Dream of Fair to middling Women*, came directly from St. Augustine's *Confessions*. Belacqua Shua, for instance, describes the Smeraldina-Rima: "She is, she exists in one and the same way, she is every way like her herself, in no way can she be injured or changed, she is not subject to time, she cannot at one time be other than at another" (*Dream* 41). James Knowlson informs us that, "These are the *precise words* that St. Augustine used to define true Being" (112, emphasis added). It should come as little surprise then, as critics are slowly discovering, that most of *Dream* may indeed be quotation or allusion of one sort or another, what today we might call pastiche. Similarly, Beckett read Thomas Dekker's *Old Fortunatus* "just before he wrote *Murphy*" (Knowlson, 198), and he copied into the *Whoroscope* Notebook the dilemma of Agripyne which would become the pattern of Neary's yearnings for Miss Counihan and Miss Dwyer, "Whether more torment to love a lady & never enjoy her, or always to enjoy a lady you cannot choose but hate."

Scholars had begun to connect Beckett's reading and his creative methods before the details in the diaries and chapbooks were available. As early as his first separately published work, the longish poem, *Whoroscope* (1930), Beckett had set the pattern of relying heavily on standard texts and reference books. The received wisdom about *Whoroscope* was that Beckett's primary source was Adrien Baillet's *La Vie de Monsieur Des-Cartes* (1691), which Beckett acknowledged having read just before composing the poem. But Francis Doherty has discovered a more immediate source. As he convincingly demonstrates in his essay 'Mahaffy's *Whoroscope*,' "Some of the footnotes Beckett gave to the poem seem to be drawn, often verbatim," from J. P. Mahaffy's *Descartes* (1880), "and some of the poem's text could well have been generated from the same source" (*Journal of Beckett Studies*, n.s. 2.1 [autumn 1992]: 28). Mahaffy was not only a more current and shorter source for Beckett (Baillet's is a two volume work), but he was a member of the Trinity College teaching faculty. Doherty's detailed reading of *Whoroscope* demonstrates that Beckett's direct and heavy debt to Mahaffy is incontestable. In C. J. Ackerley's words, "the *Whoroscope* poem, as impressive and witty as it is, makes on-going, flagrant use of Mahaffy's short life of Descartes and almost everything in it can be found there."

The essay that follows Doherty's in the same issue of the *Journal of Beckett Studies* is J. D. O'Hara's "Freud and the Narrative of 'Moran'" (47-63), in which O'Hara demonstrated that Beckett's method of relying heavily on sources was not restricted to his earliest work but carried over into what is generally considered his most important novel, the diptych, *Molloy*. The O'Hara essay on "Moran" was actually the second part of his study of *Molloy*. The first half, "Jung and the Narratives of 'Molloy,'" appeared a decade earlier in the *Journal of Beckett Studies*, 7 (spring 1982): 19-47, and then in a revised and expanded form as "Jung and the 'Molloy' Narrative" in *The Beckett Studies Reader* (1993, 129-145). These essays, however, were merely an aperçu for O'Hara's *summa, Samuel Beckett's Hidden Drives: Structural Uses of Depth Psychology* (1997). As comprehensive a study of Samuel Beckett's use of source material for *Molloy* as exists in print, *Hidden Drives* focuses particularly on works of Freud and Jung (and their predecessor Schopenhauer), which Beckett used extensively as what O'Hara calls "scaffolding" or "structures of thought that uphold Beckett's literary works." What O'Hara details in his parallel readings is something like Beckett's own "discourse on method," intensely through *Molloy*, and then sporadically to the mid-1950s in the short story, *From an Abandoned Work* (1954-55) and the play *All that Fall* (1957).

With confirmation from the chapbook of the 1930s, John Pilling finds (in the lead essay of the critical anthology he edited with Mary Bryden, *The Ideal Core of the Onion: Reading Beckett Archive*) traces of Beckett's composite compositional technique as late as the 1981 novel *Company*:

> The *Murphy* notebook was obviously plundered intermittently, or served as *aide-mémoire*, in such diverse cases as the *nouvelle Premier amour* (the paradoxical two-line epitaph), *Waiting for Godot* ("neither despair nor presume," which Beckett was later to attribute to St. Augustine), the radio play *All that Fall* (whose hinny is revealed here as prompted by reading a passage of Darwin's *Origin of Species*) and—perhaps most remarkable of all—the late

fiction *Company*, the Aspirate Aitch section of which was half adumbrated more than forty years earlier by the use of the letter H to designate the persona of the horoscope section of the notebook. (6)

To this developing pattern of impressive scholarship we now add Chris Ackerley's *Demented Particulars*, which details the "unacknowledged references," Beckett's graftings, in *Murphy* to an unprecedented degree. The range of allusion, quotation, "distant echo and semi-allusion" Ackerley discovers and discusses in *Murphy* defies summary here. Very clearly the annotations speak for themselves. Their very pervasiveness is testimony not only to Ackerley's scholarly diligence and acumen but also to Beckett's determination to situate his work firmly within the complexities of European intellectual discourse.

As Ackerley demonstrates, such "grafting technique . . . almost runs wild" in *Murphy*, a novel whose technique, we now discover, comes close to what today we might call assemblage, but these methodological discoveries have left more than one critic uneasy about their implications for Beckett's "originality." Knowlson for one raises the specter (only to dismisse it) of plagiarism: "It is not that he plagiarizes; he makes no attempt to hide what he is doing. Anyone familiar with Augustine's book would recognize the passages involved" (112). Ackerley too is sensitive to the issue and argues that Beckett's method is "not so much plagiarism as part of a private dialogue." In fact, we might go further to declare that Beckett's technique is the very opposite of plagiary, the intent of which is to conceal and deceive. On the contrary, Beckett's renderings are played against his sources, the recognition of which is imperative to the full effect of the prose. In the 1930s when Beckett was inventing the technique, as he was inventing himself as a novelist, the critical vocabulary integral to its exegesis was yet to be developed. It would take another generation before Roland Barthes and Jacques Derrida would reconstitute Dada and Surrealist theory to begin celebrating such intertextuality. Beckett's splicing his reading onto his own stock of prose produces patterns of utterances which Gilles Deleuze would call rhizomatic or a technique Fredric Jameson might call pastiche. That is, these early works are finally assemblages, intertextual layerings, palimpsests, the effect of which is to produce (if not reproduce) multiplicity of meanings in a manner that will come to be thought in the second half of the century as Postmodern. Beckett may have dismissed the neo-Dadaist "cut-up" techniques of William Burroughs and Brian Gysin in the 1950s as not writing but plumbing, but Beckett himself may have begun artistic life as a plumber. What Beckett rejected in both Surrealist and post-Surrealist technique like that of Burroughs and Gysin is the overtness and exaltation of the method and the reduction if not the destruction of the agency of author. What Beckett missed in both Surrealist methods and the Burroughs/Gysin process was cerebration. Beckett remained too much the Modernist to abandon authorship (and its ally humanism) entirely, although he dabbled in near-automatic writing himself with the short prose piece called 'Lessness.'

Beckett's own development of pastiche was, then, less Postmodernist than Modernist, less a means of destroying the hierarchy of culture, erasing the distinctions between high and low art as it would develop later in the century (as it does in the Pop Art of Andy Warhol, say), nor was it an attempt to obliterate style, that mark of coherent and discrete individuality, as was much Surrealist technique. Postmodern pastiche would suggest that the only style possible in contemporary culture is travesty or mimicry of past styles—quite the opposite of what Beckett was developing. Intertext or assemblage or pastiche allowed Beckett to develop his distinct early style, even as its rejection, particularly through his three great French novels of the Post-World War II period, made possible Beckett's late style, a minimalism whose complexity resides in the rigor with which complexity is eschewed. Ackerley's reading Beckett's reading allows us to watch Beckett developing techniques which would become emblematic of Postmodernism, while Beckett himself remained within the liminal space of Modernism, a space of illimitable transition, transformation and multiplicity, yet subject to the agency of authorship. What Ackerley's *Demented Particulars* makes clear is that *Murphy* may be the peak of that grafting technique through which Beckett discovered his own authorial voice, and as such these "demented particulars" will form the starting point of all *Murphy* and much Beckett scholarship well into the twenty-first century.

S. E. Gontarski

Introduction

a. *In which the Reader is Introduced to the Text.*

> "Why the ————," said Neary, "is light given to a man whose way is hid?"
> "Pardon," said Cathleen.
>
> —*Murphy* [46].

Samuel Beckett's *Murphy* is a vast, rollicking *jeu d'esprit* in the tradition that runs from Cervantes and Rabelais through Burton and Fielding to *Ulysses*, and it maintains itself proudly in that company. Yet it has never received the attention it deserves. For all its mere 282 pages (158 in the Calder edition), it has an intricacy which justifies its place among these giants of philosophical comedy, and cries out for the kind of close scrutiny that has not yet been made of it. There are two book-length studies of *Murphy*, both distressingly poor, and general accounts of the fiction have paid too little attention to the particulars, demented and otherwise, that for Beckett constitute the only possible straws of understanding, philosophical or fictional. The *esse* of the book, a gigantic joke made up of an infinitude of tiny ones, has been sometimes acknowledged, but the tiny jokes too rarely perceived. To use Beckett's term, words constitute "phrase-bombs," verbal and philosophical land-mines laid all through the text; and if these have not exploded it is because readers have moved too lightly.

These readings offer many new insights, some trivial but others profound. Scrutiny of the texts that Beckett read leads to a reconsideration of the use made of them, and thus of his mode of working. Particularity should not mean narrowing of vision. *Murphy* matters, not just because of its own recondite merits (I must reject Cronin's dismissal of it as an apprentice piece), but because it represents the fullest achievement of the first decade of Beckett's writing (1926-36). It draws on the intense cerebration of those years yet avoids the manifest flaws and arrogance of other early works. *Murphy* is a culmination of one stage in Beckett's career, but equally the beginning of another, the matrix in which many later works were formed: the first text he did not consistently reject, and to which he returned in his later writings. After *Murphy*, he moved from the Joycean manner toward the sparer style of the later fiction and drama; yet while the rejection of allusive compression and the decision to write in French led to a different mode of expression many of the later concerns (word, theme and detail) are implicit in the earlier novel. The glosses will point these out, thereby defining *Murphy* not simply as an isolated freak (which in a way it is) but relating it to Beckett's later and greater achievement. The annotations open out the range of intricate particulars that went into its making, the quips and quibbles, allusions and curiosities, rags, tags, jests and profundities which frustrate and enhance the pleasures of the way, be it a journey of discovery or a wandering to find home. *Murphy* is a rare delight, but not infrequently a difficult one; a *vade mecum* that responds to it both in earnest and in jest may prove tolerable company.

b. *The Critical Debate.*

> I feel that the only line is to refuse to be involved in exegesis of any kind. And to insist on the extreme simplicity of dramatic situation and issue. If that's not enough for them, and it obviously isn't, it's enough for us, and we have no elucidations to offer of mysteries that are all of their own making. My work is a matter of fundamental sounds (no joke intended) made as fully as possible, and I accept responsibility for nothing else. If people want to have headaches among the overtones, let them. And provide their own aspirin.
>
> —Samuel Beckett to Alan Schneider.

Murphy had a difficult birth, and the critical rattle has not entirely made amends. Early reviews were few and mostly uncomprehending, but Kate O'Brien saw it as "magnificent and a treasure" [see #195.4], and Dylan Thomas appreciated its quirkiness. Sir Herbert Read praised its "rare and right combination of learning and license," but as Knowlson says [217], his perception has been almost totally ignored ever since. Not until the reissue by Grove Press in 1957 was there a stirring of interest, largely in the USA and led by Hugh Kenner (1961) and Ruby Cohn (1962), who accentuated the Cartesian and comic elements. They had been anticipated in 1959 by Samuel Mintz, whose view of the action as a "Cartesian catastrophe" (Hesla's later phrase, 36) brought to light its Occasionalist qualities, and, in what is still a relevant study, set a trend to see the novel in terms of its dualist component. The culmination of this tendency was Edouard Morot-Sir's excellent 'Samuel Beckett and Cartesian Emblems' (1975).

Several general surveys of Beckett's fiction appeared over the next two decades, most seeing *Murphy* as a point of departure for the later works. These include books by Federman, Fletcher, Coe, Robinson, Webb, and Pilling. A good introduction is Doherty (1971), and the best critical study Hesla (1976), whose shaping of the chaos has not been bettered. Harvey's invaluable study of the poetry curiously ignores *Murphy*. Elsewhere, a preoccupation with the drama led to a discounting of the fiction as prelude to it. *Murphy* received little individual attention until 1968 when Robert Harrison's poor monograph appeared, followed in 1971 by Sighle Kennedy's unfortunate study, which, for all its isolated insights (she was the first to recognize the use of Whitaker) lacks an ironic perspective (as is evidenced by her publishing Beckett's polite note, in which he is quite obviously telling her that she has lost the plot).

A new era in Beckett studies began with the publication in 1978 of Deirdre Bair's biography, which, for all its dreadful errors, set Beckett's work in the context of his life and drew attention to early pieces. Several good studies appeared about this time, the *Journal of Beckett Studies* leading the way: Jim Acheson's articles on Murphy's metaphysics (1978 and 1979; his 1997 book adds little to these); John Pilling's 'Beckett's Proust' (1976); Nicholas Zurbrugg's *Beckett and Proust* (1984); three excellent studies by J. C. C. Mays, identifying the Dublin background and personalities; Mooney's 'Pre-Socratic Skepticism' (1982); Sylvie Henning's 'The Guffaw of the Abderite' (1985) and her *Critical Complicity* (1988). Rubin Rabinovitz's best work is in *The Development of Samuel Beckett's Fiction* (1984), where he draws attention to Beckett's extensive use of echoes and parallels. His *KWIC Concordance*, edited with Michèle Barale (1990), is useful in this respect, but his later book (1992) is a disappointment. There are some nice idiosyncratic touches from those who knew Beckett, such as Vivien Mercier, Ludovic Janvier, and Con Leventhal, published in various memoirs and festschrifts. And in a class of its own is Eoin O'Brien's *The Beckett Country* (1986).

More recently, there have been new approaches to Beckett's early work. These include the expected rash of feminist and theoretical studies, but even the best have not coped well with *Murphy*. Attempts to reclaim Beckett for the Irish, from Harrington to Cronin, have proved unconvincing. Farrow's study (1991) is thin, but the publication of *Dream* in 1992 activated interest in the earlier work. Rabaté's *The Ghosts of Modernity* and O'Hara's *Hidden Drives* draw attention, each in its inimitable way, to Beckett's knowledge of psychology. We choose our predecessors, Borges noted, and this commentary would acknowledge, in addition to the best of the above, a trend beginning with Terence McQueeny's unpublished dissertation (1977), and moving through practitioners of the particular to James Knowlson's biography and John Pilling's *Beckett before Godot*, the emphasis being upon that element in Beckett's fiction which is at last being recognised, its roots in his reading and the close relationship to the European and Classical traditions, literary and philosophical, upon which it draws.

c. *History and Composition of the Text.*

> I hold fit to lay down this general Maxim. Whatever Reader desires to have a thorow Comprehension of an Author's Thoughts, cannot take a better Method, than by putting himself into the Circumstances and Postures of Life, that the Writer was in, upon every important Passage as it flow'd from his Pen; for this will introduce a Parity and strict Correspondence of Ideas between the Reader and the Author.
>
> —Swift, Preface to *A Tale of a Tub*, 44.

The aetiology of *Murphy* must remain obscure, yet some things can be documented. Beckett lived in London for six weeks (July-August 1932), at 4 Ampton Street, just off Gray's Inn Road, reading eclectically and walking the streets, and, as the McGreevy correspondence shows, details from this period would enter the novel. However, *Murphy* draws more directly on his sojourn there from Christmas 1933 to late 1935, when he was undergoing an intensive course of psychotherapy at the Tavistock Centre, scraping a living with occasional reviews and half-heartedly looking for work. He had not recovered from the shock of his father's death; his health was poor; he had little money; and his decision to abandon the academic life was only dubiously validated by the wretched sales of *More Pricks than Kicks* and the difficulties with his collected poems (*Echo's Bones and other Precipitates* had been accepted but the limited edition did not emerge until December 1935, and then to gloomy silence).

Beckett took a furnished room at 48 Paulton's Square, close to McGreevy at Cheyne Walk Gardens, and the two spent much time walking, talking, visiting galleries and concerts, and reading. Beckett underwent therapy and read about the psychoanalytic process; a visit home in August 1934 confirmed the need to continue, much as he disliked certain aspects of London. This time, in early September, he took a room with the Frost family at 34 Gertrude Street, where he would remain for fifteen months. At some point thereafter, I assume, *Murphy* was conceived, and quickened in the *Whoroscope* Notebook. The precise date and sequence is impossible to determine: Bair's assumption [196] that the novel had begun by September 1934, and that Beckett had 1600 words written when he returned to Ireland, is based on her mis-dating the McGreevy letters and painfully prolongs the maieutic process; equally, some of Beckett's notes and 'Lightning Calculation' must pre-date actual composition, and testify to an intention formed but not yet worked out in detail. Knowlson notes, for instance [744], that Beckett toured the wards of Bedlam on September 23, 1935; details immediately entered the notebook, but took their place among others that had been there for some time.

Knowlson records [203, 743] that a holograph manuscript entitled 'Sasha Murphy' was begun on August 20, 1935, and written over the next ten months into six notebooks (five red, one blue), some 800 pages in all; it remains in private hands and is not available for consultation. Not seeing it has restricted this commentary. However, the fossil record of the *Whoroscope* Notebook, on one side, and the Austin typescript on the other, makes possible some assumptions about what lies between. Knowlson says the manuscript differs radically from the finished text at many points, but my guess is that it would not vary *significantly* from the typescript, save in length, Beckett's final revisions (June 9-27, 1936, according to the McGreevy letters) being a condensation rather than a rewriting; but that some other elements, perhaps a Volpone-like sub-plot (the peregrinations of Neary's first wife) would have been present, and, perhaps, more clues as to the derivation of the detail. Time may tell.

The best source of information is Beckett's correspondence with Thomas McGreevy. The letters of 1930 to 1936 reveal a private world shown to nobody else, much of which went into *Murphy*. They give valuable indications of Beckett's reading, but the first mention of the novel (unnamed) is on September 8, 1935, where he confesses to have been working "at some other stuff I fear involuntairement trivial." He tells of watching in Kensington Gardens the old men with their kites, and of his resolution that this should be the final image [see #25.1]. The same letter reports the seizure of the "old boy" in the house opposite [see #69.2]. Two weeks later (undated), Beckett complains that he has to force himself to keep at the book, but that he has done "about 9000 words" of "poor stuff" in which he has little interest. He confirms that the book "closes with an old man flying his kite," as if to suggest an ending done. On October 8 he notes that the book "goes very slowly," but he has no doubt it will be finished, and that he has done about 20,000 words (Pilling estimates the published version at some 80,000 words). Silence ensues until January 9, 1936 [misdated as "9/1/35"], Beckett in Dublin and McGreevy in London, when he names it *Murphy* and talks of the need to "penetrate more deeply" by going in search of Geulincx at TCD; a week later ["16/1/36"] he states that he can suddenly see *Murphy* as a breakdown between Geulincx's *ubi nihil vales* [see #178.9] and Malraux's *Il est difficile* [see #156.1]. He says that he has done "next to no work" on *Murphy*, but by February 6 reports that "There only remain three chapters of mechanical writing," which he lacks the courage to begin. On March 6 he complains that "*Murphy* will not budge," and on March 25 that it "goes from bad to worse." He tells of a trip with his brother Frank to Lough Corrib, a vision of which he gives to Neary [see #267.4]. On May 7, he reports being busy with *Murphy*, "which gets near to its first end, at least, at last, thanks be to God"; and on June 6 he writes: "I have finished *Murphy*, meaning I have put down last words of first version. Now I have to go through it again. It reads something horrid. One should have a continuity-girl..." The revision was quick, for on June 27 he writes: "*Murphy* is finished & I shall send off three copies on Monday . . . I could do more work on it but do not intend to . . . it has been hard work the past month & I am very tired, of it & words generally."

McGreevy obviously read one copy quickly, for on July 7 Beckett expressed his relief: "I find the people so hateful myself, even Celia, that to have you find them lovable surprises and delights me." McGreevy must have had reservations about chapter 12, for Beckett justifies, politely but firmly, his decision to allow so much to follow Murphy's end, and eloquently defends the post-mortem burlesque [see #259.2]. There would be minor changes to the typescript, a few more raisins in the pudding to enrich the texture [see, for instance, #24.3], and other points emerged eventuated as a consequence of his 1936-37 visit to Germany [Leibniz's garret, #162.1, and the Pergamene Barlach, #239.1], but these were few. The text was finished; the battle had just begun.

Beckett's efforts to publish *Murphy* are the stuff of tragic farce. Bair is in error about the dates of submission and rejection (the McGreevy letters do not support her attributions), and fantasizes about Beckett spending so much on postage that he was forced to turn to George Reavey as agent [230], but her general account is valid: immediate rejection by Chatto and Windus, his previous publisher, followed quickly by several others, including Heinemann in London and Simon and Schuster in America ("5% appeal"). Houghton Mifflin wanted a new title and cuts to chapter 6, which provoked Beckett's anguished howl [Knowlson, 248]: "Do they not understand that if the book is slightly obscure, it is so because it is a compression, and that to compress it further can only result in making it more obscure?" He refused to touch chapter 6, the horoscope or the game of chess. Beckett's despair grew as the rejections mounted; he was willing to turn to "the Hogarth Private Lunatic Asylum," or (almost) to compromise: "Quigley, Tromhebereschleim, Eliot, or any name the publishers fancy" [Bair, 243]. Dent, Faber, Secker and even Hogarth turned it down; the reader for Hamish Hamilton found it "as obscure as I feared," and felt he couldn't make an offer ("Many thanks all the same").

Yet something was taking its course. After 42 rejections [Bair, 269; this number is improbable], by which time he had moved permanently to Paris, Beckett learned [December 9, 1937] that Routledge had accepted *Murphy* for publication in the spring, with a £25 advance. Knowlson indicates [292] that Jack Yeats had suggested the book to T. M. Ragg, who recommended it with enthusiasm, bypassing Herbert Read, the firm's regular reader, who saw it only after the contract was signed and the proofs made ready. Beckett corrected the proofs from his hospital bed, having been stabbed in the interim by a Parisian pimp (almost a Murphy-like catastrophe).

The novel was published on March 7, 1938. The order form (7/6, postage 6d extra) made curious reading:

> To define some things is to kill them; no less this novel. Its meaning is implicit and symbolic, never concrete. To attempt to extract it would be to damp its spirit . . . But if the theme of the book defies description, not so the writing. The portrayal of scenes is masterly; there is a diversity of simile which could only proceed from a mind well-stocked with many seemingly antagonistic branches of knowledge, and the author possesses an encyclopaedic vocabulary. The style is leavened with a Celtic waywardness which is as attractive as it is elusive and leaves the reader questioning the source of his enjoyment.

Never concrete, indeed. Celtic waywardness, God blast you. Little wonder that the novel did not attract many subscriptions. There were reviews in the most important English publications, and most were positive, if cautious, but with the exception of Kate O'Brien's they did not please Beckett, nor do anything for sales. None appeared in Dublin, saving Austin Clarke's understandably negative opinion in the *Dublin Magazine*. Immediate sales were few, and when Beckett returned to London after the war, it was to find the book out of print, some 750 copies having been sold to an untraced buyer (perhaps destroyed by enemy bombing). There were no waiting royalties, though some came in belatedly [Knowlson, 770].

Before and during the war Beckett with the aid of Alfred Péron worked on a translation of *Murphy* into French (he had given a copy to Raymond Queneau, hoping that Gallimard might take it, but Queneau, curiously, thought the English too arcane). The outcome was an embarrassment, but it would be (excepting one critical essay) Beckett's first published work in French. In October 1946 he accepted a contract for the translation [Knowlson, 362], Routledge having sold the world rights to *Murphy* and options on other books to Bordas; but by June 1948 only a handful of copies had sold, and in 1951, when Jérôme Lindon of Minuit acquired the rights and unsold stock for the price of the paper they were printed on, only 95 out of a run of 3,000 had gone.

All in all, an inauspicious start. Poor sales in England, worse in Ireland, mediocre reviews, a disastrous French translation, and a failure to interest any American publisher. Not until the success of *Waiting for Godot* would there be a retrospective interest in the novel, and had the pimp's knife struck a fraction differently *Murphy* and this commentary might have existed only in an alternative universe.

d. *Beckett's Reading*.

> This figure, owing to the glittering vitrine behind which the canvas cowers, can be only apprehended in sections. Patience, however, and a retentive memory have been known to elicit a total statement approximating to the intention of the painter.
>
> —'Love and Lethe,' 87

It would be an extravagance to list all the books Beckett is known to have read in the years leading up to *Murphy*; indeed, I tried at one point to do so, and, like Neary [55], soon left off, appalled. And it would be an even greater impertinence to imagine that by so doing one might track the maieutic mysteries to their dark zone. No, the aim must be to create an *Image* of that process. For more complete accounts, see my Bibliography (C) and the relevant chapters and footnotes of Knowlson's biography, not the least of its achievements being his detailed accounts of what Beckett was reading, when and where. Relevant details will be noted in the commentary; here, the intention is to sketch a broad picture.

At Trinity, Beckett's passion for words, literature and art developed under the influence of his Professor of French, Thomas Rudmose-Brown, who passed on his deep love of and witty irreverence for the texts he taught [Knowlson, 47-51]. "Ruddy" was unusual in that his courses and affections combined a respect for the canon with a relish for what was happening in the world: a mixture of the traditional (Villon, Rabelais, Ronsard, Racine, Corneille, Molière), the recent (Rimbaud, Baudelaire, Mallarmé, Valéry, Hugo), and the contemporary (Proust, Vielé-Griffin, Fargue, Le Cardonnel, Larbaud, Jammes, Malraux, Gide). This integration of the past and present, long before Beckett had heard of Eliot's 'Tradition and the Individual Talent,' would henceforth characterize his way of reading. The Trinity syllabus was demanding and thorough. The system encouraged wide reading: not just *Andromaque*, but all of Racine; not just the *Drapier Letters*, but all of Swift. Beckett's love of Dante (a third year course) grew under the external guidance of Bianca Esposito, but he absorbed Petrarch, d'Annunzio, Machiavelli, Leopardi, Ariosto . . . . He took courses in English: Shakespeare, Spenser, Donne, Milton, More, Bacon, Pope, and Swift, each of whom would leave a mark on *Murphy*. Like many of his contemporaries, he rejected the Victorians and "the ineluctable gangrene of Romanticism" [*Proust*, 80], excepting always Keats: "that crouching brooding quality" [Knowlson, 117]. And like Joyce before him he reacted against the Twilighters, saving only Yeats (O'Casey and Synge were a separate love). Beckett gained not so much a degree in literature as an opening to the mind of western Europe, with German (Hölderlin, Goethe) and Spanish (Calderón, Cervantes) natural extensions, as were the Greek thinkers, Latin poets and post-Cartesian philosophers he would later study. Trinity was not so much an education as a corner stone of knowledge. Beckett's next ten years would build upon that, the love remaining even as the skeptical distrust of its value grew.

Paris was the crucible in which Beckett's reading turned to writing. He went to the École Normale Supérieure (1928-30) with the intention of working on Jouve and an interest in Jules Romains and Unanimisme. The "composite consciousness" of that movement might seem to have little to attract Beckett, but he liked the way that Romains fixed with an unusual intensity on ordinary details [Pilling, *Beckett before Godot*, 26-28]: *Murphy* could be described as the death of a nobody. In Paris Beckett met McGreevy and Joyce, learned to drink, published his first *essais*, and came back a writer. Several elements contributed to the transition. The École was a stimulating environment, and Beckett loved its fine old library and magnificent books; he cultivated there his life-long habit of working closely with reference books, commentaries and dictionaries. He read widely in Descartes, Bruno, Vico and other writers he knew only superficially. While not close to the Surrealists he could absorb the atmosphere of experiment and become involved in the literary scene with its private presses and little magazines, as well as enjoy theater and galleries: "He was imbibing a heady mixture indeed" [Knowlson, 107].

Beckett began to write his first small pieces and poems, somewhat in the surrealist idiom, his major triumphs being the essay contributed to the *transition* tribute to Joyce (1929) and the award of a £10 prize, plus publication, in a competition run by the Hours Press (1930). Both are indicative of his mode of composition at this time. The *Exagmination* essay is erudite, compelling—and totally derivative. McQueeny has shown its reliance on McIntyre, Croce, de Sanctis, Michelet and Symonds, all of whom were in the École library: "a brilliant mosaic of secondary sources done by a rushed apprentice" [60]. The *Whoroscope* poem, impressive and witty as it is, makes flagrant use of Mahaffy's short life of Descartes, and almost everything in it can be found there. The indebtedness of these first works to unacknowledged writers is not usually admitted, but the method would remain Beckett's *modus operandi* over the next few years, yet, as McQueeny makes clear, with a growing mastery of material and technique. The *Proust* essay of 1931, for example, was based on an intensive reading over the summer of 1930 of *A la recherche* (twice), but also of a number of recent critics: Curtius, Benoist-Méchin and Dandieu in particular, Schopenhauer filtered through the latter. McQueeny shows that the *Proust* essay differs significantly from the earlier one, in that Beckett engages in an implicit dialogue with his sources and himself. His synthesis of Dandieu's *Proust* is less a statement of psychology than of aesthetics and epistemology [107], the doctrines of pessimism increasingly forming part of his own attitude to art [154]. *Murphy* is in direct descent from *Proust* in this respect, its unacknowledged references not so much plagiarisms as parts of a private dialogue.

Joyce was a major force, but Beckett's response to the maestro may be defined as much in terms of resistance as influence. Joyce, Beckett would repeat, made him realize artistic integrity [Bair, 73]. He adopted Joyce's technique of reading for the sake of his own writing, copying out phrases to be grafted into his own writings, ticking them off to show they had been incorporated. The Dream Notebook of the early 1930s quotes liberally (and often obscurely) from Augustine's *Confessions*, Thomas à Kempis's *Imitation* and Burton's *Anatomy*, among others, and the *Whoroscope* Notebook, begun a little later, illustrates the same tendency. *Dream* and the early poems are the works most obviously shaped by this accretive method, but much of *Murphy* originates in phrases culled in this manner (Beckett called such xenia "helps"). His practice differed from Joyce's in that he resisted the universal music of *Finnegans Wake* and cultivated instead a technique of distant echo and semi-allusion, a mode he would make increasingly his own. Borrowings in *Murphy* from Joyce are relatively few, and those from *Ulysses* are mostly from 'Ithaca' and 'Eumaeus,' where style obfuscates certainty. Beckett's stylistic evolution was indeed a reaction against Joyce, but in terms of what became a central theme in *Murphy*, the fundamental unheroic. Knowlson [105] quotes Beckett in 1989, looking back on the relationship: "I do remember speaking about Joyce's heroic achievement. I had a great admiration for him. That's what it was, epic, heroic, what he achieved. But I realised that I couldn't go down that same road." *Murphy*, in time, went its own way.

Beckett's time in Paris was broken by his return to Ireland to take up his teaching post at Trinity. This he found little to his liking ("exhibiting myself"), and after his resignation he returned to Europe (1931-33). The Trinity experience was by no means wasted. His teaching of Racine taught him much about dramatic structure, and would shape the comic novel as yet unconceived. His Rimbaud lectures may not have impressed his students, but they informed his own understanding. A major discovery was Jules Renard [see #208.2]: Beckett was fascinated by the intimacy of the *Journal*, and the total honesty of Renard's scrutiny of himself and his world, but it would be some time before he could realize this quality in his own writing. During this period a number of poems were written, as well as some of the stories that would become *More Pricks than Kicks*. These fed indirectly into *Murphy*: 'Yellow,' based on his operations in 1932 and 1933, is a prototype of the future novel, anticipating the irreverent guffaw of the Abderite with its one appalling joke made up of countless smaller ones (of the early stories, 'Yellow' remained Beckett's favorite). 'Echo's Bones' was turned down after the other stories were accepted by Charles Prentice in 1933, and so was available for reworking. And this was true of the major piece of work done in the years 1932-33, the novel published in 1992 as *Dream of Fair to middling Women*, which was thoroughly cannibalized for *More Pricks than Kicks* and *Murphy*. These years were not good ones for Beckett, with his physical problems (the irrational heart of *Murphy*) very much the product of a morbid obsession in self [Knowlson, 180], but the eclectic reading and accumulation of straws of knowledge that took place formed a necessary apprenticeship for the work to come.

Psychotherapy was an important part of the process during the London years (1933-35). Knowlson has shown [177-78] how widely Beckett read about psychoanalysis, taking detailed notes from Ernest Jones's *Papers on Psycho-analysis* and books by Alfred Adler, Otto Rank, Karin Stephens and Wilhelm Stekel: following these hints I found a number of details used in *Murphy* [for example, #119.2, the origin of Cooper's acasthisia]. Freud was a major force, Beckett's interest centering upon narcissism, neuroses and the psychopathology of daily life rather than the familiar dreams of totems and taboos. He found in these studies, curiously dated as they now seem, confirmation of his own intrauterine attraction and psychosomatic problems, and insights into the fraught relationship with his mother (yet there is only one reference to Murphy's birth, 71, or parents, 251); but he retained a skepticism about their potential. On October 2, 1935 he attended the third Tavistock lecture [Bair, 208, and Knowlson, 176], at which Jung referred to a diagram of the unconscious which became part of the model of Murphy's mind [see #111.3], showed how complexes may appear in visions and speak in voices [see #185.2], and made the comment which Beckett never forgot about the little girl who "had never been born entirely." As well as attending the one lecture, Beckett read the others when they were published later that year. Yet for the writing of *Murphy* he turned to Robert Woodworth's *Contemporary Schools of Psychology* (1931), which he exploited as a "help" [see #80.3], and to Ernst Haeckel's *The Riddle of the Universe* (1900), for the image of the embryonic soul [see #66.1]. Again, this illustrates a tendency to take relatively minor works and use them as consistent points of reference.

Beckett's confidant at this time was Thomas McGreevy, and in a remarkable letter of March 10, 1935 Beckett links his physical symptoms with the feelings of arrogance that had characterized his dealings with others, and would likely have continued to do so were it not for his "old internal combustion heart" [see #3.9]. Knowlson argues [179] that this letter offers the first convincing explanation of how the arrogant, narcissistic young man of the early 1930s could evolve into someone noted later for his extraordinary kindness, courtesy and almost saintly good works. *Murphy* is a crucial text in this transition, and McGreevy's Catholicism contributed to its ethos. Beckett the religious writer is not the contradiction it seems, for his agnosticism always found expression in the images of the Christian faith; his later dismissal of this as a familiar mythology [Duckworth, lvii] is a little too easy. Extensive notes taken from Augustine, close readings of the Bible (Luke his preference), and his curiosity about the theological impasses into which the 17th century rationalists fell all bear witness to his fascination with religious matters. The letters to McGreevy, often signed "God bless," detail such matters as sending his mother H. V. Morton's *In the Steps of the Master* ["10/3/35"], comments on the second lesson at church that evening ["5/5/35"], and his attraction to Geulincx's conviction that the *sub specie aeternitatis* vision is the only excuse for remaining alive ["6/3/36"]. In that letter of March 10 (badly misread by Bair [197]), Beckett responds to McGreevy's recommendation that he should find comfort in Thomas à Kempis's *De Imitatione Christi* by admitting that he had replaced the plenitude which Thomas calls God by a *pleroma* to be sought among his own feathers and entrails, but doubted that the *Imitation* could be twisted into "a programme of self-sufficiency." He admits that it had served only to reinforce his deliberate immersion in self, and that any "Christlike imitative pentimenti" could not redeem a composition invalid from the word go [see #99.5 and #103.3]. I read this not as a rejection of the *Imitation* but as an acknowledgment of its fundamental principle of quietism [the "precious margarita" cited in the Dream Notebook], which might yet receive consolation "from the waste that splutters most when the bath is nearly empty." Beckett is talking about his heart in its physical and metaphorical manifestations, and with skepticism ("If I cod myself with all this, I cod myself & that is all"), but the feeling that emerges from his absorption in the *Imitation* is that of a quiet acceptance of the way mapped out by Thomas à Kempis. That he could not believe in it (*impossibile est*) was no more of a paradox than his feelings for the 17th century artists and philosophers whom he also loved but in whom he could no longer have faith.

Chapter 6 of *Murphy* offers the necessary critique. The novel is premised on Cartesian dualism, but Descartes is less an active presence than a *deus absconditus*; references are to the system rather than specific works. As the chapter moves from Cartesian clarity to Schopenhauer's willlessness, the texts on which it relies are surprisingly few. It begins with Spinoza's *Ethics*; moves to Leibniz's *Monadology*; then makes extensive use of Geulincx's *Ethica*, which Beckett read, in the Latin of the three-volume Land edition, in the Long Room at Trinity during the early months of 1936. Other writers, such as Rousseau, sneak in, but the direction is clear and distinct: Murphy's wish to apperceive himself in the third zone of his mind is a Kantian one, but moderated by the pessimism of Schopenhauer, *The Critique of Pure Reason* as qualified by *The World as Will and Idea* (which Beckett had read in the Haldane translation). The simple outline is complicated, as my notes to the chapter reveal, by similar paradigms created from Greek philosophy, Christian mysticism, depth psychology and post-Newtonian physics [see #107.2]; but the structure of the novel as a whole arises from a distrust of Cartesian rationalism, and its controlling irony from the incommensurabilty of Murphy's declared goal and its realization in a universe which is unclear and indistinct—in a word, absurd.

Beckett found in the Atomists (Leucippus, Democritus, Epicurus and Lucretius) an ironic anticipation of this, and a school at odds with the mainstream of Greek philosophy (Socrates, Plato, and Aristotle), whose affirmation of the immortal soul fueled the tradition of Christian rationalism. His distance from the prevailing mood may be gauged by a meeting of the Trinity College Classical Society of November 13, 1925, as reported in *TCD: A College Miscellany* (xxxii.550 [November 19, 1925], 36-37): Mr. C. F. Doyle's paper on "The Belief in Immortality among the Ancients" traced that belief from the doctrines of Orphism and the Pythagoreans, through the Eleusinian Mysteries (death as "the passage to brighter and better things unknown") and Plato (who "predicates eternity of universal soul and metempsychosis of individual souls"). It met with the approval of all present, the Chairman in putting the vote of thanks adding that "Aristotle was the only philosopher who gives us a systematic account of the soul and its relation to the body." The Atomists were despised and ignored. Lesley Daiken's 1930 notes are indicative of how they were taught at Trinity, in one orthodox lecture, "The School of the Sophists." A definition of *to apeiron* was offered, and related to "infinite" and "indefinite," the better to dismiss it as "An ideology of negative attributes ... Reactionary became Agnostic." Then followed a list of said negatives: Infinitude, Indefinable, Indefinite, Incomprehensible, Inapprehensible, Unattainable, Unknowable; leading to a rejection of any system founded upon the principle of it is not, and concluding, "The exponents of this school are on a low intellectual level." These notes are indicative of a certain dismissive attitude, but Beckett, as one who preferred goats to sheep, found in the Atomists a lasting fascination. His interest was rekindled at the École Normale, enflamed during his London visit of 1932, and as part of the agenda for *Murphy* he read systematically through standard commentaries such as John Burnet's *Early Greek Philosophy* and *Greek Philosphy*, Beare's *Greek Theories of Elementary Cognition*, Bailey's studies of Epicurus, Windelband's *History of Philosophy*, whatever he could find on Democritus, and, probably, Hermann Diels's *Die Fragmente der Vorsokratiker*, the standard authority. The end of *Murphy* is a huge Democritean guffaw, but its insistence on the soul's dissolution is not just an Atomist joke.

Murphy is firmly set in the London of 1935, and even if Beckett had felt there "the way a slug-ridden cabbage might be expected to be," there were compensating moments, such as the little steamers dipping their funnels to get under Tower bridge: "Très émouvant" [letter to McGreevy, August 4, 1932]. The Chelsea embankment, Tyburnia, the street scenes of chapter 5, Hyde Park, and Bethlem Royal Hospital are closely observed; and yet, as Knowlson remarks [116], *Murphy* evolved out of Beckett's reading as much as of his experience of the place. Thus, the Embankment is invested with elements of Dante's *Purgatory* [see #14.7]; Tyburn is inseparable from Magistrate Fielding; Murphy's various addresses are a provocative affront to Joyce's realism [follow the trail from #1.3]; the Park invokes a Pastoral tradition; and the Hospital forms an 18th-century image of Bedlam. London has an air of grubby plausibility, yet so much of the incidental detail arises directly from Whitaker's *Almanac 1935*, Beckett using it to plot the time-space co-ordinates of his novel in much the way that Joyce had used Thom's *Directory 1904* for *Ulysses*.

Early in 1935 Beckett set about reading more widely, with an emphasis on the novel and authors who could improve his technique. Although Knowlson [216] includes Stendhal, Rousseau, Lesage, Balzac, Mann, and Rabelais among those read at this time, Beckett mostly followed the English tradition: Jane Austen's exquisite detail, George Eliot's profound genius, Thackeray's puppet-mastery, and Meredith's *The Egoist* with its exquisitely patterned action and celebration of Bergson's Comic Spirit. Eke a rich vein of 18th century sirreverence: Smollet and the picaresque, Fielding's bum-baillifs, Swift's *A Tale of a Tub,* and Boswell's *Life of Johnson*: as Beckett said to Deirdre Bair [257], "They can put me wherever they want, but it's Johnson, always Johnson, who is with me. And if I follow any tradition, it is his." His reading for *Human Wishes* was beginning even as *Murphy* drew to an end.

At some point, I believe, the action of *Murphy* was reconceived in terms of a City Comedy, and a decision taken to "Londonize" the novel: this is reflected in the expected echoes of Shakespeare and Marlowe (many from Bartlett), and the use of Jonson's *Volpone* to characterize Celia and define much of the action [see #10.1]; but also in the several pages of Elizabethan and Jacobean quotations recorded in the *Whoroscope* Notebook, some ticked off to show they had been included. Many are so recondite that one must ask why they were chosen, particularly when the impetus for so doing is not allusion in the usual sense. Some details identify specific editions ("*girl* 2 syllables in John Ford" pinpoints the Mermaid); others remain evasive ("Pudenda of the soul" is still a bashful mystery). My annotations note chunks of Robert Greene and George Peele [235]; a passage from Beaumont and Fletcher's *The Maid's Tragedy* [106]; a detail from Nashe's *The Unfortunate Traveller*; bits of Dekker, Marston, and Jonson; a snatch of Fletcher's *Sullen Shepherd*; and Augustine's Two Thieves stolen from Greene's *Repentance* [see #213.2]. This is not so much "casually erudite" [Knowlson, 217] as wilfully obscure, an act of Joycean arrogance which is also private homage to the literary tradition to which the novel belonged. Beckett had written for his own delectation as much as anybody's, but the example of *Ulysses* could hardly be ignored. He probably believed that his novel should do for his London (the dear indelible world of the 16th, 18th, and 20th centuries) what *Ulysses* had done for Dublin. It was not to be.

e. *The Comic Cosmos.*

> As for those other faults of barbarism, Doric dialect, extemporanean style, tautologies, apish imitation, a rhapsody of rags gathered together from several dung-hills, excrements of authors, toys and fopperies confusedly tumbled out, without art, invention, judgement, wit, learning, harsh, raw, rude, fantastical, absurd, insolent, indiscreet, ill-composed, indigested, vain, scurrile, idle, dull, and dry; I confess all ('tis partly affected), thou canst not think worse of me than I do of myself.
> —Burton, *Anatomy*, 'Democritus to the Reader,' 8.

Like the *Anatomy*, to borrow Johnson's opinion, *Murphy* is a valuable book, if perhaps overloaded with quotation. A decade went into its making, and that "rhapsody of rags" [above] is but a small part of the whole. A full study of Beckett's "reading" would include not only other novels (Fontane's *Effi Briest* had a lasting impact), but the authors (O'Casey, Pound, Jack Yeats) he reviewed at the time, as well as those (A.E., Austin Clarke, Frank O'Connor, Frederick Higgins) on whom he sharpened his talons. And Synge, whose poetic influence was inestimable. Such a study would consider the impact made upon his writing by the visual arts, and the growing dialectic between his reverence for the Old Masters, and his sense that they would no longer do [see #196.2, and the treatment of that theme by Knowlson, 196-97]. It would venture into film: Neary and Wylie as hardy laurels, Cooper's hat raised to Chaplin, the funny walks and slapstick comedy of so many scenes [see #259.2]. It would consider music and theater, semiotics of the London scene, spiritualism, astrology, kites, dogs, chess, and mathematics, and the way Beckett got bogged down, as he said to McGreevy [April 19, 1936], in "the absurdist difficulties of detail." All facets of the world encompassing him about afforded demented particulars, the straws of understanding with which his imagination might build, or break. These are better treated in the annotations.

Yet out of the blooming buzzing confusion of the Big World [see #4.3] the figure of *Murphy* emerged as an organized whole. Despite the infinitude of sources, those that actually shaped the *kosmos* were few. I have noted how unexpected texts (Schopenhauer's *The World as Will and Idea*, Geulincx's *Ethica*, Burnet's *Greek Philosophy*, Woodworth's *Contemporary Schools*, Windelband's *History of Philosophy*, and Whitaker's *Almanac* 1935, to name the big six) contributed to the fictional world. Initially, the novel may be defined as a Cartesian machine, a cosmos governed by laws that are clear and distinct. Accordingly, its inhabitants must recognize the rationalist tradition, in which the right pursuit of reason is the highest activity of the immortal soul, and leads to the love and understanding of God. Beckett's gospel is Geulincx's *Ethica*, the opening sentence of which affirms that virtue is uniquely the love of right reason, with its consequence, *Ubi nihil vales, ibi nihil velis* [see #178.9], which Beckett in his note to Sighle Kennedy underlined as one of his two points of departure. So much of Beckett's reading affirms this principle, from Pythagoras, Socrates, Plato, and Aristotle among the Greeks, through Augustine and Thomas à Kempis, to Descartes and Berkeley and beyond.

Yet in his study of Descartes, which Beckett used as a crib for *Whoroscope*, Mahaffy identifies the chief difficulty of the Cartesian method, as summed up by Thomas Hobbes [96]: that what Descartes conceived as clear and distinct may well have seemed to him to be so and thus provide a foundation for thought, but such clarity can be at best metaphorical, which may be why a man holds and defends with obstinacy some opinion, "but it cannot tell him with certainty that the opinion is true." Beckett's recognition of this constitutes his foundation of doubt with respect to the earthball: if his universe is Cartesian, its entelechy is dubious. Mintz's sense of the action as a Cartesian catastrophe is just: the premise is the dualism of body and mind, with Murphy's attempt (by the agency of Geulincx) to live exclusively in the little world where alone he can be free [see #109.1]; but his endeavour ends in chaos.

The microbes in the ointment are the Atomists, the Classical ones and the physicists of Beckett's own day, whose discovery of relativity, sub-atomic particles and the world of quanta posed a challenge to the rationalist universe, physically and metaphysically, for in their new found land Newtonian principles demonstrably do not apply (there is a long extract on this theme in the *Whoroscope* Notebook copied from Henri Poincaré's *La Valeur de la science*). This is the 20th century equivalent to the challenge made to the mainstream of Greek thought by Leucippus and Democritus, whose denial of the immortality of the soul was a direct threat to the teaching of Plato and Aristotle. Hence Beckett's second point of departure, the dictum of Democritus that *Nothing is more real than nothing* [see #246.5], with its affirmation (if that is the word) of the reality of the Void. In sum, the cosmos of *Murphy* may be seen as a would-be Occasionalist universe which is blown apart by the guffaw of the Abderite [see #246.6].

This paradigm applies to the monads within the macrocosm. Hippasos is an emblem [see #47.7]: drowned in a puddle for divulging the incommensurability of side and diagonal; or, in other words, for revealing a fatal flaw in the theory of Pythagorean harmony he was drowned at sea in what the, er, *pious* would call just retribution, and the skeptical an accident of the kind that 2,400 years later would befall Murphy. In the rationalist tradition, of which Descartes can act as emblem, the soul seeks God by cultivating the highest activity of the mind; in the mystical tradition, Christian vision or Cartesian dream, the seeker confronts the paradox of an enlightenment which is not of this world, and returns with knowledge of that experience to communicate to others. For Murphy, the "necessary journey" [see #4.2] is into his own dark, where, loving himself, he can be free; but a "deplorable susceptibility" to ginger biscuits and Celia [179] holds him in the Big World of the body and prevents his retreat to the little world of the mind. Murphy discovers in his confrontation with Mr. Endon that he cannot take the final step into the serenity or otherwise of the microcosmopolitan world because—and only Beckett could have come up with this twist, and all its attendant ironies—the cost would be his sanity. This is a price he is not prepared to pay, for if he can no longer apperceive himself then he can no longer exist. This is an irresolvable antinomy, and one to which Beckett would return in later works, such as *Film*.

The key word is 'irrationality' in all its manifestations: philosophical, mathematical, psychological, and literary. Windelband notes, #43, 'The Metaphysics of the Irrational,' that the "dialectic of history" has willed that the System of Reason should change into its opposite, and the attempt to deduce all phenomena from one fundamental principle gives rise to other theories which are thereby forced to maintain what is translated rather awkwardly as "the unreason of the Word-ground" [615]: that which cannot be comprehended by reason should be thought of as the irrational. He notes the influence of Schelling, who transferred the irrational to the essence of the Absolute itself [618]; and the manifestation of that impulse in Schopenhauer, who asserted "the absolute unreason of an objectless will" [620], grounding pessimism metaphysically in the unhappy will within a world of misery and suffering. Beckett's argument, articulated in *Proust* and repeated in *Murphy*, that pleasure is but the removal of pain and that man's best lot is never to be born, is the consequence of this metaphysic, spelled out in precisely these terms by Windelband.

In Hesla's neat formulation, Beckett creates a Cartesian cosmos with Proustian characters. Yet that cosmos is not what it seems, for its "clear and distinct" qualities become increasingly confused. The action of the novel, for instance, is meticulously plotted (with the disposition of Whitaker and others ancillary) in terms of time and place: the days can be matched against the 1935 calendar, with phases of the moon, tides, and even the weather matching the "real" world [but see #276.1]; the chronology, though initially confusing, can be reasoned out in a satisfactory manner; and the observation of London testifies to an exact sense of place. Time and space thus form the Cartesian co-ordinates or analytical grid of the mechanical world: *Murphy* is more beastly circumstantial [13] than almost any novel in the realist tradition. Yet time and again, in one place or another, the text is problematical. Those who have noticed this [Kennedy, Rabinovitz, Acheson] usually voice a fashionable thesis about unreliable narrative and gentle skimmers ("obstacles to be sidestepped, irrelevancies to be hurdled" [Ben-Zvi, 45]), but the issue is more complex. Unreliability creates the comedy of absurdity, and synthetic reasoning in a contingent world [see #168.9] leads to peculiar paradoxes indeed. Even such a basic question as, *How did Murphy die?*, runs into impossible difficulties [see #262.3, for a classical case of misadventure]. The combination of particularity *and* absurdity, I argue, gives the world of *Murphy* its demented definition.

I am not convinced that this was Beckett's pre-established intention. The *Whoroscope* Notebook identifies (§1) 'H' (the horoscope) and 'X' (who became Murphy), in terms of the impetus given by H (a "1/- corpus of motives") to X (who has no motive). The germ of the novel seems to be the horoscope as the director of action, and although Beckett states the "Dynamist ethic of X. Keep moving the only virtue" (§2), the first notes indicate that H, "any old oracle to begin with," gradually acquires a fatality until it is "No longer a guide to be consulted but a force to be obeyed" (§3). The notes are cryptic, and difficult to read, but they testify to a process whereby X and H will be clarified side by side, as "monads in the arcanum of circumstance, each apperceiving in the other till no more of the *petites perceptions* that are life" (an echo of Leibniz's *Monadology*), until they perish together, "fire *oder was*." Others mention "Racinian lighting" (§5), and "Purgatorial atmosphere sustained throughout" (§6), with instructions to choose "caresses" carefully (§8), the Dantesque analogy kept out of sight. A Dantean schema ("Peccati d'amore") is separately given, and elaborated (§§10-12), but it is difficult to relate more than the odd word ('cornice') to the final action. However, §13 brings in "The picaresque inverted": *Gil Blas* "realised" by his encounters, but X by his failure to encounter (this suggests Stephen Dedalus at the end of *Portrait* seeking to encounter the reality of experience). §14 mentions the difficulty of the caress, and §15 "Correspondences with solar spectrum" (the iridescence would give way to tones of green and yellow). Mahaffy [157] notes Descartes's *reductio* of physical science to the mathematical laws of figure and motion: "Give me extension and motion," Descartes exclaims in his *Monde*, "and I will construct the world." What emerges from Beckett's anthill of motion and extension is the image of Murphy as a monad [see #72.5].

Recognizable bits of the novel begin at §16, with X bound with silk scarves to a chair, the chimes and street cries, *quid pro quo*, "all the colours of the rainbow on floor beyond curtain," and the telephone ringing: it is his fiancée, with something for him (the horoscope), but he does not want her round yet, so puts her off with a story about a man paying him a visit *on business*, leaves the receiver hanging, and binds himself up tightly for another spell. Night. Fiancée arrives and finds him trussed up, delivery of H, "coyness of this, she insisting on reading out titbits." They separate (tragic touch), "& this is the prologue. But call it not so."

There follow several pages of notes, mostly taken from the *Britannica*, testifying to an early intention of defining the action seriously in astrological terms. This faded. Traces would remain, of course, but the Notebook gives little evidence of perhaps the most magnificent jest in the later novel, the replacement of the Cartesian or Occasionalist God by the stars, to regulate the machinery of the Big World (the joke taking particular point from Descartes's refusal to let astrologers know his date of birth). There are other pertinent entries, which indicate the way that *Murphy* began as a patchwork piece, if not a cento: §20, the dialogue between Celia and Willoughby K. ("You are all I have"), which mentions Murphy for the first time; §21, where Murphy says he is of the little world, and mangles Geulincx, *ubi nihil valeo, ibi nihil velo* ("I quote from memory"); §22, the *naevus*, by which Celia will identify the body (an indication that the plot was complete); §23, a summary of the Neary sub-plot, introducing "Miss C" and the unnamed tout, with "lead-face & scarlet muffler"; §24, Neary in Dublin, his school improbably named 'Naedlarks,' but closed down as he departs for London; §§25-28, Neary's search for Murphy, Celia and the tout, "Brewery St" [*sic*]; §29, giving details from Beckett's visit to the Bethlem Royal, which Knowlson [744] dates as September 23, 1935; §§30-33, details such as music MUSIC MUSIC, Celia alone, the old boy's suicide, ginger biscuits, and Celia's wild afternoon of whoring in which she meets Cooper (now named); and §34, which cites Malraux's "Il est difficile" [see #156.1], then offers a rare piece of actual composition, the irrrefragable comments of the coroner concerning "the cause of death and identity of the ~~deceased~~ accused, I beg your pardon, the deceased." These notes were surely compiled in London before Beckett returned home in late 1935, but thereafter the entries are more random, and undated save for one interesting comment ["4/12/35"]: "The wise man will not marry the sister of a bleeder" [see #24.3]. The Elizabethan details (at the back of the Notebook) cannot be dated in this manner, and Beckett did not use the pages sequentially.

Comedy is notoriously impossible to define, and the above indicates only some of the forces that went into the shaping of *Murphy*. Yet the novel may be placed, tentatively, within a tradition. Knowlson has shown [217] that the composition of the first 10,000 words coincided with Beckett's reading of *Pantagruel*, from which he took 23 pages of notes; he indicates that the Rabelasian "blend of erudition and humour" might have contributed to *Murphy's* making. My notes indicate a range of affinities, from Jacobean City comedies to Jonathan Swift, *Tom Jones,* and *The Egoist*, to say nothing of the rags and tags from Burton and countless others. And yet, were I to "place" *Murphy* with respect to any one forbear, I would consider *Candide* but instead choose Racine, his drama perhaps the supreme literary achievement of the 17th century and as such a creative complement to Descartes. Beckett's admiration for Racine is known; the "situation circle" he used in his Trinity lectures has been defined; the way that *Murphy* enacts the Racinian plot has been noted by Mercier; and I cannot imagine a better brief summary of the novel than Ludovic Janvier's "*Andromaque* jouée par les Marx Brothers" [see #5.5]. Were I to be taxed with the obvious, the incongruity of offering a tragedian as a model for comedy, I might add a comment from Schopenhauer [*WWI*, I.iv §58, 415-16]:

> The life of every individual, if we survey it as a whole and in general, and only lay stress upon its most significant features, is really always a tragedy, but gone through in detail, it has the character of a comedy. For the deeds and vexations of the day, the restless irritation of the moment, the mishaps of every hour, are all through chance, which is ever bent upon some jest, scenes of a comedy. But the never-satisfied wishes, the frustrated efforts, the hopes unmercifully crushed by fate, the unfortunate errors of the whole life, with increasing suffering and death at the end, are always a tragedy. Thus, as if fate would add derision to the misery of our existence, our life must contain all the woes of tragedy, and yet we cannot even assert the dignity of tragic characters, but in the broad detail of life must inevitably be the foolish characters of a comedy.

There is an incongruity with respect to the above: if it is true, as Beckett believed, that Racine had transposed the notion of a Supreme Will with heredity [I am citing Leslie

Daiken's 1930 lecture notes, probably taken from Beckett], replacing the "mediaeval preoccupation with predestination as being an exterior force responsible for doom and the phenomena of catastrophe" with the promptings of an interior being (Phèdre's consciousness of sin)—then, surely, *Murphy* is written deliberately across that grain. One of the curiosities of this novel, devoted obsessively to the little world of the mind, is its eschewal of interior consciousness; even the one broken dream [175-76] is painted on a flat surface. Likewise, almost every speech act is a simple "said": a few sneers and cries and calls and groans, the odd ejaculation or shriek or murmur, but by and large a deadpan approach to conversation. This is classical detachment taken to an extreme.

J. C. C. Mays has shown how far Beckett's style evolved between *Dream* and *Murphy*: "Though the novel incorporates themes and allusions endemic in the writing of the five or so years that preceded its composition, it establishes a new attitude towards them and thereby a new relationship with them" ['Mythologized Presences,' 215]. Mays discusses the linking of the two plots of *Murphy* by echo and repetition, parallels of sound and action; and unlike Rabinovitz, whose approach to this aspect of the novel is doggedly mechanical, he shows how the geometrical principle of its structure controls the humor and leaves room for exploitation of emotions like savagery and tenderness. The overall organization could be called a Gestalt one, with geometrical shapes (e.g. circles, from situations to prisons and ponds) standing out. *Murphy* is a novel of surfaces rather than symbols, and its modular principle (not unlike that of *Watt*, though better connected) is the paragraph centered on a particular theme (*voyeurism*, 90), which integrates the images. Or on an image which integrates a theme (the *voltaic pile*, 207). This is a method essentially visual in its conception, though the images and themes may be drawn from various fields. I would add to this only the ironic subversion of the commonplace, cliché and received idea pinned with deadly accuracy; and the importance of the pun, that syzygetic device that mocks even as it creates.

Murphy is a very funny novel. A Pythagorean academy in Cork, Neary doing battle with Cuchulain, the touching little argonautic in the Park . . . these are wonderful conceits. More debatable, perhaps, is the erratic genius of chapters 10 and 12, but Beckett's letter to George Reavey of November 13, 1936 [Bair, 243] makes the case: "The wild and unreal dialogues, it seems to me, cannot be removed without darkening and dulling the whole thing. They are the comic exaggeration of what elsewhere is expressed in elegy, namely, if you like, the Hermeticism of the spirit." He justified to Tom McGreevy [July 7, 1936] the post-mortem farce [see #259.2], obviously well aware just how the absurdity accentuates the tragedy. Most of all, I adjure you, Neary is a comic triumph, a huge Falstaffian creation whose every utterance is a magnificent mangling of the entire western philosophical and literary tradition. His fantasia on the Apmonia has sometimes been seen as a sign of superficiality; Neary has his problems, to be sure, but a lack of wit is not one of them. He tries to live in the rationalist world, as both a Pythagorean and a Newtonian, attempting to establish "a rapport between the logical operations of the mind and the universe outside that mind" [Farrow, 12]; but he comes to grief through the Proustian principle which *defunges* his system, and that of the entire world of the novel, the subversion of reason by desire. At the end of the story he is a sadder and wiser figure, perhaps as a consequence of an absurdity which he alone might appreciate, when he interrupts the coroner and Dr. Killiekrankie with a comment that causes stupefaction: "An accident?" [see #262.2]. It is perhaps the first time that Neary has used this word in anything but its metaphysical sense, yet the coroner's reaction underlines for him what in Cartesian terms (or their psychoanalytical equivalents) is an irrational heresy, that man is not substance *per se* but rather *per accidens*. Hence he admits, at the end of the day, something previously impossible to him as a Pythagorean: "Life is all rather irregular"—a termitary that annihilates, perchance, if not the visible universe then most of its rationalist foundations.

A Note on Methodology

You must choose, between the things not worth mentioning and those even less so. For if you set out to mention everything you would never be done.
                                                                              —*Molloy*, 41.

My title, *Demented Particulars*, is borrowed from Mr. Willoughby Kelly [see #13.2], but underlying his dismissal of the beastly circumstantial is one of Beckett's most important statements, to the effect that the only things that can be known are the straws and the flotsam of human history, and that any attempt to rationalize them is a futile form of animism. Hence the ethical axiom of Arnold Geulincx: *Ubi nihil vales, ibi nihil velis*. Yet, just as Murphy could not want nothing where he was worth nothing, and Beckett was driven by the inexplicable need to express, so these notes respond to the critical prurit, or academic urge to scratch the spot that itches [see #193.1]. On the one parched palm, the hermeneutical incommensurability of the part and the whole: for each interpretative problem, the need to choose what is almost worth mentioning, then define the horizon of relevant meaning in which it operates—a logical conundrum, in that each is needed for the proper definition of the other. On the other, an unsatisfactory response to the antinomy: the rough rule, or principle of sufficient reason (to echo Schopenhauer), that the weighting of interpretation should be roughly in proportion to the significance of the detail in the text. Hence, a cautious use of modals, derogating from the indicative and assertive when I am tolerably certain of what I say, through various degrees of "could" and "should," to "possibly" and "perhaps" when speculation seems warranted but the evidence equivocal, or the insight valuable despite the tenuous nature of the proof.

References to *Murphy* are keyed to the 1957 Grove Press edition, which matches the Routledge first edition. They are sequential, and followed by a number in square brackets which refers to the British (Calder) edition of 1963, in turn the matrix of the Picador text. Translations, if not otherwise specified, are my own. Cross-references are in the form of "[see #138.1]"; parenthetical references to other texts (listed in the Bibliography) are by author's name or short title. For the sake of clarity some conventions have been adopted, *if the compositor would be so kind*:

• Quotations retain their original spelling and punctuation. This may lead to the apparent incongruity of British and American usage in the one paragraph.

• Double quotation marks are preferred if they can be used without ambiguity, but single marks used for citations of (usually) single words, and for titles of poems and articles. With so much borrowed the distinction is useful, and often necessary.

• Round brackets are used for normal parentheses, but square brackets for authorial intrusions [mine], cross-references and bibliographical citations.

• Greek and Latin forms of names (Heraklites, Heraclitus) are not standardized, but used in the manner of the writer cited.

• I have preferred 'McGreevy' to 'MacGreevy' since Beckett's friend did not adopt the Hibernian spelling until 1938; I use the later form if following another who has done so.

Chronology

<table>
<tr><td>1934:</td><td>• Murphy is a student at Neary's Pythagorean Academy, in Cork.
• Murphy conducts his amours with Miss Counihan [49].
• (June) Wylie worships Miss Counihan from afar [60].</td></tr>
<tr><td>1935:</td><td></td></tr>
<tr><td>February:</td><td>• Murphy's memorable farewell to Neary [4, 50].
• Neary thinks of Miss Dwyer [4], who at last makes him happy, then becomes one with the ground against which she had figured so prettily [48].</td></tr>
<tr><td>March:</td><td>• Neary meets Miss Counihan "in the month of March" [48].
• He besieges her with mangoes, orchids, Cuban cigars, and a copy of his tractate [50].
• Murphy is in London [52], living in West Brompton [1].</td></tr>
<tr><td>April 18:</td><td>• (Maundy Thursday) Murphy is seen [by whom?] supine on the grass in the Cockpit of Hyde Park [50].</td></tr>
<tr><td>June 24:</td><td>• (Midsummer Night) Murphy meets Celia and is accosted in form [15].</td></tr>
<tr><td>June 30:</td><td>• Murphy proposes in Battersea Park [16].</td></tr>
<tr><td>August:</td><td>• Miss Counihan knocks skillfully into Neary in the Mall [53].
• ("The next morning") Neary closes the Gymnasium and leaves for Dublin [54].
• Cooper is dispatched to London to find Murphy [55].
• The blockade begins [65].</td></tr>
<tr><td>Sept. 12:</td><td>• (Thursday) Murphy sits naked in his rocking chair [1].
• Celia telephones Murphy, having obtained the horoscope [7-8].
• Celia confides in Mr. Kelly [11-25].
• Cooper, having picked up Murphy in the Cockpit [120], tracks him to the mew, pauses to admire the pub, and (five hours later) finds him in an appalling position [121].
• (Evening) Celia enters as Cooper exits [26] and rescues Murphy.</td></tr>
<tr><td>Sept. 13:</td><td>• Murphy tells Celia all, keeping back nothing that might alarm her [30].
• Celia hands Murphy his little bull of incommunication [31].
• Murphy asks for a clean shirt [41].</td></tr>
<tr><td>Sept. 14-19:</td><td>• Cooper drinks for a week [121], then telegraphs Neary, twice [122].
• Celia and Murphy begin the new life [63-64].
• Murphy on the jobpath [70-74].</td></tr>
<tr><td>Sept. 19:</td><td>• (Thursday, "a week later") Wylie encounters Neary in the GPO [42].
• Neary leaves for the Great Wen [59].</td></tr>
</table>

Oct. 7:	• (Monday) Summer time ends [114]. • Mr. Kelly mends his kite [115]. • Neary sits in Glasshouse Street [115-17]. • Miss Counihan sits on Wylie's knees, *not* in Wynn's Hotel [117]. • Enter Cooper [118]. • Plans are made to take the Saturday B. & I. to Liverpool [129].
Oct. 11:	• (Friday) Murphy meets the chandlers, Vera, Ticklepenny and Miss Dew [75-106]. • The Old Boy severs the connection [134-35].
Oct. 12:	• Celia is in mourning for herself [136].
Oct. 13:	• (Sunday) Murphy tells his joke about the stout porter [139]. • Miss Counihan, Wylie and Cooper break their fast on the Liverpool-London express [139]. • Murphy sets out for the MMM [142-43]; meets Bim [156-59]; moves into his garret [162]; begins work [170]; and finds his fire [172-76].
Oct. 13-18:	• Murphy on day-shift at the MMM [176-89]. • Miss Counihan in Gower Street [195]; Wylie in Earl's Court [203].
Oct. 19:	• (Saturday) Celia goes out, and is seen by Cooper [150-53]. • Cooper reports to Miss Counihan [203-04], and Wylie [204-07]. • Murphy returns to Brewery Road for his chair [154]. • Ticklepenny intrudes upon his rest [191-94]. • (Evening) Miss Counihan then Wylie visit Neary [208]. • Murphy has his last good night [194].
Oct. 20:	• (Sunday) Neary's hair turns white [224]. • Wylie, Neary, Miss Counihan, and Cooper (?) go to Brewery Road [225]. • Murphy begins his night duty [236]. • Celia "at this point" tells her story [233 & 236].
Oct 20/21:	• (Night) Murphy encounters Mr. Endon, returns to his garret, and dies [240-53].
Oct. 21-23:	• Wylie, Cooper, Neary, Miss Counihan, and Celia stay with Miss Carriage for "two days and three nights" [256].
Oct. 23:	• News of Murphy's death reaches Brewery Road [256]. • The post-mortem takes place [259-69]; Murphy is cremated [271]. • Neary pays off the others [271]; Cooper sits on his hat [273]. • The body, mind, and soul of Murphy are distributed over the floor of the saloon [275].
Oct. 26:	• Celia and Mr. Kelly are at the Round Pond [276]. • The kite string breaks [281-82].

Demented Particulars: The Annotated *Murphy*

Title

Murphy: what's in a name? As Stephen Dedalus says to Leopold Bloom, "Shakespeares were as common as Murphies" [*Ulysses*, 578]. Neary's experience [55] is salutary: "He began feebly to look for a thread that might lead him to Murphy among the nobility, tradesmen and gentry of that name in Dublin, but soon left off, appalled." Critical offerings are equally discouraging: a "morphe" or form; translation of that morpheme to Morpheus, God of Sleep ("wrapped in the arms of Murphy" [*Ulysses*, 614]); a cause of such sleep being (since 1829) the Cork stout of that name (our Murphy is Dublin-brewed); a name beginning with the 13th letter of the alphabet; indeed, the surgical quality of that most common of Irish surnames (Christian unknown). Less likely: Uncle Sam's folding bed, patently manufactured by Sighle Kennedy; an Irish potato, an irrational root [O'Hara, *Hidden Drives*, 48], *le grand peut-être*; homage to Fritz Lang's *M* [Bair, 242]; *Mr. Murphy's Island*, a 1921 comedy by Elizabeth Harts, performed at the Abbey 16.8.26 (not ticked off by Beckett as one he had seen [BIF, *1227/1/2/6*]); and "Murphystown" with its ruined castle near Beckett's Foxrock home [O'Brien, 23]. Quite possibly: Dr. Johnson's friend Arthur Murphy, who appears with Hugo Kelly in Beckett's 'Human Wishes' [BIF, *3461/1*]. My preferences are simple: μορφάς, atomic shapes which generate all objects of sense [Beare, 163]; the pseudangelic sailor of 'Eumaeus'; the chessy eye of Paul Morphy [see #242.1]; a hint of *Finnegans Wake* [see #105.5]; and the determinism implied by Murphy's Law: if anything can go wrong it will.

1

1.1 [5]: *The sun shone, having no alternative, on the nothing new*: in accordance with the scriptural conclusion, "there is no new thing under the sun" [Ecclesiastes 1:9], or the dictum of Heraklites, Fragment #32: "The sun is new every day" [Burnet, *Early Greek Philosophy*, 135]. From the beginning of the novel (September 12, 1935) to its end (October 26) sun and moon are "bound" by inexorable laws: on the foredawn of Murphy's death (October 21) [250-51], the moon "had been obliged" to set, and the sun "could not rise" for an hour to come. The Big World is a deterministic machine, if not an "infernal machine," or an anarchist bomb, set to explode at a given time. The opening sentence encapsulates both its workings and its indifference to the little world of man, and mind.

1.2 [5]: *as though he were free*: the mood is conditional, for the only way "out of it" (i.e., the condition of contingency imposed by the Big World) is to retreat into the freedom of the mind, and, when that proves impossible, by death.

1.3 [5]: *West Brompton*: a district of London between Chelsea and Earl's Court, South Kensington and Fulham Park. Beckett lived from September 1934 until late 1935 with the Frost family at 34 Gertrude Street, SW10, technically in Chelsea. This is the first setting of 'Lightning Calculation,' an early draft of *Murphy*, in which one Quigley looks out from his balcony into the hospital opposite. Murphy's mew, in the French translation to be located in "l'Impasse de l'Enfant-Jésus," a ruelle near *des Favorites* [Knowlson, 363], is to the west; curiously, in a novel where so much is detailed, no precise location is given [see #63.1].

1.4 [5]: *in a mew . . . a medium-sized cage*: a mew (usually pluralized) is a small blind alley, often used as a stables, but originally a cage in which molting hawks and hunting birds were held; from the outset, then, cages and enclosures circumscribe Murphy's body, and thus his hopes or delusions of freedom. This is suggested by 'fondly,' with its identified contraries of "lovingly" and "foolishly" [Webb, 44]. That limitation, as well as the restricted SE aspect, is implied in the echo of *Hamlet* [II.ii.405]: "I am but mad north north-west: when the wind is southerly I know a hawk from a handsaw." The Alba, *nec cincta nec nuda* [L. "neither draped nor naked"], sits in her peignoir, and calls for more brandy: "Shall I be mewed up like a hawk?" [*Dream*, 54]. Both phrases are in the Dream Notebook [#851, #780], and derive from Burton's *Anatomy* [III.2.2.iii, 524, and I.2.3.xv, 201], hawking considered as a relief from melancholy.

1.5 [5]: *He sat naked in his rocking-chair*: as Mintz suggests [157], Murphy's nakedness (and hence the puns on "undressed teak" and need to "buckle to") derives from L. *nudus*, "merely," and the sentiment in Geulincx's *Ethica* [I.II.ii §8, 33]: "Sum igitur nudus speculator hujus machinae. In ea nihil ego fingo vel refingo; nec struo quidquam hîc, nec destruo; totam id alterius cujusdam opus est." [L. "I am therefore merely the spectator of this machine. In it I produce nothing, nor reproduce nothing; nor do I construct here, nor deconstruct; all that is the work of someone else."] In the 'Annotata' [§21, 212], the machinery is identified as the world; in the novel the chair is referred to as a machine [30]. For other Occasionalist implications of Murphy's position, see #2.3, #109.1, and #178.9. In the *Whoroscope* Notebook, after some Astrological and Dantean preliminaries, §16 begins: "Exordium 1: X, naked, bound with silk scarves to a chair, behind curtain or hanging, hears endless chime of cuckoo (echo of what street cry) *quid pro quo*, sees all the colours of the rainbow on floor beyond curtain." Then follows an outline recognizably that of the first chapter, plus a few coy details when the horoscope is delivered: "this is the prologue. But call it not so" (the pun, perhaps, on *pro*, as in "prostitute").

2.1 [5]: *in the Virgin again for the billionth time*: affirming the inevitable even as it hints at the redemption of time, through the unique Incarnation of Christ in Mary; Beckett reflects in the *Whoroscope* Notebook that the "Virgin was born in the Virgin" (September 8). For Astrology as the machinery of the Big World, see #32.2.

2.2 [5]: *Seven scarves*: 2 + 1 + 2 + 1 = 6: where is the seventh, and how was it tied? Beckett told Deirdre Bair [669-70] it was an oversight, but when the mistake was called to his attention he found it amusing and decided to leave it. This is improbable. The error is so basic that it challenges the reader's sense of logic, and there is no easy resolution. O'Hara asserts ingeniously that the seventh scarf represses his penis [*Hidden Drives*, 69]. This might have been news to Beckett, even though he had written to Mary Manning [January 1, 1937; Knowlson, 751]: "provoked by belated romantic German novels I find new planes of justification for the bondage in the chair that were not present to me at the time. Or rather for the figure of the bondage in the chair. If I am not careful I shall become clear as to what I have written." Compare the opening sentence of part IV of Spinoza's *Ethics*: "Human infirmity in moderating and checking the emotions I name bondage" [see also #4.2].

2.3 [5]: *local movements*: those conditioned by the nervous system, such as reflexes, tics and blinking, localized at one place of the body. The phrase is repeated [28]: "a licking of the lips, a turning of the other cheek to the dust, and so on." There is a metaphysical underpinning to this: before his "Sum igitur nudus speculator hujus machinae" [see #1.5], Geulincx states that the nervous system "acts" in a localized manner between body and mind, using paralysis and other medical conditions to demonstrate that motion requires another agency [*Ethica*, I.II.i-vii, 31-33, and 'Annotata' §§5-21, 204-12]. This is a consequence of the mechanical universe, the only movement being local movement [Brunschvicg, 158: "Il n'y a qu'une espèce de mouvement, le mouvement local"]. Murphy in his chair is a *reductio* of such arguments.

2.4 [5]: *as a gull's*: an echo of Proust's description of Albertine [*Le Temps retrouvé*, I.210]: "indifférent à tous, et marine, comme une mouette" [Fr. "indifferent to everything, sea-like, like a seagull"]. The image haunts Malone as he tells his story of Sapo [*Malone Dies*, 192]: "I don't like those gull's eyes. They remind me of an old shipwreck, I forget which. I know it is a small thing. But I am easily frightened now."

2.5 [5]: *an iridescence splashed over the cornice moulding*: a discoloration in the plaster as wall meets ceiling; but 'cornice' is redolent of Belacqua's rocky lee in Antepurgatory, and thus anticipates the final image of the chapter. 'Iridescence' refracts the spectrum of the Big World, linked to the little world by the eye, or iris [see #248.3]. The novel was originally to have been decorated by the colors of the spectrum, perhaps with the paradox that these, accelerated, become white (the Void is colorless); this faded to Braque-like tonalities of green and yellow.

2.6 [5]: *the echo of a street-cry*: not simply the voices of the street, the myriad voices, but rather the cries of hawkers invested with a tonality and musical phasing, each with its own individuality. Thus, the chimes and calls of the hawkers keep Marcel awake in his cool dark room at Combray, as invoked by Beckett in *Proust* [83].

2.7 [5]: *Quid pro quo!*: L. "something for something," tit for tat, a return as good as that given: the cry of the mercantile gehenna, with a once-obvious pun on 'quid,' or £1. Murphy makes a concession to the marketplace when he describes his chair as "guaranteed not to crack, warp, shrink, corrode, or creak at night." Beckett observed as a working principle that the inner nature of man is too fearful and depressing to contemplate, and that consequently he should be distracted from such contemplation by ceaseless and pointless activity: compare Pascal on Diversion [*Pensées*, §139], or Schopenhauer's vanity of existence [*Parerga*, §146, 287]. This is a first step along the Jobpath. Diderot's *Jacques le fataliste* disputes "the quiproquo of living" [DN, #1086].

2.8 [6]: *detained*: in *Portrait*, Stephen Dedalus distinguishes between this word in the literary tradition and its use in the marketplace [187]. Beckett is aware of the distinction: see #87.3 for 'tundish,' which is used in the same scene. En route to the Knott house, Watt is *detained* in the ditch by a mixed choir [*Watt*, 35].

2.9 [6]: *pleasure*: the life of the mind in chapter 6 is anticipated here by the emphasis on pleasure: Murphy's activity may be unusual, but he is not off his rocker. The touch of Epicurus is not accidental: post-atomist epicureanism asserted pleasure as the end of life but denied immaterial reality, final causes, immortality of the soul and universal ideas. It accepted the duality of body and soul, and with that (contrary to the Stoic doctrine of fate) the choice of freedom in the soul's activity; in Windelband's words (165), "To rest unmoved within one's self." Yet the view of pleasure as a good was pessimistic: pleasure, said Epicurus, "as a distinctive thing is a kind of excess, a reaction from pain. Life swings like a pendulum from extreme to extreme, pain is a motion and pleasure is a motion, but not to move is best" [Brett, 190; see also #9.1 and 'Epicurus to Menoeceus,' *Epicurus*, 83-93]. Hence the paradox: the perfect pleasure of equilibrium, but the rocking chair (motion) as the means of achieving rest. Behind this may lie the dictum of Spinoza [*Ethica* III.xl, n], that pleasure signifies a state wherein the mind passes to a greater perfection, and pain wherein it passes to a lesser. In the French translation Beckett was more explicit: "un tel plaisir que c'était presque une absence de douleur" [Fr. "such a pleasure that it was almost an absence of pain"]. Here Schopenhauer is marked, more so than in the original, but what Beckett discovered in the Greek atomists was ratified in the German pessimist, and vice versa.

2.10 [6]: *it set him free*: the nature of that freedom will be considered later, in terms of Geulincx's Occasionalism [see #109.1], but its condition is defined in Schopenhauer as the transition from Will to Contemplation. *The World as Will and Idea* [III.2.xxv, 67-69] articulates his central paradox: the world, and all in it, as an aimless and incomprehensible play of external necessity, an inscrutable and inexorable Ἀνάγκƞ. In one aspect it is phenomenon (or Idea), and in another Will, "and indeed absolutely *free will*, for necessity only arises through the forms which belong entirely to the phenomenon" [67]. But if the Idea is conditioned by necessity, and the Will alone is free, how then is freedom possible? One has the choice of seeing the world as "a mere machine which runs on of necessity" [68], or of recognizing a free will as its inner being. This riddle, he suggests, can be resolved only "by placing the whole *necessity* in the *acting and doing (Operari)*, and the whole *freedom* in the *being and nature (Esse)*" [68]. In his words: "To save freedom from fate and chance, it had to be transferred from the action to the existence" [69]. The key to freedom is thus the knowledge of the Will in one's self-consciousness by apperception [see #21.1 and #113.3], and this vital condition allows Beckett to move between the phenomenal worlds of Kant and Schopenhauer and consciousness of and in the little worlds of Descartes and Geulincx.

2.11 [6]: *as described in section six*: an affront to the conventions of realism, accentuating the move towards the mind. Beckett noted to McGreevy [October 8, 1932] that one thing he admired in Fielding was "the giving away of the show pari passu with the show." Kurt Koffka's preface to his *Principles of Gestalt Psychology* [1935] anticipates the "perceptual constancies" of its sixth chapter, but says that they are not essential, so the reader not sufficiently interested may skip without losing the thread of the argument. Beckett allows no such concession.

3.1 [6]: *Cork*: from Gaelic *Corcaigh*, "marshy ground"; an etymology underlying the Dublin jest of a Pythagorean academy in that second city of spires and ships and bumpkins from the skerries, hills and bogs. Cork represents the Irish "prosodoturfy" [89] to be sucked from a mug of Beamish, writers such as Daniel Corkery and Frank O'Connor working to undermine the Anglo-Irish ascendancy.

3.2 [6]: *Neary*: suggesting Neary's Bar in Dublin, in Chatham Street close to the Gaiety Theatre, with two splendid cast-iron lanterns, the name of *Neary's* inscribed thereon, projecting from its brick and limestone front. Here "the legendary Macran" (Henry S.), an eccentric, hard-drinking, tough-talking Hegelian scholar, Professor of Moral Philosphy at Trinity and part-model for Neary, held court. This identification, made by Mays in 'Young Beckett's Irish Roots' [23], seems sufficient; that it is an anagram of 'yearn' is a useful accident. Rabaté favors Beckett's psychiatrist, Wilfred Bion, pointing to his neo-Hegelian interests, his sense of the centrality of desire, and his coming to London from India ['Fluxions,' 6].

3.3 [6]: *could stop his heart*: although a fairground trick of fakirs and fakers, the condition is not unknown, and is called *bradycardia* (Gk. βραδύς, "slow," and καρδία, "heart"), either *idiopathic* (controlled) or *essential* (congenital). Cardiac rhythm is reflexive, but the relation between heart rate and respiration permits the individual to exercise some control by means of sustained expiration. This is difficult with stress, which is why Neary loses the knack [56].

3.4 [6]: *the Nerbudda*: otherwise the Narbada, a river in India, traditionally the boundary between Hindustan and the Deccan, rising from the central plateau and flowing westwards to the Gulf of Cambray near Bombay. It ranks second in sanctity only to the Ganges. The name merges Neary into the Buddha, whose teachings that the highest state is attained when normal consciousness is transcended are often considered analogous to the Western mystical tradition, the natural development of Greek philosophy from the Pythagoreans through Plato to the Christian conception of the soul. The Buddhist dimension, touched on so lightly here, is significant in that its goals of enlightenment and the merging of the individual into the cosmic soul must be seen as a parallel to yet the inverse of Murphy's quest for his own dark.

3.5 [6]: *fell among Gaels*: an echo of the Bibical parable of the man who went down from Jerusalem to Jericho, and fell among thieves [Luke 10:30]. Less obviously, Beckett's review of 'Recent Irish Poetry' [*Disjecta*, 70], where the "antiquarians" are accused of "delivering with the altitudinous complacency of the Victorian Gael the Ossianic goods."

3.6 [6]: *to sit at Neary's feet*: 'Upanishad' refers to the philosophical treatises elaborating the earlier Vedas, or sacred texts of the Hindus, with the literal sense of "sitting at the feet."

3.7 [6]: *a Pythagorean*: Beckett took some details in the *Whoroscope* Notebook from an unidentified French encyclopaedia:

> Pythagoras (b. Samos 569—d. Tarentum 470): Circumcised by priests of Diospolis in Thebes; settled in Greater Greece, taught at Tarentum, set up school at Crotona. At 60 married the beautiful Theano, daughter of the doctor Brontinus. Led Crotona in war against Sybarites (Sybaris), who were defeated. Rewarded with gift of magnificent garden where he built a college on Egyptian and Chaldean lines. This the famous Institute of Pythagoras. Neophytes only admitted after novitiate of several years in absolute silence. Stages of initiation: auditor, speaker, mathematician, magisterum, Secrète des dogmes de rigueur comme dans les mystères. No meat, wine or love. His doctrine of metempsychosis. Dieu unité primordiale, s'unissant un nombre pair (néant), produit nombre impair (être, monade): as result of popular revolution in Crotona Pythagoras slaughtered or banished. P. himself, at 80, found refuge in Tarentum.

Little of this, perhaps the garden as Neary's Grove and a hint of his *Doctrine of the Limit* [see #50.5], made its way into *Murphy*, Beckett drawing upon Burnet [see #3.8] for what more he needed. Pythagoras founded the society at Krotona c. 529 BC as a religious fraternity, and assumed authority in Archaia until disturbances led to his exile at Metaponion. The Order is speculative, accentuating such notions as metempsychosis, abstention from animal flesh and beans, and curious prohibitions such as not to touch a white cock or the insistence on stirring the ashes after cooking, to leave no trace of the pot (compare the disposal of Murphy's remains). Pythagoras wrote little, and though the discoveries of the musical ratios of the octave and of the theorem that bears his name were probably his own most of the scientific and mystical doctrines associated with the School are those of his followers.

3.8 [6]: *Apmonia . . . Isonomy . . . Attunement*: terms arising from Beckett's reading of the pre-Socratics, specifically John Burnet's *Early Greek Philosophy*. The joke turns on the witty Greek letter *rho* masquerading as a Roman 'p'; Kennedy observes [302] that Burnet's *Greek Philosophy* offers the capitalized form, APMONIA [45]. O'Hara, curiously, calls Neary's philosophical knowledge superficial [*Hidden Drives*, 45]. *Apmonia* has the clear shape of our "harmony" but its sense in Greek is akin to "octave." The great contribution of Pythagoras to acoustics was his discovery that the concordant intervals of the musical scale could be expressed by simple mathematical ratios. Burnet notes [112]:

> In principle, at least, that suggests an entirely new view of the relation between the traditional 'opposites.' If a perfect attunement (ἁρμονία) of the high and the low can be attained by observing these ratios, it is clear that other opposites may be similarly harmonised.

From this it follows that wisdom is not a knowledge of many things, but the perception of the underlying unity of warring opposites (basic constitutive principles of so much of pre-Socratic thought): "The 'strife of opposites' is really an 'attunement' (ἁρμονία)" [Burnet, 143]. The hot and cold, wet and dry, could be blended to attain a medical harmony associated with Alkmaion and termed the *isonomy*, as Burnet observes [195-96], since the soul's attunement is intimately connected with the four elements and the theory of the human body as a microcosm of the greater harmony (Alkmaion differed from the Pythagoreans in regarding the brain rather than the heart as the seat of consciousness). For Plato's Socrates [*Phaedo*, 36 §85E, 296-99], the harmony of body and soul was like a lyre, and the question arose: if the body were too tightly strung by diseases or other ills, must the soul necessarily perish? These various notions were blended in Burnet's later *Greek Philosophy* [50]:

> We still speak of "tonics" in medicine as well as music. Now the medical school of Kroton, which is represented for us by Alkmaion, based its theory on a very similar doctrine. According to him, health depended on the "isonomy" (ἰσονομίη) of the opposites in the body, and disease was just the undue predominance of one or the other. We need not be surprised, then, to find that Alkmaion was intimately associated with the Pythagoreans, and that he dedicated his medical treatise to some of the leading members of the society. Health, in fact, was an "attunement" (ἁρμονία) depending on a due blend of opposites.

Beckett found this an effective condensation of Burnet's earlier work, since it more succinctly emphasizes the medical condition from which Murphy suffers, one for which Neary with his Pythagorean sense of the closed circle and perfect attunement can offer no relief, until Neary himself suffers the condition [224] and understands that life is all rather irregular [271].

3.9 [6]: *an irrational heart*: the phrase blends the medical extensions of Pythagoras with the mathematical ones [see #47.8], to introduce the irrationality which is a central philosophical and psychological concern in the novel. Aspects of the theme will be discussed as they occur; here, it suffices to note that the irrational infiltrates every cornice of the work and goes to the heart of the absurdist vision of existence against which the comic action is played. Murphy's condition is based upon Beckett's own, as Knowlson makes clear [64]:

> In April 1926, while he was still living at Foxrock, he first experienced what he later came to describe as 'the old internal combustion heart.' During the night his heart started to race faster and faster, fast enough to keep him awake. At first, this caused him relatively little anxiety. But, later, the attacks were to become more frequent and far more distressing. Soon they were accompanied by dreadful night sweats and feelings of panic that eventually became so serious that Beckett felt he was being paralysed by them and was forced to seek medical help. The problem was to plague him for very many years.

The metaphors of "seizing" and "ebullition" are a direct emission of this "old internal combustion heart." Beckett cited in his Dream Notebook [#571]: "His heart taketh not rest in the night" [see also Burton, *Anatomy*, 'Democritus to the Reader,' 17, and Ecclesiastes 2:23], but the condition is less spiritual than physical. His father had died recently of cardiac complications, and Beckett accordingly had used the condition in 'Lightning Condition,' where Quigley feels pains in his chest. These, he is convinced, are the prologue to angina pectoris, "from which disease his father had died and Stalin was said to suffer, so that he (Quigley, not Stalin) lived in the constant fear of being convulsed." In 'A Case in a Thousand' Dr. Nye is given a heart "that knocked and misfired for no reason known to the medical profession" [41]. The irrational heart is an essential component of the fundamental unheroic.

3.10 [6]: *auscultated*: diagnosed by listening, as with a stethescope, for the *tick douloureux*, that one might be stimulated back into the diastole-systole of life. In 'Yellow' [*MPTK*, 186] Belacqua dies on the operating table ("By Christ!"), because they had clean forgotten to auscultate him.

3.11 [6]: *Petrouchka*: after the Russian Ballet's success with *The Firebird* (1910), Diaghilev commisioned Stravinsky to write on the Petroushka [Calder spelling] theme. The ballet grew out of a musical composition in which the piano represents a mischievous puppet playing tricks to make the orchestra retaliate. Set in a fairground of old St. Petersburg during Carnival, it is remarkable for its musical ingenuity and brilliant orchestration. The premiere was in Paris (January 13, 1911), with Nijinsky and Karsavina in the leading roles. Beckett saw several ballets during his London years, including two *Petroushkas*, one with Léonide Massine and the Ballet Russe, which he liked; the other a Polish production with Léon Woizikowsky [Knowlson, 193-94], which he described in a letter to McGreevy [October 23, 1935] as "positively ammonia."

4.1 [6]: *figure and ground*: to the Behaviorist, a Gestalt is a secondary product, built up by previous associations. The triumph of the rats over the configurationists is to some a sad regret; but in its day Gestalt psychology was one of the more vigorous emerging movements. Robert Woodworth's *Contemporary Schools of Psychology* (1931) describes it as a reaction against associationism and notes its insistence upon pattern and form, elements largely ignored by other schools. Knowlson [737] has drawn attention to the extensive notes Beckett took from Woodworth; these include a paraphrased version of this passage [107-08]:

> The distinction of figure and ground is regarded by the Gestalt psychologists as absolutely fundamental in the process of seeing. Some figure is sure to be

seen if the field offers any possibility of it. The figure is typically compact, but at any rate it appears as having form and outline, while the background appears like unlimited space. The figure is more apt to attract attention than the ground . . . Figure and ground are not peculiar to the sense of light. A rhythmical drumbeat or the chugging of a motorboat stands out as a figure against the general background of less distinct noises; and something moving on the skin stands out from the general mass of cutaneous sensations . . . Gestalt psychology has seized upon this distinction of figure and ground as a fundamental principle in the organization of experience and behavior.

This was revised in later editions as Woodworth's enthusiasm for the School became subdued. For Beckett, however, the distinctions remained fundamental, as is evidenced by the number of citations in *Murphy*, but also by Watt's puzzlement over point and circle in Erskine's room [*Watt*, 128-30], and by Winnie's experience of "formication" in *Happy Days* [30].

4.2 [6]: *But a wandering to find home*: as Ruby Cohn noted [*Comic Gamut*, 46], this is from *The Witch of Edmonton*, by William Rowley, Thomas Dekker, and John Ford. Beckett's source was probably the *Dekker* volume in the old Mermaid series. Frank Thornley, regretting his bigamy and the murder of one wife, contemplates his own death [IV.ii.28-34]:

> For when a man has been an hundred years
> Hard travelling o'er the tottering bridge of age,
> He's not the thousand part upon his way:
> All life is but a wandering to find home;
> When we're gone we're there. Happy were man
> Could here his voyage end; he should not, then,
> Answer how well or ill he steered his soul . . .

In Gestaltist terms Murphy implies the need to fix the figure, to prevent it reverting to the ground. Reversing tomb-womb, J. D. O'Hara sees "home" as a return to the matrix ['Beckett Backs Down,' 38, 54]. Then, a musical offering from Schopenhauer [*WWI*, I.iv §58, 414]:

> Melody is always a deviation from the keynote through a thousand capricious wanderings, even to the most painful discord, and then a final return to the keynote which expresses the satisfaction and appeasing of the will, but with which nothing can then be done, and the continuance of which any longer would only be a wearisome and unmeaning monotony corresponding to ennui.

There may be also an awareness of *Ulysses*, in terms of the image of Bloom's homecoming or Stephen's journey to meet the self he is ineluctably predestined to become. This is what Walther Bauer termed "die notwendige Reise" [Ger. "the necessary journey"], i.e., to the Self. Beckett noted of that journey [German Diary 4, January 18, 1937; Knowlson, 247]:

> Journey anyway is the wrong figure. How can one travel to that from which one cannot move away? *Das notwendige Bleiben* [The Necessary Staying Put] is more like it. That is also in the figure of *Murphy* in the chair, surrender to the thongs of self, a simple materialisation of self-bondage, acceptance of

which is the fundamental unheroic. In the end it is better to perish than be freed. But the heroic, the *nosce te ipsum* [know thyself], that these Germans see as a journey, is merely a different attitude to the thongs and chair, a setting of will and muscles and fingers against them, a slow creation of the desire and power to stand up and walk away, a life consecrated to the possibility of escape, if not necessarily the fact, to a real freedom of choice when the fire comes. Murphy has no freedom of choice, i.e., he is not free to act *against* his inclination. The point is that the *nosce te ipsum* is no more mobile than the *carpe te ipsum* [gather thyself] of Murphy. The difference is that in the one motionless there is the seed of motion, and in the other not. And so on. And so on.

4.3 [6]: *the big blooming buzzing confusion*: the celebrated dictum of William James, cited by Woodworth [107] as a first principle of Gestalt perception:

> When the baby first opens his eyes upon the world, while he certainly does not see a world of objects such as adults know and see, he may not, on the other hand, see a mere chaos of miscellaneous points, a "big, blooming, buzzing confusion," as James thought. If there is some compact bright mass of color in his field of view, such as a face bending over his crib, this probably stands out as a figure against the general background. The baby cannot be supposed to see the face accurately, nor to have any notion of what the blotch is, but at least, so the Gestalt psychologists believe, he singles out the face as a compact visual unit, and so makes an important start toward coming to know the face. If it were no easier for him to see the compact figure as a unit than to lump together miscellaneous points from all over the field, his progress in knowing objects at sight would be much slower than it actually is.

This leads directly into what Neary says a little later [see #6.1]. It is tempting to interpret his sense of *face* in terms of Pound's 'In a Station of the Metro,' where the apparition of faces in the crowd stands out as a figure from its ground, but Neary is presumably not conscious of that reading (the common ground is, probably, William James).

4.4 [7]: *Miss Counihan*: the name has teasing intimations of the summit (or cornice) of desire, in both French and English. O'Brien suggests [189] she is "the contemporary embodiment of Cathleen ni Houlihan"; quickly contracted it might be heard this way. The hint of 'Cunard' (as in Nancy Cunard) is audible, but more pertinent is Voltaire's Counégonde, beloved of Candide, victim and proponent of the best of all possible worlds.

4.5 [7]: *one short hour*: an echo of Doctor Faustus's famous speech of despair at the end of the play: "Now, Faustus, thou hast but one bare hour to live"; since Faustus has surrendered his immortal soul for sensory satisfaction [see #5.2]. Neary's half hour and 15 minutes may enact Faustus's sense of time ticking away.

4.6 [7]: *position . . . negation . . . sublation*: a parody of Hegelian dialectic, perhaps in deference to Professor Macran [see #3.2]. Murphy anticipates Neary's achieving a transition of his knowledge from lower to higher in three phases of activity and the movement of one to the other: first, the *position*, or, in Hegel's terms, *Unmittelbar* ["immediate"], the starting-point or presupposition, the given; next, *Negativität* ["negation"], the principle of both destruction (of the previous position) and production (of a new immediacy); finally, through the exercise of negation, the effect of *Aufheben* ["sublation"], the higher category brought to light as a consequence of the dialectical process. Rabaté suggests that Neary aims at unifying Hegelian and Gestaltist features, but the "sublations" are unsatisfactory because the synthesis he expects occurs in the field of perception: "Neary's drama is the drama of human desire which abolishes its object as soon as it is satisfied" ['Fluxions,' 27]. Unlike Mr. Kelly [24], who achieves his sublation, Neary makes no synthesis but clenches his hands more violently than before. Knowlson notes [152-53] that Beckett's friend at the École Normale, Jean Beaufret, was given to similar gesticulation in philosophical dispute; his fictional analogue, Lucien, "did not know how to deal with his hands" [*Dream*, 22].

5.1 [7]: *Teneriffe and the apes*: prosaically, back to the Gymnasium and the students, in terms of Wolfgang Köhler's *The Mentality of Apes* [1925], which reported the results of his studies into the intelligence of apes at the Prussian Academy Anthropoid Station at Tenerife [*sic*], in the Canary Islands, 1913-17. Köhler was marooned there during World War I, and had time to make a thorough study [Woodworth, 114]. He was fascinated by the relationship between man and the anthropoid apes with respect to cognition, and believed we might gain knowledge of acts of intelligence and insight by observing apes becoming perplexed and making mistakes in simple situations. His work was followed by Robert Yerkes (1927; mentioned by Woodworth), who speculated that apes might learn a language of gesture, and left traces of his name in 'Yellow' [186] and *Molloy* [136]. These challenged associationist assumptions by indicating that anthropoid apes manifest intelligent behavior, to a considerable degree, of the kind found in humans; in particular, an ability to "see" pattern. In Beckett's minimalist drama, *Act without Words I* (1957/1963), action and setting draw directly upon *The Mentality of Apes*.

5.2 [7]: *all is dross*: the words of Faustus when Mephistopheles offers him the succubus of Helen of Troy and he launches into his great speech: "Was this the face . . ."; leading to the sentiment that "all is dross that is not Helena." Neary responds to the earlier apparition of *face* [see #4.3]. The profound bathos of his "for the moment at any rate" may echo Coleridge's willing suspension of disbelief which "for the moment" constitutes poetic faith.

5.3 [7]: *closed figure*: the phrase used by Woodworth [109] with respect to a figure drawn with small gaps and the mind's tendency to close the gaps and see a complete figure; adding (as if for Neary): "an imperfect figure means unbalanced brain tensions." Koffka stresses the impulse towards closure as a dominant psychological given, emphasizing how it resolves unbalanced tensions by bringing about equilibrium. In the simplest sense of Neary's words, Miss Dwyer is complete, a perfect form, which means she does not need him to make her so. Neary, however, needs her to be complete. His problem may be expressed in terms of the Platonic tenet that "Desire is a condition of the soul, and all desire is ultimately of one kind, the creature's recognition of incompleteness. Desire may be either physical or psychic in origin; but its satisfaction requires an idea of the object" [Brett, 95]. Or, as Beckett writes in *Proust* [55]: "It represents our demand for a whole. Its inception and its continuance imply the consciousness that something is lacking. 'One only loves that which one does not possess entirely'" ["on n'aime qu'on ne possède pas," *La Prisonnière*, II.247]. Neary ails to attain harmony and equilibrium. He will be at the end of the book a sadder and wiser figure, but perhaps more complete: free of both fear (the Cox is dead) and desire (he no longer even dislikes Miss Counihan). The closed figure is important in *Watt*, with respect to Watt's experience of circle and center [128-30], or the human figure seen against the ground of the sky above and the waste below.

5.4 [7]: *my tetrakyt*: more correctly, 'tetractys' or 'tetraktys,' for the Pythagoreans a figure formed by fire (hence, without dross, or perfectly closed):

```
        .

      .   .

    .   .   .

  .   .   .   .
```

The figure may be defined by as ten points in four lines that form "the tetrality of the
dekade" [Burnet, *Early Greek Philosophy*, 102], an equilateral triangle, 1 + 2 + 3 + 4
= 10, combining in perfect form all the mystical numbers. Either wittingly or undone by
the unreason of love, Neary fails to give it the right name, but in so erring suggests
another closed figure, the kite.

5.5 [7]: *Neary's love for Miss Dwyer*: the figures form a closed circuit—in fact, if displayed geometrically, a hexagon, than which little can be more closed (the stability of
this one is quickly shattered). Elmar Tophaven's German translation (1959) offers a
pleasing alternation of "der" and "die" that the English "who" and French "qui" cannot
provide. Some names are innocent, others less so:

Miss Dwyer: an innocent party, but a circuit can be shortened by, er, a *missed wire*.

Flight-Lieutenant Elliman: whose embrocation, rubbed on by the Unnamable
[320], eases the aching liniments of desire, and gives him the strength to go on.

Miss Farren: the name is probably taken from Mary Farren, housemaid at
Cooldrinagh mentioned by Knowlson [265]. *Ringsakiddy* might be Ringaskiddy, "the
headland of the Skiddies" (a family originally from Skye), near the mouth of the Lee,
County Cork.

Father Fitt: a merry Chaucerian name begotten on Ballin[a]clashet ["town of the
trench"], Oysterhaven, Kinsdale, Cork. Perhaps a collateral relative of the Miss Fitt of
All That Fall [1956].

Mrs. West of Passage: Passage (West) is a small port in County Cork, on the
estuary of the Lee between Cork and Cobh. The North-West passage was another
short-circuit, avidly sought.

As Mercier notes [39], this parodies the "situation circle," a phrase Beckett used
in his lectures at Trinity of a Racine plot (perhaps *Andromaque*). Notes taken and dia-
grams made by Rachel Dobbin validate this suggestion: "A loves B, and B loves C,
and C loves D. The great pagan tiger of sexuality chasing its tail in outer darkness"
[Interview, 6]. Or, in the words of Ludovic Janvier [27], "*Andromaque* jouée par les
Marx Brothers" [Fr. "*Andromaque* played by the Marx Brothers"]. Knowlson notes [208]
that Beckett had Racine in mind as he planned the structure of his narrative, in that
something has "taken its course" and the characters are brought to a preordained ending. Ironically, the "situation" is of little relevance to the plot that follows, which may
imply a critique of such racination. Yet there is for both writers a complex relationship
of inner and outer action, the machinery of the plot and conflicting impulses of the
characters. Beckett describes this as the relationship between the desiring subject
and the object of desire: "two separate and immanent dynamisms . . . related by no
system of synchronisation"—adding, as first serve in the next sparkling rally, that "our
thirst for possession is, by definition, insatiable" [*Proust*, 17].

5.6 [7]: *a short circuit*: compare André Breton's likening of consciousness to a generator
with linked poles: "En poésie, en peinture, le surréalisme a fait l'impossible, pour multi-

plier ces courts-circuits" [Fr. "In poetry, in painting, surealism has done the impossible, to multiply these short-circuits," *Deuxième manifeste,* 809]. See #29.5 and #207.6.

5.7 [7]: *The love that lifts up its eyes*: from Luke 16:22-26, the story of the rich man (traditionally but without biblical sanction named *Dives*) and the beggar at his gate:

> 22. And it came to pass that the beggar died, and was carried by the angels into Abraham's bosom; the rich man also died, and was buried.
> 23. And in hell he lift up his eyes, being in torments, and seeth Abraham afar off, and Lazarus in his bosom.
> 24. And he cried and said, Father Abraham, have mercy on me, and send Lazarus, that he may dip the tip of his finger in water, and cool my tongue; for I am tormented in this flame.
> 25. But Abraham said, Son, remember that thou in thy lifetime receivedst thy good things, and likewise Lazarus evil things; but now he is comforted, and thou art tormented.
> 26. And beside all this, between us and you there is a great gulf fixed, so that they who would pass from hence to you cannot; neither can they pass to us, that would come from thence.

In the *Whoroscope* Notebook this passage exists in two versions, French and Italian, with a curious little preface to the former [see also #107.6]:

> Luke XVI: Dives—Lazarus, prayer from virtual to actual in entelechy . . . petites perceptions to apperceived in monad—poem. Père A. Aie pitié de moi, et envoie Lazare, afin qu'il trempe dans l'eau le bout de son doigt, pour me refraîcher la langue, car je suis extrèment tourmenté dans cette flame. Mais A. lui répondit: Mon fils, souviens-toi que tu avais tes biens pendant la vie, et Lazare y a eu des maux; et maintenant il est consolé et tu es dans les tourments. Outré cela, il y a un grand abîme entre vous et nous, de sorte que ceux qui voudraient passer d'ici vers nous ne le peuvent non plus que ceux qui voudraient passer de là ici.

The image arises from the custom at a feast of allowing a dear friend to recline on one's bosom, as the belovèd John upon the bosom of Christ; Miss Counihan embraces the phrase [48-49]. The "gulf" separates Murphy from those living in their little worlds [see #177.3 and #236.4]. The *conte cruel* is compelling, with similarities to the well with two buckets [58] and parable of the two thieves [213]. Beckett was intrigued by what he called in his 'Denis Devlin' review [1938] "the Dives-Lazarus symbiosis . . . as intimate as that of fungoid and algoid in lichen" [*Disjecta*, 92; taken, he noted, from the *Concise New Oxford*]. He used it in *Dream* [3, 105 and 229], but the final stroke in the sparkling rally was not delivered until 1964, with an admirable aposiopesis, in *How It Is* [64]:

> blessed day last of the journey all goes without a hitch the joke dies too the convulsions die I come back to the open air to serious things had I only the little finger to raise to be wafted straight to Abraham's bosom I'd tell him to stick it up

5.8 [7]: *"Greek," said Murphy*: as in "It's all Greek to me" (in translation, "du Turc"). In *Julius Caesar* [I.ii.288], Casca says: "But, for my own part, it was Greek to me" (which is what Casca is speaking). Molloy comments [37]: "Tears and laughter, they are so much Gaelic to me." Murphy perhaps implies Wilde's infamous "The love that dares not speak its name," from *The Picture of Dorian Gray*, with its sublimation of Greek ways.

6.1 [7]: *blotch*: the word used by Woodworth [106; see also #4.3] for the experience that takes place when figures are formed and objects recognized:

> Suppose as we open our eyes on a certain occasion we have nothing before us but a green blotch on a gray background. We unhesitatingly take the blotch as a coherent whole, as a vague shape standing out from its background. We can scarcely force ourselves to take half of the green blotch along with a part of the adjacent gray as a unit, still less to take part of the green blotch along with distant parts of the gray.

6.2 [7]: *heterogeneous stimulation*: Neary's witty variation on Woodworth's sense of the blotch [107]: "the area of homogenous stimulation is a dynamic system and not an aggregation of separately active points." This is the *Gesetz der Prägnanz* [Ger. "law of pregnancy," or fullness], whereby different stimuli combine to produce that psychological organization that will be as "good" as conditions allow, in terms of such properties as regularity, symmetry and simplicity, which lead to homogenity [Koffka, 110-13]. 'Heterogenous' has thus a double articulation: (a), the tumult or welter of disparate stimuli which fail to render such fullness, and (b), the tumult or welter of Neary's heterosexual attraction to the figure of Miss Dwyer.

6.3 [7]: *there is a Miss Counihan*: weighted with the force of Neary's Pythagorean investigations into the nature of Being, the vital question of which is a concern for the reality or non-reality of what **Is**, and thus the non-reality or reality of what **Is-Not**. The pre-Socratics emerge variously from this abyss of Being. The issue is discussed from Thales to Heidegger, but Beckett (or Neary) may have in mind Burnet's *Greek Philosophy* [67], which is headed "IS IT OR IS IT NOT?" and deals with the difference between ἐστί νοεῖν, that which can be thought, and ἐστί εἶναι, that which can be: "It is impossible to think what is not, and it is impossible for what cannot be thought to be. The great question, *Is it or is it not?* is therefore equivalent to the question, *Can it be thought or not?*" In the novel this is subverted by the guffaw of Democritus, for whom the Void or Nothing is as real as that which Is [see #246.5]. Knowlson [109] tips the issue towards Augustine, whom Beckett had incorporated into *Dream*: Belacqua [42] describes the Loved One in terms used by the Saint to define true Being [*Confessions*, I.i-iv, 2-9]: "She is, she exists in one and the same way, she is everyway like herself, in no way can she be injured or changed, she is not subject to time, she cannot at one time be other than at another" [DN, #136]. Neary, speaking *secundum carnem*, intimates something of Augustine's incarnated spirit tempted by the flesh.

6.4 [8]: *commerce*: intercourse that, in both the sexual and mercantile sense, implies a bonding to the Big World. Celia's profession, the oldest one, is *work* reduced to its fundamental chime, *quid pro quo*.

6.5 [8]: *Precordial*: from L. *praecordia*, "before the heart," i.e., the thoracic area. The word is commonly used in Geulincx. The *OED* offers the obsolete sense of exceedingly cordial, very hearty, but Murphy uses it transparently as pertaining to the heart, hence not heart-felt. The logic seems to be: precordial, therefore tired; Cork County, hence depraved.

6.6 [8]: *there is no other*: Neary's position is the *reductio* of that outlined in Beckett's *Proust* [41-42], in turn the *summa* of Proust himself: "We imagine that the object of our desire is a being that can be laid before us, enclosed within a body. Alas! it is the extension of that being to all the points of space and time that it has occupied and will occupy. If we do not possess contact with such a place and with such an hour we do not possess that being." Love, accordingly, is defined as "Time and Space made perceptible to the heart" [c.f. *La Prisonnière*, II.249]. Given that God (as Love) is the full extension of Time and Space, and the heart is the seat of such knowing, it follows that Neary claims to be loving "whole-heartedly." Hence his nod to Murphy's "God bless my soul," and the comment on why Murphy cannot love. Murphy's conarium having shrunk to nothing [see #6.7], he cannot be open to the extension of any being outside himself. In *Dream* [99-103], Belacqua mocks the Mandarin's sense of love ("The need to live, to be authentically and seriously and totally involved in the life of my heart") as using a woman as a private convenience; to which the Mandarin, espousing a position akin to Neary's, replies: "If such . . . be her desire" [101]; then, going further: "What's wrong" he said suddenly "may I ask, with you and Beatrice happy in the Mystic Rose at say five o'clock and happy again in No. 69 at say one minute past" [102-03]; to which Belacqua can only reiterate his inchoate conviction that there can be no such thing as love. Neary's sentiment has degenerated by the end of 'First Love': "But there it is, either you love or you don't"; and reaches its nadir when Molloy wonders [57], is it true love, in the rectum?

6.7 [8]: *Your conarium has shrunk to nothing*: the conarium is the pineal gland, for Descartes the place in the human body where body and soul have commerce, with the mingling of animal spirits and metaphysical essences. In the words of Baillet [153]: "Son sentiment touchant la siège de l'Ame dans le cerveau, qu'il établissait dans la petite glande appellée *conaire* ou *pinéale*" [Fr. "His sentiment concerning the seat of the Soul in the brain, that it was settled in the little gland called the *conarium* or *pineal gland*"]. Descartes uses 'conaire' in his *Treatise of the Foetus* and in his letter to Mersenne of April 1, 1640, and the action of "la petite glande" is discussed in 'Des passions en général' [Fr. "Of the Passions in General"]. It epitomises his dualism: Descartes had asserted that all changes of matter-in-motion are accounted for by reference to extension, while all psychic matters are referred to the nature of the mind; however, this did not account for confused ideas (as opposed to *claires et distinctes*), nor for the passions and emotions connected with them. Here was an exception, it being proposed that God had arranged in man a co-existence of the two substances, so that a disturbance of the "animal spirits" (centered in the conarium) excited in the mind an unclear idea, whether sensation, passion or emotion. As Mahaffy says [177]: "At this point, in some inexplicable way, and by special arrangement of the Deity, the mind is specially in contact with the nervous organism." As the Occasionalists pointed out, even if it were correct to identify the conarium as the place where the infusion of animal and metaphysical spirits took place this did not explain *how* the union took place, however precisely the locale was pin-pointed (the French translation reads that Murphy's conarium "se suit réduit aux dimensions d'une tête d'épingle" [Fr. "felt itself reduced to the head of a pin"]). It also left unresolved the question of what felt the passion, the body or the mind. Geulincx accepted the Cartesian position, but carefully extricated himself from the tangle winding about the conarium [see #109.1 and #178.9].

7.1 [8]: *where he could love himself*: for clarification of this ethical proposition, see #107.1.

7.2 [8]: *the telephone*: a link to the Big World, since its rail and crake (raucous birds, both) demand an answer. Murphy's mew, with a landlady, lodgers, telephone, door hanging from its hinges, and only a curtain separating him from the sun, is an unsatisfactory monad.

7.3 [8]: *harlot . . . scarlet*: c.f. Isaiah 1:18: "Come now, and let us reason together—though your sins be as scarlet, they shall be as white as snow" (echoed by Robert Greene, whose 'Repentance' provided Beckett with other details). In the typescript, the last occupant was a "molly" whose past had been "excellent." The change is less a tribute to the Scarlet Woman of *Revelation* than a cheap rhyme, that of Hilaire Belloc's 'On his Books': "When I am dead, I hope it may be said: / His sins were scarlet, but his books were read."

7.4 [8]: *crake*: the cry of the corncrake, or land-rail (*Crex crex*), heard as a death-rattle by Belacqua, who to his later regret puts no store in omens ['Walking Out,' *MPTK* 119]. Molloy hears their awful cries [16], and associates them with his mother's death. In *Dream* (70) the narrator dismisses Belacqua's poem as "the corncrakes' Chinese chromatisms." In Robert Greene's *The Comicall Historie of Alphonsus, King of Arragon* Melpomine, Muse of Tragedy, reproaches Calliope, Muse of Epic:

> Calliope, thou which so oft didst crake
> How that such clients clustred to thy Court
> By thick and threefold, as not any one
> Of all thy sisters might compare with thee;
> Where be thy schollers now become, I troe?

7.5 [8]: *God blast you*: in anger, or Irish, indistinct from "God bless you," a common greeting to which Celia may or may not be responding.

7.6 [8]: *Celia*: the name is a gift from heaven: she is celestial, and so part of the astrological system outside Murphy's own; yet the pun on her name, sadly expanded by Mr. Kelly in his excellent French [see #115.1] throws the starry concave into doubt. There is a remote conjunction of a Celia and Murphy in Fielding's *Amelia*, some chapters apart. More visible is Ben Jonson's *Volpone*, which Beckett admired [letter to McGreevy, January 18, 1935], and which enters the tableau of chapter 2. Celia resembles Dekker's Bellafront in *The Honest Whore* [II.i]: "therein I'll prove an honest whore, / In being true to one, and to no more." The point of the multiple references [for others, see #10.1] is not to pin Celia down, but to indicate that she is part of a literary and comic tradition which *Murphy in sui* stands outside.

8.1 [9]: *lamented against his flesh*: in accordance with the Biblical teaching [Mark 14:38, Matthew 26:41] that the spirit is willing (or ready), but the flesh is weak. Murphy would find little consolation in Thomas à Kempis, *De Imitatione Christi* [III.xxxiv.3]:

> Adhuc, proh dolor! vivit in me vetus homo, non est totus crucifixus, non est perfecte mortuus: adhuc concupiscit fortiter contra spiritum, bella movet intestina, nec regnum animal partitur esse quietum.

[L. "Still, alas! the Old Man doth live in me, he is not wholly crucified, is not perfectly dead. Still lusteth he mightily against the Spirit, and stirreth up inward wars, nor suffereth the kingdom of the soul to be in peace."] The old serpent reappears in III.xii.5, but Murphy would not be impressed with the advice: "insuper et labore utili aditus ei magnus obstructur" [L. "by any useful employment thou shalt greatly stop the way against him"].

8.2 [9]: *what you told me*: Celia for professional reasons cannot utter the word, as Mr. Kelly also observes [23]. In *Whoroscope* (1930), Beckett exploited the same pun.

8.3 [9]: *the usual at the usual*: exigencies of time and space reduced to the *petites perceptions* of habit. In the typescript she was to meet him at the usual at nine; instead she arrives at the mew at ten. The French text reads: "Sois au coin de la rue ce soir comme la première fois" [Fr. "Be at the corner of the street this evening like the first time"]. Her lateness is explained by Murphy not turning up at the usual at the usual, thus obliging her to seek him elsewhere.

8.4 [9]: *a funny old chap*: the French translation evades the impossible nuances by creating others not present in English: "un vieux type qui joue aux échecs. Un vieux monsieur délicieux. Propre, sourd et muet" [Fr. "an old fellow who plays chess. A delicious old gent. Neat, deaf and dumb"], i.e., a clean old man.

9.1 [9]: *the freedom of that light and dark*: Murphy's retreat into his inner darkness is a paradox of motion, the chair gathering speed until it stops. Epicurus, whom Beckett relies on, follows Aristippus in recognizing three terms: gentle motion, violent motion, absence of motion [see #2.9: "not to move is best"], and says that the latter can be called freedom from disturbance (ataraxy), for it is a state of persistent equipoise [Brett, 190]. This for Beckett represents the state of complete indifference from all contingency. The same paradox lies at the heart of one of Bruno's identified contraries, as invoked in Beckett's *Exagmination* [6]: "Maximal speed is a state of rest."

9.2 [9]: *the moon got slower and slower*: traditionally, nothing is constant beneath the moon, yet the suspicion of lunacy must be discounted. The goal is a state beyond what Murphy terms his Belacqua fantasy [78], for even that is subject to mutability; rather, the desideratum is a lapse from time and consciousness that seems absolute. It is important that the opening chapter, an overture, should finish on this (apparent) note of attained freedom, for without an achieved sense of the validity of Murphy's end the time-bound reader (or chandler) cannot respond sympathetically to the means by which he attempts to reach it.

2

10.1 [10]: *Age . . . weight*: the catalogue of vital statistics parodies traditions of storytelling in which the physical features of the heroine are carefully listed. Unlike Murphy, about whom little is learnt (his eyes are like a gull's, he has a birth-mark, and his countenance changes from yellow to white if work is mentioned), Celia's externals are given with demented particularity. Bryden suggests [30] that she becomes "no more than an objectified and quantified mass of flesh"; but in the Cartesian schema she represents Body, as Murphy does Mind. Nor would Beckett expect his reader to be ignorant of Swift's poems which celebrate the beautiful Caelia, whose heavenly name is at odds with the physical necessities she observes: while it would be crass to insist on an undercurrent, there is a small awkward eddy. The list appears in the *Whoroscope* Notebook, headed by an enigmatic "Venus de Milo"—presumably a jest, given that it includes measurements for Upper arm, Forearm and Wrist; unless Beckett intended the Venus de Medici, in the Uffizi, Florence, often assumed as the standard of female beauty, as in the description of Sophia [*Tom Jones*, IV.iv]. Celia's is the frame desired by Volpone, whose most celebrated song is Jonson's imitation of Catullus's *Vivamus, mea Lesbia* [L. "Let us live, my Lesbia"], sung in Act IV by the libidinous villain to win the chaste maid. That scene probably suggested the tableau here:

> Come, my Celia, let us prove
> While we may the sports of love;
> Time will not be ours forever,
> He, at length, our goods will sever;
> Spend not then his gifts in vain.
> Suns that set will rise again:
> But if once we lose this light
> 'Tis with us eternal night.

10.2 [10]: *Eyes . . . Green*: as those of most of Beckett's heroines, notably the Smeraldina of *Dream*, her very name derived from Dante's *Purgatorio* XXXI.116-17: "li smeraldi / ond' Amor già ti trasse le sue armi" [It. "the emeralds from which Love once shot his darts at you"].

11.1 [10]: *fiery darts*: Cupid's, obviously, but the rhythm and "encompassing about" suggest an unidentified source, a pentameter missing its pot. 'Tow' is old rope, which, smothered in pitch, might serve as a torch.

11.2 [11]: *a Chef and Brewer*: there is a mystery here: the Chef and Brewer chain, familiar in the 1960s and '70s, did not exist in the '30s; nothing by that name appears in the 1935 Post Office Directory, nor in the Trade or Commercial listings. Even if there were a Chef and Brewer near Marble Arch, the name suggests a pint and pie, not a prawn and tomato sandwich and "a dock glass of white port off the zinc"; i.e., a small glass of a fine aperitif, at the counter [Scots *doch-an-dorach*, a stirrup-cup drink taken standing up]. The Lyons chain had at the Arch a corner-house where alcoholic drinks were available, and owned the Cumberland Hotel nearby [Vada Hart to CA]; Beckett may be mocking the inexplicable splendor of Lyonian white and gold [see #80.2]. There is little mention of food in *Murphy*, saving Murphy's biscuits and Neary's Chinese meal; food implying the body's bondage to the contingent world. The suspicion remains that a small joke has evaded precise definition.

11.3 [11]: *four football pools collectors*: touts who collect the coupons that clients have filled in, predicting the weekly wins, losses and (especially) draws in the English soccer league. The unlikely 4/- in the £1 commission (20%) suggests that some punters will never see their winnings. The jest contributes to the cozening background.

11.4 [11]: *Tyburnia*: the area between Bayswater Road, Sussex Gardens, Oxford and Cambridge Terraces, and Edgware Road; named for the Tyburn Stream that once flowed into Hyde Park. By 1935 the name was little used because of its association with the public gallows at Tyburn, until 1783 the place of public execution at the crossroads just outside the park. The huge triangular structure could hang twenty-one at a time, and frequently did so. An echo of 'Hibernia' may be heard, the area then as now with a considerable Irish population. Noting this, Acheson comments [48] that while the Chef and Brewer and football pools collectors are accurately observed, 'Tyburnia' is invented; from this erroneous tripod he asserts that Beckett's unreliability challenges his readers' assumptions about fiction. The conventions of realism are subverted in *Murphy*, but I would qualify this fashionable thesis and first affirm the novel's thorough grounding in the observed particulars of London, past and present.

11.5 [11]: *Mr. Willoughby Kelly*: in Ireland Kellies are almost as common as Murphies. Cohn suggests that it may derive from 'kell' as a variant of 'caul' [*Comic Gamut*, 54]; the word is used in Burton's *Anatomy* [e.g., I.1.1.iv, 88]. In Beckett's unfinished 'Human Wishes' Mr. Kelly was to have been reborn, if that is the phrase, as the author of *False Delicacy*, a "drunken staymaker Hugo Kelly, dead and damned these five years" [see #276.4]. Willoughbies are rare birds on either side of the Irish Channel, but one may be spotted in a novel Beckett enjoyed in the early 1930s, George Meredith's *The Egoist*, the attraction less the Willow Pattern of tragic love and philosophical comedy than the title itself. This is the first of a number of what Rabinovitz [*Development*, 77] has aptly termed levees, from the ceremonial rising of *le Roi Soleil* in France, at which a character of relative importance holds court in bed. Other instances are the preliminaries to Neary's breaking his bed [210-12], and the imperfect quincunx centered about Celia [232-33].

11.6 [11]: *his brain-body ratio*: in the typescript the phrase was "mind-body ratio," but the change accords with the avian imagery following. Mr. Kelly, with his fine bulb of skull and embedded eyes, is like Mr. Endon, if not so deeply entrenched as a denizen of the mind.

11.7 [11]: *"You . . . and possibly Murphy"*: in the *Whoroscope* Notebook, this exchange was to take place in Hyde Park, as Celia and Mr. Kelly wait for "the Star" (Venus) to appear.

12.1 [11]: *as though he were a doll*: Culik discusses Mr. Kelly's lack of "doll's eye movement," seeing it as a symptom of pineal disturbance and relating it to hydrocephalia, ataxia, somnolence, exophthalamia and nystagmia ['Medical Allusions,' 95-98]. I prefer to call it "old age," but conarial shrinkage, linking him to Murphy, is an alternative diagnosis.

12.2 [11]: *The friendship of a pair of hands*: compare Belacqua in *Dream* [5], "wringing his hands faute de mieux." Later in that novel [176], as the Alba clasps and unclasps her hands, her "inner spectator" yawns and turns over; in Occasionalist terms, there is lacking an essential synchronization of mind and body to resolve the impasse and initiate decisive movement. Beckett was fascinated by the expressive power of gesture [Knowlson, 56]. Watt reflects [33]: "The parts of the body are really very friendly at such times, towards one another." The *Whoroscope* Notebook records, with no source indicated: "una mano lava l'altra, e tutte e due lavano il viso" [It. "one hand washes the other, and both wash the face"].

12.3 [11]: *Celia's account*: the words "expurgated, accelerated, improved and reduced" (repeated 119) were added to the typescript, and reflect a sentence in 'Echo's Bones' [16]: "to divide, multiply, contract, enlarge, order, disarrange or in any other way image in the mind by thinking." This appears in the Dream Notebook [#141] amidst several items from the *Confessions*, but derives from Pusey's note (138; "Aug. de vera Relig. c. 10") to VII.xvii, distinguishing images of the essential soul from phantasms.

12.4 [11]: *Mr. and Mrs. Quentin Kelly*: nothing more is heard of either, but 'Quentin' reflects Beckett's predilection for the Quintilian 'Q,' which in turn invites logical speculation about "respective partners" and "being an only child."

12.5 [11]: *the ill-fated Morro Castle*: this ship, named for the "Moorish Castle" of Havana harbor, on September 8, 1934 at 2.45 a.m. was destroyed by fire off the New

Jersey coast, with a considerable loss of life. There were theories that the vessel was struck by lightning, that fires were intentionally set, or that carelessness and drunkenness by passengers and crew contributed. It remains a mystery of the sea, which did not inhibit the *British Journal of Astrology* [May 1935, 145] from offering an astrological reading (hence, 'ill-fated'). Celia has thus been on the streets a few months only before meeting Murphy.

12.6 [11]: *midsummer's night*: June 24, Shakespeare's night of love and the feast of St. John the Baptist, which Malone hopes to survive [179]. Sunset in London was at 20.19 GMT, but with an extra hour of Summer Time twilight would linger much longer [Whitaker, 102]. Celia's encounter with Murphy, though some have assumed it to take place in the morning [Farrow, 17], when all good Beckettians are in bed, is perfectly met in terms of the half-light.

12.7 [11]: *the sun being then in the Crab*: the Sun entered Cancer at the solstice on June 22, 1935, at 9 a.m. [Whitaker, 104]. In the crudest astrological sense, the first meeting of Celia and Murphy does not take place under an auspicious sign.

12.8 [11]: *Edith Grove . . . Cremorne Road . . . Lot's Road . . . Stadium Street*: in Chelsea, near the Embankment, and a short distance only from where Beckett was living in Gertrude Street, from which direction Celia is coming. Murphy presumably is attempting at the precise hour of sunset (on June 24, 21:19, adjusted time) to correlate his personal stars with those about to appear in the sky. The "beastly circumstantial" junction in space is curiously at odds with the lack of precise co-ordinates concerning the hour of his birth [see #23.3].

12.9 [11]: *the Reach*: the Chelsea Reach, that stretch of the Thames between Battersea Park and the Embankment, its restorative qualities a matter of opinion. In the days of Charles II it was a fashionable rendezvous for pleasure craft and elegant barges, and the setting for spectacular aquatic and fireworks displays. For Beckett the area retained much of that charm.

13.1 [12]: *declension*: literally, a fall, or coming from, as in the Alba's similar movement from light to dark [*Dream*, 166]. The effort required by Murphy to despatch his head upwards after the fall is similar to that exerted by some of the inhabitants of Dante's lower depths.

13.2 [12]: *demented particulars*: c.f. William Blake's *Annotations to Sir Joshua Reynold's Discourses* [1808], as cited in Bartlett: "To generalize is to be an idiot. To particularize is the alone distinction of merit." A like sentiment underlies Beckett's rejection of attempts to "unify" or "clarify" the historical chaos, or, worse, to anthropomorphize the inhuman necessities that provoke such chaos [German Diaries 4, January 15, 1937; Knowlson, 244]:

> What I want is the straws, flotsam, etc., names, dates, births and deaths, because that is all I can know. Meier says the background is more important than the foreground, the causes than the effects, the causes than their representatives and opponents. I say the background and the causes are an inhuman and incomprehensible machinery and venture to wonder what kind of appetite it is that can be appeased by the modern animism that consists in rationalising them. Rationalism is the last form of animism. Whereas the pure incoherence of times and men and places is at least amusing.

As Windelband notes [296], the *metaphysics of individualism* that accompany such a theory of knowledge assert that only particulars can be regarded as truly real (he invokes Roscellinus), and this is a position (a form of Nominalist irony) Beckett accepted, one that acknowledges the immediacy of "demented particulars."

14.1 [12]: *she suffered this gladly*: an echo of the wading girl scene in Joyce's *Portrait* [172]: "Long, long, she suffered his gaze." Murphy's encounter with Celia lacks Stephen's language of ecstasy but shares his sense of profane joy.

14.2 [12]: *Brava!*: the self-conscious approbation of one aware of the infelicity of '*Bravo!*'

14.3 [12]: *the Roussel dummy in Regent Street*: designed by John Nash in the early 1800s to connect Marylebone Park to the Regent's Palace and upgrade the Pall Mall and Haymarket areas, Regent Street quickly became one of the elegant areas of London, devoted to "shops appropriated to articles of fashion and taste." These included in the 1930s the establishment of J. Maison Roussel, elastic belt makers, 173 and 177 Regent Street, WI, retailers of trusses, corsetry and intimate apparel. Conspicuously featured in their shop window was a dummy with outstretched arms, a figure that was used as their logo [Phil Baker to CA].

14.4 [12]: *the hypogastrium*: from Gk. ὑπό, "under," and γαστήρ, "the stomach"; hence, the lowest part of the abdomen. Beckett probably took the word from Burton [*Anatomy*, I.1.2.iv, 96], where it is related to the physiology of melancholy.

14.5 [12]: *the brightness of the firmament*: the heavens of Genesis 1:6-8. In Augustine's *Confessions* [XIII.xv, 402-05; DN, #202], the Firmament is God's book, stretched over us like a skin, as in *Dream* [26]. Also in *Dream* [16], there is a scintillating rhapsody to the night firmament, an "abstract density of music, symphony without end, illumination without end," and the "tense passional intelligence" that traces it but "shall never be co-ordinate." O'Hara comments of the drama of narcissism played out here, that Murphy's indifference is what motivates Celia to accost him at second sight [*Hidden Drives*, 147].

14.6 [12]: *Celia's course was clear: the water*: literally, the Reach, but with an awareness that the decorous end of a harlot past her prime is the leap from a bridge of sighs into the Thames. "There would be time for that": comment on dit en anglais, "*à l'eau, c'est l'heure.*"

14.7 [12]: *the Battersea and Albert Bridges*: crossing the Thames within the Chelsea Reach. The embankment is lined with benches, for respite of the weary and sleep of the homeless. In the *Whoroscope* Notebook Beckett wrote: "Purgatorial atmosphere sustained throughout." As Knowlson has pointed out [205, 743], there is a Dantesque element about the setting that lifts it above the purely local and humdrum.

14.8 [12]: *a Chelsea pensioner*: an "emerited" soldier from the Royal Chelsea Hospital, further up the Embankment. The Hospital was founded by Charles II in 1682, built by Sir Christopher Wren, opened in 1694, and completed in 1702; the legend that it began at the instigation of Nell Gwynne is without foundation. It takes in old and disabled soldiers, offering board and lodging, and a small 'baccy allowance. The pensioners in their tunics are a conspicuous part of the Chelsea scene: blue in winter, but lobster-scarlet in the summer. The apothegm, "Hell roast this weather," contributes to the Dantesque soulscape.

14.9 [12]: *an Eldorado hokey-pokey man*: as Richard Coe notes ['Beckett's English,' 47-48]:

> In Murphy's London, two firms vied for the juvenile ice-cream market: Wall's and Eldorado. Both employed disabled former service-men to pedal round the streets on delivery-tricycles fitted with refrigerated containers. Wall's (blue-and-white, with the slogan 'Stop Me and Buy One') was reputed to have the better quality; but it was also more expensive. Eldorado (red-and-white) was the cheaper, inferior product, and cheap ice-cream was then known as 'hokey-pokey.'

Hokey-pokey ('Hoc est corpus' declining to 'Hocus-pocus') is not cheap ice-cream but a variety with bits of caramel in it. Beckett's choice hints at an interlude of paradise: the golden city of the conquistadors reduced to the "Eldorado Ice-Cream Co., Ltd, ice-cream manufacturers and merchants, 64 to 76 Stanford St., SE 1, T. A. 'Nysice.'" The "cruel machine" intimates the torments of Hell, with the "short interlude" of sleep a brief respite only. The bicycle was for Beckett so often an emblem of the body-mind dualism (what Hugh Kenner has called "the Cartesian centaur" of man and machine); but this is the only one mentioned in the novel.

14.10 [12]: *devils*: malebrachian overtones are to the fore, yet with a cloven foothold in the reality of artistic Chelsea: 'devils' are *printers' devils*, or apprentices in the printing trade; 'ghosts' are those who write under the names of others.

15.1 [13]: *A funnel vailed*: the boats are dipping their funnels (as if in salute) to pass beneath Battersea Bridge and enter the Reach; a sight which Beckett in a letter to McGreevy [August 4, 1932] said that he had often observed while sitting on the Albert Bridge, and which he found "très émouvant." He used it in 'Serena I': "I surprise me moved by the many a funnel hinged / for the obeisance to Tower Bridge." *Vails* are tips a servant might anticipate, deriving from the archaic sense of 'dips,' as to doff one's hat. Beckett may have taken the word from 'The Complaint' of Young's *Night Thoughts*: "Time lodged in their hands is Folly's Vails"; this appears on Blake's illustration to the passage in the nearby Tate.

15.2 [13]: *coupled abreast*: as is the small boy's kite [152]: that Celia notes such syzygy indicates her inner need for Murphy, perhaps even for a child of her own.

15.3 [13]: *Chelsea Old Church*: otherwise All Saints, on the Embankment at Old Church Road, its chapels dating back to the 13th century, with a Jacobean altar table, Holbein columns, and a long association with Nicholas Breakspear (Pope Adrian IV) and Sir Thomas More, whose statue now stands outside. Henry VIII married Jane Seymour here privately, before the state wedding in 1536. The bells Celia hears date back to the reign of Elizabeth I, although the campanile was partly demolished in 1667, to be rebuilt in a new steeple with a peel of six.

15.4 [13]: *He was still in the mouth of Stadium Street*: there is in Murphy's posture an ironic parallel with Socrates. As Burnet notes [*Greek Philosophy*, 130]:

> Socrates was subject to ecstatic trances. He would stand still for hours together buried in thought, and quite forgetful of the outer world. His friends

were accustomed to this and knew better than to disturb him when it happened. They simply left him alone until he came to himself.

It would be foolish to exaggerate the likeness (Murphy comes from, not to), and Beckett might have disowned the comparison, but there is an affinity between his later espousal of ignorance and impotence (but *after* years of intense study) and the reluctant recognition by Socrates that he perhaps knew more than his fellows, for unlike them he was conscious of his ignorance.

15.5 [13]: *accosted him in form*: in the expected manner; for other implications, see #90.6.

16.1 [13]: *It was the condition of their walking away*: the key to this enigmatic exposition is the time-honored system of mnemonics used to determine condition and mood of logical syllogisms ('accident' is used in the scholastic sense). Mercier recalls [33-34] their use Trinity Exhibition examinations in scholastic logic, but suggests that the terms are imperfectly recalled; this would be ironic were it so. 'Barbara,' 'Baroko' and 'Bramantip' are authentic, but 'Baccardi' for 'Bokardo' is a witty variant of Bacardi rum (in 'Echo's Bones' [5] Belacqua is invited to the lodgings of Zaborovna for a repast of garlic and white Cuban rum). The terms are those of Aristotelian logic, which prevailed for 2,000 years until challenged in the 19th century by Boolean and other systems. The categorical statements are of four kinds:

All <u>A</u>s are <u>B</u>s	'A-Statements'
No <u>A</u>s are <u>B</u>s	'E-Statements'
Some <u>A</u>s are <u>B</u>s	'I-Statements'
Some <u>A</u>s are not <u>B</u>s	'O-Statements'

The A-E-I-O derive from the vowels of 'Affirmo' and 'Nego' respectively, 'A' and 'I' affirming and 'E' and 'O' negating. In syllogisms, if 'S' is the subject-term, 'P' the predicate-term, and 'M' the middle term, and the conclusion always S—P, then 'S,' 'P' and 'M' can be arranged in four ways (these are called the four *figures*, or shapes of the syllogism):

1	2	3	4
M—P	P—M	M—P	P—M
S—M	S—M	M—S	M—S

Each of the three statements in a syllogism (S, M or P) is one of four categories (AAA, AAE, etc); these are *moods* or *forms* of the syllogism. For each figure there are (4.4.4) = 64 syllogistic forms; and since there are four figures (4.64) = 256 possibilities (512 if the premises are transposed). Aristotle found only 24 of these to be valid, and in the 13th century, tradition maintains, Pope John XXI composed a Latin verse saying which they were:

Barbara, Celarent, Darii, Ferioque prioris
Cesare, Camestres, Festino, Baroco secundae,
Tertia, Darapti, Disamis, Datisi, Felapton
Bocardo, Ferison, habet; Quartia insuper addit
Bramantip, Camenes, Dimaris, Fesapo, Fresison.

The three vowels tell which propositions are involved; thus 'Barbara' names the first mood of the first figure (the consonants reflect how Aristotle proved the validity of the named argument, but that is another matter). The verse names 19 of the 24 forms, the other five being 'weakened forms' (AAI and EAO in Fig. 1, EAO and AEO in Fig. 2, AEO in Fig. 4), i.e., with particular conclusions where, in the same figure, there are moods with the same premises and general conclusions (e.g., AAA instead of AAI).

In his *Methodus Inveniendi Argumenti* [1663], Geulincx proposes a logical method in Dispute of working from definitions and first principles towards what can be known, applying the system of mnemonics to various syllogisms considering the statement *Homo est animal* [L. "Man is an animal"], the categories mentioned by Murphy being [*Opera* 2, VIII §4, 92-95]:

Barbara: *Omne animal sentit, omnis homo est animal; ergo omnis homo sentit* ["Every animal is sensible (i.e., has senses), every man is an animal; therefore every man is sensible."]

Baroco: *Omnis homo est animal, aliquod vivens non est animal; ergo aliquod vivens non est homo* ["Every man is an animal, some living thing is not an animal; therefore some living thing is not a man."]

Bocardo: *Aliquod animal non est homo, omne animal sentit; ergo aliquod sentiens non est homo* ["Some animal is not a man, every animal is sensible; therefore, some sensible being is not a man."]

Applied to the present situation, various possibilities arise; from *barbara*: "Murphy is a man. All men love Celia. Therefore, Murphy loves Celia"; to *baroco*: "Murphy is a long lingering looker. Some who walk away are not long lingering lookers. Therefore, some who walk away are not Murphy"; and *bocardo*: "Some long lingering lookers do not walk away. All long lingering lookers love Celia. Therefore, some who love Celia do not walk away." *Baccardi* is not a legitimate term, but (implicitly) the weakened AAI form: "All men love Celia. All Murphies are men. Therefore, Murphy loves Celia" (it may be an appropriate short-circuit). *Bramantip*, as Murphy points out, is not applicable. In the French translation, Beckett substituted 'Baralipton,' which is not a reference to a nice cup of tea but a legitimate alternative (used from the 16th century) for complex syllogisms of the fourth class which may or may not be valid according to how the middle negative term is distributed.

16.2 [13]: *What is my life now but Celia?*: in tone, a response to Neary's "all is dross" [#5.2] and Volpone's "Come, my Celia" [#10.1]: eternal night might seem not the worst of fates.

16.3 [13]: *the moon being at conjunction*: this is the Sunday of June 30th, and Whitaker confirms [102] that the moon was indeed New, that is, sun and moon aligned with respect to the earth on the same celestial longitude and thus reflecting minimal light.

16.4 [13]: *the Battersea Park sub-tropical garden*: previously, Battersea Gardens, south of the Thames directly opposite the Chelsea Embankment. Once frequented by cabbage growers and asparagus planters, it was purchased in 1825 by the Marquess of Winchester, who turned the 200 acres into a park, at a cost of £238,620. It was opened to the public in 1858, featuring horticultural displays, woodland walks, trees (3,000 varieties), a boating lake, a deer park, a wolery [see #106.2], and, later, sporting facilities, a children's zoo, and peace pagoda. The Sub-Tropical Garden, some four acres in the middle of the Park, still exists, but no longer as what it was. Created in 1863 as an emblem of Empire upon which the sun never set, it was an attempt to form a micro-climate by means of rounded hills and sheltered belts, to encourage the growing of such exotica as palms, pineapples, and bananas. Over the years (in sympathy with the Empire) it gradually declined to a country garden, sub-tropical in name only (in 1998 there remained one last lonely palm), forsaking its romantic qualities yet retaining its charm.

16.5 [13]: *the ringing of the bell*: this took place in Battersea Park precisely at the hour of dusk, on June 30, 1935 at 21:18 p.m., adjusted Summer Time [Whitaker, 102]. Murphy's waiting for this exact moment may be conditioned by advice given in the 'Daily Guide' of the *British Journal of Astrology*, June 1935 [162]:

> *24th: Push business. Make contacts.*   [Celia "meets" Murphy]
> *30th: Evil for all things till evening. Then make plans.*   [Murphy proposes after dusk]

The coincidence is, I submit, too striking to be accidental. Beckett was aware of this monthly prognostication [see #216.3], and in a novel where little is accidental no other explanation seems more likely.

17.1 [14]: *Campanella's City of the Sun*: Murphy "rests" on this tome in the figurative sense of letting its astrological prognostications determine his future. Tommaso Campanella (1568-1639) was an Italian historian, astrologer and political visionary who spent half his three score and ten in prison, frequently under torture, as punishment for his revolutionary views (he was incarcerated with Bruno when the latter was led out to the stake, and escaped a similar fate only by feigning madness). He wrote some 100 works, ranging from politics and theology to astrology, but is best known for his *Città del sole*, or *Civitatis Solas*, the "City of the Sun," written in prison and Italian in 1602, but published in Latin, 1623, and thereafter frequently over the next 300 years. His was a vision of a Republican utopia based on the laws of Reason and Theology and governed by Astrology, Campanella seeing no conflict in these; Windelband [377] identifies the "inner contradiction" in his work; Burton in the *Anatomy* describes it as a witty fiction, but a mere chimera ['Democritus to the Reader,' 58]. As such it forms an ironic model for Murphy's Big World, with Our Hero an unlikely Solarian, given Campanella's emphasis on organized work and a regimented community of womanhood for purposes of sexual relief and procreation; the act of intercourse determined by favorable signs, yes, but directed by *il maestro* and *la maestra*, who ensure that those paired off have prepared themselves for three nights, properly digested their food and said their prayers, before their cell doors are opened at the auspicious hour.

17.2 [14]: *by hook or by crook*: by foul means or fair, deriving from the ancient right of peasants to gather such firewood as might be obtained by use of a stick with an iron crook [Brewer]; but assumed to refer to marriage either compelled or blessed by a bishop's crozier. Cromwell boasted that Waterford would fall "by Hook or Crooke," the reference being to two adjacent landing places in Counties Wexford and Waterford. Murphy's wish to marry seems less social conformity than astrological imperative. Campanella has much to say about the favorable alignment of the heavenly bodies to ensure healthy issue, but nothing in the *Città del sole* suggests the need to unite before the moon is in opposition, i.e., on the other side of the earth from the sun, thus reflecting maximal light (a Full Moon), as next on July 16th. There seems no reason for Murphy's urgency, in the event not acted on, unless he is worried that the next Full Moon will be eclipsed [Whitaker, 106]. Rather, the mention of Campanella (not in the French translation) acknowledges the utopic desire for uxoric bliss governed by astrology.

17.3 [14]: *find a Quintilian*: Marcus Fabius Quintilianus, Roman rhetorician c. 35-95 AD and head of the School of Oratory. His twelve-volume *Institutio Oratoria*, or Training of an Orator, forms the standard classical treatise on oratorical composition and the devices of rhetoric. He was known for the mode of inquisition rehearsed by Mr. Kelly, who begins, though he loses the thread, by invoking the classical categories or *memoria technica* of scholasticism, whereby any subject might be divided into all possible parts for analysis [*Institutio Oratoria* III.vi.23ff]. The seven terms are set out in Geulincx's *Ethica* [VI.I.1, 141]: *Quis? quid? ubi? quibus auxiliis? cur? quomodo? quando?* ["Who? what? where? by what means? why? in what way? when?"]. Beckett would use these as first principle of the early drafts of *Watt*, where a figure named Quin arises against the waste and void. In *Godot*, Lucky's application of reason to the extension of God (if He is infinite, how can He have a long white beard?) degenerates to "quaquaquaqua." The categories go back beyond Quintilian to Aristotle [*Categoriae*, 4], and to the process of reasoning traditionally applied to the proposition that "Socrates is a man": Celia, responding in an orderly manner, concludes that Murphy of necessity is Murphy (which invalidates her later attempts to "make a man" of him).

17.4 [14]: *prospects*: the Hibernian equivalent of Johnson's comment to Boswell, that the noblest prospect a Scotchman ever sees is the highroad to England [*Life*, July 6, 1763, 145].

17.5 [14]: *Mr. Quigley*: the name suggests Oscar Quigley, a well-known Dublin chessplayer of the time. Beckett used it for the protagonist of 'Lightning Calculation,' which encapsulates several key moments in the story. Like Mr. Quin of *Watt*, Mr. Quigley gradually faded from the scene until little was left save his name and role as *Deus ex machina*. Given the Cartesian structure of the Big World as a machine, there is a need for something—someone—to provide for Murphy. Mr. Quigley's existence is a consequence of his residency in Holland, i.e., he is a Dutch Uncle, an excessively candid or stern guide and adviser, as in Horace [*Odes* 3.xii.3]: "mentuentes patruae verbera linguae" [L. "dreading the castigations of an uncle's tongue"]. The reasoning, like the income, is as necessary as it is sufficient. After his father's death Beckett was given what he called "a Protestant income," enough to survive on but not to enjoy.

18.1 [14]: *never ripped up old stories*: an indirect admonition to forget the past and accept the present. The phrase was copied into the *Whoroscope* Notebook from Sheridan's 1777 dramaticule, *A Trip to Scarborough* [John Pilling to CA]. In Act IV.i, disguised as his wealthy brother Lord Foppington, the penniless Tom Fashion woos Miss Hoyden, whose Nurse tells stories of her childhood, and is rounded on smartly: "Pr'ythee, nurse, don't stand ripping up old stories, to make one ashamed before one's love . . . If you have a mind to make him have a good opinion of a woman, don't tell him of what one did then, tell him what one can do now." Admittedly, it is rather uncertain what Murphy can do now. Lord Gall used the phrase in 'Echo's Bones' [13], but that story getting "no forrader" Beckett recycled it in *Murphy*. More literally, Beckett himself rarely ripped up drafts.

18.2 [14]: *his bolt was shot*: "a fool's bolt is soon shot" [Bartlett], and "Justice must be done, though the heavens fall"; the two combined in the image of a Tyburnian trapdoor.

18.3 [14]: *as though by clockwork*: an Occasionalist conceit [see #109.1 and #178.9]; i.e., it would be a miracle. The comparison of Mr. Kelly's immense cerebrum and Celia's not very large brain is less a statement of misogyny than a crack at phrenology.

19.1 [15]: *its caecum*: from L. *caecus*, "blind"; hence, the blind gut, a pouch at the beginning of the large intestine. Mr. Kelly's scraping together of his *disjecta membra* caricatures the principles of Associationism, the elements not held together (bricks without mortar): he is not an organized whole [Woodworth, 95; see #56.4]. There may echo *Confessions* [X.xi, 106-07], where Augustine says of the images brought to the soul by the senses: "et cogenda rursus, ut sciri possint, id est velut ex quandam dispersione colligenda, unde dictum est cogitare" [L. "and they must be rallied and drawn together again, that they may be known; that is to say, they must as it were be collected and gathered together from their dispersions; whence the word cogitation is derived"]. Compare Beckett's comment in the German Diaries: "The point is that the *nosce te ipsum* [know thyself] is no more mobile than the *carpe te ipsum* [gather thyself] of Murphy" [*GD* 4, January 18, 1937; see also #4.2].

19.2 [15]: *to consume away*: an ironic echo of Yeats's 'Sailing to Byzantium':

> Consume my heart away; sick with desire
> And fastened to a dying animal
> It knows not what it is; and gather me
> Into the artifice of eternity.

19.3 [15]: *it was certain*: one of the few things in the novel that is, such certainty being the consequence of the analytic given that Mr. Quigley is a "Dutch uncle" [see #17.5].

20.1 [15]: *the imponderables of personality*: a phrase derived from the Introduction to Alfred Adler's *The Neurotic Constitution*. Knowlson notes of Beckett [86], that "not unlike his character, Belacqua, in this respect at least, he saw the sexual act as not necessarily related to love." Murphy seems to share this view, but Celia (curiously, given her profession) does not. There are serious consequences for him of her returning to work (the disruption of the pattern of serenade, nocturne and alba), but the attitude maintained is the logical consequence of his dualism. For the "normal" reader, however, whatever imponderable that might be, the miscarriage of the tribute ensures some degree of ironic detachment from Murphy.

20.2 [16]: *the Archaeus*: the archei are, for followers of Paracelsus, immaterial principles presiding over the animal and vegetable economy, thus energizing all living substances. The chief archeus was situated in the stomach, with subordinate archei regulating other organs. Thus, Murphy respects the bodily necessities; and by so doing conforms to Geulincx's third Obligation [*Ethica* I.ii.6 §1, 44], to eat, sleep and drink in moderation. For Geulincx, acknowledging the body as a machine did not negate the obligation to keep it in reasonable working order; in the 'Annotata' relating to this section [§§20-21, 243-44] he reconciles this with the prime ethical axiom, *Ubi nihil vales, nihil velis* [see #178.9].

21.1 [16]: *apperceiving himself*: 'apperception' is for Leibniz and Kant the active process of the mind's reflecting upon itself, the mind's perception of itself as a conscious agent, the consciousness of being conscious. This implies the faculty to perceive the logical paradox thereof: as Brett notes [123-24]: "If I do not perceive that I see in one indivisible act, there will be that which sees and that which perceives, and these will require a third faculty to unite them. To cut short this infinite process we assert that the sense perceives itself." In Kant's terms, this is the synthetic unity of apperception; to which Schopenhauer pays special attention in *The Fourfold Root of the Principle of Sufficient Reason* [§§40-45, 165-76]. In his 'Recent Irish Poetry' [*Disjecta*, 70], Beckett commented on "the cold comforts of apperception," but in such a way as to suggest few, if any, valid alternatives.

21.2 [16]: *the starry concave*: compare the conclusion to Kant's *Critique of Pure Reason*, as cited in Bartlett: "Two things fill the mind with ever-increasing wonder and awe, the more often and the more intensely the mind of thought is drawn to them: the starry heavens above me, and the moral law within me." To which Schopenhauer, at the end of his main argument, responds: "but conversely, to those in whom the will has turned and has denied itself, this our world, which is so real, with all its suns and milky-ways—is nothing" [*WWI*, I.iv §71, 532].

Schopenhauer's theme finds its clearest expression in a passage [*WWI*, I.iii §38, 266] that may underlie Murphy's "metaphysical considerations" at this point (or moment):

> If we lose ourselves in the contemplation of the infinite greatness of the universe in space and time, meditate on the thousands of years that are past or to come, or if the heavens at night actually bring before our eyes innumerable worlds and so force upon our consciousness the immensity of the universe, we feel ourselves dwindle to nothing . . . But at once there rises this ghost of our own nothingness, against such lying impossibility, the immediate consciousness that all these worlds exist only as our idea, only as modifications of the subject of pure knowing . . . The vastness of the world which disquieted us before, rests now in us; our dependence upon it is annulled by its dependence upon us.

This, Schopenhauer concludes, is the sense of the sublime arising through the consciousness of the vanishing nothingness of our own body in the presence of a vastness which, from another point of view, itself exists only in our idea, and of which we are the knowing subject.

More mundanely: closer inspection reveals an unexplained absence of the letter 'l' (in 'conclave'). This might be Beckett's tribute to Martha's "I do not like that other wor[l]d" [*Ulysses*, 74]; or a response to André Breton's advice [*Manifeste* 1924, 47-48], on how to write a surrealist composition: "A la suite du mot dont l'origine vous semble suspecte, posez une lettre quelconque, la lettre *l* par example, toujours la lettre *l*, et ramenez l'arbitraire en imposant cette lettre pour initiale du mot qui suivra." [Fr. "at the end of a word whose origin seems suspect to you, place some letter or other, the letter *l* for example, always the letter *l*, and create an arbitrary effect by imposing this letter as first of the word following"]. The advice is not taken literally, but Mr. Kelly's "pythonic glaze" [24] may owe its fixity to this suggestion.

21.3 [16]: *a chronic emeritus*: an *emeritus* is one honorably discharged from active duty, yet retained on the rolls; *chronic*, from Gk. χρόνος, "time," suggests long-ailing. Schopenhauer uses *emeritus* of one who has attained true absence of will [*WWI*, I.iv §65, 467].

21.4 [16]: *Ixion . . . Tantalus*: denizens of the gloom, as described by Beckett in the *Whoroscope* Notebook (December 1935), the almost-illegible notes deriving (in part) from Lemprière:

> *Ixion*: King of Thessaly. Married Dia daughter of Eioneus. Father by her of Pirithous. Murdered Eioneus treacherously at a banquet, precipitating him into fiery pit. Zeus took pity on him, purified him, carried him to heaven & had him sit at his table. But Ixion courted Hera. Zeus created a phantom resembling her, by which Ixion begot a centaur. Chained by Hermes to a wheel which he rolled perpetually in lower world, scourged & ejaculating "Benefactors should be honoured."

Tantalus: Son of Zeus & Pluto, Father of Pelops & Niobe. King of Lydia or Corinth. Having divulged confidences of Zeus, made to him at table of the God, he was punished in lower world by being afflicted with a raging thirst & placed in a lake whose waters receded as soon as he made to drink. Above his head branches of fruit likewise receded. And a boulder ever threatened to crush him. According to other traditions, this punishment was for having served his son Pelops to Gods as a repast, in order to test them. Or that he stole nectar and ambrosia from table of Gods & gave them to his friends, or finally that he tricked Paleaus & received golden dog of Zeus.

Beckett commented in *Proust* [13]: "So that we are rather in the position of Tantalus, with this difference, that we allow ourselves to be tantalised." He would return to the theme himself in his *Act without Words I* (1957/1963), the mute character reaching for the receding fruit with all the simian vulgarity of Köhler's anthropoid apes [see #5.1].

21.5 [16]: *Providence will provide*: turning the synthetic sentence "the Lord will provide" into its analytic equivalent, and meeting in the empirical world a logical impasse. In *Exagmination* [4-5], Beckett has Vico define Providence as (I paraphrase Croce's untranslated Italian) a mind both diverse and with all contraries but always superior to the humanity whose ends it thereby serves more fully, adding: "What could be more definitely utilitarianism?"

22.1 [16]: *the Earl's Court Exhibition*: Earl's Court is the aspect of London SW a little to the NW of West Brompton; the first and most celebrated of its exhibitions was held in 1887, but they continued until 1914 when the military requisitioned the grounds. The use of "transports" is unusual, the normal collocation being of joy.

22.2 [16]: *the hireling fleeth*: as in John 10:13: "The hireling fleeth, because he is an hireling, and careth not for the sheep." The context suggests when the wolf comes; i.e, to the door.

22.3 [16]: *What shall a man give*: although it is cynically observed in Job 2:4 that "Skin for skin, yea, all that a man hath will he give for his life," the reference is to the New Testament refiguration of this, in Matthew 16:26: "For what is a man profited, if he shall gain the whole world, and lose his own soul? or what shall a man give in exchange for his soul?" By logical transposition the conclusion follows: Murphy gives up his soul for Celia.

22.4 [16]: *a point*: a nice and knotty point [see #131.3], rather than one scored. Murphy wants to live in the mind; work is done by the body, so the mind must flee the thought; Murphy's body wants Celia; Celia requires work; *ergo*, Murphy must give up his mind for Celia. Mr. Kelly's "Points one and two" refer to the Biblical quotations.

22.5 [17]: *a corpus of incentives*: the request to "procure" such an object rephrases the legal injunction of *habeas corpus* [L. "produce the body"] in the idiom of the pimp. In the *Whoroscope* Notebook the phrase is "corpus of motives," which reflects more directly its source in Schopenhauer's "Law of Motives," or *motivation* [*Fourfold Root*, §43, 171, and elsewhere]. He proclaims this as the cornerstone to his entire Metaphysic, the point being that the *Law* is causality from within, whereas the *corpus*, or body, is without.

23.1 [17]: *Berwick Market*: this began in the 18th century when shop-keepers in the street (which cuts north across Oxford Street, near the Tottenham Court Road) began to display their wares on the pavement, but the market was not officially recognized until 1892. By then it had become a seedy crowded area, with cut prices on every-thing, particularly materials and silks, nightgowns, gloves, etc., and the inevitable red-light bargains. The market was affected by the growth of Oxford Street as a shopping center, but remained active in 1935.

23.2 [17]: *a swami*: a Hindu holy man, with the gift of prophecy. In the *Whoroscope* Notebook Beckett conceived the action in terms of a protagonist, 'X,' and a horoscope, 'H,' the latter acquiring an authority and fatality that would make it no longer a guide to be consulted but a force to be reckoned with. For the confidence Murphy feels in any system outside his own, and the irony of replacing the Cartesian God with Astrology, see #109.1.

23.3 [17]: *the science that had got over Jacob and Esau*: 'science' is used with a 17th century intonation, but an irony arises from the etymology of 'horoscope' [Gk. ὥρα, "hour" and σκοπέω, "I look at"], for the precise position of the stars and planets at the moment of birth is of utmost importance. However, as the *British Journal of Astrology* repeatedly stated, it was possible to get over the problem by working back from the observed qualities of the native to the "certain" hour of his birth, i.e., when the condi-tions were such as to condition said qualities (chess players might call this retrograde analysis). Twins complicated matters should the gemels display marked difference, as most famously in the instance of Jacob and Esau, the latter an hairy man who pref-ered goats to sheep. Having sold his birthright for a mess of pottage, Esau deceived his father into giving him the blessing rightly his brother's [Genesis 25:27 to 27:35]. The problem was propounded in Augustine [*Confessions*, VII.vi, 358-59; DN, #131], to illustrate the futility of such prediction; but the science of Astrology got over that, as Tommaso Campanella does in the Preface to his *Astrologia* [5], by insisting that at the moment of nativity the heart ("*principium vitae*") of Esau lay "*in diverso situ*" to the hori-zon and the stars as compared with that of Jacob, which assumed a better disposition. This seems to be Dante's understanding [*Paradiso* VIII.130-31].

23.4 [17]: *It*: i.e., the [W]horoscope, the pun also celebrated in Beckett's poem of that name.

23.5 [17]: *Approach, my child*: as Christ to Mary Magdalene, it has been suggested; an attractive notion (given Celia's response [24]), but unsupported by the Word.

24.1 [17]: *the classic pythonic glaze*: the fixed gaze (the wandering 'I' returns; see #21.2) of a Pythoness, or Priestess of Delphi, in trance before transmitting the words of the oracle. The 'python' was a huge serpent hatched from the mud of Deucalion's flood and slain by Apollo near Delphi, the sacred *omphalos* whose vestals were named accordingly. Pythagoras was so called because a pythic oracle had predicted his birth.

24.2 [17]: *pronate*: palm down, here literally on the 'nates' or temple. Unlike Neary [4-5], Mr. Kelly brings his dialectic to a satisfactory sublation.

24.3 [17]: *sever your connexion*: the typescript reads "sever your connexion with this ~~bleeder~~," with 'Murphy' substituted for the final word. In like vein, Bloom advises Stephen to "sever his connection" with Buck Mulligan [*Ulysses*, 618]. There is in the

Whoroscope Notebook a maieutic saw: "The wise man will not marry the sister of a bleeder"; significant not only because it anticipates the haemophilia of *Watt* [102] but as one of the few dated entries ["4/12/35"]. Beckett had returned to Ireland by December; the entry dates other items in the same ink and indicates what he was reading then. The deletion makes the link to the Old Boy's death less explicit [138-39], conceals the vulpine pun on Time's severing our good [see #10.1], and obscures the connexion with the final snapping of the string of the kite [281].

25.1 [18]: *his kite*: a Cartesian emblem, the kite of the mind tenuously attached to the hand of the body (Mr. Kelly's "out of sight" has the corollary, "out of mind"). The kite, Moody suggests [220-22], is like an unseen speck or atomic mote in the void, the sky a macroscopic image of Murphy's little world. The novel germinated from Beckett's watching the old men with their kites in Kensington Gardens, and his resolution that this should be the final image. In a letter to McGreevy [September 8, 1935], he tells of the discovery:

> I begin to think I have gerontophilia on top of the rest. The little shabby respectable men you see on a Saturday afternoon and Sunday, pottering about doing odd jobs in the garden, or flying kites immense distances at the Round Pond, Kensington. Yesterday there was a regular club of the latter, with a sprinkling of grandchildren, sitting in a crescent waiting for a wind. The kites lying in the grass with their long tails beautifully cared for, all assembled and ready. For they bring them in separate pieces, the sticks and tail all rolled up in the canvas and a huge spool of string. Some have boats as well, but not the real enthusiasts. Then great perturbation to get them off at the first breath of wind. They fly them almost out of sight, yesterday it was over the trees to the south, into an absolutely cloudless iridescent evening sky. Then when the string is run out they simply sit there watching them, chucking at the string, the way coachmen do at a reins, presumably to keep them from losing height. There seems to be no competition at all involved. Then after about an hour they wind them gently in and go home. I was really rooted to the spot yesterday, unable to go away and wondering what was keeping me. Extraordinary effect too of birds flying close to the kites but beneath them. My next old man, or young old man, not of the big world but of the little world, must be a kite-flyer. So absolutely disinterested, like a poem, or useful in the depths where demand and supply coincide, and the prayer is the god. Yes, prayers rather than poem, in order to be quite clear, because poems are prayers, of Dives and Lazarus one flesh.

3

26.1 [19]: *full and at perigee*: this is the night of September 12, as is later revealed. Rabinovitz [*Developments*, 120 n15] errs in supposing the evening to be September 11 [see #114.1], and the passage to be full of deliberate error [see, however, #26.3]. According to Whitaker [114], the moon was full at 20 hours 18.3 minutes, having achieved perigee, or its position during the lunar month closest to the earth, at 18.1 hours. The coincidence of full moon and perigee is not particularly striking, occurring on the average about once a year (as it had on July 26, 1934 and would again on October 30, 1936 [Whitaker 1934, 106 and 1936, 134; noted by Kennedy, 126n]).

26.2 [19]: *by a striking coincidence*: the echo of 'Eumaeus' and Bloom's "struck him ... as a striking coincidence" [*Ulysses*, 615] adds the requisite note of mockery, there being for Beckett a significant difference between a coincidence and a striking one.

26.3 [19]: *29,000 miles nearer the earth*: the figure is impossible: at *apogee* (farthest from earth), September 26, the moon was 252,590 miles from the earth; at *perigee* (closest), 221,740 miles. Sighle Kennedy, who first addressed the problem, adds [162-63]: "the figure Mr. Beckett gives is so high that it destroys the sense of perigee and apogee. The greatest distance that the moon ever gets from the earth is 252,710 miles; the closest it ever gets to earth is 221,463 miles—a total difference of only 31,247 miles." The mean distance is 239,000 miles [Whitaker, 152]. Kennedy sees the error as deliberate (as does Rabinovitz), put there to see if the reader is awake ("gentle skimmer" predictably follows). The error was translated in the French version, but the mistake may represent an approximate difference between apogee and perigee, 29,000 being a handy figure (the height of Mount Everest in feet, a useless tag which every schoolboy knew), Beckett misunderstanding and therefore misrepresenting the position. The error could be an affront to logic and rationality, as others are, but Beckett usually has reasons for misrepresentation and they are lacking here.

26.4 [19]: *for four years*: another error: in April 1932, perigee was 221,730 miles [Whitaker 1932, 14], a difference of ten miles. Rabinovitz again assumes intention [*Development*, 107], but no reader could readily verify this; I suspect Beckett overlooked this entry as he checked back to March 1931, when the distance was 221,600 miles [Whitaker 1931, 10].

26.5 [19]: *Exceptional tides were expected*: the details are from Whitaker: the dates *September 13-15 starred [116] in accordance with an earlier note [89] explaining that "days thus indicated throughout the Almanac are those on which High Tides may be expected" (in September, during the early hours of the morning). There is elsewhere a description of such tides [155]:

> These extremes do not usually coincide with the times of these phases of the Moon, but occur later, by an interval known as the *age* of the tide—then, at London Bridge, the highest of spring tide occurs 2 1/2 days after New or Full Moon, and the neap tide is similarly delayed . . . Besides this there are differences due to the varying distance of the Moon from the Earth, and when the Moon is at or near perigee at New or Full the tide is specially high.

26.6 [19]: *The Port of London Authority was calm*: i.e., at the thought of flooding, this being likely should high tides and lunar conditions combine with strong northerly winds in the North Sea and heavy rains in the Thames basin to cause a dangerous rise in the river [Whitaker, 89]. There was an urban myth, before elaborate flood-gates and controls were established against precisely that eventuality, that England was slowly tilting downwards in the east and that one day in the geological future the City of London and its Underground would be flooded.

The Port of London Authority was established under the Port of London Act in 1908, for the purpose of "administering, preserving and improving the Port of London," working the docks, and with the duty to "diminish the evils of casual employment." The Port, operating calmly under the Chairmanship of Lord Ritchie of Dundee, comprised in 1935 the tidal portion of the Thames from Teddington to the sea (some 69 miles of wharves), with five dock systems covering 4,203 acres, "of which 722 are water" [Whitaker, 479-81].

26.7 [19]: *scarlet muffler*: a sudden flash of color. The phrasing that follows ("It was after ten" . . . "a man smelling strongly of drink") is in marked contrast with the ironic tone of the first paragraph, and suggestive of a Victorian mystery—perhaps Conan Doyle's *A Study in Scarlet*, with its "scarlet thread of murder running through the colourless skein of life."

27.1 [19]: *stigmatised*: used in the casual sense of "defined dismissively," and only remotely suggesting a laborer's bleeding hands. The word is repeated [249].

27.2 [19]: *a fake jossy*: from 'joss,' in iggorant opinion, the house-god of the heathen Chinee, a temple hence known as a 'joss-house.'

27.3 [19]: *a Fury*: one of the three *Erinyes*, avengers of wrong done to natural piety and murder within the family, often punishing the guilty by inflicting madness [see #175.2]: Tisiphone, the Avenger of blood; Alecto, the Implacable; and Megaera, the Disputacious. They were also known as the 'Eumenides' or "gracious ones," an apotropaic term to turn away wrath. For Beckett there is a private pun, as implied by the narrator of 'Ding-Dong' when he says that his sometime friend Belacqua "could give what he called the Furies the slip by merely setting himself in motion" [*MPTK*, 39]; this implies avoiding the bailiffs.

27.4 [19]: *a tipstaff*: an officer of the King's Bench, attending the judges, possessing a staff of office tipped in silver, the touch of which designated a prisoner to be taken into custody. The warrant "to distrain" is that permitting the seizing or holding of goods.

27.5 [20]: *the bailiff . . . the bum-bailiff*: from Turk. *bajalus*, one in charge of the imperial children, as transferred to the Venetian ambassador at Constantinople, or 'balio,' and thence to any magistrate. A 'bum-bailiff' is a lower officer, one who initiates arrests by touching on the back. Beckett copied 'bumtrap' from Magistrate Fielding into the *Whoroscope* Notebook, but did not use it.

27.6 [20]: *the usual auspices*: here, the sounds of silence (the phrase presumably adjectival).

27.7 [20]: *The gentle passion*: compare "the gentle sin," as used by Romeo of the love that will destroy the star-cross'd lovers [*Romeo and Juliet*, I.v.96].

28.1 [20]: *devil's finger*: the middle finger, or *digitus infamis*, as flourished in the *Clouds* of Aristophanes [651-52], and glossed in the Dream Notebook [#748]: "digitus tertius, digitus diaboli" [L. "third finger, devil's finger"]. The source is unknown. Beckett had used it in 'Walking Out' [*MPTK*, 115], where Belacqua draws designs on the jennet's coat; he would do so again in 'First Love' [34], where the narrator recalls tracing the letters of 'Lulu' with his devil's finger into an old cowclap. This supports Harvey's gloss [152] of the phrase "His finger" in 'Serena III' as the finger of Christ that "wrote love in the dust."

28.2 [20]: *as last heard of*: the paradox of motion, of things getting faster and faster until they stopped [see #9.1], has been short-circuited unexpectedly.

28.3 [20]: *a turning of the other cheek*: as appropriate to one in the crucified position, this being Christ's injuction to resist not evil [Matthew 5:39], but rather walk an extra mile.

28.4 [20]: *idle speculation*: a sentiment echoed in *Waiting for Godot* [51], when Vladimir contemplates Pozzo lying in a heap, and says, "Let us not waste our time in idle discourse"—before launching into his longest speech.

29.1 [20]: *A huge pink naevus*: a congenital discoloration, such as a birthmark, the consequence of the grouping of blood vessels too near the skin: "an extensive capillary angioma" [266]. According to Adler, such "peripheral stigmata" as naevi may indicate "more profound organ-inferiorities" [*Neurotic Constitution*, 8]. Murphy's birthmark becomes, in the end, his deathmark and the *modus morendi* of his being identified, just as (or rather, not as) Fielding's Joseph Andrews is restored to fortune by his strawberry blemish.

29.2 [20]: *an old Girl Guide*: one anxious to gain her First-Aid badge by knowing the right thing to do, rather than doing the right thing. The mechanics of getting Murphy onto the bed, admittedly, show an Archimedean ingenuity.

29.3 [21]: *the face*: the compact visual unit emerging from the blotch [see #4.3].

29.4 [21]: *her yellow hair*: as in Yeats's 'For Anne Gregory': to "Love you for yourself alone, / And not your yellow hair." The color is commended by Burton [*Anatomy*, III.2.2.ii, 517] as the type of beauty, that of the Virgin Mary [DN, #842].

29.5 [21]: *the short circuit*: love requited [see #5.5]. The position may owe something to Paul Éluard's 'L'Amour' in *L'Immaculée conception* (1930) [*Oeuvres complètes*, 345-48], where postures adopted by lovers during "l'amour réciproque" [Fr. "requited love"] are given poetic names; Celia's lying "athwart" Murphy could be added to the list.

30.1 [21]: *machine*: the echo of Geulincx made explicit [see #1.5].

30.2 [21]: *had cracked the mirror*: a sign of bad luck, traditionally of death in the family.

31.1 [22]: *this neap*: picking up the metaphor of 'ebbed' and 'strand': the neap is the tide just after the first and third quarters of the lunar month, when the difference between high and low is least. Beckett copied the phrase "he turned a little yellow—as well he might" from Burton's *Anatomy* [III.3.1.ii, 634; DN, #946], and employed it in *Dream* [182, 235].

31.2 [22]: *little bull of incommunication*: the "life-warrant" is likened to the Papal Bull of Excommunication, so-called from the *bulla*, or leaden capsule of the Seal appended to the document, and as such more weighty than the Brief, which was sealed in wax with the Pope's private Seal. The Bull of Excommunication could affirm the Lesser, sequestration of the individual from services of the Church, or the Greater, exclusion from the sacraments and all intercourse with the faithful.

31.3 [22]: *Mercury*: according to Brewer, the planet Mercury "signifieth subtill men, ingenious, inconstant, rymers, poets, advocates, orators, phylosophers, arithmeticians, and basic fellowes." No explanation of "planet par excellence" is offered, but Beckett had copied the phrase into the *Whoroscope* Notebook from the *Britannica* of 1911 or 1926 (it remained until the 1954 edition). Associations between the planets, metals and colors are there outlined: Mercury is affiliated with quicksilver, the entry stating that it has no fixed color but rather assumes that of any other planet conjoined.

32.1 [22]: *blackmail*: delivered by Mercury, postman of the Gods; originally, "black rent" [OE *mal*, "payment"], or tribute in the form of goods demanded for immunity from pillage (as opposed to "white rent," or silver), whence the sense of extortion.

32.2 [22]: *THEMA COELI*: L. "theme of the heavens," a common flourish, with overtones of Aristotle's *De caelo*. 'Thema' assumes the meaning of "Chart" or picture of the sky at a particular date, with the Sun at the Ascendant, or on the eastern horizon. Jung insisted upon his patients having their horoscopes cast, and Dr. Wilfred Bion, from whom Beckett was receiving treatment, took a keen interest in them; Beckett may have had his drawn up at Bion's request [Knowlson, 207-08]. Harrison [76-77] argues for a pattern within the novel based on Murphy's journey through the twelve houses; this is nonsense, but astrological sigla (Goats, Twins, a Scorpion) appear erratically. Athough lacking any sense of irony, Kennedy has come up with a few good things, including the opinion of a professional astrologer [253] to the effect that as a whole the horoscope is not coherent, but there are vague implications, none of them good: "Murphy's horoscope presents almost every planet in the position noted as most uncongenial for astrological rating." This will be touched on in the notes to follow, after a four-fold caveat: astrology is not an exact science, and every "authority" differs on detail; Beckett is working with a competent command of the jargon but is parodying the methodology; the reader need not know more than is necessary for the purpose; and, finally, since Descartes would not have his birth date known [Baillet, 4-5], one should not overlook the jest of a Big World structured according to Cartesian dualism, in which Astrology takes the place of God. Beckett would not say with Burton: "Astra regunt homines, et regit astra Deus" [L. "the stars rule men, but God rules the stars"; *Anatomy*, I.2.1.iv, 133n].

The model for Murphy's horoscope may be that offered by the *British Journal of Astrology*, itself the reincarnation of *Old Moore's Monthly Messenger* [see #93.2 and #216.3], and sold at 6d, the price of Suk's nativity (in the *Whoroscope* Notebook, the "corpus of motives" was priced at 1/-). In 'The Student's Page' of the issue of April 1935, E. H. Bailey, Editor of the *BJA*, outlined the four principles involved in the casting of horoscopes:

1. The personal nature, or the disposition, life, character and mind of the subject.
2. The physical nature, temporal and physical conditions, health, disease, and death.
3. The worldly position, relating to all temporal and material conditions of life, such as finance, marriage, profession, etc.
4. The progress of the life, particulars of good and bad fortune as shown by the directions operating after birth.

For each of the above Bailey insists upon the importance of the Ascendant [see #33.4], the fixed point around which the entire horoscope revolves. Beckett does not imitate the *BJA* closely; rather, he has taken its procedures and parodied them ruthlessly, incorporating materials from other penny pamphlets that may never be found. As a final irony, the *BJA* claimed to have been founded for two purposes: to combat "the growing menace of cheap and so-called horoscopes offered by pretenders with no knowledge of the science"; and to enable the public "to obtain reliable astrological calculations, from Certified members of the Institute." These were offered at the Special Rate, far beyond Murphy's means, of 21/- (full horoscope), or 10/6 (delineations only).

32.3 [22]: *Delineations*: the identification of aspects of character, from the positions of the zodiacal signs; as opposed to "directional influences" relating to the prediction of future events. There was debate as to whether one's fate was written in the stars or the signs, with respect to which the *BJA* was unequivocal: "The twelve signs of the zodiac are the basis for all horoscopical calculation" [February 1935, 90]. From the

Britannica, Beckett recorded the difference between "natural" and "judicial" astrology, the former predicting the motion of heavenly bodies and occurrences such as eclipses, the latter their influence upon human destiny.

32.4 [22]: *Ramaswami Krishnaswami Narayanswami Suk*: an improbable concatenation of Hindu sacred names, each suffixed by *swami*, or holy man: *Rama*, the 6th, 7th and 8th incarnation of Vishnu; *Krishna*, the well-beloved, the 8th atavar of Vishnu, most worshiped of the Hindu deities; *Narayan*, an alternative name of Vishnu. A constant theme in the *BJA*, 1934-36, was the attraction of "Hindu methods." By fateful conjunction, R. K. Narayan's *Swami and Friends* was published in 1935. 'Suk' is out of place: the word (also *souk*, *suq*, or *sukh*) is Arabic for a market-place or bazaar.

32.5 [22]: *genethliac*: from Gk. γενεθλιακός, "of one's birth"; i.e., a caster of nativities, *genethlialogy*, or Natal Astrology, being that branch of the science which deals with the preparation of individual horoscopes.

32.6 [22]: *"Then I defy you, Stars"*: Romeo's response [*Romeo and Juliet*, V.i.24] to the false news of Juliet's death, whereupon he seeks an opportune apothecary and buys a dram of poison to dispatch himself beside her. In *Finnegans Wake* [467], Joyce refers to an "ill-starred punster"; this is usually assumed to be Beckett, though Knowlson [723] questions this.

32.7 [22]: *The Goat*: Capricorn, tenth sign of the zodiac, ruled by Saturn; Murphy's birthday is thus between December 22 and January 19. Rabinovitz notes [*Development*, 106] that Suk could not have given the position so accurately without knowledge of the time of birth to a few minutes, and sees this as another instance of intentional unreliability. He may have missed the joke, for there is another way of reading the rather casual account, as Kennedy has done [251], though she misses the enormity of what she has found: Murphy's birthday may be four days *into* Capricorn, or December 25 (the date is never directly stated, let alone the hour or minute). Harrison [28] in a lucid moment sees Murphy as the *pharmakos*, or scapegoat of Christian tradition. Thus emerge some magnificent ironies: Murphy's life and death as an Imitation of Christ's; the Good Shepherd born under the sign of the Goat; the prominence of an Intense Love nature rarely suspicioning the Nasty; an inclination to Purity; the hypostatic impulse to be in two places at a time; and heights of glory injurious of the Native's prospects.

32.8 [22]: *this Native*: the subject, whose natal day is under scrutiny.

32.9 [22]: *clairaudience*: the supposed faculty of hearing what is not audible to the human ear.

32.10 [22]: *The Moon twenty-three degrees of the Serpent*: E. H. Bailey indicates [*BJA*, June 1935, 170], that after the rising sign and House is identified the next step is to determine if there are any rising planets (the Moon considered as such). A degree is one 360th of the circle of the heavens; hence, at our native's birth the Moon was 23° into the constellation of Draco, the Serpent, which circles the North Pole between 63° and 80° of the equator. Mercury would be in Scorpio from November 10 to December 28 1935; Murphy dies on October 23, when the sun first moves into Scorpio. The significance seems unclear, beyond an affinity between Murphy's personality and the Moon, and a hint of the pythonic glaze [see #24.1].

32.11 [22]: *great Magical Ability of the Eye*: and yet, when Murphy looks into Mr. Endon's eyes [183], he is the one who succumbs, not unlike the squirrel fascinated by the serpent in the mesmerising account by Schopenhauer [*WWI*, III.2.xxviii, 113n].

32.12 [22]: *suspicioning the Nasty*: consider Swift's 'Meditation on a Broomstick': "by a capricious kind of Fate, destin'd to make other Things Clean, and be Nasty itself" (the pun on 'capricious' is a bonus).

32.13 [22]: *Mars having just set in the East*: Rabinovitz thinks this an "unlikely proposition," since the earth's rotation creates the illusion of planets and stars rising in the east and setting in the west [*Development*, 106]. Kennedy says [255] the phrase merely indicates that the planet is beneath the eastern horizon at the time of birth—as in the astral vision of Virgil's *Fourth Eclogue* which is commonly assumed to have predicted the birth of Christ. Either way, it denotes our Native's great desire not to engage in any pursuit, particularly the martial kind.

32.14 [23]: *a wish to be in two places at once*: perhaps, body and mind.

32.15 [23]: *Harmony*: Murphy's irregular heart has sought the Apmonia [see #3.8].

32.16 [23]: *publishers, quadrupeds and tropical swamps*: Beckett would have immense difficulty in getting the manuscript accepted; Murphy will have problems with Nelly [100]; and his troubles began in the sub-tropical garden of Battersea Park [see #16.4]. He is also in danger of a fit [139], brought on by his imperfect sense of humor.

33.1 [23]: *Mercury sesquiquadrate with the Anarete*: Mercury is our Native's ruling planet, being in aspect of 135° of the Anarete, "the Destroyer" or House of Death. Kennedy is correct to claim [257] that this would be Saturn, which bodes not well. The term 'sesquiquadrate,' i.e., 90° plus half the quadrate, or 45° = 135° (sometimes termed "the aspect of agitation"), is not used in Hindu astrology, but Beckett would have met it in the *Britannica* entry.

33.2 [23]: *The Square of Moon and Solar Orb*: at the moment of nativity, the Sun and the Moon were "square," or at a right-angle to one another; since planets separated by 90° are "opposed" they interact inharmoniously. E. H. Bailey comments [*BJA*, February 1935, 86] that when the Moon is in Scorpio or Capricorn the effect of square or opposition is exceptionally adverse; Kennedy suggests [253] that such cross-currents intimate affliction. The implications are confused, but not good.

33.3 [23]: *Herschel in Aquarius stops the Water*: 'Herschel' is another name for Uranus, after Sir John Herschel who discovered it in 1781, thereby complicating centuries of astrology, based on a set number of planets (the science that got over Jacob and Esau got over that). These are the last words muttered by Murphy [252], when he is least on his guard.

33.4 [23]: *the Hyleg*: otherwise the 'Hylech,' or Ascendant, the ruling planet of nativity crossing the eastern horizon at the moment of birth; for Murphy, Mercury. Beckett copied into the *Whoroscope* Notebook from the *Britannica*: "Star rising at moment of birth called the Ascendant." It is considered the giver or sustainer of life, and as such beneficent (unlike the Anarete); but should it cross into an unfortunate aspect the individual may be threatened. Saturn may have thus affected Murphy [see #33.1]. As Bailey points out [*BJA*, February 1935, 91], the conjunction of Capricorn rising with

Saturn as ascendant is most unfortunate: "a child born under such a configuration would have had a very poor chance of surviving infancy."

33.5 [23]: *Neptune and Venus in the Bull*: as Rabinovitz notes [*Development*, 107, 120], Neptune was in Taurus from 1874 until 1889, but would not return to that constellation in the twentieth century; whereas Uranus was in Acquarius from 1912 to 1920; hence, the two positions are mutually exclusive. It may be a incommunicable bull: a glance at the myth of Pasiphaë, Queen of Crete, who fell in love with the white bull, the gift of Poseidon (Neptune); to fulfill her lust she commissioned the fabulous artificer Dedalus to make a bronze cow, into which she crept, to be serviced by the bull and give birth to the Minotaur.

33.6 [23]: *a fiery triplicy*: the twelve signs of the Zodiac form four triplicities, or trigons, three signs set 120° from one another in equilateral triangles, one associated with each of the elements: a fiery triplicity of Aries, Leo and Sagittarius (the "Bowman"), ruled by the Sun by day and Jupiter by night; an earthly triplicity of Taurus, Virgo and Capricorn, ruled by Venus by day and the Moon by night; an airy triplicity of Gemini, Libra and Aquarius, ruled by Saturn by day and Mercury by night; and a watery triplicity of Cancer, Scorpio, and Pisces, ruled by Venus by day and the Moon by night. This aspect is usually regarded as beneficent.

33.7 [23]: *Bright's Disease*: first investigated by the English physician, Dr. Richard Bright (1789-1858): a granular degeneration of the kidneys to fat (*proteinuria*), giving the patient a flabby bloodless appearance, with drowsiness and easy fatigue.

33.8 [23]: *Grave's Disease*: exophthalmic goitre, a thyroid disorder occurring mostly in women, and characterized by bulging eyes, fatigue and emotional irritability. It was identified (1843) and named after Dr. Robert Graves, physician to the Meath Hospital in Dublin. One of Beckett's teachers at Earlsford House suffered from this disease [Knowlson, 35].

33.9 [23]: *Lucky Gems*: sporting an amethyst, an antidote to intoxication, seems unnecessary in one who never touches the stuff. In 'Echo's Bones' [21] the groundsman, Mick Doyle, considers amethyst bottles a great mistake: "They don't give the drink a fair chance." The diamond, that adamant which can be cut or polished only by itself, may have been suggested by Jean Beaufret's phrase, "black diamond of pessimism," which Beckett admired and used in *Dream* [47; see Knowlson, 152]. Lemon is Lucky, for it is the color of Faith, and mentioned as such in the description of the Bovril sign in 'Ding-Dong' [*MPTK*, 42]. The possibilities of four as Lucky Number are inexhaustible; it is neither the dualist 2, nor Dante's 3 (these axiomatic to the novel). Sunday is an odd Lucky Day, for in nursery wisdom: "The child that is born on the Sabbath day / Is bonny and blythe and happy and gay." As for the Lucky Years: 1936 is the first year after the demise of Murphy, and 1990 the first after that of his creator (Murphy sneaking into Scorpio, and Beckett sneaking out).

33.10 [23]: *Is it even so*: see #32.6: the opening words of the line from *Romeo and Juliet* [V.i.24] that the horoscope cites, Murphy accepting his fate as written in the stars.

34.1 [23]: *Pandit*: from Skr. *pandita*, "learned, conversant with": strictly, a Hindu polyhistor learned in Sanskrit, philosophy, literature and law; less strictly, a teacher or expert in any field; less respectfully, one not reluctant to give an opinion on any matter, a ponderous *pundit*.

34.2 [34]: *The very first fourth to fall on a Sunday in 1936*: the first such day is October 4, 1936, as Murphy has gathered [75]; a fact he might have found in Whitaker [130].

34.3 [24]: *the stone*: "Calculous concretion in the kidneys or bladder" [Johnson's *Dictionary*]. The link to the horoscope is painful: "Herschel in Acquarius *stops the water*." As Swift wrote to Stella [*Letter* xxxi, September 25, 1711]: "Arbuthnot made us all melancholy, by some symptoms of bloody urine: he expects a cruel fit of the stone in twelve hours; he says he is never mistaken, and he appeared like a man that was to be racked tomorrow." Beckett wrote to Mary Manning [May 22, 1937]: "Pelorson used to talk about the stone in his heart. I didn't know what he meant till I felt it myself. Cardiac calculus." Epicurus, it is said, died of the stone.

35.1 [24]: *resolved it quite legitimately*: see #4.6: it is uncertain why the resolution is legitimate, as no Hegelian sublation has been achieved, unless Murphy considers the return to the original a higher category, or new position achieved as a consequence of the process.

36.1 [25]: *met*: an anticipation of the later Polite Conversation [see #221.1]; though the echo of Oberon's "Ill met by moonlight, proud Titania" [*A Midsummer Night's Dream*, II.i.60], is more obvious here, our two having met on Midsummer's Night.

36.2 [25]: *love with a function*: in his essay on *Proust*, Beckett defines love as a function of man's sadness [63], this being the conclusion of a long passage concerning the intensity of Marcel's love for Albertine, which can co-exist only with a state of dissatisfaction: "One only loves that which one does not possess entirely" [55]. Farrow comments [44]: "A lover therefore is someone who is degraded from the position of end in himself to a means to an end, a satellite revolving around his beloved, in terms of a series of contingency." Celia's brief replies are the best response to this kind of bilge, however true it may be.

36.3 [25]: *a pain in the neck . . . the feet*: Beckett suffered considerably from an anthrax (his "faithful impetigo") on the neck and recurrent problems with his feet. Belacqua also suffers from a spavined gait (cramps, corns and hammer-toes) and a growth on the neck; in 'Yellow' he is hospitalized to be trimmed like a carrot [182], his toe (he requests) to be given to the cat.

36.4 [25]: *You can want what does not exist*: an anticipation of Geulincx's *Ubi nihil vales* [see #178.9], with ironic reference to Murphy's self-love [see #107.1].

37.1 [25]: *the charVenus and her sausage and mash sex*: for a different class of invective, compare the untranslatable French version: "Putain de putain, ce que ça m'emmerde, la Vénus de chambre et son Éros comme chez grand'mère." Sausage and mash is a working-class delight, whatever its Freudian possibilities.

37.2 [25]: *I am what I do*: the bodily equivalent of "I am that I am"; the words of God unto Moses [Exodus 3:14]. The eternal tautology is found elsewhere: in the Vedas, Beckett having copied into the *Whoroscope* Notebook Schopenhauer's "tat twam asi" [Skr. "this thou art," *WWI*, I.iii §44, 284 and iv §63, 459]; and St. Paul's "by the grace of God I am what I am" [I Corinthians 15:10]. Thus Belacqua to himself in 'Yellow' [172]; and Quigley of 'Lightning Calculation' to his sweetheart, the laundress: "'Darling' Quigley would protest, 'I am what I am', and would have liked, but did not dare, to add,

'Take me or leave me.' But the laundress would only reply, 'There is such a thing as room for improvement. I'll be saying goodnight.'"

37.3 [25]: *Bollitoes*: more accurately, 'Ballitoes,' as in the corrected Calder text; silk stockings secured with suspenders to corset or belt. The brand was widely advertised for some years thereafter [Vada Hart to CA].

38.1 [26]: *the days of nuts, balls and sparrows*: St. Augustine's "a nucibus et pilulis et passeribus" [*Confessions*, I.xix], as entered into the Dream Notebook [#79] and used in 'Echo's Bones.' Belacqua, in the *au-delà*, feels himself restored for the moment by a lousy fate to "the nuts and balls and sparrows of the low stature of animation." Augustine is talking about childhood play and deceit, which matches Murphy's sense, but he follows it with a nod towards humility, which isn't Murphy's intention.

38.2 [26]: *To die fighting*: again, the fundamental unheroic. Zurbrugg suggests [84] the parallel with Proust's "inertie absolue," the ablation of all desire.

39.1 [26]: *Father forgive her*: she knows not what she says [Luke 23:34].

39.2 [26]: *than a parrot into its profanities*: the parrot for Beckett, in keeping with a long tradition, was an emblem of the relationship between thought and speech, the feathered biped capable of the latter but not the former. The image first appears in *Whoroscope* ("Pale abusive parakeets in the windows of the mind"), as glossed by Mahaffy [179], whose little treatise on Descartes Beckett had plucked for the poem:

> In fine, there is not a single external action which can convince those who examine it that our body is not merely a machine which moves by itself, but has in it a thinking mind, except the use of words, or other signs (such as those of mutes) made in relation to whatever presents itself, without any regard for the passions. This excludes the talking of parrots, and includes that of the insane, as the latter may be *à propos*, though it be absurd, while the former is not.

The bird appears fleetingly in Beckett's work, the Smeraldina (on occasions that is) looking like a parrot in a Pietà [*Dream*, 70]. The most colorful specimen, undoubtedly, is Jackson's pink and grey parrot in *Malone Dies* [see #108.2].

39.3 [26]: *great magical ability*: as in the later encounter with Mr. Endon, and in defiance of the horoscope, Murphy fails; here, however, the failure arises from the paradoxical success of entering the eyes of other, rather than seeing the reflection of himself unseen.

40.1 [26]: *this monstrous proposition*: Shame! Kick his arse! Throw him out! A violation of the very first section of *The World as Will and Idea*, where Schopenhauer is at pains to stress that subject and object cannot be separated this way [see #109.1 and #218.1].

40.2 [26]: *the mercantile gehenna*: the world of commerce as the biblical Valley of Hinnom, where sacrifices to Moloch were offered and refuse of all kinds cast, for the consumption of which fires constantly burnt; for Milton, the very "type of hell" [*Paradise Lost*, I.405].

40.3 [27]: *if my mind, then all*: the plot is simple: by falling in love, Murphy loses his mind, and can come to his senses only by accepting a job in a mental home, where he will discover that he is not so much free as contingent; his death resolves the problem by short-circuiting it. O'Hara underlines the oddity of the psychological love affair in terms of a lover who is himself his loved one's rival, presenting his self's case to that beloved [*Hidden Drives*, 62].

40.4 [27]: *difficult music*: Beckett noted that for Schopenhauer and Proust, "music is the Idea itself, unaware of the world of phenomena, existing ideally outside the universe, apprehended not in Space but in Time only, and consequently untouched by the teleological hypothesis" [*Proust*, 92]. The catalytic element in the work of Proust, it asserts his unbelief in the permanence of personality but his belief in art, with a unique beauty and "invisible reality" that "damns the life of the body on earth as a pensum and reveals the meaning of the word: 'defunctus'." This derives from Schopenhauer's 'Doctrine of Suffering' [*Parerga*, §156, 300], but equally pertinent are two sections in *The World as Will and Idea* [I.4 §52, 330-46, and III.2.xxxix, 231-44], dealing with the metaphysics of music, the salient points of which are the contention that if music is too closely tied to words it strives to speak a language which is not its own, and the conviction that music is an objectification of the Will. Pity poor [Ce]celia: she just wants Murphy to find work, and cannot hear the complex orchestration, Schopenhauer's base to Proust's melody, that would damn it as defunctus.

40.5 [27]: *he pinioned her wrists*: as had Mr. Kelly [24], in a similar attempt to dissuade.

41.1 [27]: *the eternal tautology*: like unto the paradox that Love makes One of Two, phoenices of turtles; or, more cynically, as Beckett observed of Jeremy Taylor's *Holy Living and Holy Dying*, that one of the two was surely redundant.

4

42.1 [28]: *September 19th*: the first mention of the date, so only retrospectively may the previous action be placed in any temporal perspective.

42.2 [28]: *General Post Office*: an imposing granite building in Sackville Street (now O'Connell Street), built in the Ionic mode with "a noble hexastyle portico of Portland stone," impressive columns and, above the pediment, sizable statues of Hibernia flanked by Mercury and Fidelity. Designed by Francis Johnston, and completed in 1817 at a cost of more than £50,000 [O'Brien, 367], it is most famously associated with the events of Easter 1916, when the resentment of English rule in Ireland erupted into violent rebellion. Led by Padraic Pearse and James Connolly, members of the Irish Volunteers and Citizens' Army seized fourteen key buildings in Dublin, notably the Post Office, which became the rebels' headquarters. On the steps of the GPO Pearse defiantly read out a proclamation declaring the independence of Eire and calling upon his fellow citizens to rise and fight for that freedom. Six days of bitter fighting took place between the rebels and some 20,000 British troops, with the gunboat *Helga* entering the Liffey to shell the city strongholds. Some 64 rebels, 134 police and soldiers, and 200 civilians died in the uprising. Because of the senseless destruction it was not a popular cause until the British, in a typical display of military intelligence, turned the populace around with the executions of fifteen rebel leaders by firing squad in Kilmainham Jail, a dying Connolly wheeled in for execution in his chair. As Pearse had probably known, the uprising could not succeed in military terms, but the sacrifice (the word is mocked at the end of the paragraph) gave the cause the martyrs it had been seeking, and made eventual independence, on whatever terms, inevitable.

42.3 [28]: *the statue of Cuchulain*: the memorial to those who died in the Easter upris-ing, carved by Oliver Sheppard, RHA, and unveiled April 21, 1935 (it is thus very recent, which makes the indignity Neary offers on "holy ground" the more provocative). The bronze statue depicts the Red Branch hero defiantly meeting his end, and is inscribed with the names of the seven signatories to the Proclamation of the Irish Republic. For years the statue was placed in the center of the GPO, where, like that of St. Peter in the Vatican, the hero's foot was polished by people touching it as a tal-isman. Cuchulain, the "hound of Ulster", was one of the principal heroes of the Ulster Cycle, and the nephew of Conchubar. His strength and valor won him the love of many women, but he was beguiled into the tragic situations (such as killing his son) that are the subject of Yeats's poems and plays.

42.4 [28]: *his buttocks, such as they are*: the insult is calculated: the number who claimed to be inside the GPO during Easter 1916 outmatches the capacity of the build-ing to hold them, and Sean O'Casey had caused offence by his irreverent treatment of the uprising in *The Plough and the Stars* (1928). The detail is otherwise calculated: Con Leventhal recalled a peculiar request: "Would I betake me to the Dublin Post Office and measure the height from the ground to Cuchulain's arse" [*Beckett at 60*, xx]. He tells of kneeling with a tape to carry out his task, lucky to get away without being arrested, but stated it was essential for Beckett to know "whether this violent gesture was in fact possible" (Joyce had made similar demands). The buttock [*sic*] is not obvi-ously callipygian, being protected by the hero's sword and the spikes of his tunic, which account for "the breaches of surface" tended by Wylie [45].

42.5 [28]: *The Civic Guard*: a term used of the domestic police following independ-ence, then gradually replaced by 'Garda' [Gael. *Gard Siochána*, "Guardians of the Peace"], the Irish equivalent. Beckett's CG, so nobly proportioned, is not a "rough grit-ty man" like the wharfinger and jarveys of *Dream* (or the missing policeman of *Godot*, 11), but more like Flann O'Brien's *Third Policeman*, a typical Mr. Plod. Belacqua has a comparable encounter with a CG at the end of *Dream* [226], and with a Dogberry in 'A Wet Night' [*MPTK*, 77].

42.6 [28]: *as rapid as a zebra's*: in the Dream Notebook [#239] Beckett wrote: "rapid as a zebra's thought," i.e., darting from one thing to another, as in Belacqua's medita-tion [*Dream*, 184]. This derives from Renard's *Journal* [January 27, 1905]. Wylie's street savvy as a bookmaker's stand, or taker of illegal bets, invites the Gestaltist joke: a zebra crossing a zebra crossing (now you see it, now you don't).

43.1 [28]: *John o' God's*: i.e., from the asylum for the docile at Stillorgan (not far from Beckett's Foxrock home), rather than criminally insane and from the state asylum at Dundrum [O'Brien, 242]. St. John of God's forms the setting of *Malone Dies*.

43.2 [29]: *shod with orange-peel*: shambling and perspiring: a joke from the days of the *École Normale* and the complaint of Beckett's friend, Georges Pelorson, who might say: "J'ai les pieds en marmalade" [Fr. "my feet are in marmalade"], a variation of his grandmother's "J'ai les pieds en compote" ["in jam"; Knowlson, 135-36]. The jest is anticipated in *Dream* [87]: "Lean on the orange-peel wonderfully made by the Lemon-sole that your . . . er . . . soul may arise from its weariness"; and is explicit in 'Enueg II': "feet in marmalade / perspiring profusely / heart in marmalade / smoke more fruit / the old heart the old heart." Beckett's favorite marmalade was Cooper's, which might account for the spavined gait of that individual.

44.1 [29]: *the single diastole-systole which is all the law requires*: the metaphor of dilation and contraction, the movement of the heart, may hint at an obscure pre-Socratic joke: in his *Greek Philosophy* [73], Burnet defines the doctrine of Empedokles, whose belief that "respiration depended on the systole and diastole of the heart" was expressed as Law of Love and Strife, a cosmic breathing which makes up "the life of the world."

44.2 [29]: *Yes, sergeant*: the obsequious promotion that seeks forgiveness for the offence; Belacqua in 'A Wet Night' [*MPTK*, 76], but not in the parallel passage in *Dream* [226], takes out the same insurance, having wiped them boots of the Civic Guard after catting all over them.

44.3 [29]: *next best thing to never being born*: the classical dictum, as copied by Beckett into the *Whoroscope* Notebook: "Optimum non nasci, aut cito mori" [L. "the best is not to be born, but to die quickly"]. It appears in Geulincx's *Ethica* [I.II.10 §1, 54]; Burton's *Anatomy* [I.2.3.x, 184n.]; and as the epigraph to Otto Rank's *The Trauma of Birth*, cited from Nietzsche's *The Birth of Tragedy*, where the wise Silenus, compelled to tell King Midas what is best for man, finally replies: "Miserable ephemeral species, children of chance and of hardship, why do you compel me to tell you what is most profitable for you not to hear? The very best is quite unattainable for you: it is, not to be born, not to exist, to be Nothing. But the next best for you is—to die soon." Freud recounts the dictum in *Jokes and the Relation to the Unconscious*, adding that "hardly one man in a hundred thousand has this luck." The pun on *Stillorgan*, that area of Dublin close to where Beckett was born, needs little elaboration. For Neary's anguished cursing on the theme, see #46.3; for the temperature of the cell, see p. 181.

44.4 [29]: *no fisc*: from L. *fiscus*, "a basket" (of a tax-collector); the treasury of a kingdom or state, or, as implied here, enforced contributions thereto.

44.5 [29]: *the poor little man*: not a hardy laurel (a favorite pun), but the silent movie action is to be noted. Neary (large and round) and Wylie (small and thin) reflect the comic duo in their make-up.

45.1 [29]: *a Dalkey tram*: the Dublin tramway system had at its zenith nineteen routes with some 61 miles of track, spreading radially from Nelson's Pillar [see #46.2]. It started with horse-cars in 1872, but was electrified between 1897 and 1901. From 1932, the system was (to Beckett's regret) gradually replaced by buses, the #8 line to Dalkey lasting till 1949 [O'Brien, 367]. Dalkey, on bend of bay south of Dublin, was once a medieval walled town; it is best known outside Ireland as the setting of chapter 2 of *Ulysses* and Flann O'Brien's *The Dalkey Archives*.

45.2 [29]: *a theme very near to his heart*: an ironic echo of Yeats's 'Easter 1916' and its reference to Major John MacBride as one who had done great wrong to "some who are near my heart"; i.e., he had married Maud Gonne.

45.3 [29]: *the jug and bottles*: the bottle-store attached to the pub, for home purchases.

46.1 [30]: *Mooney's clock*: the clock of the Abbey Mooney [56], at 1 Lower Abbey Street, and visible from the Pillar. There were several Mooneys in Dublin, each with a conspicuous clock outside. The news is sad, because in Dublin (though not the rest of Ireland) pubs were compelled to close between 2.30 and 3.30 p.m., a stretch known universally as "holy hour."

46.2 [30]: *the Pillar railings*: Nelson's Pillar, in O'Connell Street, a little north of the GPO; from its erection in 1808 until its blasting by the IRA in 1966 a conspicuous Dublin landmark. Built at a cost of £6,856, raised by public subscription, to commemorate the one-handled admiral, it consisted of a solid pedestal (30'), a fluted Doric column, hollow, with 168 steps (71' 8"), leading to a platform from which rose a capital (7') and podium (12' 6"), surmounted by a colossal statue of Nelson (13'); a total of 134 feet [O'Brien, 368]. From the platform there was a view of the city, less plum than plumstone for two old ladies in the 'Aeolus' episode of *Ulysses*, and of dubious satisfaction to the obscure figure 'C' in *Molloy* [9]. A railing indeed surrounded the plinth for such as Neary to lean against.

46.3 [30]: *cursed . . . the day in which he was born*: a frequent sentiment in Beckett, deriving from Job 3:3: "Let the day perish wherein I was born, and the night in which it was said, There is a man child conceived." Swift read this passage each year on his birthday [Schopenhauer, *WWI*, III.4.xlvi, 399]. Robert Greene laments in his 'Repentance' [XII.166]: "Oh woe is mee, why doe I liue? nay rather why was I borne? Cursed be the day wherein I was born, and haplesse be the brests that gaue me sucke." Beckett's favorite version came from Calderón's *La Vida es sueño* [Sp. "Life is a Dream"], via Schopenhauer [*WWI*, I.iii §51, 328, and iv §63, 458], and as repeated in *Proust* [67]: "Pues el delito mayor / Del hombre es haber nacido" [Sp. "For the greatest crime of man is to have been born"].

46.4 [30]: *an underground café*: unidentified.

46.5 [30]: *Cathleen na Hennessey*: the embodiment of Cathleen ni Houlihan, the "little old lady" representing the spirit of Ireland; compare Yeats's Countess Cathleen, or the old milk-woman of the opening of *Ulysses*. Hence the efficacy of the coffee, Hennessey's Three Star Brandy also being the Alba's favorite painkiller [*Dream*, 138].

46.6 [30]: *a man whose light is hid*: Neary continues to quote Job, here 3:23: "Why is light given to a man whose way is hid, and whom the Lord hath hedged in?"

46.7 [30]: *the Red Branch bum*: Neary's periphrastic last straw. The 'Red Branch' refers to the Ulster Cycle of Irish mythology, centering about such heroes as Concubar and his nephew Cuchulain [see #42.3], or recounting the tragic love of Deirdre and Naiose. The most polished of the four legendary cycles, the Red Branch tales were a constant source of inspiration to the Twilighters, whose limits of endurance Beckett is sorely trying.

47.1 [30]: *this kip*: the Dublin equivalent of a London stew [see #55.1]. "The Kips" were the Dublin red-light district, popularly known as "Monto" (Montgomery Street), and said to be in earlier years "one of the most dreadful dens of immorality in Europe" [O'Brien, 176].

47.2 [30]: *My grove on Grand Parade*: for the Platonic Academy, see #54.2. Grand Parade is a wide avenue in the heart of the commercial area of Cork, running northward from the River Lee and Southern Mall [see #53.2] to St. Patrick's Street.

47.3 [30]: *as a man wipeth a plate*: the gentle words of the Lord [II Kings 21:13]: "I will wipe Jerusalem as a man wipeth a dish, wiping it, and turning it upside down."

47.4 [31]: *turned his cup upside down*: completing the action, as at the end of Synge's *Riders to the Sea*, but without Maurya's accompanying denial of desire: "and we must be satisfied."

47.5 [31]: *the pudenda of my psyche*: among the Jacobean references in the *Whoroscope* Notebook listed for inclusion in *Murphy*, but the reference too intimate to reveal (Ford may be incriminated). Beckett was tickled by Schopenhauer's opinion that plants were shameless, exposing their genitals to the common view, a sentiment echoed in *Proust* [89].

47.6 [31]: *But betray me*: compare the advice given in the 'Daily Guide' of the *BJA* for September 19, 1935: "Sign papers, make plans, but guard against deception."

47.7 [31]: *Hippasos*: a follower of Pythagoras, who flourished about 500 BC, but was expelled from the Order for betraying its mysteries [see #47.8]; after his expulsion, a tombstone was erected to him as if he were dead. He founded a branch of the School with followers termed Ἀκουσματικοί, held to be the successors of the outer ring, or auditors, rather than those initiated (after five years of silence) into the advanced doctrines. His *Mystical Doctrine* (affirming that the first principle was a material being and not a number) was written with the intention of discrediting Pythagoras, but his fate confirmed to followers of the latter the impiety of that claim.

47.8 [31]: *the incommensurability of side and diagonal*: the Pythagoreans contended that any number was either a whole, or could be expressed as the ratio of two wholes, so that $^{43}/_{100}$ could be seen as 43 parts, each one-hundredth long. However, the square root of two, that length obtained by the theorem of Pythagoras from a right-angled triangle with two sides each of length 1, could not be so expressed, but only approximated as $^{14}/_{10}$, $^{141}/_{100}$, $^{1414}/_{1000}$, etc. Pythagorean initiates were forbidden upon pain of death to reveal such incommensurabilty, or the existence of the surd, as this was "a scandalous exception" to the laws of Harmony that regulated the octave and the music of the spheres. The secret was supposedly betrayed by Hippasos, whose death at sea was seen as divine retribution. Neary's words are cited almost verbatim from Burnet's *Greek Philosophy* [55]: "Tradition represented Hippassos as the man who divulged Pythagorean secrets, and one story says he was drowned at sea for revealing the incommensurability of side and diagonal, another that he met with the same fate for publishing the construction of the regular dodecahedron."

47.9 [31]: *the regular dodeca—hic—dodecahedron*: Burnet describes [*Greek Philosophy,* 55] the principles underlying the construction of the dodecahedron, which of the regular solids "approaches most nearly to the sphere." Each of the twelve "panels" of the dodecahedron is formed by the regular pentagon, the figure thus incorporating the mystical attributes of 3, 4 and 5. Just as the cube represented the element of earth, the pyramid fire, the octahedron air, and the icosahedron water, the regular dodecahedron stood for the mystical quintessence. Freeman suggests [85] that Hippasos may have discovered how to construct the Dodecahedron from the Pentagon, and the inscribability of the former in a perfect sphere, by finding its center. Neary's "hic" is attributable to brandy, not beans, so need not constitute a betrayal of the vital spirits. In Plato's *Phaedo* [59 §110B, 378-79], the earth seen from above is said to look like ὥσπερ αἱ δωδεκάσκυτοι σφαίραι [Gr. "those twelve-sided balls"], which applies the Idea of its perfection in terms of a vision of loveliness denied to those who live in its mud and hollows.

48.1 [31]: *Herr Kurt Koffka*: Kurt Koffka (1886-1941) a founder of the Gestalt school of psychology. His *Grundlagen der psychischen Entwicklung* (1921) [Ger. "Principles of psychological development"], translated as *The Growth of the Mind* (1925), applied Gestalt notions to learning psychology, stressing the relationship between innate capacities and environmental conditions, which Koffka called the convergence factor. His *Principles of Gestalt Psychology* (1935), immediately became a classic; had Neary applied to it he might have found in chapter 5 [198], "Why is the Ground Simpler than the Figure?", an answer to his problem: "the after-effect is one primarily in the conditions of the process rather than in the process itself, i.e., in those processes which give rise to organization, and not in the organization itself." For Miss Dwyer to stand out from the background she must form a compact visual unit, an organized whole. The perception of that whole is by virtue of filtering and transforming the various stimuli; when these no longer stimulate, the ability to form the Gestalt and distinguish it from the homogenous surface or background (or the intrusion of another figure) will be impaired. For Neary, this happens rather quickly.

Neary could have resorted to the *De Imitatione Christi* of Thomas à Kempis [III.xxxix.3], the voice of Christ:

Fili, saepe homo rem aliquam vehementer agitat, quam desiderat: sed cum ad eam pervenerit, aliter sentire incipit, quia affectiones circa idem non sun durabiles, sed magis de uno ad aliud nos impellunt.

[L. "My son, oftentimes a man vehemently struggleth for somewhat he desireth, but when he hath arrived at it he beginneth to be of another mind; for the affections do not remain long on one object, but rather urge us from one thing to another"]. Hesla ['Being,' 12] suggests that Neary would do better to apply to the author of *Proust*, who argued [13] that the aspirations of yesterday were valid for yesterday's ego, but not today's: "We are disappointed at the nullity of what we are pleased to call attainment. But what is attainment? The identification of the subject with his desire. The subject has died—and perhaps many times—on the way." The ego named Neary that yearns for Miss Dwyer (Hesla suggests) is not the ego that attains her.

48.2 [31]: *the morsel of chaos*: a neat integration of the Gestalt figure with the Democritean atom, or monad, standing out against the void.

48.3 [31]: *The plaisir de rompre*: Fr. "the pleasure of breaking," i.e., of taking the active part in ending a relationship. *Le Plaisir de rompre* is the title of an 1897 play by Jules Renard.

48.4 [31]: *that post-mortem of Dives to Lazarus*: the rich man in the torments of Hell, with the consciousness of the great gulf between him and the poor man in heaven [see #5.7].

49.1 [31]: *preoccupied*: in the literal sense of "already or previously occupied," as of Father Abraham's bosom [see #5.7].

49.2 32]: *would press his bosom to the thorn*: as in the 'Ode to the West Wind': "I fall upon the thorns of life! I bleed!" Neary's heart, like Shelley's, both pants and bleeds.

49.3 [32]: *That long hank of Apollonian asthenia*: Murphy's asthenia, or degeneration of the vital spirits (from Gk. ἀσθενής, "without strength"; DN, #1028), is not a neo-Nietzschean debility but a condition attributable to Diogenes of Apollonia, for whom the primary substance or substrate of the universe was air, from which by condensation, rarefaction and change of state the form of everything else arises [Burnet, *Early Greek Philosophy*, 352-58; see also Diogenes Laertius, IX.57-58]. The interaction between the air in the body and that outside is thus the type of all vital action; this theory of respiration, with an acute understanding of the veins and arteries, was propounded in his *On Natural Science*, and satirized by Aristophanes in *The Clouds*. In the words of Brett [118]: "Diogenes of Apollonia makes the air in the organism the medium by which all sense-affections are brought to consciousness. Thus air comes to be at once the inner principle of organic and rational life." Hence the rarified wit that follows.

49.4 [32]: *that schizoidal spasmophile*: one expressing the wish to be in two places at once [see #32.14]; and displaying undue contractions of the muscles, due to excessive irritability of the neuro-muscular junction. Beckett may have picked up 'spasmophilia' from Alfred Adler's *The Neurotic Constitution* [4]. The *OED* Supplement illustrates the rare use of 'spasmophile' by Beckett's unique example.

49.5 [32]: *a notable wet*: usually, one who drinks too much (Murphy is a non-drinker), and hence appears foolish. But for Diogenes of Apollonia [see #49.3], thought is the activity of dry air and moisture detrimental to thinking; hence the irony of . . .

49.6 [32]: *a Drinker machine*: after Philip Drinker, American health engineer (1894-1972); a respirator, or iron lung, used to treat polio. A metal tank encloses the patient's body, leaving the head exposed, and artificial respiration is provided by alternating negative and positive pressure.

49.7 [32]: *bottle of hay*: Fr. "botte de paille"; but hinting at *A Midsummer Night's Dream* IV.i.31, where Titania asks her sweet love what he will eat; i.e, Wylie is being told he is an ass.

49.8 [32]: *Fletcher's Sullen Shepherd*: the embittered villain of John Fletcher's *The Faithfull Shepherdesse* (1610?), introduced as "One that lusts after every severall beauty, / But never yet was knowne to love or like" [I.ii.200-01]. The pastoral tragi-comedy has a situation circle more complex than that embracing Miss Dwyer and Flight-Lieutenant Elliman, but the action is short-circuited and sparks begin to fly when the Sullen Shepherd, who lives "by the More," is engaged by Amarillis (in love with Perigot who has a tryst with Amoret who is otherwise inclined) to befoul the fair, which he does by expounding then acting on his feelings for shepherdesses [II.iii.11-20], for which perfidy he is banished from the Downes:

> all to me in sight
> Are equall; be they faire, or blacke, or browne,
> Virgin, or carelesse wanton, I can crowne
> My appetite with any: swear as oft,
> And weepe as any, melt my words as soft
> Into a maidens eares, and tell how long
> My heart has bene her servant, and how strong
> My passions are: call her unkinde and cruell,
> Offer her all I have to gaine the jewell
> Maidens so highly prise: then loath and fly:
> This do I hold a blessed destenie.

50.1 [32]: *the Gymnasium*: for the Platonic implications of the name, see #54.2.

50.2 [32]: *Maundy Thursday*: the Thursday closest to the Paschal Moon, the Full Moon used to determine the dating of the Easter festivities; in 1935, April 18th [Whitaker, 94].

50.3 [32]: *the cockpit in Hyde Park*: a natural amphitheater, where Murphy is later discovered prone, rather than (as here) supine [see #96.1].

50.4 [32]: *Neary besieged Miss Counihan with attentions*: the import of which passes
her by:
 mangoes: obviously, the tropical fruit, but perhaps pertinent is a passage in
Beckett's *Proust* [91]: "the horrible pomegranates of 'Il Fuoco,' bursting and bleeding,
dripping the red ooze of their seed, putrid on the putrid water." This was identified by
John Pilling as Croce's allusion to d'Annunzio's *Il fuoco* (Milan: Fratelli Treves, 1904,
92), and may be described as Beckett's critique of fly-blown prose.
 orchids: in the language of flowers somewhat ambiguous, for the word derives
from Gk. ὄρχις, "testicle." Knowlson [117-18], cites Beckett to McGreevy [July 7, 1930]
on d'Annunzio: "I think it is all balls and mean nasty balls . . . Proust's floral obses-
sions. D'A seems to think that they are *merely* pausing between fucks. Horrible. He
has a dirty squelchy mind, bleeding and bursting, like his celebrated pomegranates."
 Cuban cigarettes: as befits a lady; but the best Cuban cigars (e.g., the *Romeo y
Julieta* Belacqua smokes in 'Echo's Bones') are rolled on a dark sensuous thigh.

50.5 [32]: *his tractate, The Doctrine of the Limit*: the Pythagoreans regarded the Limit
(πέρας) and the Unlimited (τὸ ἄπειρον) as the elements of number, and therefore the
elements of things [Burnet, *Greek Philosophy*, 44]. From this, all flows: Odd and Even
numbers with the Limit and the Unlimited; the spatial character of geometry as
opposed to the linear nature of arithmetic; aspects of the musical scale; the relation of
the Doctrine to the theory of 'Αρμονία or Attunement [see #3.8]; the distinction of Being
and Becoming; problems of the One and the Many; the identification by Pythagoras of
the Limit with Fire and the Unlimited with Darkness; the debate as to how the Limit
gave form to the Unlimited (a central problem of Greek thought); or the theory of creation implicit in the notion that after the first unit was formed the Limitless was drawn
in, the Boundless thus inhaled keeping units (*monads*) separate from each other
[Burnet, *GP* 108]. For Democritus, the Doctrine was the basis of atomism, for unless
there were such a limit (Gk. ἄτομος, "that which cannot be divided"), things would pass
out of existence [Bailey, 282]. Burnet's two studies of Greek philosophy and Bailey's
The Greek Atomists are the requisite points of departure, but Neary's treatise, should
the manuscript be recovered from Miss Counihan, would doubtless throw light on
much of the above.

50.6 [32]: *Father Prout*: Francis Sylvester Mahony (1804-66), Irish priest and humorous
writer. Born in Cork, the son of a woolens manufacturer in Blarney, he became a Jesuit
seminarian, was educated and in turn taught at Clongowes Wood College, but was
expelled from the school and Order after a late-night escapade when he and someboys
returned intoxicated. Despite the Jesuits' efforts to convince Mahony that, whatever his
calling, it came not from God, he persisted in his pursuit and was ordained at Lucca in
1832, but not long after recognized their wisdom in barring him from holy ranks
[O'Brien, 296]. He abandoned the clerical life for one of literary bohemianism, moved
to London, and contributed regularly to *Fraser's Magazine* and *Bentley's Miscellany*.
Assuming the nom-de-plume of Father Prout, and introducing himself to the literary
world as the kidnapped by-blow of Swift and Stella, cruelly abandoned on the bleak
summit of Watergrasshill and taken to the Cork Foundling Hospital, the heir to Swift's
genius escaped his cruel confinement in a milk-churn to begin his literary career, most
famously in the *Reliques* where he unleashed his satire and indulged his frivolous erudition. He is best remembered for his poem, 'The Bells of Shandon,' celebrating Cork

and the River Lee [see #54.3]. Following his death in Paris, he was buried in the Church of St. Anne in Shandon, where Beckett attended his grave (an outside vault, to the left of the front door) en route to Germany in 1936, sketching it as the first entry in his German Diary ("Cork 29/8/36"); this confirms the detail in the novel, as he had visited Cork in August 1928 en route to Peggy Sinclair in Kassel.

50.7 [32]: *cattleyas*: a genus of orchid, native to Central America, named for an English patron of botany, William Cattley, and bearing a profusion of violet, rose-colored or yellow flowers. They are celebrated in *A la recherche* [*Swann*, II.26], Swann in frantic pursuit of Odette:

> Elle tenait à la main un bouquet de catleyas et Swann vit, sous sa fanchon de dentelle, qu'elle avait dans les cheveux des fleurs de cette même orchidée attachées à une aigrette en plumes de cynge.

[Fr. "She had in her hand a bouquet of cattleyas, and Swann saw, beneath her kerchief of lace, that she had in her hair the flowers of this same orchid attached to a swansdown plume."] Odette does not always encourage his attentions, but Swann's pursuit on this occasion meets with success, so much so that the phrase "faire cattleyas" is used henceforth to signify the act of physical possession; Neary is at best left with the sentiment of his loved one's refusal: "Alors, pas de cattleyas ce soir" [Fr. "Alas, no cattleyas tonight"; II.82].

51.1 [33]: *on his own bottom*: i.e., by his fundamental character, or basic merits; an innocent phrase, with but distant echoes of Titania and her ass.

51.2 [33]: *his second communion*: a sentiment associated with one's first communion, as notably in Joyce's *Portrait* [47], when the young Stephen Dedalus is told what Napoleon said to his generals: "Gentlemen, the happiest day of my life was the day on which I made my first holy communion." Years later Beckett said to Tom Driver: "I have no religious feeling. Once I had a religious emotion. It was at my first Communion. No more." Its efficacy at times of crisis was, he suggested, that of an old-school tie [Driver, 'Beckett by the Madelaine'; cited by Doherty, 15].

52.1 [33]: *Two in distress . . . make sorrow less*: proverbial; the corollary, perhaps, to the neo-Epicurean sentiment that a pleasure shared is a pleasure halved.

53.1 [34]: *The Mecca*: birthplace of Mohammed and holy city of the Moslems; the faithful are expected to make a pilgrimage there at least once in a lifetime.

53.2 [34]: *the Mall*: the South Mall in Cork City, running at a right angle off Grand Parade.

53.3 [34]: *between Amsterdam and Scheveningen*: the latter, a coastal nexus of The Hague, is some distance south of Amsterdam; Mr. Quigley's shuttling between the two is vaguely suggestive of Descartes, whose years in Holland were marked by frequent changes of abode.

53.4 [34]: *superlative reasons for doing*: the Grove edition omits the next word 'so,' which was added by Beckett's hand to the typescript.

54.1 [34]: *Wynn's Hotel*: at 35-36 Lower Abbey Street, opposite and a little along from the old Abbey Mooney, and then as now one of the better-class establishments. Largely destroyed in the fighting of Easter 1916, it was rebuilt in 1926. In *Ulysses* [687] Wynn's Hotel is bracketed as Murphy's, the 1904 proprietor being one D. J. Murphy [Gifford, 605].

54.2 [34]: *the Gymnasium . . . the Grove*: names redolent of Plato's Academy: a school taught at a *gymnasium*, or public place for athletic sports, outside the walls of Athens, in the *grove* of Academus, where Plato had a home and garden. Other schools, such as those of the later Pythagoreans and the German academies, adopted the model.

54.3 [34]: *the Lee*: the River Lee, "softly flowing" through the city of Cork, as celebrated by Father Prout (F. S. Mahony), the sentiment presumably not passing through Neary's mind:

> On this I ponder, where'er I wander,
> And thus grow fonder, sweet Cork, of thee;
> With thy Bells of Shandon that sound so grand on
> The pleasant waters of the River Lee.

54.4 [34]: *âme damnée*: Fr. "damned soul," one who shares his master's fate. Here, a man-of-all-work (i.e., *à tout faire*); hence, a tout. Compare Jules Verne's Passepartout, servant of Phineas Fogg in *Around the World in Eighty Days*.

54.5 [34]: *Cooper*: four associations seem apt: the brew, half-stout and half-porter, named from the practice of allowing coopers (or barrel-makers) a daily portion of each, which they would mingle; Becky Cooper's, the Dublin house of ill-fame, illustrations from Dante upon its walls [Knowlson, 139-40]; William M. Cooper, author of *Flagellation and the Flagellants*, which Beckett had cited repeatedly in *Dream*; and Cooper's Marmalade, which was Beckett's favorite [see #43.2]. Cooper's morbid craving for alcohol depressant (*humane*, rather than *human*), his triorchitricity, his degeneracy and his curious haunted walk suggest the pertinence of each.

54.6 [34]: *triorchous*: from Gk. ὄρχις, "testicle"; having three testicles. Diderot mentions this condition in "Le Rêve de d'Alembert" [325]. Kennedy [85] assumes "hovering like a hawk," which is an odd flight of fancy; while Culik ['Medical Allusions,' 93] attributes the third to a painful knot of the intestines pushing past Cooper's fascia in a hernia, accounting for his reluctance to sit; this illustrates the danger of realist diagnoses of surrealist symptoms. Better the bucket and well theory: since Cooper has only one eye, he needs another orb to compensate.

54.7 [34]: *a destitute diabetic*: a remarkable image added by hand to the typescript, and anticipating the young Fellow of Trinity [58]. The French translation reads: "un diabétique continental sans resources dans une grande ville des Iles Britanniques" ["a resourceless continental diabetic in a large town in the British Isles"].

54.8 [34]: *never took off his hat*: unlike Murphy, who never wears one. Cooper and Murphy are bound by such syzygies, and the suggestion of the caul implies that Cooper is another not properly born. Murphy's death frees Cooper not only to sit, but to do so on his hat [see #273.1].

55.1 [35]: *the usual stew*: the London equivalent of a Dublin kip [see #47.1].

55.2 [35]: *the happy beds*: a pathetic fallacy (the *Whoroscope* Notebook invites "benevolent pisspot"), usually attributed to chairs or bicycle seats blessed by the posteriors of young ladies. There is, however, a hint of Keats's euphoria: "Ah, happy, happy boughs! that cannot shed / Your leaves, nor ever bid the Spring adieu" ['Ode on a Grecian Urn'].

55.3 [35]: *the nearest station doss*: one of the flophouses in the vicinity of the Amiens Street station, then a run-down area; e.g., Mrs. Maloney's in Marlborough Street [*Ulysses*, 573].

55.4 [35]: *salts of lemon*: potassium hydrogen oxalate, a deadly poison, used to remove ink-stains and iron-mold from linen.

56.1 [35]: *Mooney's*: the Abbey Mooney [see #46.1], then at 1 Lower Abbey Street, a little down from Wynn's Hotel. On Sundays, the weary pun: all is doss that is not Miss Counihan.

56.2 [35]: *moving slowly from one stool to another*: a curious parallel to Neary's winding and unwinding is suggested by Zurbrugg [87-88], with the inertia of Proust's *tante Léonie* [*Swann*, I.242-43], like a water-lily driven by the current from bank to bank, "refaisant éternellement la double traversée" [Fr. "eternally repeating the double crossing"]; reaching its point of departure only to repeat the antithetical manoeuvre, "pareil aussi à quelqu'un de ces malheureux dont le tourment singulier, qui se répète indéfiniment durant l'éternité, excitait la curiosité de Dante" [Fr. "also like one of these unhappy ones whose particular torment, repeated indefinitely throughout eternity, aroused Dante's curiosity"].

56.3 [35]: *the curates*: those who serve; as explained in the *TLS* review of *Dubliners*, June 18, 1914: "The reader's difficulty will be advanced if he is ignorant of Dublin customs; if he does not know, for instance, that a 'curate' is a man who brings strong waters." Porter (the preference of the heavily laden) is a bitter dark-brown beer brewed from malt that has been first mildly charred by drying at a high temperature; in Dublin, a rougher version of stout.

56.4 [36]: *an organised whole*: as Woodworth notes [97-100], "Gestalt Psychology Stresses Organized Wholes"; i.e., any system, from a soap bubble or rolling wheel to the human or animal organism, and even the solar system, is a Gestalt greater than the mere sum of its parts. The standard example is the human face. Woodworth considers the matter of facial expression of emotion and character, which other psychologists had approached analytically [97-98]:

> They have taken each feature separately and considered the different positions it takes, seeking to discover what is expressed by each. Brow elevated, brow depressed, eyes wide, eyes half-closed, lips protruded, lips retracted— each such detail probably means some relatively simple emotional state, and adding them together we get the expression of a complex emotional state. The Gestalt psychologist approaches this matter with the idea that the face must be taken as a whole . . . He finds that the apparent expression of a part may change, in a picture, when the rest of the face is changed without any objective change in that particular part . . . Evidently the shape of the face resides in the face as a whole, and the expression of the face likewise. In the same vein, the Gestalt psychologist urges that we get no true picture of a person's character by listing the various personality traits . . . The personality is not a mere sum of traits, but an organized whole, a gestalt.

57.1 [36]: *that deathless rump*: the Yeats touch, as in 'The Statues,' where the poet, recalling Easter 1916, summons immortal Cuchulain to his side. The sentiment is subverted by Cromwellian crudity: the Rump was the remnant of the Long Parliament enduring after the purge of 1648, and the term given to that body during the Protectorate. Given Cromwell's barbarity in Ireland, such a gathering would have little chance in the GPO [see #42.2].

57.2 [36]: *palliation*: relief from suffering when there is no cure. Even in extremis Neary is quibbling: the sentiment derives from Chamfort's Maxim §113 [see #79.4]: "Vivre est une maladie dont le sommeil nous soulage toutes les seize heures. C'est un palliatif. La mort est le remède" [Fr. "Living is an illness from which sleep relieves us every sixteen hours. This is a palliative. Death is the remedy"]. Beckett would later translate the maxim as one of eight from Chamfort: "Sleep till death / healeth / come ease / this life disease" [*Collected Poems*, 134-35].
 Windelband [620], in a passage that Beckett had clearly read, offers the metaphysics of pessimism in terms of Schopenhauer's sense of the conflict of will and desire. This leads to the predominance of pain in the life of the will: "Compare the pleasure of the beast that devours with the torture of the one that is being devoured— and you will be able to estimate with approximate correctness the proportion of pleasure and pain in the world." Various conclusions follow: that the best lot of man is never to have been born; and that if life is suffering then only sympathy can be a fundamental ethical feeling; but this alleviation of the hurt is but a palliative for it does not abolish the will, and with the will unhappiness remains.

57.3 [36]: *The horse leech's daughter*: a curious passage from Proverbs 30:15-16:

 The horseleach hath two daughters, crying, Give, give. There are three
 things that are never satisfied, yea, four things say not, It is enough.
 The grave; and the barren womb; the earth that is not filled with water;
 and the fire that saith not, It is enough.

This is the sole mention of the leech (Heb. *alu-qah*) in the Bible, the "daughters" being either its greed or the bilingual blood-sucking disk at the head of the body (a leech can consume three times its own weight in blood, a strong anticoagulant in its saliva ensuring a continuous flow from its victim). The suggestion is that of the torments of insatiable desire. See also the diagnosis of Proust [*Jeunes filles*, III.207]: "Au commencement d'un amour comme à sa fin, nous ne sommes pas exclusivement attachés à l'objet de cet amour, mais plutôt le désir d'aimer" [Fr. "At the start of a love affair as at its end, we are not exclusively attached to the object of that love, but rather the desire to love"]. The consequences are spelt out by Morel to Baron Charlus in *La Prisonnière* [I.69], to the effect that when "la personne" is no longer a source of pleasure she becomes immediately "l'objet d'une apathie" [Fr. "the object of an apathy"], neurasthenic in nature, which disengages one from all obligation. Neary's dilemma is thus a Proustian one.

57.4 [36]: *a closed system*: with respect to the physical universe, one in which basic laws of the conservation of matter and energy hold sway, and Newtonian physics are valid. As Bailey points out [277], this has its origins in Epicurus, who emphasized the change but not cessation of existence: "the sum of things always was such as it is now and always will be the same." Lucretius likewise saw the universe as birthless, deathless and immutable [*De rerum natura*, II.304ff]. Wylie extends the principle to the metaphysics of desire. The assumption will be challenged by the tumult of non-

Newtonian motion (quanta) in the third zone of Murphy's mind [see #113.1]; but is perhaps validated on Murphy's death by Cooper's new-found freedom to sit and take off his hat [see #254.2], one loss balanced by another gain.

57.5 [36]: *Her quantum of wantum*: elemental units of sub-atomic movement (*quanta*) and the shell beads used by North American Indians in lieu of money (*wampum*). The phrasing derives from Windelband [546], who argues that in Nature substance is permanent, "its quantum can neither be increased nor diminished"; or [416], that God has communicated to the corporeal world "a *quantum* of motion which changes only in its distribution among the individual corpuscles."

58.1 [36]: *the young Fellow of Trinity College*: either a reference to Bishop Berkeley, past Fellow of Trinity, or a shaggy-dog story. Insulin is the active substance in secretions from the pancreatic cells that form the islets of Langerhans, and is essential for controlling metabolism of carbohydrates and fats; in its absence, excess of sugar may cause *diabetes mellitus*. Insulin had only recently been isolated (Banting and Best, Toronto, 1921) and its properties determined (Sanger, Cambridge, 1925-28), but insulin coma-therapy was then used at the Bethlem Royal as a means of controlling schizophrenia, controlled doses producing effects similar to electro-convulsive therapy (ECT). The relief implied is death by means of insulin injection.

58.2 [36]: *Berkeley*: George Berkeley (1685-1753), Bishop of Cloyne and Fellow at Trinity. His first book, *A New Theory of Vision* was published in Dublin in 1709, when he was twenty-four, and *A Treatise Concerning the Principles of Human Knowledge*, his greatest work, followed in 1710. Berkeley discerned in Locke a scientific world-view and the idea that mathematics and mechanics are the keys to understanding nature; in other words, that all matter is atomic or "corpuscular" in nature, and its properties a matter of mechanical interactions. He believed this idea to be fatal to religion and morality, and thought he could show it to be untenable. Berkeley denied the ultimate existence of matter (Neary's "Immaterialise or bust"). He contended that perception was not causal but rather that the "proper objects" of vision are purely visual ideas "in the mind," the cause of these being ever the will of God [see #246.3]. To balance Wylie's optimistic trust in equilibrium, Neary reminds him that Berkeley's cosmos could vanish on the instant, if the mind but change its theme.

58.3 [37]: *Deus det!*: L. "Let God give it," the verb in the jussive mood; as in the formula of Grace, *Deus det nobis suam pacem* [L. "May God give us his peace"; in Rabelais, II.xli, 242].

58.4 [37]: *an aching void to the same amount*: an Archimedean joke, elaborated in the French translation:

> —Et de tout cela, dit Neary, corrige-moi si je me trompe, je dois inférer que la possession—*Deus det!*—de volume correspondant. Il se tut, mécontent de sa phrase. Il reprit: Déplacerait sa propre masse de—comment dirai-je—de
> —Gale, dit Wylie.
> —En effet, dit Neary. Cela démange presque au sens propre.

> [Fr. "And from all that," said Neary, "correct me if I am wrong, I should infer that the possession—*Deus det!*—of equivalent volume." He stopped speaking, unhappy with the phrase. He started again: "Will displace its own

weight of—what shall I say?—of . . ."
"Scurf," said Wylie.
"Indeed," said Neary. "That scrapes almost the right meaning."]

58.5 [37]: *Humanity is a well with two buckets*: this memorable image of *exhalantion* (in Sir Thomas Browne's sense of drawing truth from the bottom of a well), or the closed system of desire and possession (as the one increases, the other decreases), is attributed by Beckett in the *Whoroscope* Notebook to Marston. It is from *The Malcontent* [III.iii.60-62], the words of Malevole to Mendoza, on the buffets of Fortune: "Did you e're see a well with two buckets, whilst one comes up full to be emptied, another goes down empty to be filled? Such is the state of all humanity." Marston in turn drew the image from Shakespeare's *Richard II* [IV.i.184]:

Now is this golden crown like a deep well
That owes two buckets filling one another,
The emptier ever dancing in the air,
The other down, unseen and full of water:
That bucket down and full of tears am I,
Drinking my grief, whilst you mount up on high.

The image is cited in Burton's *Anatomy* as an emblem of how men prey upon one another: "like so many buckets in a well, as one riseth another falleth, one's empty, another's full " ['Democritus to the Reader,' 33]. In *Watt* [55], Mary's one hand on its way down to be filled meets the other on its way up to be emptied. Likewise in *Malone Dies* [185], there are two pots, one for soup and the other for bodily needs, the second filling as the first is emptied; Malone's decline is signaled when the one remains full even as the other is filling [252].

59.1 [37]: *this Coney Eastern Island*: a frenetic mingling of New York's amusement park at Coney Island (swings and roundabouts) with Frederick Higgins's effusive description of his native land as "an Easter Island in the Western Sea" ['Recent Irish Poetry,' *Disjecta,* 73], and with the plea for "celestial" attractions other than the somatic Miss Counihan.

59.2 [37]: *heal-all*: literally, panacea.

59.3 [37]: *derogating from the general to the particular*: for all his faults, Neary does not do this, despite Schopenhauer's assumption that the systematic form of knowledge is based upon "the gradual descent from the general to the particular" [*WWI*, I.i §14, 83]. See #13.2, and Beckett's insistence upon the straws and flotsam of existence (demented particulars) as the only things that can be known (Schopenhauer at least insisted on the immediacy of perception).

59.4 [37]: *the Great Wen*: a growth or cystic excrescence on the scalp or body of man, beast or tree. The term 'great wen' was applied to London by William Cobbett in his *Rural Rides* (1822) through the outskirts of the growing city; this detail is given in the *OED*.

60.1 [37]: *to wipe her—er—feet on*: as Rabinovitz says [*Development*, 75], Wylie's use of 'er' followed by an implied obscenity is a small joke at Miss Counihan's expense, this being her invariable manner. For the joke itself, compare *Molloy* [20], our man accosted by a policeman:

Your papers, he said, I knew it a minute later. Not at all, I said, not at all. Your papers! he cried. Ah my papers. Now the only papers I carry with me are bits of newspaper to wipe myself, you understand, when I have a stool. Oh I don't say I wipe myself every time I have a stool, no, but I like to be in a position to do so, if I have to. Nothing strange about that, it seems to me. In a panic I took this paper from my pocket and thrust it under his nose. The weather was fine.

60.2 [38]: *Zeiss glasses*: German field-glasses, reputedly the best of their kind. They originated in Jena, at the University of which Hegel was Professor. The "watering place" is less likely to be a German spa than the Lucan Spa Hotel, mentioned in *Dream* [183]. Wylie's reverence is, er, germane in that it anticipates the more complex account of the theme in chapter 6, while it picks up the discussion of Beauty in *Dream* [35]. It activates the dictum, *ubi amor ibi occulus* [L. "where I love I look"], from Burton's *Anatomy* [III.2.3, 554; DN, #867].

60.3 [38]: *All centre and no circumference*: as in the famous definition of God: "a sphere of which the center is everywhere, the circumference nowhere." Beckett cites this in the Dream Notebook [#672], with a cryptic "St. Bonaventura" that perhaps indicates its source in W. R. Inge's *Christian Mysticism* [28]. The dictum goes back at least to the 12th century, and perhaps even to the One of Empedocles [Freeman, *Ancilla* #31]. It has been repeated by Alan de Lille, Dante and Meister Eckhardt, each of whom links it with the idea of God as Monad, complete in every part of Himself, so as to signify that in every moment and every place God constitutes the center of all moments and all places. The definition is found in Rabelais [III.xiii] and Leibniz [*Monadology*, 420], but Neary's intended reference is probably the *Pensées* [#72], the long meditation on man's disproportion wherein Pascal comments that it is the greatest sensible mark of the mighty power of God that imagination loses itself in that thought, and that our little body is imperceptible in the *bosom* of the whole.

61.1 [38]: *Bray*: a small town in Wicklow County, on the coast south of Dalkey, at "the square end" of the "Slow and Easy," the local rail service from Harcourt Street ("the round end") which passed through Foxrock and is featured in *Watt*. The name epitomizes changes of loyalties, but not affections; in the words of the old satire, "Let who will be king, I will be Vicar of Bray still."

61.2 [38]: *née Cox*: the rhythm suggests 'praecox,' or dementia, but too little is given in the novel to draw conclusions [see #272.2]. The first deserted wife, by gemination, may be *née Box*, as in the French translation.

61.3 [38]: *Calcutta*: as the diverb goes, "the woman you wronged in Calcutta." Neary cannot, in the circumstances, make the obvious retort: "But that was in another country, / And, besides, the wench is dead" (this, from Marlowe's *Jew of Malta*, was marked for interpolation in the *Whoroscope* Notebook, but not finally included). Beckett's fraught association with Kenneth Tynan's *Oh Calcutta* ["Oh quel cul tu as"] was yet far in the future.

62.1 [38]: *the worst*: eight nips at 6d each, plus two more at 8d (why?), should add up to 4/- plus 1/4, for a total of 5/4. Even if this is not what Cathleen means ("forty-eight" pence equal 4/-, and 16/- more make up a pound), Neary is being gently skinned.

62.2 [39]: *out of his government*: the metaphor is drawn from the stars, the displacement of reason within Neary throwing the microcosm into chaos.

62.3 [39]: *His surgical quality*: his detached impersonality [Webb, 49]. The phrase occurs in the 'Ithaca' chapter of Joyce's *Ulysses* [627], where Mr. Bloom's hand, about to make cocoa, is described as having "the operative surgical quality." Thus the inescapable if inappropriate patter of *The Merchant of Venice* [IV.i.179-81], as the gentle rain tries not to fall:

> *Portia*: The quality of mercy is not strain'd,
> It droppeth as the gentle rain from heaven
> Upon the place beneath:

Shylock's insistence upon his pound of flesh makes a neat transition to the Cattle Market of the next chapter. It all adds up to a mildly muddled ending to a nicely confused episode.

5

63.1 [40]: *Brewery Road*: running between the York and Caledonian Roads, in a depressed area north of King's Cross and on the edge of Islington. In the *Whoroscope Notebook*, Beckett registered his decision to set part of the action there, between slaughter-house and prison, which tie in with other aspects of mews and cages. In this chapter the big theme is JOB, and close observation of the physical realities of the mercantile gehenna is critical; the London scene is surveyed meticulously to contrast its big buzzing confusion with the little world of the mind. Yet despite the exact observation, a critical address is suppressed: Miss Counihan later asks: "What number again in Brewery Road did you say?", but receives no answer [see #120.2]. One might guess an address midway on the north side of the street [see #74.6], but the jest relates to Joyce's *Ulysses*, where Bloom is domiciled precisely at 7 Eccles Street; thus, conventions of realism are mocked even as they are most closely observed.

63.2 [40]: *Pentonville Prison*: the prison is technically in Barnsbury, an area once notorious as a venue for brutalizing sports. As Clunn notes [301], "the habits of the population were generally of that low order then commonly found on the borders of a great city." The Pentonville Act of the early 1800s called for a model prison, but the first stone was not laid until April 10, 1840. The cost was £84,168.12.2, and the official opening December 1, 1872, though it was operative long before that. It was designed to take 520 convicts under sentence of transportation; they were to be kept silent and separated for the first eighteen months of the sentence, before being transported "in one of three classes depending upon their behaviour, industry and moral outlook." By the standards of the day the prison was innovative and clean, but the rigidity of the "silent system" and the harsh discipline drove many convicts mad, some ending their days in the asylum. With the cessation of transportation it became grossly overcrowded. The system was modified over the years, but in the 1930s the prison was still overfull, and its walls (about which Murphy walks, as an exteriorization of his inner world) grimly threatening.

63.3 [40] *the Metropolitan Cattle Market*: in the 1930s a bustling complex. There remains only the clock tower and a notice near the old entrance, from which I quote:

> In 1852 the City of London bought the area of Copenhagen Fields, which now forms Caledonian Park and the Market Road Estate, to build a cattle

market to replace Smithfields which was in the centre of the city. Islington at that time was still outside the city and cattle could easily be driven to the new market along the Caledonian Road to the north.

The new market was designed by J. B. Bunning, leading architect, and opened in 1855. The centre piece was the clock tower and it could take 42,000 sheep & 7,000 cattle as well as numerous pigs and calves.

The cattle market was held on Mondays and Thursdays and on Fridays there was a flea market. By the beginning of this century the cattle market had decreased drastically and the market became famous for its antique stalls. On one Friday in 1930 a census showed 2,000 stalls.

The market closed in 1940 and did not reopen after the war. In 1965 the area was eventually cleared and the present part and housing estate were built.

An amalgam of Bartholemew and Vanity Fairs, the Caledonian Market offered everything from silver and antiques to chintz and junk. Its frenzied variety makes it an ideal emblem of what Murphy calls the Big World, where everything is, as Celia observes [67], an end to means.

63.4 [40]: *those killed under him by Balzac*: Honoré de Balzac (1799-1850), French novelist associated with the realistic tradition of *La Comédie humaine*, which Beckett dismissed as "a chloroformed world" planted with "clockwork cabbages" [*Dream*, 119]. His style is parodied in *Malone Dies*, with the story of Big Lambert and Saposcat's time among the peasants. The catabasis is not identified in life or fiction, but bulky Balzac began his new life as a writer (1819-20) in a little garret with yellow walls and flimsy furniture.

63.5 [40]: *a linoleum of exquisite design*: as Knowlson notes [199], Beckett conferred upon the room that he invented for Celia and Murphy in Brewery Road many of the qualities of his room at Mrs. Frost's, including its linoleum floor with a design (he wrote to McGreevy) "like Braque seen from a great distance" [September 8, 1934]. In the first outline of the novel, in the *Whoroscope* Notebook, the linoleum, then back at the mew, was to be invested with all the iridescent qualities of the rainbow. See also #140.1.

63.6 [40]: *Braque*: Georges Braque (1882-1963), friend and contemporary of Picasso, with whom he conspired and competed to establish a new mode of expression called Cubism, the celebrated designs of guitars and harlequins typically portrayed in abrupt geometrical patterns of multiple perspective and subdued color (the novel's green and yellow motif reflects something of his tonalities). Braque was the first modernist to introduce collage, and, unlike Picasso, he remained more or less true to Cubist principles for the rest of his career.

63.7 [40]: *distempered*: a process in which pigments are mixed with a glue or casein binder, as used for flat wall decoration or poster art; the word also has overtones of high fever.

64.1 [40]: *the new life*: the life that begins after receiving Christ into one's heart, as, most famously, in the *Vita nuova* of Dante, in which the poet tells Guido Calvacanti the story of his love for Beatrice, his grief at her death, the visit from the Lady Philosophy, and his resolve to celebrate his lost love in *La Divina commedia*.

64.2 [40]: *the hegira*: from Ar. *hejîra*, "departure"; the flight of Mahomet from Mecca to Medina, when he was expelled by the Magistrates; the date of July 16, 622 (by infidel reckoning) marking the beginning of the Mohammedan calendar. The word was used by Joyce to describe his frequent changes of abode in Paris [Cronin, 152].

64.3 [41]: *a Doric pelvis*: i.e., narrow and unadorned. The description derives in part from Beckett's childhood neighbor, Mrs. Coote, the "small thin sour woman" identified in *Company* [28; O'Brien, 15]. For a remote connection, see Beare [134-35]: "'Most odour emanates,' says Empedocles, 'from bodies that are fine in texture and of light weight.'"

64.4 [41]: *Miss Carriage*: an abortive pun.

64.5 [41]: *P.G.s*: Paying Guests, a landlady's perogative.

64.6 [41]: *a fence sold out*: informed on, rather than having disposed of his property (a 'fence' being one who receives and sells stolen goods).

64.7 [41]: *The antinomies of unmarried love*: 'antinomy' is used by Kant to define the basic contradictions in which Reason finds itself, and by Schopenhauer [*WWI*, I.1 §7, 37-39] as a contradiction which develops entirely of itself and can neither be escaped or resolved; above all, he argues, that of "no object without a subject" [38] renders materialism impossible, the existence of the world dependent, on the one hand, upon the first conscious being, who is in turn dependent upon a long chain of causes and effects preceding. Without this antinomy, the very notions of Time and Space (to say nothing of the Lover and the Loved One) are meaningless; hence, perhaps, Murphy's sense of the annihilated universe which follows.

65.1 [41]: *to annihilate . . . the visible universe*: despite the underpinnings of Schopenhauer, the phrasing suggests the apocalyptic vision of William Blake as imagined by Stephen Dedalus at the beginning of 'Nestor' [*Ulysses*, 24]: in the thud of Blake's wings of excess, the ruin of all space, and time one livid final flame.

65.2 [41]: *no willing and no nilling*: i.e., no sexual shenanigans; but a return to the dominant, *nolens volens*, the annihilation of the world as Will, whether Murphy likes it or not ("Then there will be nothing . . ."). This ironically qualifies Schopenhauer's sense of the sexual drive as an expression of the Will. The Dream Notebook [#127] notes a like phrase from Augustine's *Confessions* VII.iii, asserting free will as the cause of doing ill, and invoking the sense of self that might draw the soul's vision from the deep pit.

65.3 [41]: *Joe Miller*: a stale jest, taking in vain the name of Joe Miller (1684-1738), an actor of farce and "facetious memory" from the age of Congreve. After his death, "his lamentable Friend and former Companion, Elijah Jenkin, Esq." set forth *Joe Miller's Jest-Book, or the Wit's Vade Mecum, being, A Collection of the most Brilliant Jests; the Politest Repartees; the most Elegant Bons Mots, and most pleasant Short Stories in the English Language* (1739), Price 1/-; in reality, a basket of 198 tired old conkers, well-roasted even in their time. The subscribers, "those Choice Spirits of the Age," included Captain Bodens, Mr. Alexander Pope, Mr. Professor Lacy, Mr. Orator Henley, and Job Baker, the Kettle-Drummer.

65.4 [41]: *In the beginning was the pun*: from the opening of the Gospel of St. John: Ἐν ἀρχῇ ἦν ὁ Λόγος [Gk. "In the beginning was the word"]; the *New Testament* response to the creation myth of Genesis, in which God created the universe (from chaos, or *ex nihilo*, the matter is in dispute). The *logos* was equated with Reason, and its antonym, ἄλογος, was used by Euclid to express mathematical irrationality; this was translated into Latin by 'surdus,' "deaf," and hence ridiculous, or *absurd* [see #77.2]. A complex etymology thus links the Word to the Theater of the Absurd, and Beckett's quibble becomes what he described to McGreevy as a "phrase-bomb" [February 3, 1931].

For Schopenhauer, the cause of laughter is the sudden perception of incongruity between a concept and the real objects that have been thought through it in some relation: "All laughter then is accompanied by paradox" [*WWI*, I.I §13, 77]. This would account for Murphy's clonic fit [139-40], were it not for Schopenhauer's insistence [79] that the play upon words, the *calembourg*, the pun, is a spurious kind of wit, and closer to folly, because it brings two different concepts by the assistance of accident under one word (this, for Freud, would be a key insight into wit and its relation to the unconscious). Behind Beckett's jesting there is a qualification of Schopenhauer's assumed gap between "real objects" and "words," the gulf not so easily bridged, and the pun, however appalling, an expression of an absurdist creation largely structured (or perceived) by language.

65.5 [41]: *to make a man of Murphy*: Beckett had noted in the *Whoroscope* Notebook: "No surer mark of folly than an attempt to correct the natural infirmities of those we love." This is from *Tom Jones* [II.vii], and Squire Allworthy's failure to register certain deficiencies in the person of Captain Blifil. Knowlson says [215] that Celia is quoting the exact words that Beckett's mother had used to him, and that Murphy's reply vents Beckett's own frustration and tension. Alfred Adler's discussion of the neurotic constitution defines as "the fictitious goal" of masculine protest the wish to be "a complete man"; this is not one shared by Murphy.

65.6 [41]: *almost five month's experience*: well, yes, inclusively; the relationship beginning June 24, and it being now early October. But really, even counting in the blockade (lifted September 12), a little over three complete months. Counting in the blockade.

66.1 [41]: *a larval experience*: in the life-cycle of the insect, the *larval* stage is that of the grub, before that of the *chrysalis* and *imago*, or adult form (as in the myth of Psyche). In *The Riddle of the Universe*, source of Buck Mulligan's description of God as "the gaseous vertebrate" [*Ulysses*, 189], Ernst Haeckel likens the development of the soul to that of the insect, for in the womb, surrounded by placenta and amnion, it remains in a state of embryonic slumber similar to the chrysalis stage. This is preceded by a "condition of the free larva (caterpillar, grub or maggot)," which is characterized by "highly-developed psychic activity." This metaphor of birth is sustained over the next two pages, and continued [183], when Murphy considers his own projection, "larval and dark," into the world [consider also Celia's experience, #149.3]. The same image is invoked in the Addenda of *Watt* [248], where: "the foetal soul is full grown (Cangiamilla's *Sacred Embryology* and Pope Benedict XIV's *De Synodo Diocesana*, Bk. 7, Chap. 4, Sect. 6"). That reference, slightly inaccurate, is to Benedict's approval (1748) of the minor Sicilian theologian's teachings on the salvation of the soul in difficult circumstances such as Caesarian birth. Beckett's concern for the soul that had never been properly born (a case he heard about at one of Jung's Tavistock lectures) would be a major preoccupation henceforth.

66.2 [42]: *intact*: "untouched": not the right word [compare L. *virgo tintacta*, "pin-up girl"].

66.3 [42]: *a peristalsis*: an automatic vermicular muscular movement, usually associated with the oesophagus but here with uterus and vagina. A traditional image for the immaculate conception of Christ is that of light passing through a window. The scene of Celia sitting in her chair inside a tiny room has affinities to the later setting of *Endgame*, the chief difference being that she is inside the womb rather than the skull.

67.1 [42]: *amnion*: the innermost membrane about the unborn foetus, continuing the imagery of the embryonic soul; in this sense, as Haeckel remarks [67], "man is a true amnionite."

67.2 [42]: *life as an end to means*: an inversion of the Platonic ideal that the first and greatest condition of successful life is a knowledge of the End (i.e., the highest Good); and of the Kantian proposition, wearily repeated by Schopenhauer [*WWI*, I.4 §62, 450]: "man must always be treated as an end, never as a means."

67.3 [42]: *imbedded in a jelly of light*: again, the amniotic image. 'Trembling' (as of a veil), in neo-Platonic thought is an attribute of the soul on the verge of entering the generative world, as in Blake's *Book of Thel*. Beckett encountered in Otto Rank's *The Trauma of Birth* the "re-birth fantasy" as the flight of the libido to the intrauterine stage [5]; the sense of being alone in a dark room as the experiencing of the primal trauma [11]; and the contention that "every pleasure has as its final aim the re-establishment of the intrauterine primal pleasure" [17].

67.4 [42]: *a nucleus*: as of a cell or blastula, even one destined to miscarry. The continuity with the previous paragraph may be deliberate: in his Preface to *The Trauma of Birth* [xiii], Rank comments: "we are led to recognise in the birth trauma the ultimate biological basis of the psychical. In this way we get a fundamental insight into the nucleus of the Unconscious."

67.5 [42]: *the nice strong cup of tea*: in polite society, 'strong' or 'hot' are optional attributives, but 'nice' is obligatory. When he first came to Gertrude Street, Beckett noted to McGreevy [September 8, 1934], he produced his own Lapsang in favor of Mrs Frost's Lipton's.

67.6 [42]: *having left undone*: i.e., fired by a conviction of righteousness unlike that admitted by the penitents during Confession in the Anglican service, as induced by *The Book of Common Prayer*: "We have left undone those things which we ought to have done; And we have done those things which we ought not to have done; And there is no health in us."

68.1 [43]: *coagulates*: a common clinch, the moot point being whether the Transylvanian translation is Miss Carriage's or Celia's.

68.2 [43]: *Lapsang Souchong*: to cite the label: "Fine tea from the province of Fujian in China; COLOUR: Burnished brown CHARACTER: Smoky STRENGTH: Medium."

69.1 [43]: *padding*: perhaps, the motion of the monad.

69.2 [43]: *the old boy*: a character suggested partly by an "old boy" who died of a seizure in the house opposite Mrs. Frost in Gertrude Street, and partly by an item which Beckett had read about in the newspaper [Knowlson, 206, 743; see also

#196.4]. Although little is seen or known of him, his behavior has something in common with Murphy's, but with a quiet desperation lacking in the latter. As Farrow notes well [22], a butler is an attendant occupation, depending for definition upon the existence of another.

69.3 [43]: *The punctuality with which Murphy returned*: the precision emulates that of Kant, whose daily constitutional at precisely three o'clock enabled his neighbors in Königsburg to reset their watches.

70.1 [44]: *Lombard Street*: not the Dublin street of sanitary engineers, mentioned in 'Ding-Dong' [*MPTK*, 43], but the banking area in the City of London, as noted in Clunn [39]: "This world-famous banking thoroughfare derives its names from the Lombards, merchants, moneylenders, and bankers who settled here in the twelfth century from the Italian republics of Genoa, Venice, and Florence. Because of their usurious practices they were ordered by Queen Elizabeth to leave the country."

70.2 [44]: *her ruelle*: literally, a little "rue" or alley, but the usual sense is well defined in an editorial note to Swift's *A Tale of a Tub* [82]: "It was customary under Louis XIV for ladies to receive morning visitors in their bedrooms; hence 'ruelle,' the passage by the side of a bed, came to signify a boudoir of ladies of fashion." The word was applied to a secret passage by means of which courtesans could be smuggled into the royal bed.

70.3 [44]: *Murphy on the jobpath*: Murphy's work-related affliction, the agony of Job, derives equally from the biblical *Book of Job* and William Blake's twenty-one engravings thereof. Blake's *Job* was published in 1825, but languished until 1910, when Joseph Wicksteed produced *Blake's Vision of the Book of Job*. There was an immense interest in Blake in the 1920s, when Geoffrey Keynes's three-volume edition of the works appeared, as well as many illustrated texts and facsimiles. *The Book of Job* disputes the theory that material misfortunes are punishments for sin. Job is perfect and upright, prosperous and faithful, blessing the Lord. Satan enters into contract with God to test that faith by destroying his prosperity, yet Job will not curse God. He persists in his faith, though he laments loudly and rues the day he was born. After great tribulation, Job's faith and the justice of God are reaffirmed, and Job is restored to double his former possessions, and to live out his old age in happiness and prosperity.

70.4 [44] *the Blake League*: there was in 1935 no such conspiracy, but a Blake Society is listed in Whitaker, "Sec. T. Wright, Olney, Bucks." Since then, the Blake Trust has promoted the works of the Master, bringing out some beautiful reproductions. With the occasional by-blow: Gulley Jimson, in Joyce Cary's *The Horse's Mouth*, tries to sell a subscription for such a society to an ex-naval officer, who thinks he is talking about Admiral Blake.

70.5 [44]: *Bildad the Shuhite*: with Eliphaz the Temanite and Zophar the Naamanthite, one of the three friends who offer false comfort (as God is just, so must Job have sinned). That is, they apply God's retributive justice to Job's sufferings, translating his agony into the clichés of orthodoxy. They are depicted in Illustration VII of Blake's *Job*, dressed in robes vaguely resembling Murphy's coat, left foot forward to indicate their folly.

70.6 [44]: *Zophar*: third of Job's miserable comforters and friends. He and Bildad are described as "fragments of Job" in accordance with the idea, first promoted by Joseph Wicksteed in 1924, that Blake's illustrations are best interpreted as a drama enacted in Job's soul, his sin being spiritual pride. The accusing friends are thus part of him, "as they speak for his submerged sense of guilt."

71.1 [44]: *on the qui vive*: the cry of the look-out [Fr. "who lives?"], modulating into the Italian: *Qui vive la pièta quando è ben mortà* [*Inferno*, XX.28], that untranslatable fragment of Dante [It. "There lives . . ."] which provokes the wretched Belacqua in 'Dante and the Lobster' to ponder the relationship between God's piety and pity, Dante's "rare movements of compassion in Hell" [*MPTK*, 18].

71.2 [44]: *maieutic saws*: the sentiment derives from Job's "What is man, that he should be clean?" [15:14]; or "how can he be clean that is born of a woman? [25:4]; or their New Testament antiphon: "he which is filthy let him be filthy still" [Revelation 22:11]. 'Maieutic' refers to the process of Socratic reasoning that brings into consciousness concepts latent in the mind, punning upon the Greek meaning of "midwifery." In Burnet's words [*Greek Philosophy*, 139-40], Socrates "had a way of speaking of the birth of thoughts in the soul in language derived from his mother's calling. He professed, of course, that he himself was incapable of giving birth to wisdom, but he claimed to be an excellent man-midwife, well skilled in the art of bringing new thoughts to birth."

71.3 [44]: *no other butt*: i.e, no other object of derision or contempt, but (for the reader) with retrospective reference to Neary's encounter with the Red Branch bum.

71.4 [44]: *the vagitus*: the first cry of the newly-born child. A favorite word for Beckett, and summed up (post-obit) by Belacqua in 'Echo's Bones' [25]: "scarcely had my cord been clumsily severed than I struggled to reintegrate the matrix, nor did I relax those newborn efforts until death came and undid me."

71.5 [44]: *the proper A of international concert pitch*: until 1859 there was no recognized standard of pitch, and there had been since classical times an unintended and uncontrolled rise in orchestral pitch, as measured (traditionally by the oboe) by tuning for 'A' in the treble stave; this might, and did, lead to serious misrepresentations of classical works. In 1859 the French government adopted diapason normal (from the Gk. διὰ πασῶν χορδῶν συμφονία, "through all the strings of the lyre," or the interval of the octave), defined as 870 vibrations or 435 double-vibrations (cycles) per second. The physicist Lissajous was commissioned to make a tuning fork (at 15 degrees C, or 59 degrees F) of exactly that pitch. A committee of physicists accepted this in 1886 as the International Normal Musical Pitch. Unfortunately, the British and Americans did not adopt the standard, preferring for organ and orchestra to redefine diapason normal (which also meant 'tuning fork') at the typical concert-hall temperature of 68 degrees F, or an 'A' of 439 cps. This became the de facto norm, certainly during Beckett's early concert-going years, and in December 1939 British Standard Pitch was more or less universally adopted, based on a frequency of 440 cps for 'A' in the treble stave. The "double flat" of 'A' means the lowering of the note by two semitones, effectively to G-natural on the scale of C-major. Something of the effect of the singular larynx, and the honest obstetrician's anguish, may be gauged even by the unmusical by singing 'la' at the pitch of 'so' on the Julie Andrews *Sound of Music* scale. Watt's sense of pitch is also a tone flat.

71.6 [44]: *the Old Dublin Orchestral Society*: the first Dublin Orchestral Society was founded in 1899 by Michele Esposito, Professor of pianoforte at the Royal Irish Academy of Music since 1882 (his daughter, Bianca, taught Beckett Italian), with 70 players and regular Sunday performances in the Antient Concert Rooms until the outbreak of war in 1914. The "honest obstretician" may be Beckett's invention; Brian Boydell, retired Professor of Music at Trinity, recalls no such flautist, but notes that many members of the professional classes played as amateurs [letter to CA]. After the War the Society lapsed, until Colonel Fritz Brase, a German-born conductor of the Army Band, founded the Dublin Philharmonic Society Orchestra in 1927, with 75 players. It began with the Beethoven 9th, and performed regularly until 1936. Beckett in various letters refers to these performances, his comments often less than flattering.

71.7 [44]: *his rattle will make amends*: punning upon the pacifying effects of the baby's bauble and death. Yet audible too are the words of Francis Bacon's 'The World' [1629]:

What then remains but that we still should cry
For being born, and, being born, to die?

71.8 [44]: *not green, but aeruginous*: the color of copper having been exposed to air, and darkened. The point to emphasize to the Blake League is that Murphy, accordingly, is not part of the vegetative world, or realm of generation. Compare the use of 'aerugo' for the colors of the sky in 'Ding-Dong' [*MPTK*, 41].

72.1 [44]: *Bishop Bouvier's Supplementum ad Tractatum de Matrimonio*: more fully, Jean-Baptiste Bouvier's *Dissertatio in sextum decalogi praeceptum, et supplementum ad tractatum de matrimonio* (Le Mans, 1827). The good Monseigneur's piety did not prevent after his death several volumes forged by one Maurice la Châtre, dealing with secrets and mysteries of the confessional or marriage-bed, and other scurvy betrayals. Henning suggests [*Complicity*, 44] that Murphy, as a theological student, meditated upon how man, fragmented by his fall, might be redeemed by the "it is consummated" of conjugal love; this, however, is at odds with the *Ciné Bleu* (or "blue movie") scenario that immediately suggests itself.

72.2 [44]: *goatish Latin*: goats were common Elizabethan emblems of the libidinous. Beckett presumably picked up the capricious phrase from Beaumont and Lecher's *Philaster* [V.iii.153], the diatribe of Dion against the rebels, which concludes: "may they have many children and none like the father! May they know no language but that gibberish they prattle to their parcels, unless it be the goatish Latin they write in their bonds." Compare Dyce's footnote to this: "the ranke sauour of gotes is applied to them that will not come out of theyr baudy latyn."

72.3 [45]: *Christ's parthian shot*: the Parthians reputedly turned in the saddle to shoot arrows backwards; hence, in the demotic, a parting shot. The last words of Christ, *Consummatum est,* were delivered as He gave up the ghost and left this world. The phrase "finished, it is nearly finished" would later be used at the outset of *Endgame*. Murphy's parting shaft: the expected supplement to marriage is, of course, consummation.

72.4 [72]: *It made him feel like a woman*: ah, don't we all . . . I beg your pardon, this is a serious theological jest, with reference to Adam's rib and the propensity of the waist-coat to pinch the rib-cage. In the *Whoroscope* Notebook, Beckett defined woman as "a constipated mammal with a pain in the right side," another of those early comments to make certain critics wish he had never written such caustic passages. Another mysogynist, Jonathan Swift, wrote that he had to get the Duchess of Hamilton to make him pockets "like a woman's, with a Belt and Buckle, for ye know I wear no waistcoat in Summer" [*Letter to Stella*, LII].

72.5 [45]: *the material of this suit*: Murphy in his overcoat forms the image of peripatetic motion, monad as nomad, and the terms of the coat's composition and qualities are the very materials of scholastic disputation. At the outset of the *Whoroscope Notebook* [§2], before Murphy had even been named, Beckett had noted the "Dynamist ethic of X. Keep moving the only virtue." That ethic remained an essential force, linking atomists such as Democritus to central precepts of Geulincx, and beyond that, to the quanta of non-Newtonian tumult. Thus, Murphy on the jobpath is the embodiment of the Democritean atom in ceaseless motion, his suit "non-porous" in the atomist sense of precluding the penetration of the Unlimited [see #246.8]. It allows no "vapours" to escape, vapores being the Cartesian and Occasionalist term for the animal spirits commingling in the conarium with spiritual essences [Geulincx, 'De Microcosmo' §4, *Physica Vera* VI, *Opera* 2, 441-42]. That it feels like "felt" and much "size" has entered into its composition suggests the visible world as extension and the sensory agents that permit its perception. Murphy is thus a Microcosm, illustrating in human terms the central law of the physical universe as iterated in the *Physica* ('Peripatetica' and 'Verum') of Geulincx: *Mundus est Corpus in Motu* [L. "the World is a Body in Motion"]. Yet lest one take this bilge too seriously, Beckett would have found in Swift's *A Tale of a Tub* [78], in that splendid puff of clothes and appearances over inner essences, a wonderful anticipation of Murphy in the sartorial saw: "what is Man himself, but a *Microcoat*."

73.1 [45]: *a collar and dicky combination*: the makings of what appears to be a shirt, for elegant evening wear, but in popular tradition the refuge of the shirtless seeking to impress. That it is "without seam" is an irreverent comparison to the immaculate garment of Christ.

73.2 [45]: *Murphy never wore a hat*: the reason is suggested in Otto Rank's *The Trauma of Birth* [91 n.2]: "the embryonal caul, as also our hat today, the loss of which in dream signifies separation from a part of one's ego." Thus, the narrator of 'Sanies I' laments: "ah to be back in the caul now with no trusts"; a sentiment echoed by Belacqua in 'Fingal' [*MPTK*, 31]: "I want very much to be back in the caul, on my back in the dark forever."

73.3 [45]: *to abandon hope*: an unavoidable (if futile) echo of Dante's "Lasciate ogne speranza" [It. "Abandon all hope"], at the entrance to Hell [*Inferno*, III.8].

73.4 [45]: *the toil from King's Cross*: a steady uphill haul, a goodly walk up the Caledonian Road from the railway, and thus (faintly, faintly) reminiscent of the way of the Stations of the Cross. King's Cross is a major terminal for the London Underground and British Railway; built on the site of a former smallpox hospital, it was opened on October 14, 1852, replacing the temporary terminus of the Great Northern Line in York Road.

73.5 [45]: *St. Lazare up Rue d'Amsterdam*: the Gare St Lazare serves northern Normandy and the Dieppe area; it is thus the Parisian equivalent of King's Cross. Thence one may walk up the steep *Rue d'Amsterdam* towards the *Place de Clichy*, the indifferent junction of the *Boulevard de Clichy* and the *Rue des Batignolles*, before moving toward Monmârtre, head of the pimple, passing en route that place of asylum, *la Cimitière de Monmârtre*.

73.6 [45]: *asylum*: "The word splits in two and squints sceptically at itself" [Hill, 15]. I term these 'Bruno words,' or identified contraries: Murphy will not find refuge in the mad-house.

73.7 [45]: *the little shelter*: for many years this wooden rotunda was a central feature of the little gardens on "Lumpy Hill" in Market Road, but it was demolished in the early 1980s. Murphy's aromatic location, with its faint susurrus of Milton as Tripe, is precisely located.

73.8 [45]: *the Tripe Factory*: the indelicate comestible from the lining of a cow's stomach was obviously in demand, for there were a number of tripe factories and wholesalers in the vicinity of the Cattle Market; that appreciated by Murphy was the establishment of J. L. Hewson, tripe dresser and owner of a string of tripe shops, at 18 Market Road directly opposite the gardens.

73.9 [45]: *Milton House*: the headquarters of Milton Proprietary, Ltd., 10-12 Brewery Road, makers, even now, of a popular disinfectant. The firm has long moved elsewhere.

73.10 [45]: *stalled cattle*: there were stables directly behind the Perseverance and Temperance Yards, with a path leading through them to the Market; an unromantic setting, despite the touch of the Wild West in the use of 'corral.'

73.11 [45]: *night's young thoughts*: those of Edward Young (1683-1765), in his day ranked as one of the greatest poets on account of the phenomenal success of his *Night Thoughts* (1742-45), which instituted the school of graveyard poetry. These begin with the sleepless poet, in the darkness of the night, lamenting his misfortunes and meditating upon the mysteries of mortality. They gave eloquence to orthodoxy, and Young had the knack of condensing his thoughts into resonant pentameters (Murphy is unlikely to be impressed by "Procrastination is the thief of time"). Although Young's system is in many ways the antithesis of Blake's, the 537 watercolors and 43 engravings to the poem are testimony to the impression made on him by Young; Beckett may have seen some at the Tate.

74.1 [45]: *back an hour*: as noted in Whitaker [118], for October 6, 1935: "Summer Time ends 2 a.m. (G.M.T.)." Daylight saving (like income tax) had been introduced as a temporary measure during World War I, an Act of May 17, 1916 ordaining that for a defined period of the year the legal time for general purposes should be one hour in advance of Greenwich Mean Time. A further Act of July 20, 1922 specified that the period should begin at 2 o'clock in the morning of the day following the third Saturday in April, or if that day is Easter Day, the day following the second Saturday; and should end at 2 o'clock GMT in the morning of the day following the third Saturday of September. This was made permanent (August 7, 1925), and modified by substituting the first for the last Saturday in September [Whitaker, 158].

74.2 [46]: *the multis latebra opportuna*: L. "the convenient haunts of many"; the words of Ovid's Narcissus to the woods around him, as he pines away for love of himself [*Metamorphoses*, III.443]. The phrase is cited in the Dream Notebook [#1112], with a cynical flourish: "Bois de Vincennes." Belacqua visits Vienna in the hope of such lurking opportunities [*Dream*, 13].

74.3 [46]: *the clock in the prison tower*: there is a small mystery here, for there is no such clock, nor was there in 1935. The prison when built in the 1840s was crowned by a grand Italian clock, which was a landmark for years, but in 1853 the clock tower and a fine portcullis were demolished to build a fourth floor. Beckett may have been guided by older illustrations, which show the clock visible from the mouth of Brewery Road; this seems more likely than having the Market clock, which is mentioned separately, assume two locations. Unless, of course, it is an Occasionalist joke. There is a further mystery, for even Murphy's slow regress could not take quarter of an hour to get home from the mouth of Brewery Road; however, from the little garden in Market Road, whence the magnificent clock tower in the Cattle Market is visible, the timing is right. There seems to be a small slip here, with no good fictional reason for the departure from fact. Unless, of course . . .

74.4 [46]: *he had walked round and round cathedrals*: the French translation adds: "en attendant l'ouverture des bordels" [Fr. "waiting for the brothels to open"]. This is indicative of a certain nastiness that entered the later rendition.

74.5 [46]: *the last bourns*: from which no Hamlet returns [III.i.79-80], and thus anticipating the "traveller's joy" at the mortuary [165]. The names are as listed in the London Post Office Directory for 1935 on the north side of Brewery Road, though not in the order transgressed.

74.6 [46]: *the Perseverance and Temperance Yards*: now Blenheim Court, a spacious yard rebuilt in the 1980s after years of dereliction; about the mid-point of Brewery Road. Miss Carriage's putative dwelling would be close by.

74.7 [46]: *The Vis Vitae Bread Co*: then at 16-24 Brewery Road, and listed as "*V.V. (Vis Vitae) Bread Co*", the "Vigor of Life" bakery in the war becoming a munitions factory.

74.8 [46]: *the Marx Cork Bath Mat Company*: listed as "62 Marx L. Cork Co. Ltd cork bath mat mkrs"; now dematerialized. Other points of interest on Brewery Road: two chandler's shops, one owned by Mrs. Laura Ketley at No. 4, and the other by Mrs. Edith Maud Jones; "Wylie-Harris & Co biscuit mfrs" at No. 52; and "Blake Jn. boot rpr" at No. 114.

74.9 [46]: *serenade, nocturne and albada*: songs of evening, morning and dawn. In *Proust* [92], Beckett celebrates Schopenhauer's sense of music as the highest form of art, the Idea itself, independent of the phenomenal world [see #40.4]. That aesthetic is counterpointed against the physical and sexual delights of the body, the closest (perhaps) that it may come to the mind's aesthetic awareness (to short-circuit the Cartesian conundrum, as to whether such pleasure is of the body or the mind). This contingency will re-emerge after Murphy's unfortunate experience with Mr. Endon [252], when he must resolve once and for all whether to return and face the music.

75.1 [46]: *lest he fell into the hands of the enemy*: according to Stekel [16], "the enemy" is produced by the fantasies of the neurotic. As all good schoolboy spy manuals know, the way to cope with this problem is to shave the head, have the secret written on it with indelible ink, let the hair grow again, and make one's way through the enemy ranks; the head may then be shaven and the message read. This bilge seems an appropriate response to Murphy's concern.

75.2 [46]: *strangury*: from Gk. στράγξ, "a drop" and οὐρία, "urine"; a slow and painful discharge of the urine, due to spasms of the uthera and bladder [see #34.3].

75.3 [46]: *Sunday, October 4th, 1936*: this is correct, as Beckett would have confirmed in Whitaker [130], where the calendar for 1936 is prominently displayed.

76.1 [47]: *the money-bags, so that they might breed*: Murphy's pirouette about a traditional figure of usury, as exemplified by the Biblical account of Laban's sheep

[Genesis 30:35], taken up in *The Merchant of Venice* [I.iii.68-97]. Shylock "takes interest" and justifies doing so by telling how Jacob, having agreed with Laban that all the "streak'd and pied" lambs were his, rewrote the laws of genetics by peeling certain wands and sticking them before the "fulsome ewes" who therefore brought forth "particolour'd lambs." Antonio replies that this was not so much Jacob's doing as fashioned by the hand of heaven, then asks: "Was this inserted to make interest good? / Or is your gold and silver ewes and lambs?"; to which Shylock craftily replies: "I cannot tell; I make it breed as fast."

76.2 [47]: *a certain disharmony*: an essential asynchronization of the two clocks that regulate the Occasionalist cosmos [see #109.1].

76.3 [47]: *their filthy synecdoche*: as defined in a vulgar limerick, the part for the whole. Beckett copied an unsullied definition into the *Whoroscope* Notebook and ticked it off to show it had been incorporated.

76.4 [47]: *a chandlery in Gray's Inn Road*: Gray's Inn Road is the major route from High Holborn to King's Cross, "a dingy and unattractive throughfare" [*Pictorial Guide*, 168]. It was named for Gray's Inn, one of the four great Inns of Court, founded for the education and lodging of law students. Its gardens and lawns were laid out by Francis Bacon, Treasurer for nine years. A chandlery was originally a store providing goods and provisions for shipping; the term in the 1930s had wider application as a general goods store. Among the several thousand listed in the London Post Office Directory for 1935 the "likely candidate" is Mr. Thos. Oldfield, 250 Gray's Inn Road, just round the corner from where Beckett had earlier lived at 4 Amforth Street, and close by the Royal Free Hospital. Nothing, alas, is known about Beckett presenting himself there for a job.

76.5 [47]: *a definite post*: the radiant aspect of a dog's life [111].

77.1 [47]: *chandlers . . . chandler's . . . chandlers'*: a crescendo of obscenity, an apostrophe to the mercantile gehenna, and a scholar's perogative.

77.2 [47]: *Thou surd!*: a surd is an irrational number, one that cannot be expressed as the ratio of two integers. There was among Pythagoreans a fear of such irrationality, which seemed to confound the very principle of harmony, and thus universal order; hence the fate of Hippasos, drowned for betraying that secret [see #47.8]. The word 'surdus,' meaning "deaf," was used in Latin translations of Euclid's ἄλογος [see #65.4], an irrational or "deaf" root (unable to move to the music of the spheres?). As Hesla concludes [7]: "The absurd is impervious to the human Logos, to human speech and reason." An essential irrationality, be it mathematical, musical, psychological or theatrical, lay at the heart of Beckett's distrust of the rationalist tradition from Plato to Descartes and beyond, with its emphasis upon Reason as the highest form of consciousness that leads the mind to God. A key moment in the novel is thus the anagnorisis experienced by Neary when he contradicts the training of a lifetime and admits that life is, after all, rather irregular [#271.3].

77.3 [47]: *the Royal Free Hospital*: founded in 1828 when a public benefactor moved by the plight of the neglected poor appealed to Parliament and the Crown to set up a free hospital for the needy, the first of several similar foundations. It is listed in Whitaker [471]: "Gray's Inn Road, W.C.1. For relief without letters of recommendation. Accidents and urgent cases received at all hours. Out-patients daily. Visiting-days: Sun, 3 to 4; Thur, 3.30 to 4.30." The Hospital moved to Hampstead in 1953, and 256 Gray's Inn Road became the Eastman Dental School. South of the Hospital lies the St. Andrew's Public Garden, now rescued from the worst of the bacteria but still blighted by a proliferation of urban tissue (Trinity Court Flats), which the park embraces like the letter **n**. Iron railings are there to rest against, and a grubby plaque states that the ground was laid out for public recreation and rest by the vestry of St. Pancras in the county of Middlesex, and declared open for public use by Lady John Manners, on the 29th day of July 1885. Murphy's refusal to sit there, let alone lie down, seems a creak in the plot to get him to Hyde Park via the tea-rooms but turns out to be a subtle joke: the park was previously a cemetery, and the tombstones are still in evidence.

77.4 [47]: *his expectation of Antepurgatory*: the region outside the gate of Dante's Purgatory, somewhat like the Limbo of the Inferno, wherein dwell the spirits of those who have died without penitence [Toynbee, 37]. There are four classes: those who died in contumacy of the Church, and only repented at the last; those who from indolence or indifference put off repentance until just before death; those who died a violent death, without absolution, but repented at the last; and kings and princes who deferred their repentance owing to the pressure of temporal interests. All are to be detained for various specified periods, unless the time be shortened by the prayers of others on their behalf.

78.1 [48]: *the lee of Belacqua's rock*: Belacqua of Florence, a maker of lutes, is of the second category [above]: for his indolence in putting off his repentance he is to be detained for a time equal to that of his life on earth. In Canto IV of the *Purgatorio*, as Dante and Virgil begin their climb, Dante wondering if he is up to the effort, they hear a voice saying: "Forse / che di sedere in pria avrai distretta" [It. "Perhaps before then you'll need to sit"]. There, in the shade of a great rock ("un gran petrone") several figures are resting, and one of them, "che mi sembrava lasso, / sedeva ed abbracciava le ginocchia, / tenendo il viso giù tra esse basso" [It. "who seemed to me weary, was sitting and clasping his knees, holding his face down low between them"]. This is the embryonal repose. Asked why he is sitting, Belacqua responds in the words Beckett much admired: "Frate, l'andare in su che porta?" [It. "Oh brother, what is the use of going up?"]. An angel would only bar his entrance, so he is content to stay where he is. This was the inspiration behind Beckett's response when, asked what he wanted out of life, he said that he wanted to do nothing but sit on his arse and fart and read Dante. See also the Dream Notebook [#305 to #315],

78.2 [48]: *the trembling of the austral sea*: from *Purgatorio* I.115-17:

L'alba vinceva l'ôra mattutina
che fuggia innanzi, sì che di lontano,
conobbi il tremolar della marina

[It. "The dawn was vanquishing the hour of morning which fled before it, so that I recognized from afar the trembling of the sea"]. The reeds are the "erbetta sparte" [I.124] on which Virgil spreads his hands, but 'austral' is not to be found in this passage, nor does it pertain to the sea: the phrase 'austral vento' [It. "south wind"] is a crux [*Purgatorio*, XXXI.71], the better reading probably being 'nostral vento' [It. "our wind," i.e., of our land]. 'Austro,' the South Wind, is mentioned later [*Purgatorio*, XXXII.99]. Dante and Virgil begin this part of their journey at dawn; Belacqua does not mention the dawn, and Dante rather than Belacqua looks down to the shores below [*Purgatorio*, IV.55]. In *Dream* [113], Beckett's Belacqua has a similar vision of the gay zephyrs of Purgatory, "slithering in across the blue tremolo of ocean with a pinnace of souls, as good as saved, to the landing stage, the reedy beach . . ."

78.3 [48]: *the sun obliquing to the north as it rose*: Dante is surprised [*Purgatorio*, IV.55-84] at seeing the sun on his left, but this is explained by Virgil, who points out that as they are at the antipodes of Zion [see #78.10] the trajectory of the sun will be seen from a different perspective. Dante, profiting from the lesson, repeats the point [82-83]: "per la ragion che di', quinci si parte / verso settentrïon" [It. "for the reason you say, departs towards the north"].

78.4 [48]: *immune from expiation*: Belacqua is unable to make amends until he has served his sentence, a period equal to his life on earth (hence the un-Beckettian wish for a long life). The vision was not without redemption. Beckett associated it with a favorite quotation: "Sedendo et quiescendo anima efficitur sapiens" [L. "Seated and in quietness the soul gains wisdom"], the first three words of which he had used as a working title of part of *Dream*. The phrase originates in Aristotle, but was attributed to Belacqua by the "Anonimo Florentino" (c. 1400), whose words were reproduced in Toynbee's *Dictionary*, Beckett's likely source (as Daniela Caselli discovered [DN, #313]). There is a variant in Rabelais [III.xlii, 33]: "Sedendo, et dormiendo fit anima prudens"; and a similar sentiment in Thomas à Kempis's dictum of quietism in *De Imitatione Christi* [I.xx.6]: "In silentio et quiete proficit anima devota" [L. "In silence and stillness the devout soul profiteth herself"].

78.5 [48]: *dreamed it all through again*: less Dante than Calderón, whose *La Vida es sueño* [Sp. "Life is a Dream"] was much admired by Schopenhauer, and is invoked in the opening pages of *The World as Will and Idea* [I.1 §5, 20-22].

78.6 [48]: *the dayspring run through its zodiac*: the sun's passage as observed by Dante and Virgil as they approach Belacqua and note "il Zodïacal rubecchio" [It. "the ruddy Zodiac"; *Purgatorio*, IV.64]. This is the only mention of the Zodiac in the *Commedia*.

78.7 [48]: *The gradient was outrageous*: the steepness of Mount Purgatory, which leads upward to Paradise, is iterated in the first stages of the climb (as the burden of sin is sloughed, the going gets easier). The precise gradient of "less than one in one" is Murphy's interpretation of *Purgatorio* IV.40-42:

> Lo sommo er' alto che vincea la vista,
>   e la costa superba più assai
>   che la mezzo quadrante a centro lista.

[It. "The summit was so high that it surpassed my sight, and the slope was even steeper than a line from mid-quadrant to the center"]; i.e., greater than 45°, the angle of a line drawn from the center of a circle to the mid-point of one of its quadrants (the angle of the quadrant being 90°).

78.8 [48]: *shorten his time with a good prayer*: the doctrine, reiterated in the *Antepurgatorio*, that time spent in Purgatory may be shortened by the intercession, through prayer, of those yet on earth. Belacqua acknowledges [IV.133-34] that he must remain there: "se orazïone in prima non maita / che surga su di cor che in grazia viva" [It. "unless prayer first aid me, arising from a heart that lives in grace"]. His prayers do not avail for they will not be heard in Heaven.

78.9 [48]: *the first landscape of freedom*: the first glimpse of the virtual dimension of the mind (as described in section six); in particular, the second zone [111], that of "Belacqua bliss."

78.10 [48]: *Zion's antipodes*: Mount Purgatory, so fatefully encountered by Dante's Ulysses [*Inferno*, XXVI]. In Dante's cosmos, Jerusalem is the central point of the northern hemisphere and the exact antipodes of Mount Purgatory (the latter near Easter Island). As antipodes, Jerusalem and Purgatory have a common horizon [*Purgatorio*, IV.70-71], in the east terminated by the Ganges in India, and in the west by Cadiz in Spain [Toynbee, 259].

79.1 [48]: *the well-known English turf*: the link to Zion is courtesy of Blake's 'Jersualem' and England's "green and pleasant land." Murphy is quite prepared to cease from mental fight.

79.2 [48]: *improved out of all knowledge*: O'Hara finely comments ['Back to Beckett,' 47]:

> The phrase is nicely balanced to generate ambivalence. Demotically it means "beyond recognition by others because so much better than before." As a superlative it means "improved beyond anyone's knowledge of the possibilities of such improvement." In the context of Murphy's objections to the world of the sense, and in the context of Valéry's description of the personality, it has yet a third meaning: Murphy as the "I," as the character improved not by additions and complications, but by being stripped of all knowledge (and therefore of the accidental and imperfect personal experience that constitutes knowledge).

There is a fourth dimension: the sentiment is straight out of Schopenhauer. The subject is the transition from the knowledge of particulars to the knowledge of the Idea: "for knowledge breaks free from the service of the will, by the subject ceasing to be merely individual, and thus becoming the pure will-less subject of knowledge" [*WWI*, I.3 §34, 230; see also #113.3].

79.3 [48]: *Lincoln's Inn Fields*: one of the four Inns of Court (the others being Gray's and the Inner and Middle Temples), offering the qualifications for a barrister and since the 14th century occupying the site of a Black Friars monastery and palace of the Bishop of Chichester. The Fields, some twelve acres, were laid out by Inigo Jones in 1618, and acquired a reputation as a dueling ground and place execution, criminals and traitors occasionally hanged from the magnificent plane trees. The Fields were purchased by the LCC in 1890 and given to the city. Beckett rouses the past with the aid of Robert Greene's 'A Notable Discovery of Coosnage: 1591,' one of five cony-catching pamphlets published in the poet's final years, hoping (on his death-bed) they might intercede for his soul as he repented of his past. The treatise concerns the dubious art of picking out a likely victim, or "conny," and cozening him by complicated enticements into a tavern, where he is tricked out of his little or much by means of cards, whores and other devious shifts. At the end of the first treatise, Greene comes to the aid of the reader bewildered by "these misteries and queynt words," offering "A table of the words of art, vsed in the effecting these base villanies proper to none but the professors thereof":

1. High law   robbing by the highway side.
2. Sacking law   lecherie.

3. Cheting law	play at false dice.
4. Cros-biting law	cosenage by whores.
5. Conycatching law	cosenage by cards.
6. Versing law	cosenage by false gold.
7. Figging law	cutting of purses, & picking of pockets.
8. Barnards law	a drunken cosenage by cards.

The pamphlet, with its companion piece 'The Second Part of Conny-Catching. 1592,' was published by John Lane as *The Art of Conny-Catching* (1923); this was probably Beckett's source, the table appearing on pp. 37-38.

79.4 [48]: *Walk before you run, sit down before you lie down*: cited in the *Whoroscope* Notebook to be included, but not identified. It reflects Chamfort's Maxim §155 [see #57.2]:

> Quand on soutient que les gens les moins sensibles sont à tout prendre, les plus heureux, je me rappelle le proverbe indien: 'Il vaut mieux être assis que debout, être couché que assis; mort que tout cela.'

[Fr. "When we find that the least sensitive people, from all accounts, are the most happy, I recall the Indian proverb: 'It is better to be seated than upright, lying down rather than seated; dead than all that.'"] Beckett offered an idiomatic translation many years later when he presented as prose-poems eight of Chamfort's maxims [*CP*, 126-27]: "Better on your arse than on your feet, / Flat on your back than either, dead than the lot." The life of Sébastien Roch Nicholas (1740-94), better known as 'Chamfort,' reflects such cynicism. Chamfort ennobled himself to compensate for the strange circumstances of his birth: of noble but disgraced origin, he had been given to a grocer's family to raise, but determined to make his way in the fashionable world, first as a libertine, then, when a mysterious illness suddenly destroyed his good looks [compare Neary's hair, 214], as a writer and misanthropist. A minor dramatist but a master of the aphorism and maxim, he acutely observed the follies of the Ancien Régime and early Revolution until he was himself denounced. To avoid the guillotine he attempted suicide by bullet and razor, shooting out his eye and inflicting on himself twenty-two deep wounds, but somehow surviving only to die from inept treatment by his doctor some five months later—an end worthy of the anecdotes he recounted so well.

79.5 [49]: *to salivate*: Beckett could have read of I. P. Pavlov's conditioned reflex in Woodworth [61-66]: his noticing that laboratory dogs would salivate before food actually appeared, provided suitable stimuli were present; the ways in which such reflexes could be conditioned; and the kinds of differentiation possible before the animal became a neurotic dog [64]. Murphy emulates the master when he gets to the Tearooms by repeating his sit, only to be disappointed; this conditioned reflex, it appears, is easily extinguished.

80.1 [49]: *vitiated*: made corrupt or impure, and without base thoughts of 'vitalism'.

80.1a [49]: *"Bring me,"*: see "Getting One's Money's Worth": an extract from the French translation of *Murphy* reprinted in *Advanced Level French Course, Book I*, by W. T. John and M. A. Crowther (London: Thomas Nelson and Sons, 1962), a shortened, slightly adapted version of the tea-room scene from "Apportez-moi une tasse de thé" to "1,83 tasse approximativement"; #21 among "Prose Passages for Translation."

80.2 [49]: *a branch of the caterers*: the fictional tea-rooms appears to be one of the four Lyons corner-houses, or one of their many tea-rooms dotted all over London. In 'Lightning Calculation,' Quigley carries out a simplified version of Murphy's ploy "to get more than his tuppence worth of tea" at a Lyons teashop. The firm of J. Lyons & Co. offered from 1894 a wide range of foods at reasonable prices; the first corner-house, with its distinctive gold on white lettering, appeared at 213 Piccadilly, and the chain eventually extended to 260 premises. The waitresses were popularly known as "nippies," a name registered by Lyons in 1924. There was no Lyons branch on Gray's Inn Road. Therein lies a recondite jest that Beckett might have expected a London public to get, had the book sold more widely: at the tea-rooms Murphy carries out behaviorist experiments, sitting and repeating the sit, then applying the stimulus proper to Vera, the waitress. According to the 1935 London Post Office Directory there was, on the east side of the street, exactly where it should be in the novel, and the only such premises of its kind, at No. 84, just past Clerkenwell Road—yes, *Skinner's Luncheon and Tea Rooms* [those unstimulated should turn to #159.2].

80.3 [49]: *the Külpe school*: a school of *Denkpsychologie* ["thought-psychology"], prominent before WWI first in Würzburg and later in Bonn under the leadership of Oswald Külpe (1862-1915), a pupil of Wundt who broke from his master's teaching by making systematic use of the combined introspective and objective methods in studying thought processes. The Würzburg School is sometimes called "the School of imageless thought" from its contention that states of awareness have neither sensory content, representation nor image. Prominent among the Külpe's followers were Marbe, Bühler, Watt and Ach [see #81.1], who took the introspective method further, seeking to understand the *experience* during associative reactions. As Knowlson observes [177-78], Beckett's source for Murphy's experiment is Robert Woodworth's *Contemporary Schools of Psychology* (1931), notably a long passage on p. 36 (omitted from later editions) exploring the proposition that in controlled associations more might be reported from the period of preparation than that of actual reaction:

> Ach and Watt agreed on the importance of preparation for a reaction—preparation, adjustment, set, Einstellung we might call it, remembering Müller's similar discovery. If we let the passage of time be represented by a horizontal line extending from left to right, and if on that line we mark a point P to denote the preparatory signal, a point S to denote the stimulus, and a point R to denote the response, then the time P-S is called the fore period of the reaction, and the time S-R the main period. The fore period is the time of preparation and the main period the time of execution. What Ach and Watt demonstrated was that most of the effort and active experience—and doubtless most of the real work—was done in the fore period. We can think of the organism as typically ready for something rather than as in a neutral, passive state. Though stimuli do sometimes surprise the organism catching it in an

> unprepared state, most reactions are prepared for, the organism being already adjusted to the situation and, in some sense, anticipating the stimuli to which it responds. This fact of preparation, set, or Einstellung is a fact of prime importance in understanding behavior. Undoubtedly, this line of facts is the most solid contribution of the Külpe group of investigators.

81.1 [49]: *Marbe and Bühler . . . Watt . . . Ach*: four followers of Külpe (the only four) who are discussed in Woodworth [33-35]:

Marbe: Karl Marbe (1869-1953), Külpe's successor at Würzburg, who sought to describe the process of judging by defining it as any response of the subject that could be characterized as true or false, seeking to discover this as an experience. His results were mainly negative, but from them arose the notion of *Bewusstseinlage*, or "conscious attitude," an awareness of the significance of hesitancy and doubt in the describing of experience.

Bühler: Karl Bühler (1879-1963), repeated Marbe's experiments a few years later but with more baffling questions, which, however, confirmed Marbe's conscious attitudes.

Watt: Henry J. Watt (1879-1925), a Scottish student in Külpe's laboratory and later professor at Glasgow, who studied a more complex form of response called the associative reaction. His was the major discovery, cherished by Murphy, that more experience was reported from the period of preparation than the period of actual reaction.

Ach: the splendidly-christened Narziss Kaspar Ach (1871-1946), who worked with Watt over reaction-time experiments, using the new introspective method. His speciality was the simple reaction, e.g., a runner's response to the starting pistol, indicating clearly that the will to move, and the effort and determination to do so, came before the stimulus and formed part of the preparation for that stimulus. This became known as "the determining tendency" and was of lasting importance in measuring the strength of mental acts, even after the Würzburg School folded with the death of Külpe.

81.2 [49]: *Vera concluded, as she thought, her performance*: i.e., her writing up the bill (the Response) is faster than her Preparation of the tea. She little knows what is to come. Murphy's preparation for the next act is elaborate, but the stimulus (mingled overtones of gratitude and mammary organs) brings the anticipated response: the larger experiment, if not the first attempt, is decidedly a success in terms of conditions imposed by the Külpe School.

81.3 [49]: *the extreme theophanism of William of Champeaux*: Guillaume de Champeaux (1070-1121), logician and theologian, Bishop of Châlon-sur-Marne and friend of Bernard of Clairvaux. Abelard studied under him in Paris, and esteemed his abilities. In 1108 William gave up his Chair to found an Augustinian house at St. Victor, inheriting the theological aims of Anselm. His *sententiae* became a systematic *summa*, characterized by their keenness of speculation and love of dialectic. A logical realist, he contended that the universe was a thing, or *res*, essentially common to all its singulars, being identically, wholly and simultaneously in each of them, individuals distinguished only by their accidents and forms. This is his "extreme theophanism": the revelation of Himself that God makes through His works, so that the world may be seen as the theophany [Gk. θεός, "God," and φαίνω, "I show"] or manifestation of the divine. This led him into dispute with Abelard, who objected that according to his theory mutually contradictory accidents would have to be ascribed to the same substance [Windelband, 294], and obliged him to restate the doctrine less extremely. The logic of his position, assuming Murphy's adherence to be more on than off, is that each biscuit is essentially the same, so that his preference for the ginger is irrational.

82.1 [50]: *a colossal league of plutomanic caterers*: the Lyons chain of tea-rooms [see #80.2], mad for money.

82.2 [50]: *a seedy solipsist*: one with the shabby belief that the world and everything in it is but a projection of his own imagination, and cannot Be without him. Schopenhauer has been accused of solipsism, by reason of his emphasis upon the World as Idea; but this is only half his story, and in his treatment of "The Objectification of the Will" [*WWI*, 1.2 §19, 135] he is at pains to point out the dangers of "theoretical egotism," whereby "a man regards and treats himself alone as a person, and all other persons as mere phantoms." This, he contends, can never be demonstrably refuted [one thinks of Johnson], but it is, he argues, no more than a skeptical sophism: "As a serious conviction, on the other hand, it could only be found in a madhouse, and as such it stands in need of a cure rather than a refutation"; hence, perhaps, "the ruthless cunning of the sane." Murphy, imagining he has met his own kind in the MMM and specifically in Mr. Endon, will need to appreciate the force of this valuable distinction between sophism and conviction before he is cured of his delusion.

83.1 [50]: *an egg and scorpion voice*: not a mixture of cream and whips, but a detail taken from Luke 11:12, and not found in the other accounts. Following the injunction to ask and it shall be given, Christ asks rhetorically that should a son ask for bread, will his father give him a stone, if for a fish then a serpent, "Or if he shall ask an egg, will he offer him a scorpion?"

83.2 [50]: *the slogan of her slavers*: i.e., that the customer is always right. Beckett had cited this, "for the artist as for the restaurateur," in his essay 'Censorship in the Saorstat' [*Disjecta*, 85].

83.3 [51]: *the cowjuice*: compare the small boy from the city, or the post-modern theorist: "But how do they get it out of the bottle and into the cow?" Rabaté notes, a little too earnestly, the underpinnings of Melanie Klein deriving from Bion's therapy, with respect to the primitive link between the truth ("Vera") and the "good breast" ['Fluxions,' 26].

84.1 [51]: *1.83$'$ cups approximately*: let X be one cup of tea. Murphy empties half in one gulp, splutters, has it filled, and gains an extra half-X. He drinks a third of X, and has the cup filled with hot. His sum is therefore X, plus half of X, plus one third of X, which comes to, um, precisely 1.8333333 . . . cups of tea. There is a semantic incommensurability: the figure works out to 1.83 repeater, exactly, but this is at best approximate.

84.2 [51]: *gentle skimmer*: more scorpion than egg, as evidenced by the scorn Beckett turned on readers of Joyce who require the divorce of form from content [*Exagmination*, 23]:

> This rapid skimming and absorption of the scant cream of sense is made possible by what I may call a continuous process of copious intellectual salivation. The form that is an arbitrary and independent phenomenon can fulfil no higher function than that of a stimulus for a tertiary or quartary conditioned reflex of dribbling comprehension.

Burton comments [*Anatomy*, 'Democritus to the Reader,' 6]: "we skin off the cream of other men's wits."

84.3 [51]: *how he would get from where he was*: Murphy's itinerary (like Belacqua's dream) unwinds backwards, from the Cockpit in Hyde Park, along Oxford Street to its junction with Tottenham Court Road, and thence to the British Museum, which is but a short clip from Lincoln's Inn Fields, Holborn and Gray's Inn Road.

84.4 [51]: *recruiting himself*: not the Imperialist theme for which the British Museum is regularly contemned by those who would prefer the Elgin Marbles to have been used as missiles against the Turks, but what Beckett termed Murphy's *carpe te ipsum* [L. "gather thyself"; see #4.2].

84.5 [51]: *the Archaic Room . . . the Harpy Tomb*: the Harpy Tomb features prominently in the British Museum's "Archaic Greece" section (pedantically not in the 'Archaic Room,' Room 3, works from 1000 to 500 BC, but Room 5). The tomb is a funerary pillar from the acropolis at Xanthos, principal city of ancient Lykia, and erected c. 480-470 BC for the ruling family. Originally it consisted of a pillar of gray-blue limestone, two meters square, on a tall plinth, with a series of Parian marble relief slabs surmounted by a heavy stepped coping at the top. This chamber contained the body and a small opening was made on the western side, so the soul could fly away. The reliefs depict offerings to seated figures, probably deified members of the family, but the tomb takes its name from the bird-like creatures with female heads, arms and breasts on two sides, who carry away diminutive human beings, perhaps the souls of the dead. These are thought to be sirens, or harpies, spirits of the storm and wind, and associated with death. There is thus an irony in Murphy's "recruiting himself" in their presence.

84.6 [51]: *Austin Ticklepenny*: the name suggests one who "tickles pennies" as another might trout, by writing doggerel and flattery for small recompense. Sheridan had such a brother-in-law by name of 'Tickell,' a poetaster and minor dramatist. Cronin's pot biography fraternally ignores the fact, but there is no doubt that the vicious portrait is Beckett's revenge upon Austin Clarke for slights real or imagined. Clarke (1896-1974) was a leading voice among the Twilighters with whom Beckett had clashed in his review of 'Recent Irish Poetry' [Knowlson, 213-14]. He was, after Yeats, the most prolific of Irish poets, but his Belvedere and UCD background set him against the Trinity heirarchy. He had learned Irish from Douglas Hyde, and his long poem, 'The Vengeance of Fionn' (1917) sounded the note he would thereafter play, the return to Irish myth and legend for inspiration (the topic of his UCD thesis), and long epics on Irish themes, integrating with the epic the melodic and assonantal qualities of traditional Irish forms. For this Beckett ridiculed him [see #117.5]. Clarke's mental and alcohol problems led to his confinement in St. Patrick's Hospital, where he was placed in a padded cell and force-fed in the manner Ticklepenny finds distressing; this shaped his later poem, 'Mnemosyne Lay in Dust' (1966). Recovering from total disintegration he moved to England in 1927, and did not return permanently until 1937, "determined not to become an exile" despite the banning in Ireland of his first novel, *The Bright Temptation* (1932). On publication of *Murphy*, Beckett was told that Clarke was going through it "with his pubic comb" [Knowlson, 213], but when Gogarty urged him to sue Clarke wisely realized that to do so would render him absurd; a decision apparently vindicated by the failure of the novel. His retaliation was a brief review in *The Dublin Magazine*: "the whole thing is a bizarre fantasy, with a nasty twist about it that its self-evident cleverness and scholarship cannot redeem."

84.7 [51]: *Pot Poet*: one who pours out pentameters for pints, a poetaster of the kind mocked by Ben Jonson, as quoted by Beckett in the *Whoroscope* Notebook:

A fellow that knows nothing but his beef,
Or how to rime his mummy guts in beer.

85.1 [51]: *The merest pawn in the game*: in fact, Ticklenny plays a considerable role in what is to follow, perhaps more than meets the eye [see #262.3]; he will remain on the board long after Murphy has been swept from it. Compare the commonplace sentiment of E. H. Bailey [*BJA*, April 1935, 122]: "I am no believer in absolute fate, which is put forward and believed in by the materialist school, an idea that we are tied and bound by planetary forces and that there is no way of escaping from it; that we are merely pawns on the great chessboard of life, moved hither and thither by every blast of planetary force."

85.2 [51]: *a child's halma*: *Halma* is a game like Chinese Checkers, played on a board of 256 squares between two people each with 19 men (or four with 13), the object being to get first to the other side by jumping over other pieces into empty squares. *Snakes and ladders*, another board-game, is here a herpetological conceit for an envenomed art of self-elevation.

85.3 [51]: *the divine son of Ariston*: Plato, whose father, Ariston, was a man of distinction who died when Plato was young, his mother Periktione afterwards marrying Pyrilampes. As Beare notes [107]: "Distinguishing λόγος (rational speech) from διάνοια (thinking), Plato cited the former as 'a stream accompanied with sound, proceeding from the soul, through the mouth.'" Beare adds that for Plato vocal sound is the shock conveyed by the air, beginning from the head and terminating in the region of the liver; details may be found in *Sophist* 263.e and *Theaetetus* 206.d. Plato himself is said to have had a thin voice.

85.4 [52]: *nulla linea sine die*: a perversion of *nulla dies sine linea* [L. "Not a day without a line"], as recorded in Pliny the Elder [*Natural History*, xxxv.36]. This the sentiment of Apelles the artist, who claimed never to have passed a day without doing at least one line, to which steady industry he owed his great success [Bartlett].

85.5 [52]: *water-tumbril*: on the wagon, but en route to the guillotine. As Horace observed, no poems can please for long or live that are written by water-drinkers [*Epistles*, I.xix.2].

85.6 [52]: *gambadoes*: from either Sp. *gambada*, a fantastic move in dancing; or It. *gamba*, "a leg," originally a long boot attached to a saddle; a syncopation of gas and gaiters. Beckett may have picked up the word from Rabelais [III.li, 68].

86.1 [52]: *the Gate*: since 1928, when it opened (October 14) with *Peer Gynt*, the rival to the Abbey [see #269.2] as the pre-eminent Dublin theater, and quickly overtaking it as a venue for experimental and international drama. The company was founded by Hilton Edwards and Mícheál mac Liammóir as the Dublin Gate Theatre Studios, working from the Peacock Theatre in the Abbey annex, but in 1930 it moved to the Old Rotunda Assembly Rooms, Parnell Square, its home ever since. Beckett saw there a "poetic comedy" by Austin Clarke, which he described to McGreevy [November 5, 1930] as "truly pernicious."

86.2 [52]: *'Take him and cut him out in little stars'*: from *Romeo and Juliet* [III.ii.20-25], where Juliet unwittingly foreshadows the death of her lover:

> Come, gentle night, come loving, black-brow'd night,
> Give me my Romeo; and, when he shall die,
> Take him and cut him out in little stars,
> And he will make the face of heaven so fine
> That all the world will be in love with night
> And pay no worship to the garish sun.

Murphy's dim recollection could be of the actor playing the apothecary from whom Romeo buys the fatal dram of poison, the desire to administer it to Ticklepenny, or a comment upon a performance which put the audience to sleep. Beckett saw the production, was unimpressed, and wrote to McGreevy [November 21, 1932]: "I saw Romeo and Juliet, all wrong, fundamentally wrong. Mac Liammoir said the lines nicely enough, but missed a lot of chances . . . the others were unspeakable, the lightings and the settings flashy and crepuscular . . ."

86.3 [52]: *snout drunk*: a variant of 'snout-fair,' i.e., superficially so, rather than snoring like a drunken pig. The phrase "merely snout-fair" derives from Burton's *Anatomy* [III.3.i.ii, 635; DN, #947].

86.4 [52]: *genustuprations*: from L. *genus*, "knee," and *stuprum*, "illicit intercourse"; hence, rape by the knees (not yet in the *OED*). Although Austin Clarke had a brief and (some said) unconsummated marriage, there was no suggestion that he was homosexual.

86.5 [52]: *dried up . . . hang up*: the missing element, *washed up*. No pun (fundamentally) intended, but how (Murphy insinuates) did he make a living? The "change of life" may be more the male menopause than a sober caesura.

86.6 [52]: *Messrs. Melpomene, Calliope, Erato and Thalia*: the muses, respectively, of Tragedy, Epic, Lyric and Comedy, 'Messrs.' being the keyword here.

87.1 [52]: *the better-class mentally deranged*: the Bethlem Royal, by its charter, excluded paupers [see #156.2].

87.2 [52]: *quantum mutatus . . . Ab illa*: L. "how much changed from that"; from Virgil's *Aeneid* [II.274], the appearance to Aeneas of Hector in a dream. The tag is applied to any change of felicity, but particularly to unregenerate man, his happiness obscured by the Fall: it is used in this sense by Burton [*Anatomy*, I.1.1.i, 81], Beckett's likely source.

87.3 [52]: *tundish*: Ticklepenny's term for a funnel; the semantic issue arising from Joyce's *Portrait* [188], where Stephen Dedalus becomes conscious of the difference of the language used by the Dean of Studies and that which is his own [see #2.8].

87.4 [52]: *shovel and bucket*: in tales of the circus, the humblest job of all: the man who follows the elephant.

87.5 [52]: *his lemon phosphate*: not a complimentary concoction, as the rattle of 'Echo's Bones' [2] makes clear: a thought bursts from Belacqua's brain "as a phosphate from the kidneys." In the French translation, Ticklepenny drinks Coca-Cola.

87.6 [53]: *where the fault lies*: the reference to the divine son of Ariston [see #85.3] is further slurred by the echo of Mark Anthony [*Julius Caesar*, I.ii.138-40]:

> Men at some time are masters of their fates:
> The fault, dear Brutus, is not in our stars,
> But in ourselves, that we are underlings.

88.1 [53]: *Dr. Fist*: i.e., Faust, as the translation into German affirms.

88.2 [53]: *copiously*: perhaps a trace of Molière's *Le Médecin volant*, iv, Sganarelle's advice to the afflicted heroine: "Faites-la pisser copieusement, copieusement."

88.3 [53]: *Killiekrrrankie*: the name of the Resident Medical Superintendent has the connotation, in English, of killing the cranky, the mentally ill; or, in fistula German, the sick [Ger. *krank*, "ill"]. See also #185.2 and #257.3.

88.4 [53]: *the Magdalen Mental Mercy Seat*: see #156.2.

88.5 [53]: *his duty to Erin*: as Beckett expounded in his 'Recent Irish Poetry' [*Disjecta*, 71], the "iridescence of themes—Oisin, Cuchulain, Maeve, Tir-nanog, the Táin Bo Cuailgne, Yoga, the Crone of Beare—segment after segment of cut-and-dried sanctity and loveliness." He castigated such as George Russell, who entered his heart's desire "with such precipitation as positively to protrude into the void" [71]; Austin Clarke for inventing formal justifications to screen "the deeper need that must not be avowed" [73]; and Frederick Higgins [see #184.5], whose modern poetry has "a good smell of dung, most refreshing after all the attar of far off, most secret and inviolate rose" [73].

88.6 [53]: *as free as a canary*: the song-bird associated, by the pun on canary wine, with the post of Laureate (the emolument for which includes a jereboam of sack). Beckett is mocking Clarke's cross-rhymes and vowel-rhyming in the latter's recent *Pilgrimage and Other Poems* (1929), in much the way that he had in 'Recent Irish Poetry' [*Disjecta*, 72]: "it is as though he were to derive in direct descent the very latest prize canary from that fabulous bird, the mesozoic pelican, addicted, though childless, to self-eviscerations."

89.1 [53]: *his own divine flatus*: from L. *afflare*, "to breathe on"; here, a catalectic *afflatus*, a creative pulse or spiration, as ructated by Swift [*A Tale of a Tub*, 151]: "For, whether you please to call the *Forma informans* of Man, by the name of *Spiritus, Animus, Afflatus*, or *Anima*; What are all these but several Appellations for Wind."

89.2 [53]: *the gaelic prosodoturfy*: prosody dug from the bogs.

89.3 [53]: *Beamish's porter*: a heavy stout of Cork origin, said by Cronin [157] to be Beckett's preference, but here associated with the Twilighters.

89.4 [53]: *seneschalesque*: from Med. L. *siniscalcus*, or from MHG *siniskalkaz*, "an old servant"; hence, pertaining to a steward. The offer, which works out at about 5d an hour, is pitiful, even with food and lodging included ("all found").

89.5 [53]: *temperate*: with the basic sense of exercising moderation and restraint; but the suggestion of descending from Olympian heights (Parnassus) to a more temperate clime.

89.6 [54]: *his pity . . . terror . . . vomit . . . catharsis*: from Aristotle's metaphor of catharsis, or purgation (Gk. καθαίρω, "to purge" or "purify"), expressed most famously in the *Poetics*, where he contends that tragedy is the imitation of an action that is serious, complete in itself, with incidents to arouse pity and fear, "wherewith to accomplish its catharsis of such emotions." *Catharsis* is used of the purging of the effects of a pent-up emotion by bringing it to the surface of consciousness [Jones, *Psycho-Analysis*, 705].

90.1 [54]: *his great master's figure of the three lives*: the figure is drawn from Burnet's *Early Greek Philosophy* [98], where it is argued that, according to Heraklites, Pythagoras first distinguished the "three lives," Theoretic, Practical, and Apolaustic, which Aristotle later used in the *Ethics*:

> In this life there are three kinds of men, just as there are three sorts of people who come to the Olympic Games. The lowest class is made up of those who come to buy and sell, and next above them are those who come to compete. Best of all, however, are those who come to look on (θεωρεῖν). The greatest purification of all is, therefore, science, and it is the man who devotes himself to that, the true philosopher, who has most effectually released himself from the "wheel of birth."

This is repeated in Burnet's *Greek Philosophy* [42], and the classification made of men into lovers of wisdom, honor and gain, which is said to imply the doctrine of the tripartite soul.

90.2 [54]: *knew nothing*: not in the supradecent sense of Socrates aware of his ignorance, but the indecent sense, as stated by Beckett in the *Whoroscope* Notebook: "Not only did he know nothing, but he was ignorant of the fact."

90.3 [54]: *as a voyeur's from a voyant's*: from Rimbaud's letter to Paul Demeny, May 15, 1871 ("La Lettre du voyant"), in which the young Rimbaud asserts his determination to be not just a poet but a visonary:

> Je dis qu'il faut être *voyant*, se faire *voyant*.
> Le Poëte se fait *voyant* par un long, immense et raisonné *déreglement* de *tous les sens*. Toutes les formes d'amour, de souffrance, de folie, il cherche lui-même, il épuise en lui les poisons, pour n'en garder que les quintessences. Ineffable torture où il a besoin de toute la foi, de toute la force surhumaine, où il devient entre tous le grande malade, le grand criminel, le grand maudit,—et le suprême Savant!—car il arrive à l'*inconnu*.

[Fr. "I say that one must be a seer, make oneself a seer. The poet makes himself visionary by a long, prodigious and reasoned disordering of all the senses. All forms of love, of suffering, of folly he seeks himself, he consumes the poisons and keeps only the quintessences. Ineffable torture, where he has need of all the faith, all the superhuman strength, where he becomes among other things the great patient, the great criminal, the greatly despised—and the great Knower—because he arrives at the Unknown"]. The Unnamable, returning from his world tour [291], his leg left in the Pacific, is like the decrepit Rimbaud returning from Abbysinia.

90.4 [54]: *the supradecent sense*: a coinage based on the prefix 'supra,' meaning "above" or "over"; hence, the antithesis of 'indecent.'

90.5 [54]: *yellow spot*: the *macula lutea* [L. "yellow spot"] of the eyeball, near the center of the retina, constituting the point of most distinct and intense vision.

90.6 [54]: *accosting him in form*: i.e., in the mind's eye, or, in terms of the theory of Forms associated with Plato, and as such satirized in Swift in *A Tale of a Tub* [193], with mad Jack's reasoning: "the Eyes of the Understanding see best, when those of the Senses are out of the way." The doctrine was expressed by Kant, to whom in turn Schopenhauer was indebted for the distinction between phenomenal and noumenal being. Considering the relation of the will as thing-in-itself to its phenomena, or the relation of the world as will to the world as idea, Schopenhauer comments [*WWI*, I.2, §24, 154-55]:

> We have learnt from Kant that time, space, and causality, with their entire constitution, and the possibility of all their forms, are present in our consciousness quite independently of the objects which appear in them, and which constitute their content; or, in other words, they can be arrived at just as well if we start from the subject as if we start from the object. Therefore, with equal accuracy, we may call them either forms of intuition or perception of the subject . . .

Murphy's Celia, therefore, is a form within his consciousness possessing a clarity that would be occluded were she a thing-in-herself. What Celia thinks about that is another matter.

92.1 [55]: *antiphony*: in musical terms, a response, as if of one side of the choir to the other; or a composition structured for alternate voices.

92.2 [55]: *squaring the circle of his shoulders*: without wishing to weigh Murphy beneath the cang of exegesis (it is only a casual quip), one might note that Ferdinand Lindemann in 1882 proved that *pi* is not only irrational (it cannot be expressed as the ratio of two integers) but transcendental (it cannot be the solution of any algebraic equation), so the quadrature of the circle is an impossibility. Dante closes the *Divine Comedy* with a reference to the problem, in terms of reconciling the human and divine in Christ, or expressing the divine vision in human language [*Paradiso*, XXXII.85-87]. Murphy might better emulate Bloom [*Ulysses*, 670, 619], and circle the square.

93.1 [55]: *syzygy*: in astronomy, or astrology, the conjunction that arises when two bodies, as seen from the perspective of a third, are aligned. Beckett uses the word in this sense in the final couplet of his underrated sonnet (a sustained single sentence), written for Peggy Sinclair and included dismissively in *Dream* [70-71]:

> Like syzygetic stars, supernly bright,
> Conjoined in the One and in the Infinite!

In 'Love and Lethe' [*MPTK*, 93], Ruby Tough mocks such an "itch for syzygy" by suggesting music and malt as the most efficacious remedy. There are metrical meanings, i.e, combining two feet in a single prosodic unit (as "-ed in the One"); and mathematical ones, involving the tendency of a diminishing series (e.g., $1/2 + 1/4 + 1/8 + 1/16 + 1/32$) to converge at an infinite point: these import an incommensurate element into the verbal equation.

93.2 [55]: *a mere monthly prognosticator's tag*: specifically, *Old Moore's Monthly Messenger* (October 1907 to September 1914); reincarnated as *The British Journal of Astrology* (October 1914 to September 1939); the broad basis of Pandit Suk's horoscope [see #32.2 and #216.3]. In his first notes for the novel, Beckett indicated that the "1/- corpus of motives" would increasingly assume authority and fatality.

94.1 [56]: *Austin*: as in Austin Clarke; but not 'Augustine,' as in the saint of that name.

94.2 [56]: *Hyde Park*: the Park was originally delimited by two Roman roads, Wattling Street (near the Edgware Road) and the Via Trinobantina (near Oxford Street and Bayswater Road), which met at its northeast corner. A Royal Park since 1536, it was once part of Henry VIII's personal hunting forest, the King having made the abbot owners an offer they couldn't refuse. Elizabeth I reviewed her troops in the Park, which remained a private hunting ground until James permitted a limited public access. The haunt of highwaymen by night, it was by day the venue for the horsey class to display their equipages. Its celebrated features include Rotten Row ("Route de Roi") for riders; the Serpentine, for boaters, swimmers and suicides; Speaker's Corner for crackpots; a monument to the public gallows at Tyburn; the Hudson memorial bird sanctuary; and delights as various as flowers and birds and bats.

94.2a [56]: *a void place and a spacious nothing*: from Augustine's *Confessions* 7.1 [DN, #125], his inability to conceive the incorruptible image of God.

94.3 [56]: *filth*: i.e., 'filthy lucre,' in its literal sense of dishonorable gain.

95.1 [56]: *the Marble Arch*: at the junction of Oxford Street, Bayswater and Edgware Roads, and Hyde Park; an entrance to the latter. The arch was modeled on Constantine's in Rome, and was intended as a grand entrance for Buckingham Palace until it was discovered to be too narrow for the state coach to pass through, whereupon it was moved to the present site.

95.2 [57]: *a nice number eleven*: the first adjective obligatory [see #67.5]. The route is still promoted on #11 buses: "Ride the best value sightseeing tour in London." It is redolent of Murphy's experience: from Liverpool Station, out along the London Wall (Balls Bros of the West End); along Old Broad Street; Threadneedle Street (a statue of that great Irishman, the Duke of Wellington); down Queen Victoria and Cannon Streets to "hideous" St. Paul's; Luggate Hill (Abbey National); Fleet Street (Scruffy Murphy's Pub near ye Olde Cheshire Cheese [DN, #1039: "it's very good cheese, but it's eating my bread"]); past Simpson's in the Strand (chess motifs about the portal), toward Trafalgar Square; St. Martin's-in-the-Fields (with its welcoming crypt); down the Mall past Westminster (bypassing the Burghers of Calais and the bridge where Arsene met the noumenal Mr. Ash); Victoria Street, Buckingham Palace Road, Pimlico Road towards Sloane Square (the Royal Court); then down the King's Road ("Uptherepublic"), bypassing the junction of Edith Grove, Cremorne Road and Stadium Street; to end at Fulham Park, south of West Brompton and just round the corner from the once delightful village of Walham, now devoured by the peristalsis of a creeping Fulham, in turn swallowed by London, with the Green reduced to such a small sward about the Parish Church of St. John with St. James that even Murphy would be hard put to lie upon it.

96.1 [57]: *the Cockpit*: so-called from its physical appearance, though cock-fights may well have taken place there: a small cupped hollow, edged by trees, just north of the Serpentine where it turns towards Long Water. It does not feature on current maps of the Park.

96.2 [57]: *Rima*: the bas-relief carved by Jacob Epstein in 1922, and unveiled in 1925 near the W. H. Hudson bird sanctuary; a cenotaph block depicting a nude female form surmounted by a flock of diagonally ascending birds, and fronted by shallow rectangular pools intended as bird-baths. The statue depicts Rima, the wild and free Brazilian girl of Hudson's *Green Mansions* (1904); it aroused great controversy as the first public London display of the naked female form, and was on several occasions tarred and feathered or defiled with green paint. Beckett's permanganate seems to be his own variation upon the theme, conditioned, Culik suggests unconvincingly, by his awareness of its use in the treatment of the urethritis associated with venereal diseases. Better is the suggestion [Phil Baker to CA] of Hudson's wild girl in the Smeraldina-Rima of *Dream*.

96.3 [57]: *the biscuits*: these appear in the early draft, 'Lightning Calculation':

> Quigley began to get engrossed by the biscuits, and therefore no longer trouble [sic] by Hobbema and his avenue and Cuyp and his birds. The packet contained five, a Ginger, an Osborne, a Digestive, a Peit Beurre and one, not signed, that he had never been able to put a name to. He put the Ginger on one side to be eaten last and began on the Osborne. He calculated, almost without realising what he was doing, that there were 120 ways in which he could eat the biscuits, there were no fewer than 120 orders in which he could take them. It was incredible. Without warning, and presumably as a result of this calculation, he felt himself flooded with happiness, with a sense of strength also. It was as though he had made a bound upward in his self-esteem. The precise quality of the emotion was not to be defined, but certainly he could not remember having experienced a more abrupt and delicious change of mood. But if he kept the Ginger till the end, as he had always been most careful to do, then there were only 24 ways of eating the biscuits. Only 24! He made the covenant with himself, never again to allow a paltry infatuation, such as his preference for the Ginger, to impoverish the nature of an assortment, whether of biscuits or of other material. He finished the Osborne and began the Ginger. It was as though his whole being were renewed.
>
> [Samuel Beckett,
> 34 Gertrude Street
> London S.W.10]

97.1 [57]: *as truly as of the stars*: Kennedy suggests [174] that underlying this passage may be the notion from popular astronomy that there are five basic star shapes, one of which was said to be that of a biscuit. Following Sir William Herschel's discovery of new galaxies and stars by means of the telescope, what seized the popular imagination was the fact that this new instrument revealed the stars not as rayed or spiky, but as round. However, the analogy between the stars and the biscuits can equally be read in terms of the extreme theophany of William of Champeaux [see #81.3]; the one interpretation need not be preferred to the other.

97.2 [57]: *the demon of gingerbread*: i.e., doubt, as of Pascal, for whom the demon of uncertainty was inseparable from the spirit of faith [*Pensées*, #434]. The demon is Cartesian, from the first book of the *Meditations* (1641), which asserts that the facts of direct observation may be but illusions and dreams, this affirming the immediacy of doubt and thus the *cogito*. Paul Shields has suggested a parallel between *Murphy* and Melville's *Bartleby*, pointing to the notion of preference and Bartleby's peculiar diet of gingernuts [Paul Shields to CA].

97.3 [58]: *Duck's disease . . . Panpygoptosis*: the former is familiar to many from the days of nuts, balls, and sparrows, i.e., bum too close to the ground; the second is Beckett's neologism, now featured uniquely in the *Supplement* to the *OED*. A putative etymology may be offered: πᾶν, "all"; πυγαίος, "of the rump"; πτῶσις, "falling"; thus, "all bottom sagging." A dachshund is (naturally) a panpygoptic canine. According to Bair [170], the original of Miss Dew was one of Geoffrey Thompson's patients at the

Rotunda Hospital, Dublin. There is a similar paean of praise to Venus Callipyge in *Dream* [97]. The aetiology, or genesis, as Beckett notes, is obscure, but the fundamental irrectitude of the jest infiltrates the paragraph, as John Pilling and James Knowlson discovered after a morning with the happy dictionaries.

97.4 [58]: *Steiss's nosonomy*: a *nosology* is a classification of diseases; the variation suggests 'Anatomy,' in Burton's sense. *Steiss* is a crude teutonism meaning "buttock."

97.5 [58]: *Dr. Busby*: Richard Busby (1606-95), Headmaster of Westminster School from 1640, with a great reputation as a teacher and a disciplinarian, and a particular penchant for whipping boys on their btms; hence the lament against Nature. He is invoked by Addison, *Spectator* #329: "Dr Busby, a very great man! he whipped my grandfather, a very great man! I should have gone to him myself, if I had not been a blockhead; a very great man" [Bartlett]. His alter ego appears in the English *Rabelais* [IV.xlviii, 228]: "the Busby of the Place," whipping the children of the Island of Papimany. Beckett cites the name (from William M. Cooper's *Flagellation*) in his Dream Notebook [#369], with a tick to show it had been used. Busby had a considerable opinion of himself: showing Charles II around the school he kept his hat on in the royal presence, since it would not do for his boys to suppose "that there existed in the world any greater man than Dr Busby." Curiously, he was himself very short. It is a Vulgar Error to suppose that the motto of Westminster is *Postera crescam laude*, usually translated as "Stick out your backside with pride"; this is rather the motto of the University of Melbourne, Down Under.

98.1 [58]: *aetiology*: the word has the specific sense of the origin of neurosis, as in Ernest Jones's discussion of Freud's "aetiology of the psycho-neuroses" [*Psycho-Analysis*, 43].

98.2 [58]: *Non me rebus sed mihi res*: L. "Not me to things but things to me." As Henning notes [*Complicity*, 47], the aetiology of this is Horace's *Epistles* [1.i.18-19]: "nunc in Aristippi furtim praecepta relabor / et mihi res, non me rebus, subiungere conor" [L. "now I slip back stealthily into the rules of Aristippas, and would bend the world to myself, not myself to the world"]. For O'Hara, the casual *bon mot* anticipates Murphy's neurotic decision [183] that his psyche is the prior system [*Hidden Drives*, 66]. Compare the claim of Stephen Dedalus that the *faubourg Saint-Patrice* matters because it matters to him [*Ulysses*, 599].

98.3 [58]: *the classical bitch's eye*: one of the less-flattering attributes of Helen of Troy.

98.4 [58]: *the ouija board*: that most essential adjunct to the medium, allowing her to soft-soap the slow by having the voices from the *au-delà* translate their vital concerns from the afterlife, the movement of an object on the board seeming to spell out some message.

99.1 [58]: *Rosie Dew*: Homer's rosy-fingered dawn, or Pope's 'Summer': "Here Bees from Blossoms sip the rosie Dew" [Smith, 'Sanctuary,' 139]. Crudely, menstruation.

99.2 [58]: *Lord Gall of Wormwood*: wormwood is the bitter shrub that sprang up along the track of the serpent as it writhed along the ground when driven forth from Paradise; and its association with gall is a common biblical symbiosis, e.g. Lamentations 3:18: "And I said, My strength and hope is perished from the Lord: remembering mine affliction and my misery, the wormwood and the gall." For Burton [*Anatomy*, II.4.1.iii, 431], wormwood or *Artemisia absinthium* is a cure for melancholy. The association with Wormwood Scrubs (the prison) is difficult to remove, and does little for his Lordship's character. However, in 'Echo's Bones,' the unpublished "recessional" tale of *MPTK*, he is not the villainous party. As the dead Belacqua sits upon the fence, he receives a stunning crack upon the eminent coccyx from a golf-ball hit by Lord Gall, a colossus with an equally great problem. He being childless and impotent ("aspermatic"), his Eden of Wormwood, one of the few terrestial Paradises outstanding in this part of the country, is in danger of falling into the hands of his enemy, the protector, Baron Extravas, "reversioner of Wormwood and fiend in human disguise," who, to make things worse, has inflicted his wife Moll with the *spirochaeta pallida*, or syphillus. The estate can be saved only if a male heir is produced. After deep discussion Belacqua ("fit as a flea") is prevailed upon to be the man in the gap; he spends the night with Moll, who becomes pregnant, and in the fullness of time a life is dropped: "Lord Gall was downstairs at the time, counting his golfballs [sperm?]. His medical advisers filed in. It was a dramatic moment. 'May it please your lordship' said the foreman, 'it is essentially a girl.' So it goes in the world."

99.3 [58]: *spado*: impotent; "long standing" is, O'Hara comments, a limp joke [*Hidden Drives*, 66]. Despite what his name implies (ejaculation outside the female vessel [DN, #478]), the reversioner, Baron Extravas, is better endowed.

99.4 [58]: *in tail male special*: the entailment upon the estate means that it may be inherited through the male line only.

99.5 [58]: *pentimenti*: from It. *pentimento*, "repentance, correction." In art, the reappearance of a design that has been painted over; here, the wish of Lord Gall for evidence from beyond that will overwrite the entailment. In a letter to McGreevy [March 10, 1935; Knowlson, 180], Beckett mocked the fatuous "picture" of himself as the superior man, not allowing "any philosophical or ethical or Christlike imitative pentimenti" that might "redeem a composition that was invalid from the word 'go' and has to be broken up altogether."

99.6 [58]: *the au-delà*: the 'beyond', as opposed to the dreary *en-deçà* [see #102.3]. 'Echos's Bones' begins with a meditation upon the theme:

> The dead die hard, they are trespassers on the beyond, they must take the place as they find it, the shafts and manholes back into the muck, till such time as the lord of the manor incurs through his long acquiescence a duty of care in respect of them. Then they are free among the dead by all means, then their troubles are over, their natural troubles. But the debt of nature, that scandalous post-obit on one's own estate, can no more be discharged by the mere fact of kicking the bucket than descent can be made into the same stream twice. This is a true saying.

99.7 [58]: *the protector*: one appointed by previous testament to administer an estate; here, the villainous Baron Extravas [see #99.2], a man of fixed principle who will not move, whatever the leverage, nor agree to any change in the conditions of the will. The problem (to extrapolate from 'Echo's Bones') is that even should the estate be disentailed and the current conditions barred, the Protector, who is also the Reversioner [see #104.1], stands to inherit.

99.8 [58]: *the Serpentine or the Long Water*: the Serpentine is a lake in Hyde Park, and the Long Water its continuation north of Rennie's Bridge [see #150.5], marking the boundary between Hyde Park and Kensington Gardens. The lake was artificially created in 1730 at the behest of Queen Caroline, at a cost said to have been £6,000 but in reality thrice that. The bed of the Westbourne Stream was enlarged, thereby linking several ponds, and a wide body of water formed. The scene of many a fête and celebration, it had become a filthy sewer by 1849, when it was drained and cleaned and the sewerage diverted elsewhere.

99.9 [58]: *Harriet*: daughter of a retired hotel keeper and school friend of the sisters of Percy Bysshe Shelly, Harriet Westbook was a well-bred, charming and sociable young lady, who met the poet shortly after he had been sent down from Oxford, eloped with him to Edinburgh in 1811, and threw herself into his idealistic schemes, as she would later into the Serpentine. The Power of Love supposed to radiate from their marriage and reconstitute mankind did not, for the Poet, survive the reality of two small children, and when it flickered in 1814 Shelly's soul found its new destiny with Mary Godwin, and Harriet was abandoned. Entirely her own fault, really, as the new lovers had invited her to share with them a Platonic idyll in Greece, and she had selfishly refused. Inconsiderate to the end, she spoiled their return by drowning herself in the Serpentine (December 1816), further contributing, the Poet felt, to his misfortunes.

99.10 [59]: *The sheep*: sheep grazed in the park until the late 1950s, mostly in the area of The Meadow, where they maintained the grass. The image has its own comic magnificence, not in the least vitiated by the base suggestion that it may have been culled from either *Don Quixote* or the curious metaphor of the souls in Antepurgatory in book III of the *Purgatorio*.

100.1 [59]: *fields of sleep*: that reading of "fields of sleep" in Wordsworth's *Immortality Ode:* [line 28] was "much debated in the pages of *Notes and Queries* at the end of the nineteenth century" [Smith, 'Sanctuary,' 132; see his 139 for details]. It is still a trap for the unwary, a slumber stealing their spirit. Wordsworth wrote several soporific songs 'To Sleep' (1816), the second beginning: "A Flock of Sheep that leisurely pass by / One after one." The worthy man was capable of further contributions to *The Stuffed Owl*. Conrad Aiken mischievously suggests that 'Daffodils' originally began: "I wandered lonely as a cow," adding, "dear William sometimes nodded; and alas, when he nodded, he snored" [*Ushant*, 56].

100.2 [59]: *turned their broody heads aside*: an echo, one of many, intended to tease by faint intimation of the Romantic tradition: here, Yeats's 'Who Will Go with Fergus?', as cited in chapter 1 of *Ulysses*: "And turn aside no more and brood / Upon love's bitter mystery"; the latter an appropriate gloss on the emetic offered. In 'Yellow,' Belacqua decides on second thoughts that anger will turn aside, "leaving him like a sheep" [*MPTK*, 183].

100.3 [59]: *argonautic*: as in Jason's quest for the Golden Fleece.

101.1 [59]: *Parmigianino*: Givolane Francesco Maria Mazzola Parmigianino (1503-40), Italian painter brought up in the traditions of Corregio, only to react against the spirit of Renaissance Classicism. Beckett would have known from the National Gallery his *Vision of St Jerome* (1521), but his more characteristic manner is reflected in such works as *La Madonna dal Colla Longa* [It. "The Madonna of the Long Neck"], in the Uffizi, and the self-portrait as reflected in a convex mirror on a convex panel, in the Kunsthistorishes Museum, Vienna. The joke follows: Parmigianino was known for his graceful distortions and elongations of the human figure, but Nelly he could have drawn from life.

101.2 [59]: *the giver and the gift*: the notion that in the act of love, as perhaps the act of perception, subject and object, are as one.

101.3 [60]: *too aggrieved not to*: this comes well from a Murphy who never speaks unless spoken to, and sometimes not then.

102.1 [59]: *hot dog*: this is no time for jokes about sausage dogs, such as the Joe Miller about the difference between a dachshund and a hot-dog vendor (the latter bawls his wares). Even the obvious jest is dubious, as America's contribution to international cuisine was not then common in England.

102.2 [60]: *rejectamenta*: presumably the gerundive (fem.) of 'rejectamata.'

102.3 [60]: *this dreary en-deçà*: the sad shadow of the *au-delà* [see #99.6].

102.4 [60]: *a closed system*: i.e., a Newtonian universe [see #57.4].

102.5 [60]: *Ipse dixit*: the Latin form of αὐτὸς ἔφα, as in Burnet's *Greek Philosophy* [43]: "The Master said so"; thus, to be taken on authority without further ado. The Master was Pythagoras, who wrote nothing down but whose word was Law. Diogenes Laertius notes [II.viii.46] that the phrase was proverbial. Rabinovitz adds [Barale, xxviii]: "According to Cicero, when they were assured that Pythagoras himself had said something ('Ipse dixit'), the Pythagoreans would accept a statement with no other proof." Fielding in one of his Prefaces [*Tom Jones*, V.i] allows the writer such authority.

102.6 [60]: *the snuff of the dip*: that which remains when the candle, or dip, is extinguished. Beckett had recently praised McGreevy in his 'Recent Irish Poetry' [*Disjecta*, 74] for the quality of inevitable unveiling by virtue of which his poems could be called elucidations, "the vision without the dip" (the comparison, presumably, with A. E.'s *The Candle of Vision*, which Miss Carriage will go back to [155]). Murphy, in the terms Beckett enunciates, is too concerned with the object (the biscuits) and not the act of perception. Hence the hyperbole that follows.

103.1 [60]: *Oh, my America*: the extremity of Murphy's anguish is to be gauged by his desperate use of John Donne's 'To his Mistress on Going to Bed,' and the bombast of likening his loss to the destruction of Atlantis.

103.2 [60]: *a critique of pure love*: discussing the nature of Love, Schopenhauer concludes it can only be knowledge of the suffering of others (Murphy was touched by the little argonautic [100]), and takes issue with Kant's assertion that true goodness and virtue can proceed only from abstract reflection. Rather, he contends, "all true and pure love is sympathy" [*WWI*, I.4 §67, 485]. Murphy may have gained threepence but he has lost all sympathy.

103.3 [60]: *left home more gladly than she now returned sadly*: an echo of Thomas à Kempis: "Laetus exitus tristem saepe reditum parit; et laeta vigilia serotina triste mane facit" [L. "All too often a merry outgoing bringeth a sad homecoming; and a gay evening maketh a rueful morning"], from the *De Imitatione Christi* [I.xx.7], which Beckett had cited in his Dream Notebook [#576], had deployed in 'Ding-Dong' [*MPTK*, 40], and had used to structure 'Sanies I,' all heaven in the sphincter (going out), but disillusionment (coming home). Beckett reread the *Imitatio* while writing *Murphy*, and corresponded about it with McGreevy, a devout Catholic, who urged him to use it to explore his own psyche. In one invaluable letter [March 10, 1935], Beckett cites "the glad going out and the sorrowful coming home," which he uses here and in *Watt* (the increeping and outbouncing house and parlor maids [50]), but states that he had replaced the plenitude à Kempis calls God, not by "goodness" (as McGreevy had urged), but by a "pleroma" (a totality of divine attributes) to be found only in his own feathers and entrails. This remarkable letter is quoted extensively by Knowlson [179-80]. The sneers and other elements of "an index of superiority" which Beckett recognized in himself and needed to set aside are attributed to Murphy. And yet, in this paragraph, despite the previous merciless panning of Miss Dew, a curious sympathy for her enters; in itself indicative of the evolution, as identified by Knowlson [179], of Beckett's concern for others.

103.4 [61]: *Victoria Gate*: the entrance to the Park, opened in 1854, at the NW corner near Kensington Gardens, and leading out into "the grey glare" of Bayswater Road. The faint sense of Miss Dew being "expelled" from the Garden is supported by the similar notion in 'Echo's Bones' [7], Belacqua experiencing similar "eructations into the Bayswater of Elysium."

103.5 [61]: *the dogs' cemetery*: the Hyde Park Pet Cemetery, a tiny plot behind the Victoria Gate Lodge adjoining Bayswater Road, started in 1880 when Prince, the dog of the wife of the Duke of Cambridge, then the Park Ranger, was run over outside and died in the Lodge. Another story insists that Cherry, a Maltese Terrier belonging to Mr. Lewis Barnard but which often visited Mr. Winbridge, the gatekeeper, died of old age and was buried in the garden, April 28, 1881. More followed, the dogs sewn up in canvas bags and interred by Mr. Winbridge. Other pets, cats, birds and monkeys, were buried as well as dogs, but the cemetery was closed in 1903 because it was full (300 graves). The pentimenti from the *au-delà* may have caused Miss Dew to catch up Nelly with greater force than strictly necessary.

104.1 [61]: *the reversioner*: the one to whom the estate will revert in the event of death; here, Baron Extravas, who stands to inherit should Lord Gall die intestate [see #99.2].

104.2 [61]: *a panpygoptic Manichee*: a Manichee, or Manichaean, is a follower of the Gnostic tradition that insists on the duality of good and evil. This was attacked as heresy by St. Augustine and the Church Fathers, who accused it of being "an extravagant mixture of materialism, mythology, and elated spiritual and intransigent rigorism" [Morot-Sir, 86]. Its principal emblem was the strife between Light and Darkness, which derived from there being two creative principles or forces in the universe, one of Good and one of Evil, as compared with the more orthodox Augustinian notion of evil as the privation of good.

104.3 [61]: *Jerome on his way through Rome from Calchis to Bethlehem*: a dramatic compression of three widely separated parts of Jerome's life:
    Calchis: 373-79: the town south-east of Antioch, to which Jerome retired after Christ reproached him in a dream with caring more to be a Ciceronian than a Christian.
    Rome: 382-85: where Jerome began his great work of revising the translation of the Bible, ultimately to form the *Vulgate*, and where he gathered about him a circle of Roman widows and maidens, to whom he taught Hebrew and the virtues of celibacy. His influence over these ladies alarmed their families and excited the suspicions of priesthood and populace. No Lena, let alone a panpygoptic Manichee, is associated with this period.

Bethlehem: from 385: Jerome, out of favor with the new Pope, left Rome for Antioch, where he was joined by two wealthy Roman ladies, Paula and her daughter Eustochium, who, accompanied by a band of Roman maidens, vowed to live a celibate life in Palestine. They settled at Bethlehem, where Jerome began to translate the *Old Testament* from Hebrew and completed the *Vulgate.*

104.4 [61]: *be of good courage*: as in Isaiah [41:6]: "They helped every one his neighbour, and everyone said to his brother, Be of good courage."

104.5 [61]: *no ordinary hack medium*: as Knowlson points out [191, 212], Miss Dew is based in the broadest sense upon Hester Dowden, "medium and psychic investigator," who was Tom McGreevy's landlady in Cheyne Walk. She had two snappy Pekinese dogs that Beckett disliked intensely, often used the Ouija board, and had been communicating for fourteen years with a spirit named Johannes, an Alexandrian Greek born in 200 BC. As Mays notes ['Mythologized Presences,' 207], she channeled *Psychic Messages from Oscar Wilde* (1924), including the information that he did not like *Ulysses.*

104.6 [61]: *ectoplasm*: that invisible spiritual substance emanating from the *au-delà*, which enwraps the sensitive soul like a transparent envelope. Anemones are another matter, precious margaritas produced with a flourish by magicians and mandrakes.

105.1 [61]: *The freedom of indifference*: a nod in the direction of Geulincx, but the rest of the sentiment, concerning the will dust in the dust of its object, appears to be from Schopenhauer. Likewise, 'sensation' and 'reflection' as "gross importunities": this is the Kantian distinction redefined as distraction. Murphy, therefore, turns to his own dark.

105.2 [61]: *detained*: i.e., in the market-place [see #2.8], the Joycean parallel further accented by the efforts "to rekindle the light" (the Dean of Studies is setting a fire).

105.3 [62]: *the pensums*: in the parlance of the Public School, the fagging, detentions, lines and small senseless demands that so intrude upon time. It was Flaubert's term for the chore of writing *Madame Bovary*. Schopenhauer uses the word in his treatment of Suffering: "Das Leben ist ein Pensum zum Arbeiten: in diesem Sinn ist defunctus ein schöner Ausdruck" [Ger. "Life is a Pensum of work; in this sense death is a fine outcome" (*Parega*, II, 300); cited by McQueeny, 106]. Beckett ends his *Proust* [93] with an evocation of this passage, the aesthetic vision that damns the life of the body on earth as a pensum and reveals the meaning of the word 'defunctus.' In like vein, Molloy laments [32]: "You invent nothing, you think you are inventing, you think you are escaping, and all you do is stammer out your lesson, the remnants of a pensum got one day by heart and long forgotten, life without tears, as it is wept." His cry is repeated, frequently, by the Unnamable.

105.4 [62]: *improved out of all knowledge*: see #79.2; O'Hara's third condition is acted out (in Hyde Park, rather than Kensington Gardens, to offer a small improvement). Swift's *A Tale of a Tub*, you may wish to know, was written "for the Universal Improvement of Mankind."

105.5 [62]: *When he came to, or rather from*: more than a casual quibble, for it represents, reduced to the most fundamental sounds, the Occasionalist dualism of body and mind, which is in turn the logical conclusion of the necessity of motion, and takes two forms, 'to' and 'from.' In the phrasing of Geulincx [*Metaphysica*, II §11, *Opera*, 2, 176]: "Motus enim duas habet partes: *abesse* et *adesse*" [L. "Motion therefore has two parts, *from being* and *to being*"]. Murphy thus affirms that he is coming *from* his mind *to* his body. Compare *Finnegans Wake* [293]: "murphy come, murphy go" (written in 1928, long before *Murphy*). In like manner, the Unnamable addresses the dogs to come: "adeste, adeste, all ye living bastards" [379].

106.1 [62]: *a drift of pale uneasy shapes*: a hint of Synge's troubles during the 1907 *Playboy* riots, when the crowd reacted to the unsentimental portrayal of "of a drift of women in their shifts alone." The offensive word was 'shifts,' as a betrayal of the purity of Irish womanhood, but, some wits would have it, the crowd should have been more upset by 'drift,' a word usually restricted to a herd of cattle or flock of sheep.

106.2 [62]: *the four caged owls in Battersea Park*: Murphy feels himself, in the words of Job 30:29, "a companion to owls." There was a hibouery in Battersea Park, between the Sub-Tropical Gardens and Power House, an artificial rock formation beneath a spreading sycamore that gave shady relief during the day. The grotto and sycamore remain, but the owls have flown, as it were, even as the thought of their sorrows returns (like the glaucous dew) to the Unnamable near the end of his soliloquy [361], his eyes opening and shutting "like the owl cooped in the grotto in Battersea Park, ah misery, will I never stop wanting a life for myself?"

106.3 [62]: *the green old days*: a further befouling of the Romantic, in shredding Cleopatra's "salad days / When I was green in thought" [*Anthony and Cleopatra*, I.v.73-74; DN, #248]. The moon as seen by Watt [30] is also "an unpleasant yellow colour."

106.4 [62]: *Gazed on unto my setting*: included for interpolation in the *Whoroscope* Notebook, and acknowledged as taken from Beaumont and Fletcher, *The Maid's Tragedy*. The play begins with a marriage, Amintor having obeyed the King and discarded his betrothed, Aspatia, to marry Evadne, but it transpires that the deceitful Evadne is marrying only to establish a cover for her liaison with the King. Act I ends with a masque, the celebration of Night, determined to create one hour of such content that Day will seem hateful henceforth; in the course of which Cynthia, Goddess of the Moon, complains that all do serve the Sun, and in vain does she lend her light, save to those few "of inquiet eyes" who gaze upon her. There is little relevance to the novel, save the rude shock that Amintor has in store in the next act. In the typescript, the passage runs directly from ". . . begin till dusk, rose and hastened back . . . ." The interpolation is ugly, and accentuates the Braque-like pattern of green and yellow to undercut the queasy Romanticism that has been so much a part of the scene.

106.5 [62]: *according to her God*: of Job, or Mammon: a distinction of little interest to Murphy.

106.6 [62]: *a shocking thing had happened*: the gentle reader will be obliged to wait until chapter 8 to find out what; even then it may not appear momentous. Even Fielding, to whom Beckett is obliged for the idea of short philosophical chapters that break up the narrative and remind the readers whose fiction they are in, doesn't do it quite like this.

6

107.1 [63]: *Amor intellectualis quo Murphy se ipsum amat*: L. "the intellectual love with which Murphy loves himself." This subverts Spinoza's *Ethica Ordine Geometrico Demonstrata*, V §35, in which is affirmed: "Deus se ipsum amore intellectuali infinito amat" [L. "God loves himself with an infinite intellectual love"], such intellectual love consisting in the understanding of His perfections and rejoicing therein, with the implication that the more the human mind understands the divine love the less it will be subject to emotion. Beckett follows not Spinoza's original but Windelband's rephrasing of it [410]. The dictum is also discussed in Brunschvicg's *Spinoza et ses contemporains* [134], which Beckett owned. V §36 continues:

> The intellectual love of the mind towards God is that very love of God whereby God loves himself, not so far as he is infinite, but in so far as he can be explained through the essence of the human mind regarded under the form of eternity; in other words, the intellectual love of the mind towards God is part of the infinite love with which God loves himself.

In Diderot's formulation, "cette espèce de Dieu" is defined as "La seule qui se conçoive" ("Le Rêve de d'Alembert," 317). Such intellectual love recognizes God as First Cause; hence Murphy's intellectual love of *himself* means that his world takes meaning from himself, and this, with all its implicit ironies, becomes a warrant for freeing himself from contingency.

Benedictus (Baruch) de Spinoza (1632-77), Portuguese-Dutch lens grinder, turned to philosophy to consider how best he might live [Brunschvicg, 1]. An heir to the Cartesians, he based his metaphysics on a monistic parallelism rather than interactionism or dualism. He considered the human body and mind as two aspects of the same reality, God. In his *Ethica*, Spinoza begins with definitions and proceeds to numbered propositions followed by 'QED,' to affirm his conviction that the order and connection of ideas is as the order and connection of things: "Ordo et connexio idearum idem est ac ordo et connexio rerum" [II §7]. This is the geometrical method, its essence demonstration. Windelband notes the naïveté of Spinoza's assumptions of the unassailable validity of the definitions and axioms [396]. Two sections discuss the nature and origin of the mind, leading to the proposition that it has an adequate knowledge of the eternal and infinite essence of God; but, as Part III contends, the passions distract and obscure our intellectual vision of the whole. Part IV is entitled "Of Human Bondage, or the Strength of the Emotions," which has a curious affinity to the image of Murphy in his chair, and asserts that we are in bondage in proportion as what happens to us is determined by outside causes and free in as much as we are self-determined. Part V concerns the definition of human freedom, as seen in the Cartesian perspective but with an insistence upon three ways of knowing, the third of which is that of the mind as it knows itself [V §31], from which arises the intellectual love of God [V §32]. Spinoza thus subverted is a convenient formulation for the rejection of the rationalist tradition, although Beckett finally relies more upon the very different *Ethica* of Geulincx, in which, however, the opposition of Ratio (reason) and Philautia (self-love) is a constant theme [see also #109.1, #178.9 and #216.6].

107.2 [63]: *Murphy's mind*: it would be equally an extravagance and impertinence to attempt to define whence Beckett's ideas derive. The chapter, brief as it is, represents a compression and distillation of his years of reading, from the pre-Socratics through the traditions of Western mysticism and reason to recent discoveries of psychology and science. Accordingly, I adopt a two-fold approach: glosses on some of the significant and problematical points, drawing on the range of Beckett's known reading and occasionally other texts; and, then, a three-fold approach to the way that these sources are "layered" in broad strata, each of the zones of light, half-light and darkness corresponding to others in turn tripartite.

i. the Greek ideal of the rational soul (Plato and Aristotle), implying an ascent to the light from the pre-Socratics, as contrasted with the Atomism of Democritus and Epicurus.

ii. the tradition of Cartesian rationalism through Newton to Kant and Schopenhauer, set against the Christian mystical tradition from Augustine to Dante, and contrasted with the post-quantum realm in which the laws of Newtonian physics no longer pertain.

iii. the image of the human psyche as popularized by Jung and Freud, with its broad divisions of the conscious, pre-conscious and unconscious [Beckett's terms; see #111.3].

These divisions represent Beckett's picturing of Murphy's mind as it feels itself to be, a construct drawing upon the range of Western philosphy and pyschology to find analogues for its rejection of the impulse towards the light of reason in favor of the deeper darkness of the mind. A model, a metaphor, is suggested by Kant's "Table of Categories" [*Critique,* I.2 §9, 107], where it is argued: "If we abstract all the content of a judgement, and consider only the mere form of understanding, we find that the function of thought in judgment can be brought under four heads, each of which contains three moments. They may be conveniently represented in the following table" [Kant gives one]:

Murphy's mind
Light (actual)
Half-light (actual <=> virtual)
Dark (virtual)

Greek thought	*Western thought*
Socrates, Plato and Aristotle	Cartesian realism
Presocratic (Pythagoreans)	Christian mysticism
Atomism (Democritus)	Non-Newtonian motion

Psychology
Conscious
Pre-conscious
Unconscious

No validity is attached to all or any of the above. At best, or at most, it is an apparatus to picture what follows.

107.3 [63]: *the gravamen*: from L. *gravis,* "heavy"; the essence of a legal complaint or accusation, the heaviest or most weighty part of an argument; but in medieval Latin (and the primary citation in the *OED*), with the medical sense of a physical inconvenience. The word is related to *gravidus,* "pregnant," and hence, perhaps, to Burton's Preface to the *Anatomy* [5], as cited in the Dream Notebook [#725]: "*gravidum cor, foedum caput,* a kind of imposthume in my head." Beckett's source may be Thomas à Kempis [*De Imitatione Christi,* III.li.1]: "Quamdiu mortale corpus geris, taedium senties et gravamen cordis" [L. "As long as thou carriest a mortal body, thou shalt feel weariness and heaviness of heart"].

107.4 [63]: *as a large hollow sphere*: a monad, from Gk. μονάς, "unit"; hence, for Leibniz, an ultimate unit of entity or elementary being: a microcosm. Gottfried Wilhelm von Leibniz (1641-1716), German mathematician and philosopher, was described by Beckett to McGreevy as "a great cod, but full of splendid little pictures" [December 6, 1933]. His was an attempt to synthesize the thought of Descartes and Spinoza with the theory of atoms and the void, which had once, he affirmed, charmed his imagination [*Monadology*, 23]. Simple being he described in terms of his theory of monads: indestructible, uncreated and inimitable elements, whose essence is activity. Although monads develop they do not effect one another. The world is an infinite set of independent monads, which precludes causation, that being merely coincidence in time and space. Hesla, who is excellent on the "impermeability of the self" [50], sums up the issue of the non-communicability of monads [75], as in Leibniz's *Monadology* [§56]: "This, for Leibnitz, is the definition of perfection. The mutual accommodations of each monad to every other, effected by the pre-established harmony, causes each monad to have relations which express all the others and consequently 'to be a perpetual living mirror of the universe.'" The fly in this ointment of microcosmology is a Proustian one, a function of the monad's existence in time (leaving aside the further complication that any notion of pre-established harmony must be premised on the problematic nature of God).

There is a theological component to Leibniz's thought, in terms of a continuous ascent towards perfection from the lowest to the highest monad, culminating in the Supreme Monad. Hence his dicum: *Deus est monas monadum gignens et in se reflectens adorem* [L. "God is the Monad of monads, engendering and reflecting in Himself His own love"]. This is cited by Beckett in *Exagmination* [6], as lifted from McIntyre's *Giordano Bruno* [McQueeny, 15], and forms a link between Spinoza's *Amor intellectualis*, the Leibniz monad, and Schopenhauer's contention [*WWI*, III.2.xxv, 74-75] that consciousness presupposes individuality, but belongs to the merely phenomenal, as opposed to the inner nature:

> Our inner nature, on the other hand, has its root in that which is no longer phenomenon, but thing in itself, to which, therefore, the forms of the phenomenon do not extend; and thus the chief forms of individuality are wanting, and with these the distinctness of consciousness falls off. In this root of existence the difference of beings ceases, like that of radii of a sphere in the centre; and as in the sphere the surface is produced by the radii ending and breaking off, so consciousness is only possible where the true inner being runs out into the phenomenon, through whose forms the separate individuality becomes possible upon which consciousness depends, which is just on that account confined to phenomena. Therefore all that is distinct and thoroughly comprehensible in our consciousness always lies without upon this surface of the sphere. Whenever, on the contrary, we withdraw entirely from this, consciousness forsakes us . . .

Schopenhauer suggests that the will as thing in itself "is whole and undivided in every being, as the centre is an integral part of every radius" [75]. This is compatible with Murphy's sense of a retreat into his center in terms of personal will-lessness [see #113.3], for the key to freedom is the surrender to the Will in self-consciousness [see #2.10]. This splendid image of the sphere with an outer surface of consciousness and a core of inner being may have given Beckett the means of moving from Leibniz's monad into Murphy's inner darkness.

107.5 [63]: *it excluded nothing that it did not itself contain*: this arises from Leibniz's sense of the monad containing potentially and ideally the universe without it

[*Monadology*, 32, 71]; yet there is a hint of Bertrand Russell's celebrated paradox concerning the set of all sets that do not contain themselves as members—is it a member of itself, given that the condition that it should contain itself is that it should not contain itself? The paradox, with its touch of tautology, may afford an ironic qualification to Murphy's assured picturing of his mind.

107.6 [63]: *virtual . . . actual*: the distinction is apparently simple, in that the virtual seems to correspond to the dark zone of the mind, and the actual to the light zone [see #111.3]. The point is made [108] that this is not a neo-Platonic distinction between form and formlessness, but rather between that of which one might have mental-and-physical experience (actual), and that of which one has mental experience only (virtual). The differentiation has complex roots in Leibniz's concept of virtuality, concerning the paradox of impressions in the monad of the external world, but a monad which (being windowless, or hermetically closed) is precluded from receiving *those* impressions from *that* world. Leibniz's resolution of the problem is (on the one hand) to invest the monad with *perception* and *appetition* [desire], then, to depict God as absolute archivist, storing the imprint of the heterogeneous phenomena that constitute the world but also programming in advance what will happen in the universe through time (the doctrine of pre-established harmony): "Thus while each monad expresses the universe in its entirety, it does so only virtually, in accordance with what Leibnitz identifies as the clear zone. Aside from what comes under the jurisdiction of the clear zone of perception, everything remains in the archival basement and is not brought into conscious perception" [Dowd].

Beckett uses the terms 'virtual' and 'actual' in the *Whoroscope* Notebook with respect to the relationship of Dives and Lazarus in Abraham's bosom: "Luke XVI: Dives—Lazarus, prayer from virtual to actual in entelechy ... petites perceptions to apperceived in monad—poem" [see #5.7]. The term *petites perceptions*, the gravamen of this distinction, is found in Leibniz's doctrine of the monad, as summed up by Baldwin ['Leibnitz']: "Activity of the mind is akin to perception. The monodal development implies the clarification of perception, and substance shows degrees of consciousness. Even the unconscious is only relatively so, for it is potentially capable of being perceived, just as the totality of countless drops of water is heard as the splash of a wave (apperception) although no single drop makes a perceptible sound (petites perceptions)." *Petites perceptions* (impossible to perceive) are thus virtual, but in their totality may become actual (apperceived); both, however, are equally real *and* ideal [see #108.3]. In Windelband's summary (424), they are akin to unconscious mental states. In Zeno's paradox, a single grain of millet falls noiselessly to the ground; a bushel poured out makes a great noise. Descartes's mistake (said Leibniz) was that his insistence on the clear and distinct took no account of perceptions which were not apperceived: "for it treats as non-existent those perceptions of which we are not consciously aware" [*Monadology*, 224]. The phrase *petites perceptions* is repeated several times in the *Whoroscope* Notebook, the action defined almost as a parody of Leibniz, X (the character) and H (the Horoscope) as separate monads in the arcanum of circumstance, "each apperceiving in the other till no more of the *petites perceptions* that are life," when the potential of each is realized in the other and they must perish together.

108.1 63]: *the idealist tar*: despite the label of a "seedy solipsist" [82], Murphy is willing to concede the existence of a material world, finding the problem of "little interest" [109]. The metaphor derives less from Uncle Remus than Berkeley's *A Chain of Philosophical Reflexions and Inquiries Concerning the Virtues of Tarwater* (1744), the Bishop's curious nostrum for ills of the material body. This came to Beckett via Fielding, as an entry in the *Whoroscope* Notebook indicates: "Dropsical: neither residence in dung (Heraclitus) nor Berkeley's Tarwater (Fielding), able to dissipate watery accumulation." The first refers to a footnote in Burnet [131], telling how Heraklites believed it was death to souls to become water, and so, when afflicted with dropsy, covered himself in dung; the second refers to the compelling account in Fielding's *A Voyage to Lisbon* [206-07] of how the writer, dying of the dropsy, turned to Berkeley's tarwater and gained immediate relief but no lasting cure.

108.2 [63]: *mental and physical experience*: Beckett attributes two citations to Gentile in the *Whoroscope* Notebook: that all consciousness is self-consciousness; and that in coming to know itself by thinking about itself, mind is adding to itself, and so making the self which it knows. This is followed by the response of Leibniz to Locke: "Nihil in intellectu, quod non prius fuerat in sensu, nisi ipse intellectus" [L. "There is nothing in the mind that was not first in the senses, except the mind itself"], Beckett underlining Leibniz's addition, which he had taken from Windelband [464]. Curiously, the first part is quoted with approval by Berkeley in his *Commonplace Book* [457]. The knotty point forms one of the highlights of *Malone Dies* [217-18], when the dubious hero takes counsel of an Israelite (named Jackson) on the subject of conation:

> But all he had to offer in the way of dumb companions was a pink and grey parrot. He used to try and teach it to say, Nihil in intellectu, etc. These first three words the bird managed well enough, but the celebrated restriction was too much for it, all you heard was a series of squawks.

108.3 [63]: *equally real*: a distinction drawing in part on Proust's registering of the ineffable effects that condition involuntary memory [*Le Temps retrouvé*, III.872], these decribed as "réels sans être actuels, ideaux sans être abstraits" [Fr. "real without being actual, ideal without being abstract"]. Beckett paraphrases this in *Proust* [75]: "imaginative and empirical, at once an evocation and a direct perception, real without being merely actual, ideal without being merely abstract, the ideal real, the essential, the extratemporal."

108.4 [64]: *the form of the kick was actual, that of the caress virtual*: for the distinction between Kick and Caress, [see #109.3]. The words 'actual' and 'virtual' appear to have reverted (in this final jest only) to the language of the market-place [compare #107.6].

108.5 [64]: *the ethical yoyo*: not so much "right forms and wrong forms," as Cartesian and Occasionalist dualism, with reference to the *Ethica* of Geulincx and the vacillation between body and mind. Compare the kite, another Cartesian toy, with similar strings attached.

108.6 [64]: *did not confer worth*: an Occasionalist use of 'confer' [see #178.9 and #194.2].

108.7 [64]: *forms with parallel*: the source of this phrase may be the discussion in Burnet's *Early Greek Philosophy* [187] of the cosmic system of Parmenides:

> Parmenides held that there were bands crossing one another[3] and encircling one another, formed of the rare and the dense elements respectively, and that between these were other mixed bands made up of light and darkness. That which surrounds them all was solid like a wall, and under it a fiery band. The central circle of the mixed bands is the cause of movement and becoming to all the rest.

The key is Burnet's footnote '3': "It seems most likely that ἐπαραλλήλους here means 'crossing one another,' as the milky way crosses the zodiac. The term ἐπαραλλήλος is opposed to παράλληλος."

109.1 [64]: *split in two, a body and a mind*: the Cartesian conundrum [see #6.7]: according to Descartes, the mind is a thinking thing (*res cogitans*), while matter is an extended thing (*res externa*); each is *sui generis* with respect to the other. Hence the dilemma: how is it possible that two incommensurates, body and mind, might interact? Faced with a paradox, he answered with a paradox: animal spirits, he asserted, mingle in the pineal gland, or conarium (that "psychosomatic fistula" referred to by Miss Counihan [see #219.1]); it being the nature of such entities that they can affect both kinds of substance. Occasionalists were quick to point out that this was an inadequate explanation, if only for the reason that substances which are *sui generis* cannot (*ipso facto*) interact (no conarium is mentioned here). Murphy's attitude towards the conundrum constitutes one of the supreme ironies in a novel predicated upon the very question: "The problem was of little interest."

For Geulincx and the Occasionalists, the problem was of supreme interest. The term *Occasionalism* derives from L. *occasio*, "an event", that is, the theory that matter and mind do not act upon each directly, but that upon occasion of changes in one God intervenes to bring about corresponding changes in the other, each thus "the occasional cause" with respect to the other. The theory was developed by Geulincx and Malebranche to deal with the problem arising from Descartes's assertion of the extreme dualism between thought and extension, with respect to the interaction of mind and matter in general, of body and soul in particular and causation in principle. Descartes had asserted that all changes of matter-in-motion are to be accounted for by reference to extension, while all psychical matters are referred to the nature of the mind; this did not explain confused ideas (as opposed to *claires et distinctes*), nor for the passions and emotions connected with them. Here was an exception, it being proposed that God had arranged in man a co-existence of the two substances, so that a disturbance of the "animal spirits" (centered in the pineal gland, or conarium) excited in the mind an unclear idea, whether sensation, passion or emotion. This doctrine of *influxus physicus* was so obviously contradictory to the rest of the system that the Occasionalists set about doing away with it.

Geulincx's response was radical: he denied efficient causality by matter, its changes being but cues upon which God effects the real results. Malebranche went further, affirming not only that one substance cannot directly influence the other but they are so heterogeneous that mind cannot even know matter; rather, we "see things in God," matter being the occasion rather than the real object of our knowledge. Their reasoning was based upon the method of doubt as expounded in the Cartesian *Cogito*, that our first knowledge is of the self as a thinking thing. This led to the principle that nothing can be done unless there is knowledge of how it is to be done; a contention with far-reaching consequences for Geulincx, who concluded that movement of the body could not in truth be attributed to the self (here he took leave of the Cartesians). In his words: "Ego non facio id, quod quamodo fiat nescia" [L. "I do not do that which I do not know how to do"]: if it is impossible for the 'I' to do what it does not know how to do, and if it does not know how it causes the arm to rise, then the 'I' does not in fact cause the arm to rise (this Occasionalist paradox is explored in Beckett's late short prose work, 'Still'). Not only are we unaware of changes in the brain, nerves and muscles necessary for such movement, but even if we were our knowledge would be *post-facto*, based on observation and not on awareness of mental activity. Thus, although we have immediate knowledge of internal activities, we cannot know how movement is initiated in the body, nor how external actions come about (paralysis and other bodily inhibitions being proof, for Geulincx, that mental volition does not lead to movement). Accordingly, the human mind is limited to knowledge of itself, and the mind is not master of the body nor cause of movement in it. The implication, or ethical corollary, accepted by Beckett, is that the 'I' is restricted to the act of thinking, where it is radically free but does not enter the *res externa*, or world of matter and extension, not even into its own body, with regard to which it is merely the spectator. Only in the little world of the mind can one be free; the body, correspondingly, may be considered a machine [see #1.5], and the 'I' should set no value upon it [see #178.9].

Geulincx offered two analogies for these theories, and for the central conviction that only through the agency of God (and according to His volition) is movement possible. The first is that of the child, wanting the cradle to rock, and finding it does so, but only because the mother has imparted motion to it; the second, more celebrated, has been called the theory of the two clocks, the idea that body and mind each run independently of the other, with God intervening upon each occasion with a miracle to calibrate the two (Leibniz also used the dual clocks analogy, but Geulincx explicitly dissociated himself from the theory of pre-established harmony). Many of Beckett's grotesques, of whom Belacqua and Cooper are forerunners, take their dyspraxic deformity, metaphysically speaking, not so much from the times being out of joint as a miscalculation in the body-mind synchronization.

As Hesla neatly puts it [39], Murphy is an Occasionalist without at the same time being a Deist. Dowd notes that Beckett's engagement with seventeenth-century thought shows an affection for the conceptual *impasses* into which the eminent figures of the Age of Reason took philosophy. Above all (as it were), his substitution of Astrology for the Occasionalist God is the *non plus ultra* of metaphysical jests. His interest in the Occasionalists did not so much wane in later years as accommodate itself to complementary theories, but the characters in *The Trilogy* return to the theories of "old Geulincx," and the Unnamable defines his sense of worthlessness in terms of the ethical absolute, *Ubi nihil vales, ibi nihil velis*, one of the two ethical principles which *Murphy* admits [see #178.9 (Geulincx) and #246.5 (Democritus)].

109.2 [64]: *as two magnitudes to a third*: a metaphor drawn from Newtonian gravitation, where the attraction between any two bodies in the universal closed system is simultaneously (and inversely) affected by the presence of any other.

109.3 [64]: *a kick*: the reflex of a malevolent deity, or donkey, when goaded; as most viciously expressed in *More Pricks than Kicks* (1934). That title is a critique of the experience of Saul on the road to Damascus [Acts 9:5, and 26:14], when he hears the voice of Jesus, saying: "it is hard for thee to kick against the pricks."

109.4 [64]: *a non-mental non-physical Kick*: the Platonic or Ideal form of a kick (small 'k'), the attenuated existence of the 'kick' as but a shadow of that form expressed in two correlative, or mutually dependent modes: *in intellectu*, in the mind; and *in re*, with reference to the thing referred to, in its physical being.

109.5 [64]: *the supreme Caress*: simply, the antithesis of the Kick, the reflex of a benevolent deity. Yet the image is more complex. Beckett had been reading *Émile*, and in a letter to McGreevy [September 16, 1934] expressed his admiration for Rousseau as the champion of the right to be alone, and as an authentically tragic figure in so far as he was denied enjoyment of that right: "not easy in a society that considered solitude a vice." Beckett qualified his praise of the "promeneur solitaire," the solitary rambler, by observing what he termed Rousseau's "infantile aspect," his fear "of the dark of his own constitution," observing that he would always fall for a show of tenderness, his great misfortune being always "de ne pouvoir résister aux caresses" [Fr. "not being able to resist caresses"]. Beckett adds: "If he had known how to trim his kite between the two positions he would have suffered less"; the words apply nicely to Murphy.

109.6 [64]: *some such process of supernatural determination*: the Occasionalist theory of the two clocks [see #109.1 and #178.9].

109.7 [64]: *his mind was a closed system*: a monad, or a miniature of a Newtonian universe. Yet Murphy will realize, in his "deplorable susceptibilty" to Celia and ginger biscuits and his encounter with Mr. Endon, that his mind is not as impermeable to the vicissitudes of the body as he might wish.

110.1 [64]: *this mental chamber*: the antechambers to Murphy's mind may be found, firstly, in the bedroom at Combray, where Marcel vainly composes his self for sleep; and, secondly, in *Dream* [44], where Belacqua, lapped in a beatitude of indolence, goes back into himself:

> The mind, dim and hushed like a sick-room, like a chapelle ardente, thronged with shades; the mind at last its own asylum, disinterested, indifferent, its miserable erethisms and discriminations and futile sallies suppressed; the mind suddenly reprieved, ceasing to be an annex of the restless body, the glare of understanding switched off. The lids of the hard aching mind close, there is suddenly gloom in the mind; not sleep, not yet, nor dream, with its sweats and terrors, but a waking ultra-cerebral obscurity, thronged with grey angels; there is nothing of him left but the umbra of grave and womb where it is fitting that the spirits of his dead and his unborn should come abroad.

This, for Belacqua, is the "real business" [44], the mind going wombtomb, the prurient heat and glare of living consumed away, the mistral of desire withdrawn [45], continent, sustenant [46]. Murphy's mind has its form with parallel here.

110.2 [64]: *motion in this world depended on rest in the world outside*: an apparent contradiction of Spinoza's *Ethica* (II §13, Lemma iii), concerning the laws of motion: "A body in motion or at rest must be determined to motion or rest by another body, which other body has been determined to motion or rest by a third body, and that third again by fourth, and so on to infinity." More simply, said Leibniz, motion and rest are entirely relative to one another [*Monadology*, 89]. According to Descartes, the earth is at rest relative to a man who might move upon it, in the same way that a man might move who yet was being carried along in a boat. In Burton's words: "as to sailors,—*terraeque urbesque recedunt*—they move, the land stands still" [*Anatomy*, 'Democritus to the Reader,' 37]. The ultimate point of rest, of course, is God, that still point of a turning world. This paradox of motion is expounded by Geulincx throughout the *Ethica*, most clearly in the image of the child willing its cradle to be rocked, but that motion imparted by the mother apparently at rest; so, Geulincx argued, God imparts to us the laws of motion which we believe we enact ['Annotata,' 227-28 nn6-7]. In this reading, Murphy's assumption is provocative, for what appears to be rest in the world outside is rather unperceived motion (God, the prime mover, imparting to the mother the motive power to rock the cradle, which the child believes it wills). The paradox, and its restriction, was for Beckett most memorably imaged in Geulincx's boat ['Annotata,' 167 n9]:

Navis ocissime vectorem abripiens versus occidentem, nihil impedit quominus ille in navi ipsa deambulat versus orientum; sic voluntas Dei omnia portans, omnia vehens fatali impetu, nihil obstat quominus nos, quantum est ex parte nostra, obluctemur voluntati ejus, liberâ et pleâ nostra deliberatione.

[L. "If a voyager is in a ship which carries him briskly westwards, there is nothing to stop him walking eastwards on board the ship; thus the will of God directs everything, carries everything along its impetuous fatality, without there being anything to stop us trying, in so far as we can, to obstruct his will through a perfectly free deliberation on our part"]. Compare *De Anima* [406.a.5-10], whence this paradox of shipboard motion derives, Aristotle concluding that the term "to be moved" has thus two senses. The image is anticipated in *Dream* [134]: "he moves forward, like the Cartesian earthball, with the moving ship, and then on his own account to the windy prow"; and would be repeated in *The Unnamable* [336], with the ship heading towards the Pillars of Hercules and the galley-man crawling towards the rising sun. Murphy's proposition (that the body must lie down that the mind may move) is valid in terms of movement relative to the bigger world apparently at rest, but problematic because the alternative to motion is homeostasis: the entire novel is predicated upon the sentiment recorded in the beginning of the *Whoroscope* Notebook: "keep moving the only virtue." As Malone concludes [232]: "In order not to die you must come and go, come and go."

110.3 [64]: *A rat is behind the wall*: Tennyson's annoying mouse behind the wainscot [*Maud*, VI.viii.9] has its savage forbear in Swift's 'To Dr. Delaney': "A rat your utmost rage defies / That safe behind the wainscot lies." The image is drawn, if not from experience, at least from *Dream* [15], where Belacqua near Vienna is living in a high dark room with rats behind the wallpaper, discreetly slithering. They return, the last rats, in *Watt* [84], and in *Endgame* [54], to be half-exterminated.

110.4 [65]: *a kind of mental tic douloureux*: literally, a trigeminal neuralgia, or twitch of the facial muscles accompanied by neuralgic pain; metaphorically, and as associated with Proust's "douloureuse synthèse" [*Swann*, I.760], a flicker of involuntary memory.

110.5 [65]: *not what he understood by consciousness*: reduced to its simplest terms, Murphy's quest for the dark is a reversal of the pattern of discovery variously termed the path of enlightenment, higher consciousness, or the ascent of the soul (by the light of Reason) towards God. Infinite glosses, drawn from all manner of writings (Buddhist, Christian, mystical, rational, psychological) might be cited, but that outlined by Brett [93], defining the three stages of the Platonic ascent to the highest Good, may stand in for others:

> . . . and as the soul is itself intermediary between Pure Forms and the Formless, so the process of development through which it goes is threefold: for there is first the process of moulding the material, irrational nature; then the intermediary stage in which concrete embodiments of law are studied; and finally the highest stage in which the laws of nature are made the subject of thought and the mind thinks over the last great law of all things, the Good in which they live and move and have their being. Plato was doubtless perfectly conscious of the latent mysticism of his doctrine; he saw that the soul in turning round from darkness to light comes finally to itself.

110.6 [65]: *privy*: in collusion with 'convenience,' an instance of what Geulincx would call *despectio sui*, or contempt of the self [see #178.9]. A like conjunction of 'privy' and 'convenience' is implied later [see #174.1].

111.1 [65]: *telekinesis*: the apparent art, or science, of producing motion in objects by mental power alone.

111.2 [65]: *the Leyden Jar*: a condensor formed by a glass jar, coated inside and out with metal foil, the inner coating connected to a conducting rod passed through an insulated stopper.

111.3 [65]: *the three zones*: parallels may be adduced from Classical doctrines of the tripartite soul to the three divisions of Dante's *Divine Comedy*, each with its sense of the dark, the half-light and the light; or Spinoza's three levels of knowledge, the third being the identification of the self with the intellectual love of God [Brunschvicg, 117]. There is Leibniz's distinction between the unconscious realm of confused perception, the conscious realm of relatively clear perception, and the self-conscious realm of apperception; and Schopenhauer's manifestations of the Will in accordance with the three forms of space, time, and causality [see #113.3]. What is striking about the tripartite division is its apparent incommensurability with Cartesian dualism. The full working out of the paradigm seems to be Beckett's own, related "not by rule of three, as two values to a third, but directly, as stages of an image" [review of Jack Yeats's *The Amaranthers* (1936), *Disjecta*, 90], as evidenced by the parallel structure in *Dream* [120-25]. This may be summarized: Belacqua at his simplest is trine. Centripetal, centrifugal, and... not. Trine. His third being is the dark gulf, the glare of will and hammer-strokes of the brain expunged; the wombtomb alive with the unanxious spirits of quiet cerebration; its center everywhere and periphery nowhere; an unsurveyed marsh of sloth [see #112.3]. There is no authority for supposing this to be the real Belacqua; but the emancipation from identity suits his complexion; he is sorry it does not happen more often; for if he were free he would take up residence in that place. Convinced (like a fool) that it must be possible to induce such pleasure, he exhausts his ingenuity experimenting; but in vain, it is impossible to switch off the inward glare. The will and the nill cannot be one. Which explains as well as anything why his temper is bad and his complexion saturnine: "He remembers the pleasant gracious bountiful tunnel, and cannot get back." There, in embryo (wombtomb) of *Dream*, is the larval stage of Murphy's mind: "Apollo, Narcissus and the anonymous third person" [124].

There was a subsequent development. On October 2, 1935 Beckett attended with his analyst Wilfred Bion a lecture given at the Tavistock Clinic, in which Jung recalled a diagram that he had used earlier, "showing the different spheres of the mind and the dark centre of the unconscious in the middle. The closer you approach that centre, the more you experience what Janet calls an *abaisement du niveau mental*: your conscious autonomy begins to disappear, and you get more and more under the fascination of unconscious contents" [Knowlson, 218, quoting Beckett's notes; Beckett is citing Jung's 'Tavistock Lecture' III, 74, after which Jung discussed the case of the little girl who had never been born entirely (94). The diagram had been used in the Second lecture (44)]. Jung adds that this process may be seen in extreme form in cases of insanity: "The fascination of unconscious contents gradually grows stronger and conscious control vanishes in proportion until finally the patient sinks into the unconscious altogether and becomes completely victimized by it. He is the victim of a new autonomous activity that does not start from his ego but starts from the dark sphere." Beckett's other notes set out and define the Id, Ego and Superego, and contain a little sketch of the "perceptual conscious," the "pre-conscious" and the "unconscious" in their relations with these. As Knowlson concludes, it is doubtful that Beckett could have made Murphy's descent into the dark zone as he did without the insights he had gleaned from his own descent into the depths with Bion; equally, he could not have conceived its structure without the aid of Jung.

111.4 [65]: *In the first*: forms with parallel, in the sense of images from the outside world, the "fiasco," conceived with consciousness and recombined so as to retain their integrity, whatever the new configuration. This zone is private, and Murphy feels free to arrange things as his mind wills, but traces of reasoned choice remain; in Proustian terms, the act is voluntary. As Brett comments [148], with reference to the Greek understanding of cognition that may have shaped Beckett's definition:

> The sense-process leaves in the mind certain forms, and imagination is the faculty of presenting the images which memory retains. Thus the mind becomes filled with forms and may be called the place of forms; when it is active it calls up by recollection the forms it requires and engages in active search for ideas connected with those present to it. The field of consciousness does not include all possible ideas; some only are present in the mind (θειόρει) out of those which, in the wider sense, it possesses (ἔχει). Thinking is therefore the actualising of ideas which otherwise exist potentially.

Where Murphy would take issue with this Aristotelian concept is the further contention that the forms thus precipitated constitute a new plurality, ascending to higher generalizations; his mind does not realize its potential in quite the way the *maestro di color che sanno* would approve.

111.5 [65]: *In the second*: forms without parallel, where the constraints of reason and consciousness are relaxed, an involuntary activity. For want of a better metaphor, this might be called the pre-Socratean, the shaping principle of which is the strife of opposites [see #3.8]. This is the Freudian pre-conscious, the realm of dreams; but the Viennese master, like Aristotle before him, would not approve of the desire to contemplate them with pleasure (a small "element of effort" [113]) before diving deeper. Psychiatry encourages the understanding of this world not as an end, but as a means of returning to the light.

111.6 [65]: *out of joint*: compare *Hamlet* I.v.189-90: "The time is out of joint. O cursed spite, / That ever I was born to set it right."

111.7 [65]: *Belacqua bliss*: the indolent pleasure of the Florentine lute-maker [see #78.1], assuming his embryonal repose, "watching the dawn break crooked" [112], and dreaming his life through once again. The word 'contemplation,' like 'beatitude' to follow, is used in unattended opposition to its more accepted sense in the traditions of Christian mysticism.

112.1 [65]: *sovereign and free*: this follows from the Occasionalist conclusion that within the little world of the mind one can be truly free [see #109.1]. Q: can one believe in free will? A: is there any alternative? Schopenhauer casts cold water over the euphoria [*WWI*, I.4.lv, 372]: "The person is never free although he is the phenomenon of a free will; for he is already the determined phenomenon of the free volition of this will . . . Since, however, it is that free volition that becomes viable in the person and the whole of his conduct, relating to himself as the concept to the definition, every individual action of the person is to be ascribed to the free will, and directly proclaims itself as such in consciousness." Schopenhauer is willing to call this freedom, subject to the stated restriction.

112.2 [65]: *to requite himself*: to return the intellectual love with which he loves himself [see #107.1, and #84.4: "recruiting himself"]. The beatitude is unparalleled because it is freed from the constraints of reason and consciousness that operate in the realm of light.

112.3 [65]: *The third, the dark*: the flux of forms manifests itself on many levels: the void of the Atomists; the Freudian unconscious; the Schopenhauerean state of will-lessness; and the world of quanta. This is Belacqua's "third being" [*Dream*, 120-21]:

> The third being was the dark gulf, when the glare of the will and the hammer-strokes of the brain doomed outside to take flight from its quarry were expunged, the Limbo and the wombtomb alive with the unanxious spirits of quiet cerebration, where there was no conflict of flight and flow and Eros was as null as Anteros and Night had no daughters. He was bogged in indolence, without identity, impervious alike to its pull and goading. The cities and forests and beings were also without identity, they were shadows, they exerted neither pull nor goad. His third being was without axis or contour, its centre everywhere and periphery nowhere, an unsurveyed marsh of sloth.

112.4 [65]: *a new manifold*: the word is used in the Kantian sense, with respect to the sum of the particulars furnished by the sense before they have been unified by the understanding, and thus a marsh containing no distinction in terms of the logical or empirical categories. Beckett cites in the *Whoroscope* Notebook another central Kantian dictum: "Zweckmässigkeit ohne Zweck" [Ger. "purposiveness without purpose," goalness without a goal]. Kant's sense is that we must act as if with purpose or intention, as if the manifold embodied some transcendent purpose, although we know it does not. Murphy in his critique seems content to accept the lack of purpose as ideal.

112.5 [66]: *neither elements nor states*: again, the Kantian manifold, but as Ellis suggests [363], the phrase may echo Heisenberg's "neither particles nor waves," to define the paradox implicit in the nature of light which generates his Principle of Uncertainty. Compare *Molloy* [31]: as identity fades, Molloy experiences the "namelessness" of "waves and particles," nameless things, thingless names.

112.6 [66]: *without love or hate*: as Mooney points out [225], Democritus denied two earlier solutions to the problem of motion for his atoms (these correspond, vaguely, to Murphy's half-light and light): that of Empedocles, who advanced "love" and "hate" as principles responsible for the animation of matter; and that of Anaxagoras, who substituted νοῦς, mind or intelligibility. The Atomists, Mooney suggests, were less concerned with the generation of motion than the coming together and passing away of atoms, or, in Murphy's words, "forms becoming and crumbling into the fragments of a new beginning." Murphy's third zone, the dark flux of forms, is defined in Atomistic terms, both those of the Ancient Greeks and the modern physicists.

112.7 [66]: *commotion*: from L. *commovere*, "to move or disturb"; used here with both the sense of recurrent motion and the more specialized meaning of mental perturbation. In a letter to Mary Manning Howe [August 30, 1937; cited in part by Knowlson, 269], Beckett used the word in further describing the "coenesthesic" state of mind, "The monad without conflict":

> There is an end to the temptation of light, its polite scorching & considerations. It is food for children and insects. There is an end of making up one's mind, like a pound of tea. An end of putting the butter of consciousness into opinions. The real consciousness is the chaos, a grey commotion of mind, with no premises or conclusions or problems or solutions or cases or judgements.

112.8 [66]: *a mote in the dark of absolute freedom*: a condition transcending (in Kant's sense) the state of being "sovereign and free" [see note #112.1]. Proust testifies [*Guermantes*, II.151] to the sense of relief one derives from Kant, "quand après la démonstration la plus rigoureuse du déterminisme on découvre qu'audessus du monde de nécessité, il y a celui de la liberté" [Fr. "when after the most rigorous demonstration of determinism one discovers that, above the world of necessity, there is that of freedom"].

112.9 [66]: *a point*: i.e., having position but not extension. Kandinsky's *Punkt und Linie zu Fläche* ["Point Line and Surface"], 1926, may underpin Murphy's experience of being a point in the passing away of line.

112.10 [66]: *matrix of surds*: the womb of irrationals, the generative principle of absurdity. The line is less effective in typescript [358]: "He called it his matrix of surds. He considered it the cat's pyjamas." Beckett claimed a clear memory of the prenatal experience [Knowlson, 2]; this he expressed by images of embryonic repose and the impulse to return to the womb. The former is exemplified by Belacqua's bliss [see #78.1]; the latter discussed memorably in Otto Rank's *The Trauma of Birth*, which insists that "every pleasure has as its final aim the re-establishment of the intrauterine primal pleasure" [17]. There Beckett might also have found that the native "wishes himself back in the place where there is no disturbance from outside" [25]; the curious notion of crucifixion as "the prevention of the embryonal position" [138]; and the contention that the pleasurable primal state is interrupted through the act of birth, the rest of life consisting in "replacing the lost paradise by complex acts of the libido, the primal state being no longer attainable" [187]. In Rank's conclusion, "the real Unconscious consists only in the libidinal relation of the embryo to the womb" [195]. Knowlson comments that Beckett "felt his solitude, sometimes very acutely. But it was a solitude that he also cultivated deliberately, obscurely aware that something was happening within him, as, eclectically, he accumulated knowledge" [200]. That "something" was conceived throughout his writings in terms of the birth of the soul, the self that had never been properly born.

Following the non-Euclidean images of point and line, 'matrix' has a mathematical dimension, as a table of figures to which values may be attributed and from which others may be generated. As Ellis notes [364], this had special application in the 1920s, following the discoveries of the worlds of quanta and sub-atomic space to which Newtonian laws no longer apply. He suggests a link to the principle of Matrix Algebra, as first presented by Heisenberg in 1925-26, "to identify and display discrete energy states in the mechanics of subatomic quanta"; the point being that the behavior of electrons might better be described in terms of matrices, or tables of variables, rather than quantities of fixed numerical value. Beckett's sense of the sums would not have been so precise, but the point seems otherwise valid.

112.11 [66]: *a missile without provenance*: i.e., moving, but without a place of origin.

113.1 [66]: *a tumult of non-Newtonian motion*: specifically, the commotion that exists in the world of quantum mechanics, in which the laws of gravitation, as defined by Newton and regulating the Big World, do not apply. The phrase does not appear in the typescript of *Murphy*, but despite being a late addition it is integral to the very texture of Murphy's mind. Beckett took in the *Whoroscope* Notebook detailed notes from Henri Poincaré's *La Valeur de la science—histoire de la physique mathématique*; in particular, from the sections dealing with the paradoxical similarities of atoms and stars: "astres infiniment petits, ce sont les atomes" [Fr. "infinitely tiny stars, these are atoms"]; a paradox that he would later use to structure the beginning of *L'Innommable*.

Poincaré discusses the laws of Newtonian gravitation, and shows that these do not apply to the movement of electrons. Among matters touched on are the laws of thermo-dynamics, conservation of energy, and the principle of action and reaction, to which are opposed Maxwell's theories of light and electro-magnetism, his Demon, Brownian motion, and Heisenberg's Principle of Uncertainty, the point being the subversion of classical physics at the sub-atomic level. Beckett found in the theories of contemporary physics other dynamics applicable to his Occasionalist definition of the little world of the mind, where one might be free, and Murphy's sensation of being a missile without provenance or target is weighted with the full wantum of quanta.

The tumult is premised on the Democritean notion of atoms continually in motion, clashing against one another, beyond which is the Real, the Void [Bailey, 296]. It is anticipated in *Dream* [138-39]: Belacqua envisions Beethoven's vespertine compositions as a blizzard of electrons eaten away with terrible silences and pitted with the stroms of silence, the "ultimately unprevisible atom threatening to come asunder," that yet create a music one and indivisible. This is a state of mind apparently attained by the Alba [*Dream*, 166]: "Alone, unlonely, unconcerned, moored in the seethe of an element in which she had no movement and from which therefore she was not doomed to filtch the daily mite that would guarantee, in a freighting and darkening of her spirit, the declension of that moment." The goal is, in Windelband's words [165]: "To rest unmoved within one's self." This is a region dimly sensed by Malone [198]: "Words and images run riot in my head, pursuing, flying, clashing, merging, endlessly. But beyond this tumult there is a great calm, and a great indifference, never really to be troubled by anything ever again."

113.2 [66]: *so pleasant that pleasant was not the word*: the phrasing (changed from the typescript's "What could be more delightful?") explicitly echoes that of the opening, implicitly linking the world of non-Newtonian motion to the post-atomist Epicurean doctrine which asserts pleasure as the end of life [see #2.9], and the similar contention of Schopenhauer that pleasure is the absence of pain [see #2.10].

113.3 [66]: *will-lessness*: a term derived explicitly from Schopenhauer, whose dualistic view of the world as will and idea forms the final critique of the various philosophies that have contributed to the picture of Murphy's mind. As such it is crucial, despite the word's absence from the typescript. A crude summary may be useful. Will is the ultimate reality of the thing-in-itself, being set against its representations. It exists out of space and time, causeless and free: "but we are not free, since the will possesses us" [O'Hara, *Hidden Drives*, 17]. Murphy's three zones correspond to Schopenhauer's manifestations of the Will in accordance with the three forms of space, time and causality. The outer zone mirrors or reflects representations of the world as interpreted by the intellect in accordance with the forms [in Beckett's terms, "actual"]; removal of the causal brings about the contemplative status (Ideas) of the second zone [Beckett's "virtual"]. The third zone expresses the paradox of Will: that of not being free yet existing as a mote in dark of absolute freedom. This is possible through the abnegation of the Will, or withdrawal into the realm of pure contemplation. Murphy favors such cosmic freedom of the third zone over the limited personal freedom of the first two; *The Trilogy* will assume as its tripartite paradigm the movement towards that realm.

In other words: in the articulation of experience, the subject's own will (desire) conditions the perceived world in a manner which conforms to it; only by renouncing the subjective aspect of will can the subject approach an appreciation of the objective Will of ultimate reality. In aesthetic contemplation, Schopenhauer says, this state of will-lessness is attainable. He outlines the conditions of such vision [*WWI*, I.3.xxxiv, 230-31]: if a man "gives the whole power of his mind to perception, sinks himself entirely in this, and lets his whole consciousness be filled with the quiet contempla-tion of the natural object actually present," losing himself in the object and forgetting his individuality but continuing to exist as the pure subject, the clear mirror, of the object, then "he can no longer separate the perceiver from perception, but both have become one, because the whole consciousness is filled and occupied with one sin-gle sensuous picture." One sunk in this perception is no longer individual, "for in such perception the individual has lost himself . . . he is *pure, will-less, painless, timeless subject of knowledge*." Or, as he says elsewhere, there is "a silence of the will so pro-found that while it lasts even the individuality vanishes from consciousness and the man remains *as the pure subject of knowing*" [*WWI*, II.2.xix, 434]. The issue is effec-tively condensed by Rabinovitz [*Development*, 94], who argues that for Schopenhauer the will is an attribute of the body, rather than the mind (the function of the mind being to transmit impulses that originate in the will); only by abnegating the will can one attain freedom; the best way to do so is through aesthetic contem-plation, which shifts the focus from the self to an impersonal concern; this if suc-cessful constitutes a denial of the will.

Schopenhauer returns to the point and paradox in a later summary, 'On the Pure Subject of Knowledge' [*WWI*, III.3.xxx, 131-32]: "With the disappearance of volition from consciousness, the individuality also, and with it its suffering and misery, is real-ly abolished . . . As the purely objective perceiver, he is the pure subject of knowledge in whose consciousness alone the objective world has its existence; as such he is *all things* so far as he perceives them, and in him is their existence without burden or inconvenience. It is *his* existence, so far as it exists in *his* idea; but it is there without will." A little later he adds [xxxi, 144]: "for, completely severed from its origin, the will, it is now the world as idea itself, concentrated in *one* consciousness." In such terms, then, Murphy apperceives his world.

113.4 [66]: *no further bulletins*: as in a hospital, where painful boils are discharged. Yet, fine as this is as a statement of intent, the virtual sentiments have yet to be accom-modated to actuality. Murphy has conceptualized his impulse towards the dark zone, but getting there is another matter: he has yet to rid his mind of its corporeal shadow. He will find in his confrontation with Mr. Endon that to do so is an impossibility, that he is engaged in "a psychic drama that has no solution" [O'Hara, *Hidden Drives*, 69], and that the issue cannot in the "real" world be so easily resolved.

7

114.1 [67]: *Thursday the 12th*: there was no problem with the date until Rabinovitz noted that Celia's triumph over Murphy, "to be pedantic," transpired the morning after, and concluded that the events of chapters 1 and 3 must take place on September 11 ['Unreliable Narration,' 61, 68]. Wrong: the given is the moon "full and at perigee" (26, 121) on the 12th, and any error is in the pedantry itself, the "triumph" technically on the morning of the 13th.

114.2 [67]: *Ember Days*: although invoked in ironic anticipation of Murphy's end, the Ember Days are given in Whitaker as the Wednesday, Friday and Saturday of the four Ember weeks (L. "Quatuor tempora"), from the first Sunday in Lent (Quadragesima), Whit Sunday, the Feast of the Exaltation of the Cross (Holyrood Day, September 14), and the Feast of St. Lucy (December 13). The September Embers commemorate the elevation the True Cross, found at Jerusalem by St. Helena; in 1935, these were the

18th, 20th and 21st [Kennedy is in error, 119, 141]. Observing these days the faithful are bound by prayer and fasting to remember those about to receive the grace of ordination.

114.3 [67]: *the sun being still in the Virgin*: a pedantic joke. The sun would pass into Libra on the 24th [Whitaker, 116], so the mistake is curious (the 19th marks the Equinox); but the action has moved from Virgo (love) towards Scorpio (death), things now in the Balance.

114.4 [67]: *Friday, October the 11th*: technically, the moon was Full on October 12, and at perigee on the 11th (222,780 miles from the earth); the coincidence is thus not so striking [Whitaker, 118]. It would be at apogee (252,160 miles) on the 23rd, the night of Murphy's dissolution [275]. Though he did not use the detail, Beckett may have appreciated Whitaker's advice [118] for October 12: "Fire Insurances must be paid."

114.5 [67]: *Time that old fornicator*: a variation of an ancient emblem, going back to Thales of Miletus (c. 600 BC), who depicted Time as an old man, bald save for one lock of hair on the forehead.

114.6 [67]: *his restitution to the bewitching Miss Greenwich*: in 1935, Summer Time began on Palm Sunday, April 14, at 2 a.m., Greenwich Mean Time, when clocks were put back one hour [see #74.1]; the lost hour is to be regained, at 2 a.m. on the night of October 6 [Whitaker, 118], pedantically the 7th (Yom Kippur, the Day of Atonement, or reconciliation). The hour is not so much restored as lost, since the clocks go forward.

114.7 [67]: *Respectable people were going to bed*: as Beckett observed in the *Whoroscope* Notebook: "Would it were bedtime & all were well." The unspecified time applies equally to the following scene with Mr. Kelly (no hour mentioned), Neary in Glasshouse Street, and Miss Counihan and Wylie, *not* in Wynn's Hotel.

115.1 [68]: *the sad pun*: see also #7.6. Piette notes [202-04] how this scene antici-pates the Unnamable's "struggles to fend off his own traces," and how "the comic abandonment of the mind by the parts of the body" is accentuated by the repetition of "he found it hard to think." He hears the acoustic echoes about the sad pun as creat-ing a cruelly sympathetic image of a mind [re]collecting its *disjecta membra*: "The superfluous feeling for the parts he denies writes the nostalgic score for the dart of the mind that imagines the present losing of them."

115.2 [68]: *lachrymatory*: from L. *lachrimare*, "to cry"; a small vase of glass or earthen-ware to hold the tears of the relatives of the departed one, for whom they were shed. According to Schopenhauer, weeping is not a direct expression of pain, for where it occurs there is little pain; rather, it is the *idea* of pain, and the belief that our own state is so deserving of sympathy that we are firmly and sincerely convinced that if another were the sufferer, we would be full of sympathy, and love to relieve him [*WWI*, I.4 §67, 486].

115.3 [68]: *Glasshouse Street*: a small loop from the north side of Piccadilly Circus to the Quadrant of Regent Street, the location perhaps chosen as much for the echo of Mrs. Hannah Glasse's *The Art of Cooking* (1747), with its apocryphal opening: "First catch your hare."

116.1 [68]: *in the tod of his troubles like an owl in ivy*: a 'tod' is a bundle of sheep-fleeces, weighing about 28 pounds; but c.f. the rhyming slang, "on your tod," or "Todd Malone," alone, as in *The Trilogy*. Brewer defines "an owl in ivy" as a horrible fright of a fellow, one with an untidy head of hair or looking inanely wise, the ivy bush a favorite haunt of owls. In the *Whoroscope* Notebook, Beckett notes for inclusion "owl in tod of ivy," supposedly from Dekker's *Old Fortunatus* (not located there). It is an Elizabethan commonplace, later used in Swift's *Polite Conversation*, Dial. 1: "He looked for all the world like an owl in an ivy bush."

116.2 [68]: *the choleric man*: in medieval terms, one governed by excessive bile, the humor leading to irrascibility. Although the repast could account for his bilious feeling, Neary's problems may arise from two fragments of Democritus: #99, "Life is not worth living for the man who has not one good friend"; and #100, "The man whose tested friends do not stay long with him is bad-tempered" [Freeman, *Ancilla*].

116.3 [68]: *a low battuta*: as used in the phrase 'a battuta' [It. "at the beat"], meaning in music the marking of time by beating, or, more strictly, a resumption of strict time after a passage has departed from its prescribed tempo. The "bones" are clappers used in a minstrel show.

116.4 [68]: *Ariadne née Cox*: Ariadne was the daughter of Minos and Pasiphae; she fell in love with Theseus, who carried her away, only to forsake her at Naxos. There are broad parallels with Neary's history: in some versions Ariadne, disconsolate at being abandoned, killed herself, as the Cox will later do [see #272.2]; in others she married Dionysius, whose followers tore Pentheus to pieces. That frenzy may be implied in the use of 'multitudinous,' which recasts the Cox as a figure of Lady Macbeth.

116.5 [68]: *vulpine endowments*: gifts of a fox, or a Volpone, in knowing what to do (*savoir faire*) or what not to do (*savoir ne pas faire*); with a misguided sense of Murphy as quarry.

116.6 [68]: *the straightening of Neary's way*: echoing the man whose way is hid [46], but mixing the metaphor ("a harder nut to crack"). The paragraph is replete with such clichés.

117.1 [68]: *a closed system*: Neary is still a Newtonian [see #57.4, #113.1 and #201.5].

117.2 [68]: *Yang Kuei-fei*: the surpassingly lovely concubine of the T'ang Emperor, Hsüan Tsung (c. 712-56), who took her from his son and neglected his state duties. Her adopted son and lover An Lu-shan rebelled against the Emperor, who was forced to flee south. En route the Imperial Guards, blaming the favorite for the debacle, forced the Emperor to order the eunuch Kao Li-shih to strangle her (some say she was hanged upon a pear tree), while her cousin and sister perished at the hands of the troops. Her fate became the stuff of poetry and legend, as in Po Chü-i's 'Everlasting Remorse.' Beckett recorded in the Dream Notebook [#522]: "Yang Kuei-fei, famous concubine, strangled by eunuch, breaking with her hands the yellow gold in the Isles of the Blest, dividing the enamel, crying over the spray of peach bloom." His source is Giles, *Civilisation of China* (85-87), the "bloom" pear rather than peach, the "gold" a hairpin and the "enamel" a brooch, broken by the concubine in the afterworld to send to the Emperor, keeping half herself.

117.3 [69]: *not in Wynn's Hotel*: the French translation reads: "*qui doit rester anonyme*" [Fr. "which must remain anonymous"], the joke untraceable. Beckett could not have anticipated his own involvement in a messy libel case, when he took the stand on behalf of his uncles Harry and Willie ('Boss') Sinclair, who had been libeled by Oliver Gogarty [Knowlson, 275-80].

117.4 [69]: *oyster kisses*: succulent varieties given by the Smeraldina to Belacqua [*Dream*, 17], here anticipating the image of the mollusc torn from its rock [118]. This instance is listed without comment in the *OED* Supplement. Beckett recorded 'oyster kiss' in the Dream Notebook [#922], from Burton's *Anatomy* [III.2.2.iv, 536, or III.2.5.v, 625]. Compare Wilenski's discussion of a motif in the paintings of Dirck Hals of private rooms in taverns where young bloods would entertain their mistresses at "oyster parties" [*Dutch Art*, 196-97], the woman typically sitting upon the man's knees. Jan Steen's 'Girl Offering Oysters' (c. 1658) is in the same tradition.

117.5 [69]: *the clapper from the bell*: a phrase used in 'Recent Irish Poetry' to mock Austin Clarke, who from the 'Cattle Drive in Connaught' to 'The Pilgrimage' continued to display the "trick of tongue or two," and remove, by ingenious metrical operations, "the clapper from the bell of rhyme" [*Disjecta*, 72]. Compare Clarke's introduction to *Pilgrimage and Other Poems*:

> Assonance, more elaborate in Gaelic than in Spanish poetry, takes the clapper from the bell of rhyme. In simple patterns, the tonic word at the end of the line is supported by a vowel rhyme in the middle of the next line. Unfortunately the internal patterns of assonance and consanance in Gaelic stanzas are so intricate that they can only be suggested in another language.
> The lack of double rhymes in English leads to an avoidance of words of more than one syllable at the end of the lyric line, except in blank alternation with rhyme. A movement constant in Continental languages is absent. But by cross-rhymes or vowel-rhyming, separately, one or more of the syllables of longer words, on or off accent, the difficulty may be turned: lovely and neglected words are advanced to the tonic place and divide their echoes.

The exaggerated acoustics that follow ("A kiss from Wylie ... this slow-motion osmosis of love's spittle"), illustrate the technique. The phrase originates in Swift's 'A Letter of Advice to a Young Poet'; Clarke was probably aware of the allusion, which "Swift gave us for jest":

> Rhiming is what I have ever counted the very Essential of a good Poet: And in that Notion I am not singular; for the aforesaid Sir P. Sidney has declar'd, That the chief Life of modern Versifying consisteth in the sounding of Words, which we call Rime; which is an Authority, either without Exception or above any Reply. Wherefore, you are ever to try a good Poem as you would a sound Pipkin, and if it rings well upon the Knuckle, be sure there is no Flaw in it. Verse without Rime is a Body without a Soul, (for the chief Life consisteth in the Rime) or a Bell without a Clapper; which, in Strictness, is no Bell, as being neither of Use nor Delight.

117.6 [69]: *a breve tied*: a "breve" is a single note equivalent to two whole notes; "tied" it is held from one bar into the next, and thus extended; "demi-semiquavers" are 32nd notes. The cultivated reader will ignore the analogy between bell and clapper, mouth and tongue; nor ponder 'osmosis' as the diffusion of fluid through a semi-permeable membrane until there is equal concentration on either side.

118.1 [69]: *exceptionally anthropoid*: an unfortunate regression to Tenerife and Köhler's discussion of the apes [see #5.1], where the word 'anthropoid' is used excessively.

118.2 [69]: *Enter Cooper*: a dramatic entrance, suitably phrased.

118.3 [69]: *turned off*: dismissed from employment, the phrase somewhat archaic even as used by Swift in his dismissal of a servant [*Letter to Stella*, XLIV]: "He is drunk every day & I design to turn him off as soon as ever I get to Ireld." It appears in *A Tale of a Tub* [61-62] as a metaphor for hanging, but is introduced here for the sake of the bad joke on the next page.

119.1 [69]: *I adjure thee*: to 'adjure' is to entreat solemnly, as in Matthew 26:63: "I adjure thee by the living God, that thou tell us whether thou be the Christ, the Son of God."

119.2 [69]: *acasthisia*: in the Supplement to the *OED* this word is defined as "the inability to sit down," and this given as the sole citation. Stekel's *Psychoanalysis and Suggestion Theory* [23] uses it of a patient with peculiar problems with his posteriors. His point is that psychoanalysis gives deeper insight into the mechanisms of neurosis that would be possible by any other method; Beckett's, perhaps, that Cooper's mechanisms of behavior are not thus explicable.

119.3 [69]: *Euston . . . to Dun Laoghaire*: the standard route from London to Dublin: by train from Euston Station to Holyhead; then by steamer to Dun Laoghaire, previously Kingston (as in the French translation), the passenger terminal for Dublin close to Beckett's Foxrock home.

119.4 [70]: *his glass eye bloodshot*: glass eyes may deteriorate because of the erosive effects of saline moisture, the roughened surface contributing to further inflammation of the socket. I trust the reader has enjoyed this note.

119.5 [70]: *a large whiskey*: as the spelling indicates, Irish rather than Scotch.

120.1 [70]: *a glorious gin-palace*: more than a pub; rather, an establishment of the kind (glass, chrome and Chelsea chintz) becoming infectious in the 1930s, and later endemic. The description combines Blake's visions with Milton's *Paradise Lost* [III.621-24] and St. John's New Jerusalem [Revelation 22:17], with the God of Genesis stretching out his hand for good measure. Turner's *The Angel Standing in the Sun*, in the Tate, is another glorious possiblity.

120.2 [70]: *a mental note of the number*: never divulged to the reader [see #153.3].

120.3 [70]: *the defence of West Brompton*: combining the idiom of a football pools collector with that of the narrator of 'From an Abandoned Work' [*Complete Short Prose*, 157], his mind "always on the alert against itself."

120.4 [70]: *Pantagruel had him by the throat*: Pantagruel, son of Gargantua, was so called "for *Panta* in Greek is as much to say as all, and *Gruel* in the Hagarene language doth signify thirsty" [Rabelais, II.2]. He was born in the great drought that lasted 36 months, 3 weeks, 4 days, 13 hours and a little more; and from his birth until the culmination of his search for the Holy Bottle was distinguished by the saltiness of his throat, which required continuous slaking. The closest echo of Beckett's phrase appears to be Rabelais [III.li, 65]: "Pantagruel held them by the George" [i.e, the 'gorge,' or throat].

121.1 [70]: *at perigree*: by striking coincidence, the same phrasing as at the start of chapter 3.

121.2 [70]: *the palatial tantalus*: the radiance is the effect of moonshine (no pun intended); the irony, that of closure: Tantalus, in the depths of Hades, was unable to drink [see #21.4].

121.3 [71]: *a fusee*: a long, large-headed match or spill, capable of burning in a wind; by striking coincidence, Cooper has one on him. Even so, he would be unaware of Baudelaire's *Fusées*, short prose-poems illuminating Parisian squalor. One might note Cooper's translation, faster than a zebra, from gin-palace to house.

121.4 [71]: *an earth closet*: a primitive water closet, with earth as the deodorizing element; more simply, a filthy "long-drop" WC.

121.5 [71]: *Wapping*: a run-down dockside area of East London, on the beach of which pirates used to be hanged, to await three turnings of the tide.

122.1 [71]: *contumely*: from L. *contumelia*, "insult"; thus, rudely and with contempt.

122.2 [71]: *begging without singing*: the typescript reads "without a licence"; Cooper's language of incarceration is that of the many Irish political prisoners obliged to be guests of His Majesty, although not all would spend their time so productively.

122.3 [71]: *the G.P. days*: Beckett listed in the *Whoroscope* Notebook several alternatives: General Practitioner, General Paralysis, Glans Penis, God Psittacus, Graduate in Pharmacy, Gloria Patri, Great Power, Gonococcus Paraclete. Cooper presumably means "Grand Parade."

122.4 [71]: *those happy days*: an anticipation of the 1962 play by that title; but here, perhaps, avoiding 'Love's Old Sweet Song' and Joyce's "dear dark days beyond recall."

122.5 [71]: *puppets*: the phrase "who is not a puppet" was added to the typescript, perhaps in response to McGreevy's comment that he found the characters lovable: Beckett was surprised and delighted, but confessed to finding them hateful [July 7, 1936]. As Leslie Daiken's Trinity notes indicate, 'puppet' was frequently used by Rudmose-Brown, and Rachel Dobbin confirms this use by Beckett when lecturing on Racine: "The artist himself was changing all the time and his material was constantly in a state of flux, hence you had to do something to organize this mess, but not make puppets and set them in motion" [*Interview*, 7]. The famous instance of author as puppeteer is Thackeray, who concludes *Vanity Fair* thus: "Come, children, let us shut up the box and the puppets, for our play is played out." O'Hara cites Valéry's phrase: "*il avait tué la marionette*" [Fr. "he had killed the puppet"; *Monsieur Teste*, 27], which Beckett had used in a 1934 review of Rilke. He points to Schopenhauer's 'On Genius' [*WWI*, III.3.xxxi, 152], which likens the intellect of the normal man to "a complex set of wires, by means of which each of these puppets is set in motion," as compared to the genius, likened to a living man playing along with the famous large puppets of Milan ['Beckett Backs Down,' 40-41]. According to Schopenhauer, only the man of genius can escape the bonds of necessity and master the Will. It is not certain that Murphy should be so differentiated: on p. 37 he was described as throwing his voice into an infant's whinge, and his end makes a mockery of his apparent free choice to return to Celia.

123.1 [72]: *You split on him . . . he splits on you*: an early instance of what was to become a defining quality in Beckett's writing, two individuals related (as Mercier to Camier, Vladimir to Estragon, Hamm to Clov) by a bond as inexplicable as it is indissoluble.

124.1 [72]: *Frankenstein's daemon . . . De Lacey*: a tale of Gothic terror, *Frankenstein, or the Modern Prometheus* was published by Mary Shelley in 1818. Frankenstein is the student who learns to impart life to inanimate matter, and makes a soulless monster out of fragments of men picked up from cemeteries, charnel houses and operating rooms, galvanizing it into life. The creature is endowed with superhuman strength, and learns something of emotion, but is revolting in appearance and inspires loathing in whoever sees it. The one exception is De Lacey, an old blind man who offers friendship and sympathy, until others drive the creature away. Lonely and miserable, it wreaks revenge upon its creator, and murders Frankenstein's brother and his bride, before fleeing to the Arctic. The student follows it there, but dies in the pursuit, and the monster, claiming that death as its last victim, disappears to end its own life.

125.1 [72]: *the effort of shedding tears*: a practical demonstration of Freud's principle of the relationship between pleasure and pain.

126.1 [73]: *lech*: neither the obsolete meaning of a look or a glance, nor the Celtic sense of the top stone of a cromlech, but a metallurgic reference to gold ore which has been worked out, washed and partially treated with lime (as such, ready to be "resolved," or further refined). The Supplement to the *OED* simply cites Beckett's usage as an early instance of a back-formation from 'lechery,' thereby missing much of the wit.

126.2 [73]: *a menstruum*: from L. 'menstruus,' "monthly"; in alchemy, a solvent, so-called because it was supposedly efficacious only at the period of Full Moon.

126.3 [73]: *her erogenous zones*: those parts of the body the stimulus of which arouses sexual desire. Beckett would refer to Freud's disciple and biographer as "Erogenous Jones."

127.1 [74]: *nothing to be done*: anticipating the famous refrain in *Waiting for Godot*.

127.2 [74]: *the Embankment*: an area of public access on the north side of the Thames, running from the City to Chelsea, its public benches traditionally a repose for the homeless and for those who forget to draw tramp—, I beg your pardon, trumps.

127.3 [74]: *St. James's Park*: the oldest Royal Park in London, once a marshy meadow and then a deer-park, with a lazary dedicated to St. James for fourteen destitute leprous maidens. It was redesigned by Charles II after the Restoration. The Park is bordered by Westminster and St. James and Buckingham Palaces, the opulence of which must be of comfort to refugees from the Embankment when enjoined (more in sorrow than in anger) to move on.

127.4 [74]: *St. Martin's in the Fields*: a celebrated church in Trafalgar Square, erected 1721-26 by James Gibbs on the site of an earlier structure and so named because it was "in the fields" between Westminster and the City; also known as "the Admiralty Church." The crypt, then bleak and cold, offers new agonies, having been converted to a cafeteria.

128.1 [74]: *this big push*: a metaphor drawn from the Western Front.

129.1 [74]: *in the middle of a fitting*: not so much a new dress as the plot tailored to meet the exigencies of the time-scheme.

129.2 [74]: *the better the day*: the proverb continues, "the better the deed"; the French translation reads, "A bon jour bonne oeuvre."

129.3 [74]: *the Saturday B. and I.*: the British and Irish Steam Packet ships, which left for Liverpool from Dublin's North Wall (scene of Eveline's paralysis in *Dubliners*). Sailings were both daylight and on the Saturday night, when berths could be booked for the nine-hour trip. Beckett's 'Che Sciagura' mentions "the B & I boat threading the eye of the Liffey on Saturday night" [*TCD: A College Miscellany*, xxxvi (November 14, 1929), 42].

130.1 [75]: *new life*: Dante's *Vita nuova* as espoused by Celia and Murphy [see #64.1].

130.2 [75]: *she stirred the fire in vain*: details in the first part of this final paragraph may be drawn from Burnet's *Early Greek Philosophy* [296-98], his discussion of Pythagorean cosmology: the "central fire" [296]; speculation about the other side of the moon [297]; and the sense of an earth suspended, rotating about its axis [298]. The pattern is repeated in his *Greek Philosophy* [92]. Miss Counihan, only just maintaining her equilibrium, may be experiencing the vertigo of finding herself no longer the center of a geo-centric universe.

131.1 [76]: *eleutheromania*: from Gk. ἐλευθερία, "freedom," and μαίνομαι, "to rage"; hence, a burning desire for freedom. Hölderlin's "Mnemosyne," from which Beckett had quoted in *Dream*, invokes "Elevtherä" as Memory's town. After the War Beckett would begin work on a play entitled *Eleuthéria*.

131.2 [76]: *which was worse*: in the *Whoroscope* Notebook Beckett had written: "Dilemma in Old Fortunatus—Give to Neary: Whether more torment to love a lady & never enjoy her, or always to enjoy a lady whom you cannot choose but hate." Thomas Dekker's *The Pleasant Comedy of Old Fortunatus* (1600), the curious recasting of a traditional tale of fortune, Virtue and Vice, presents in Act III.i Charles of Orleans, prisoner at the court of Athelstane, and very much in love with the covetous Agripyne, who amuses herself by posing him the question which Beckett (accurately) has noted. The reply of the Duke of Orleans is vehement and passionate: "But to love a lady and never enjoy her, oh it is not death, but worse than damnation, 'tis hell, 'tis—" The real-life Charles of Orleans was from 1415 until 1440 a prisoner in England, where he made a considerable reputation for himself as a poet of wit in the *amour courtois* tradition, which is invoked here. In the event, Beckett gave the sentiment to Miss Counihan, perhaps to equate her more closely with Agripyne.

131.3 [76]: *knotty points*: i.e., nice and knotty ones, quidlibets and quodlibets, paradoxes not easily resolved, as in Swift's *A Tale of a Tub* [169]: "I now proceed to unravel this Knotty Point." The ultimate knotty point, of course, is Mr. Knott of *Watt*.

131.4 [76]: *heads in the pillories of their shoulders*: provenance unknown: this is probably not Murphy's figure, even though he uses it [142]. Beckett might apply 'cang' (a Chinese wooden collar worn by criminals) to this kind of situation.

131.5 [76]: *the areas*: in many Dublin streets, the deep recesses between tenement and outer pavement. The most celebrated such area in literature is that of 7 Eccles Street, by descent into which Mr. Bloom lets himself into his house [*Ulysses*, 625-26].

131.6 [76]: *a fosse of darkness*: a 'fosse' is a ditch or trench, but in conjunction with the serrated edge spurting light there is an artistic or semi-heraldic touch to the composition, giving it a compelling beauty. The visual quality is marked, and this is the one moment in the novel that Miss Counihan is on her own, or that any sympathetic access to her feelings is granted.

8

132.1 [77]: *it came bobbing back to her*: as befits the Biblical exhortation [Ecclesiastes, 11:1]: "Cast thy bread upon the waters: for thou shalt find it after many days."

132.2 [77]: *insmell*: the Hopkins-like *haecceitus* of Miss Carriage's inscape, causing her (and others) considerable instress.

132.3 [77]: *pristine*: Miss Carriage uses the word in its accepted sense of "clean" or "spotless" rather than the precise sense of "in its earliest condition." Often casually applied to the scrubbing and restoration of public monuments.

134.1 [78]: *caper*: the Latin word, meaning "goat," assumed the sense of the smell of the armpits. The quality is here defined as "tragic", in accordance with Gk. τράγος, "goat," popular etymology deriving 'tragedy' from goat-song (according to Horace, the winner of a choral competition might receive as prize a goat).

134.2 [78]: *My poor child*: from the virgin Miss Carriage, this comes curiously.

134.3 [78]: *vermigrade*: wriggling with a worm-like movement; the earlier term was 'peristalsis' [#66.3]. The *OED* Supplement cites this as its sole example, calling it "rare."

134.4 [78]: *an Ægean nightfall*: unexpected, like a tropical nightfall (hence "suddenly"), as in the description "thirsting for heat and light" [*Molloy*, 30]. In the Dream Notebook [#715], Beckett recorded "The hour when darkness fills the streets", from Victor Bérard's *L'Odyssée*; to enter *Dream* [31] as "the Homeric dust of the dawn-dusk," and to be mocked in 'Draff': "the magic hour, Homer dusk, when the subliminal rats come abroad on their rounds" [*MPTK*, 197]. 'Ægean' thus stands in curious counterpoint to 'Homeric.'

134.5 [78]: *his throat cut in effect*: as a necessary consequence of the implicit semantic proposition, since it *is* a cut-throat razor (Beckett twice wrote in the *Whoroscope* Notebook: "Occam's cut-throat"). The incident derives from the real-life seizure of an "old boy" who lived opposite Mrs. Frost's in Gertrude Street, and an account of the suicide of an insane Chinese man in Gower Street [Knowlson, 20, 743; see also #196.4].

135.1 [79]: *the York and Caledonian Roads*: Brewery Road runs east-west between the two, the Perseverance and Temperance Yards equidistant between them [see #74.6].

136.1 [79]: *to consummate*: in compliance with Hamlet's soliloquy, suicide "a consummation / Devoutly to be wish'd" [*Hamlet*, III.i.63-64]. Felonies are more usually compounded.

137.1 [80]: *an "Oh"*: Murphy fails to appreciate that the Celia who drove him into the jaws of a job is not the same Celia who receives the announcement of his being hired with but an "Oh" [Hesla, 46]. Hesla relates this to *Proust* [13]: "we are not merely more weary because of yesterday, we are other, no longer what we were before the calamity of yesterday." The calamity here is the Old Boy's death.

137.2 [80]: *everted*: to 'evert' is to overthrow, to turn upside down or inside out, and more commonly used of the eyelid than the eye. A goat's eye is notably void, a postern to Nothing or an empty soul. Again, the motif of green and yellow.

137.3 [80]: *exalt*: from L. *exaltare*, "to raise up on high," as Job was exalted by God, or the beggar from the dunghill [I Samuel 2:7-8]. Compare the alchemical sense of purifying or refining (anticipating the excremental image to come). "New man" and "new woman" complement the "new life" on the heights of Islington [see #64.1].

138.1 80]: *the entire sublunary excrement will turn to civet*: identified by Ruby Cohn [*Comic Gamut*, 317] as deriving from Marston's *The Malcontent* [IV.v.110-11]: "the very muck-hill on which the sublunary orbs cast their excrements." A reference to "a little civet" (a musky perfume from anal secretions of the civet-cat) follows in the next scene (V.i.18). Lear longs for "an ounce of civet" to sweeten his imagination [*King Lear*, IV.vi.130]. The transformation of excrement to civet derives from Paracelsus, as refined by Sir Thomas Browne [*Vulgar Errors*, 2.iii] and picked up by Swift in *The Tale of a Tub* [165]: "*Paracelsus*, who was so famous for Chymistry, try'd an Experiment upon human Excrement, to make a Perfume of it, which when he had brought to Perfection, he called *Zibeta Occidentalis*, or *Western-Civet*, the back Parts of Man . . . being the *West*." Hence, perhaps, the immediate reference to the billions of "leatherbums," or workers in moleskin trousers. Browne, having defined the "posteriours" as the America or Western part of his Microcosm, turns to portable Boats, "made of Leather."

138.2 [80]: *more joy in heaven*: the parable of the lost sheep, as related in all the Gospels, but the wording reflecting Beckett's usual preference for Luke, here 15:4 and 15:7:

> What man of you, having an hundred sheep, if he lose one of them, doth not leave the ninety and nine in the wilderness, and go after that which is lost, until he find it?. . .
> I say unto you, that likewise joy shall be in heaven over one sinner that repenteth, more than over ninety and nine just persons, which need no repentance.

138.3 [80]: *this warren*: perhaps, a busier version of Moran's 'Hole' [*Molloy*, 141].

138.4 [80]: *a fourpenny vomitory*: a cheap means of inducing vomiting. The logic, admittedly tenuous, seems to be that if Murphy cannot hold down his perfectly balanced meal, then he will waste away until his breeches fall off.

138.5 [80]: *a marasmus*: from Gk. μαραίνω, to wither, or waste; an atrophy or wasting-away, without associated fever or apparent disease. Beckett recorded in the Dream Notebook [#464]: "baby died in a marasmus, rubbing his little thighs" (from Garnier's *Onanisme seul et à deux*, 232-34). He later used the word in a letter to Mary Manning, describing his trip to Germany as a failure [December 13, 1936]: "The physical mess is trivial, beside the emotional mess. I do not care, and don't know, whether they are connected or not. It is enough that I can't imagine anything worse than the mental marasmus, in which I totter and sweat for months. It has turned out a journey <u>from</u>, and not to, as I knew it was, before I began it."

139.1 [80]: *severs the connection*: bringing out the suppressed pun upon 'bleeder' [see #24.3], while echoing Volpone's "He at last our good will sever" [see #10.1], and preparing for the severance of kite and string at the end of the novel. That Murphy can use this expression means, presumably, that Celia has told him everything [see pp. 13 and 24].

139.2 [80]: *a niobaloo*: the hullaballoo of Niobe, daughter of Tantalus and wife of Amphion, King of Thebes, weeping for her fourteen children who were slain by Apollo and Artemis after she had boasted herself superior to Latona, who had only those two. Niobe was transformed by Zeus into a stone, which during the summer shed tears.

139.3 [81]: *XX Butler . . . Porter*: a slide down the social bannister, from Gentleman's Gentleman to the cellars. The pun (no longer an ex-butler) relates to Guinness XX, "Extra Stout Porter" (1820).

139.4 [81]: *the London-Liverpool express*: meeting the Saturday B & I [see #129.3]; more precisely, the London and North-Western Railway, running from Liverpool to Euston Station.

139.5 [81]: *clonic*: i.e., spasmophiliac [see #49.4]. The joke about the bottle of stout and a card party is lost in the suds, unless it is the old chestnut about the gambler who preferred, he said, "a full bottle in front of me to a full frontal lobotomy."

139.6 [81]: *Gilmigrim jokes*: as in *Gulliver's Travels* [I.5], where Gulliver, having drunk plentifully of a delicious wine called *glimigrim* [sic], very diuretic, is able to recycle it to good effect and put out the palace fire. Compare those Lilliputian jokes called 'Tom Swifties': "Houyhnhnms," he said, hoarsely.

140.1 [81]: *the dream of Descartes linoleum*: the "dim geometry" of exquisite design mentioned on p. 63. Descartes passed the winter of 1619 near Ulm, in Bavaria, thinking and meditating in the celebrated "poêle," a small room heated by a central stove [see #163.1]. According to Baillet [VI, 78ff], the germ of his great enterprise then developed, that of demolishing the edifice of traditional knowledge and constructing a new system upon different foundations. This endeavor caused him violent mental agitation, and, his brain on fire, he fell into a kind of rapture which prepared his exhausted mind for dreams and images and visions. On the night of November 10, having conceived the idea that the method of analytical geometry might be extended to other studies, he went to bed filled with this rapture, and had three curious dreams which confirmed both his sense of the way of life he must henceforth follow and the fundamental synthesis of mathematics and methodology.

140.2 [81]: *the gapes*: a disease in poultry, of which gaping is the obvious symptom.

140.3 [81]: *the stout porter*: when Belaqua tells this joke in 'Echo's Bones' [12], Lord Gall spoils the clonic effect by giving the right answer impatiently. The jest is omitted from the French translation, but repeated in *Watt*, the bitter stout porter appropriately named Powers (a brand of Irish whiskey).

140.4 [81]: *Tintoretto's Origin of the Milky Way*: Jacopo Robusti (1518-94), known as Tintoretto or the "little dyer," since his father was a *tintore*. He struggled for recognition, but became one of the greats of the Venetian school, celebrated for his mastery of color and depictions of the human form. The *Origin*, c. 1580, an oil in the National Gallery, London, depicts Jupiter's attempt to guarantee the immortality of his son by the mortal Alcmeme by holding up the infant Hercules to drink from the breast of the sleeping Juno, who, waking suddenly, spills her milk in two streams, one falling to form the lilies on the ground, and the other creating the milky way. Seeing countless points of light blurred by the distance, Moran thinks of "Juno's milk" [*Molloy*, 140]. In Murphy's less reverential response, but one compatible with the way Jupiter is holding the child and the look on Juno's face, the goddess has been awoken painfully by a nip on the nipple.

140.5 [81]: *gloom took its place*: in accordance with the precepts of Democritus Junior, Burton recommending mirth and laughter as a means of relieving melancholy, yet aware that such palliations can be at best temporary [*Anatomy* I.3.3, 278].

141.1 [82]: *if not this evening*: imitating Augustine's description of the non-eternal voice [*Confessions*, XI.vi], cited in the Dream Notebook [#189]: "For that voice passed by & passed away, began & ended; the syllables sounded & passed away, the second after the first, the third after the second, and so forth in order, until the last after the rest, & silence after the last."

141.2 [82]: *the pantaloons*: in the *Comedia delle arte*, a feeble old man, in spectacles and slippers, the foil of the clown, whom he abets in all knavery; the word deriving from the lower garment typically worn, with breeches and stockings all of a piece. Murphy alludes to Jaques's famous speech on the seven ages of man in *As You Like It* [II.vii.157-66]:

> The sixth age shifts
> Into the lean and slipper'd pantaloon,
> With spectacles on nose and pouch on side;
> His youthful hose well sav'd, a world too wide
> For his shrunk shank; and his big manly voice
> Turning again towards childish treble, pipes
> And whistles in his sound. Last scene of all,
> That ends this strange eventful history,
> Is second childishness and mere oblivion,
> Sans teeth, sans eyes, sans taste, sans everything.

141.3 [82]: *in Lydian mode*: one of the modes in ancient Grecian music, characterized as soft and effeminate. The Lydian is also the third of the four ecclesiastical modes, the others being Phrygian, Ionic and Doric [see #64.3].

142.1 [82]: *an execution*: hangings took place at Pentonville Prison from 1902, the last carried out on July 6, 1961; there was no particular day set aside for this [Mairi Turner to CA], but for Murphy the Good Friday image is to the fore.

142.2 [82]: *as though turned to stone*: not an allusion, but the critique of one: Schopenhauer, discussing the superiority of perception over reflection, argues that knowledge can only be new and enduring when *sight* has formed its foundation [*WWI*, II.1.vii, 246]. He illustrates his point by stating that a commonplace writer might describe profound contemplation or petrifying astonishment by saying: "He stood like a statue"; but Cervantes says: "Like a clothed statue, for the wind moved his garments." As if to outdo Schopenhauer and Cervantes in the appropriateness and originality of the expression (as *seen* by Celia, for the last time), Beckett completes the commonplace with a remarkable figure: "in the middle of a hornpipe."

143.1 [83]: *multiplied in their burlesque*: thus the capering newsboys mock Leopold Bloom, as seen from the Editor's office [*Ulysses*, 125]. There is a curious link between their playing football, Murphy's coat described as a "punctured ball" [141], and his hissing: as if to imply that the Job has penetrated the hermetically closed microcosm to release the vital element of air. A football, curiously, is the most common everyday manifestation of the dodecahedron [see #47.9]. Kennedy, even more curiously, thinks the boys are playing with an American football.

143.2 [83]: *nothing short of alms*: giving of alms is an act of charity, one of the seven corporeal works of mercy. The sentiment is repeated [154], with reference to pity.

144.1 [84]: *He gets out his razor*: as Knowlson suggests [206], the reasoning is a pastiche or parody of the Conan Doyle deductive logic. This is accentuated by the radical intrusion of the narrator into the privacy of what has been so far presented as a separate and unknowable monad (the consciousness of the Old Boy), not only to express the opinion that Miss Carriage's conclusions are all lies, but to offer precise details of the Old Boy's shaving habits.

145.1 [84]: *seizure*: the suggested punctuation makes the word sound like 'caesura.'

145.2 [84]: *Shrove Tuesday . . . Derby Day*: Shrove Tuesday, Pancake Day or Mardi Gras, is the Tuesday before Ash Wednesday, in 1935 on March 5th [Whitaker, 90]. Derby Day, when the Stakes are run (for two-year old colts and fillies), is with the Oak and the St. Leger one of the three classic races, in 1935 on Wednesday, June 5th [Whitaker, 584]. The choice of the Old Boy's festivities is perhaps explained by a fortuitous conjunction in Brewer: "Shrove Tuesday used to be the great 'Derby Day' of cockfighting in England."

145.3 [84]: *Felo-de-se*: suicide, the Anglo-Latin term meaning "felon of self." In 'Love and Lethe' Belacqua connives at his felo-de-se, but the narrator declares himself unable to discover how the resolution, finally as unsuccessful as Ronsard's *amour*, was formed, the motives being "subliminal to the point of defying expression" [*MPTK*, 95]. The Old Boy's motives are to Celia equally inexplicable.

148.1 [87]: *not of vacuum but of plenum*: the distinction is that of Democritus, as in the article on him in the *Britannica*, where the distinction between *plenum* (πλήρης) and *vacuum* (κενόν), each equally real, is carefully drawn [see #246.5].

148.2 [87]: *not of breath taken but of quiet air*: an echo of Keats's 'Ode to a Nightingale': "To take into the air my quiet breath." The line enters Belacqua's consciousness near the end of 'Dante and the Lobster.'

149.1 [87]: *the oakum of her history*: oakum is unpicked rope, used for caulking the seams of a ship when forced in with chisel and mallet, and sealed with pitch. "Picking oakum" was the common and brutal employment of those detained at His Majesty's pleasure in prison or workhouse. Doherty [120] defines the later Beckett voices as living off the scraps and fragments of a mind, picking and unpicking the "oakum of old words ill-heard ill-murmured."

149.2 [87]: *Penelope's curriculum*: the lesson given by the faithful wife of Odysseus to her suitors, whereby each night she would unpick the weaving done during the day, to keep her promise not to marry any of them until the work was done.

149.3 [87]: *hackled into tow*: retwining the metaphor of oakum in accordance with Ernst Haeckel's *The Riddle of the Universe* [see #66.1], and the formation of the foetal soul, not to be given birth, or "expelled." As were the suitors, upon the return of Odysseus. The image is associated with the post-mortem purgation of Belacqua [see #78.5], who must expiate his sins by dreaming through his life before he can attain paradisial innocence. Beckett, like Penelope, weaves various well-used threads into the one design.

150.1 [86]: *Lovely work, if you can get it*: the expected reponse from those who can't. In the original outline in the *Whoroscope* Notebook, Celia was to return to a wild afternoon of whoring, during which she would meet Cooper.

150.2 [87]: *the Round Pond*: Celia's course is clear: the water [see #14.6]. The Round Pond was artificially created when Kensington was refashioned by Queen Caroline [see #150.6]; it is perfectly circular, a few feet deep and about seven acres in area, near the intersection of several avenues running from various corners of the park (Celia contemplates taking the path southeast of the pond, but instead takes the northeast one). The pond is used by model boat enthusiasts of all ages, and is the venue for the kite-flying that so attracted Beckett's affection [see #25.1].

150.3 [87]: *the Piccadilly tube*: the best-known London Underground line. The first part of the line, Kensington to Piccadilly and thence to King's Cross, was begun in 1902 and opened in 1906; the continuation to the Caledonian Road followed shortly, and by 1932 the line reached Finsbury Park, with the extension to Cockfosters planned.

150.4 [87]: *the Serpentine*: the large body of water in Hyde Park [see #94.2], running E-W before turning north at Rennie's Bridge to form the Long Water that separates Hyde Park from Kensington Gardens. It was created by Queen Caroline in 1730 by enlarging the bed of the Westburne Stream to link several ponds into a wide straight canal, at a cost stated to be £6,000, but in reality thrice that. The scene of many a royal fête and celebration, it remained a filthy sewer until 1849 when it was drained and cleaned, and the sewerage diverted.

150.5 [87]: *Rennie's Bridge*: a five-arched stone construction, designed by George and John Rennie in 1826, dividing the Long Water from the Serpentine; effectively, the mid-point of the Hyde Park-Kensington Gardens complex.

150.6 [87]: *Kensington Gardens*: the eastern prospect of Hyde Park [see #94.2], some 275 acres. Originally a modest garden, it was enlarged and redesigned by Queen Caroline, wife of George I, and the Round Pond, Serpentine and Long Water were created. For many years the Gardens were closed to the public, but when George III moved from Kensington to Buckingham Palace the gates were opened daily to the respectably dressed. For many, they are still associated with the Edwardian elegance of J. M. Barrie, whose statue of Peter Pan (brought in overnight, so the children might think it the work of fairies) is its best-known feature.

150.7 [87]: *Victoria Gate*: a northern entrance to Hyde Park [see #103.4].

151.1 [87]: *the accident house of the Royal Humane Society*: on account of the many accidents that occurred at the Serpentine, George IV in 1794 gave a plot of land to the Royal Humane Society on the northern bank, near the Cockpit, to erect a house for rendering first-aid to drowning persons. This was replaced in 1834 by a later building, designed by J. B. Bunning in Decimus Burton style. In 1940 the building itself suffered an accident when damaged by a bomb; it was demolished in 1954, a plaque now marking the spot.

151.2 [87]: *the fountains*: there was originally a dirty duck-pond, a foot or so deep, at the head of Long Water near the Lancaster Gate, into which the Ranelagh sewer periodically discharged; it was transformed in 1860 into the present Italian Gardens, with filtering basins, fountains and ornamental works.

151.3 [87]: *the palace*: Kensington Palace, aligning the western prospect of the Gardens. The original house was acquired in 1689 for £18,000 by William III, and was rebuilt by Wren, Hawksmoor and Kent in fine brick. For some years it was the official residence of the monarch, and even after the move to Buckingham Palace it retained its Household status: Queen Victoria, whose statue stands before it [see #277.1], was born there.

152.1 [89]: *the Physical Energy of G. F. Watts, O.M., R.A.*: a twelve-foot equestrian statue in bronze, cast by George Frederick Watts (Order of Merit, member of the Royal Academy), and a replica of the central portion of the Rhodes Memorial on the slope of Table Mountain, Cape Town. It is in direct line of gaze opposite the statue of Queen Victoria, some 400 yards on the other side of the Round Pond. Beckett's phrasing, identical to that on the statue, was presumably copied from it. In a later allusion to this, Watt [20] lacks the energy to turn the other cheek.

152.2 [89]: *coupled abreast*: as tug and barge [15], again testifying to Celia's inner needs.

152.3 [89]: *the wrack*: the darkened clouds, which momentarily part. A small curiosity, for the *OED* defines 'rack' as clouds driven before the wind in the upper air, but insists that the 'w' form is erroneous ('wrack' meaning otherwise "wreck" or "ruin").

152.4 [89]: *viridescent*: i.e., slightly green; indicative of the changes throughout the novel whereby the original iridesence gave way to yellow and green [see #2.5 and #229.2]. The word is cited in the *OED* as rare, but the Supplement instructs "Delete *rare*," offering this instance.

153.1 [89]: *the Broad Walk*: a wide path, lined with lime trees, running north-south from the Black Lion Gate to the Palace Gate at the western end of Kensington Gardens [see #276.3].

153.2 [89]: *the District Railway*: the Metropolitan District line of the London Underground was an extension of the Metropolitan Railway through Notting Hill Gate and South Kensington (1867), with an extension from King's Cross and Liverpool Street into the City (1875), to form an Inner Circle linking central London to residential areas and the northern termini. Celia has a short walk from the Black Lion Gate to Notting Hill, then a longer one up the Caledonian Road, her "toil" replicating Murphy's daily struggle up that steady incline.

153.3 [89]: *a mental note of the number*: again, not communicated to the reader [see #203.3].

153.4 [89]: *to climb the stairs in the dark*: echoing Tennyson's "The great world's altar stairs, / That slope through darkness up to God" [*In Memoriam*, 55.4]. Compare *A la recherche* [*Swann*, I.45], Marcel mounting the staircase "contre-coeur" [Fr. "against his heart"].

154.1 [89]: *no bounds but alms*: see also #143.2: the sentiment is the more incongruous, given the derivation of 'alms' from the Gk. ἐλεημοσύνη, "pity."

155.1 [89]: *the steps resumed their climb*: the Purgatorial image of Celia's resumed travail is associated with Sidney's *Astrophel and Stella*, Sonnet XXXI: "With how sad steps, O Moon, thou climb'st the sky! / How silently, and with how wan a face." Wordsworth began a sonnet (XXIII) with these lines.

155.2 [89]: *The Candle of Vision*: an inspirational prose text by George Russell ('A.E.'), in which he peers through the windows of his soul (as Miss Carriage through key-holes) to see images created by the divine imagination and relate his vision of the far-off Many-Coloured Land to that of seers and writers of the sacred books. It is as bad as that sounds, an incongruous choice for the mercantile Miss Carriage to return to, having watched Celia ascend the stairs. In like manner, to while away the time and improve his mind, Mr. Case in *Watt* [228] reads *Songs by the Way*, by George Russell (A.E.), the book held out at arm's length. In the French translation, however, Beckett unveiled "*Roses de Décembre*, par Madame Rosa Caroline Mackworth Praed," but thereby lost the light of the candle which he had used in his 'Recent Irish Poetry' [*Disjecta*, 74], where he praised Thomas McGreevy for being aware that it is the act and not the object of perception which matters: "It is in virtue of this quality of inevitable unveiling that his poems may be called elucidations, the vision without the dip."

9

156.1 [90]: *Il est difficile*: from part 4 (April 11, 1927, 10:30 p.m.) of André Malraux's *La Condition humaine* (1933), a novel set in the troubled Shanghai of 1927. These are the words of Tchen, a kamikaze terrorist about to blow up the automobile of Chang Kai-Shek:

> Cette nuit de brume était sa dernière nuit, et il en était satisfait. Il allait sauter avec la voiture, dans un éclair en boule qui illuminerait une seconde cette avenue hideuse et couvrirait un mur d'une gerbe de sang. La plus vieille légende chinoise s'imposa à lui: les hommes sont la vermine de la terre. Il fallait que le terrorisme devînt une mystique. Solitude, d'abord: que le terror-iste décidât seul, executât seul; toute la force de la police est dans la déla-tion; le meutrier qui agit seul ne risque pas de se dénoncer lui-même. Solitude dernière, car il est difficile à celui qui vit hors du monde de ne pas rechercher les siens.

[Fr. "This night of fog was his last night, and he was satisfied with it. He was going to go up with the car, in a ball of light that would illuminate for a second this hideous avenue, and would cover the wall with a spray of blood. An ancient Chinese saying came to him: men are the vermin of the earth. Terrorism had to have a mystique. Solitude, first: so the terrorist might make decisions alone, carry them out alone; all the strength of the police comes from informing; the murderer who acts alone does not risk denouncing himself. Solitude to the end, because it is difficult for one who lives outside the world not to seek his own kind."] As Pilling notes [*Beckett before Godot*,

145-47], Tchen's satisfaction is bound up with his knowledge that his death has a purpose, the removal of a political adversary; whereas Murphy, who would never die for anything as vulgar as a cause, finds satisfaction hard to come by, and knows even less about his death than about his life: again, the "fundamental unheroic" [see #4.2]. What appealed to Beckett was less the political irony (the car does not contain Chang, and Tchen's death rebounds on others; he is not, as he thinks, alone) than Malraux's sense of solitude and self: *la possession complète de soi-même* [Fr. "the complete possession of one's self"], which only death can penetrate. Malraux follows the botched explosion with a terrifying account of Tchen's associates thrown live into the furnace of a train, which perhaps confirmed the *modus morendi* of Murphy's fate. In a letter to Thomas McGreevy [January 10, 1936], Beckett complained that he had been recently unable to work, but had suddenly seen how Murphy's position was a "break down" between Geulincx's *Ubi nihil vales* [see #178.9] and Malraux's assertion: the tension of the chapter is tautly strung between these two poles.

156.2 [90]: *The Magdalen Mental Mercyseat*: see Exodus 25:17-22, the description of the Ark of the Tabernacle with its mercyseat of pure gold, whence God would commune to Moses. O'Hara notes that for Murphy it replaces the rocking chair [*Hidden Drives*, 48]. The Bethlem Royal Hospital dates from 1247, when the Priory of St. Mary of Bethlehem, Bishopsgate, was founded by Simon Fitzmary. By 1329 it was a hospice, but the first reference to it as a hospital for the insane is 1403. In 1816 the first State Criminal Lunatic Asylum was opened at Bethlem. From 1857 paupers were no longer admitted, in 1863 the criminal wings were demolished, and in 1882 provision was made for paying patients. In 1925 the governors bought the Monks Orchard Estate, south of London, and in 1930 the hospital moved there (the original site is now the Imperial War Museum).

156.3 [90]: *on the boundary of two counties*: the Bethlem Royal Hospital, Monks Orchard Road, Beckenham, Kent, on the meridian of Miss Greenwich, has most of its wards in Surrey but one in Kent. The injunction to move up a little in the bed, a phrase Beckett had used in an oddly-appreciative review of Pound's *Make It New*, 'Ex Cathezra' [*Disjecta*, 79], may meet the expressed wish of our native to be in two places at once [32]. It anticipates Spike Milligan's *Puckoon* [84], where the public bar crosses the Ulster border and customers are crammed into the few square feet where the drinks are 30% cheaper.

156.4 [90]: *the one sheriffalty*: alternatively, 'shrievalty'; the word pertains to the office or jurisdiction of a sheriff, rather than the county, or shire. It applies strictly to counties ending in 'shire,' so is doubly inappropriate here.

156.5 [90]: *Mr. Thomas ("Bim") Clinch*: while the name echoes Swift's 'Clever Tom Clinch, Going to be Hanged' (1727), Beckett's choice of *Clinch* for the nepotistic clutch is otherwise appropriate. Bim has a fancy for Ticklepenny not far short of love, and Murphy finds the possibility of "clinching" (with a clench) his retreat into the little world in the service of the Clinch clan "very pretty" indeed [179]. There was, incidentally, a J. D. Clinch on the staff at TCD, but Bim's original, Brian Ryder suggests, was one Kenneth Cantle, the nurse in charge of the wards at the Bethlem Royal Hospital, whose father and uncle had founded Bethlem's orchestra; a photo of them is visible in the waiting-room (Brian Ryder to CA). Ruby Cohn has noted Beckett's fancy for the names 'Bim' and 'Bom' [*Just Play*, 177]:

> From the time of his collection of stories *More Pricks than Kicks*, written over two decades earlier, Bim and Bom recur sporadically in Beckett's work.

Russian clowns whose comic routines contained—and were allowed to contain—criticism of the Soviet regime, they became for Beckett emblems of
human cruelty, disguised under a comic garb.

The names first appear in 'Yellow' [176], when Belacqua contemplates effacing the
proper self "in favour of Bim and Bom, Grock, Democritus"; then (huge, red and
whiskered) in *Murphy*; and after that in two passages later deleted from the manuscripts of *Waiting for Godot* and *Endgame*. They emerge as 'Bom,' 'Pim' and 'Bem' in
How It Is; are heard faintly in *Ping*; and take their curtain call as 'Bam,' 'Bem,' 'Bim'
and 'Bom' in Beckett's last completed dramatic work, *What Where*, with its hints of
unspecified cruelty: "You gave him the works?" Knowlson suggests [744] that the
names may echo Richard Aldington's "Enter Bim and Bom," the Epilogue to his 1931
novel, *The Colonel's Daughter*, where the two Russian clowns are set down on an
English football field to comment upon the degeneration of English society.

As for 'Thomas': there is a tinkling asymmetry between the identical Clinch twins,
Thomas (Tom) as "Bim" and Timothy (Tim?) as "Bom" [165], but more resonant is the
echo of the celebrated bell of Christ Church, Oxford, "Great Tom." This was moved in
1545 from the center tower of Osney to St. Frideswide's steeple; recast several times
over the next hundred years; and when placed over the Faire Gate, as Tom Tower was
then known, the 17,000 pound bell bore this inscription:

> *In Thomae laude resona*
> *Bim Bom sine fraude*
> ("I sound forth in praise of Thomas, Bim! Bom! without false promise.")

The bell was recast in 1680, with a new inscription: "*Magnus Thomas Clusius
Oxoniensis Renatus Aprilis VIII Anno MDCLXXX*." It rang out on Restoration Day, May
29, 1684. "Bim! Bom!" thus faded into fable, leaving only the name "Great Tom" (alluding to that other great Becket, Thomas). Beckett does not refer again to the bell, and
rarely to Oxford (Belacqua says of families, "they make us magdalen" [*Dream*, 177]),
but the B-flat from Tom Tower mingles with the Pavlovian percussion of Skinner's in a
curiously compelling cracked tone.

157.1 [91]: *your one-six-eight*: i.e, £1.6.8, for ten days' work, which works out at about
4d an hour, menial for even a pot poet (he pleads for an extra halfpenny). As Rabinovitz
notes ['Unreliable Narrative,' 59]: "Ticklepenny accepts this offer without realizing that
after working ten days he is owed one-third of five pounds, or one-thirteen-four (one-six-
eight is a third of four pounds). The exact value of 'Bim's fancy . . . not far short of love'
may be difficult to compute, but it is clearly less than six shillings eightpence." For one
terrified of losing his pay, Ticklepenny seems strangely unaware of what he risks.

157.2 [91]: *recondite*: from L. *reconditus*, "hidden"; hence, deeply concealed, or
beyond ordinary understanding.

158.1 [91]: *He would be expected*: much of this matter is recorded in the *Whoroscope*
Notebook, Beckett taking notes from his visits there, from his talks with Geoffrey
Thompson, his friend who worked there as a psychiatrist, and from a nurse whom he
quizzed (the Notebook reads at one point "endorsed by nurse" [Knowlson, 209]). Beckett
did not work at a mental hospital (the Calder dust-jacket is wrong to say so), but his close
observation of the Bethlem Royal and his acute interest in the process of psychoanalysis he was undergoing led to the incorporation of precise details. "Sterilize when in
doubt" refers, one assumes, to the instruments of palliation rather than the patients.

158.2 [91]: *honour and obey*: an incongruous echo of the marriage service, compounded by the equally irrelevant reference to foot and mouth, a disease of cattle.

159.1 [92]: *No patient was dead*: recorded in the *Whoroscope* Notebook, as garnered by Beckett during a visit to the Bethlem Royal. There is no suggestion of "in flagrante" there.

159.2 [92]: *Skinner's House*: even in 1935, rat-infested. Although the work of Burrhus Frederic Skinner was as yet in its troubled infancy, the conflict between Behaviorism and other contemporary schools was marked, with Skinner building his reputation as heir to Watson and Pavlov, and the scourge of consciousness [see #165.3].

160.1 [92]: *certified*: as the novel implies, most inmates at the Bethlem Royal were admitted without certification, as Voluntary or Temporary patients. Dangerous and criminal psychotics were constrained at the Maudsley, Denmark Hill.

160.2 [92]: *not hopeless*: a distinction made in the admission criteria [Whitaker, 195]: "The buildings form a modern and efficiently equipped hospital for the reception and treatment of mental and nervous ills. Patients of the educated classes—presumably curable—are eligible for admission. Visiting days: Males, 1st and 3rd M; females: 2nd and 4th M. Physician Supt., J. G. Porter Phillips, M.D., F.R.C.P."

160.3 [92]: *sanguine punctilio*: confident attention to the smallest points of conduct and manners; 'punctilio' deriving from L. *punctum*, "a point," as in a nice point of honor.

161.1 [92]: *peraldehyde*: a volatile colorless fluid $(CH_3CHO)_3$ formed by the polymerization of formaldehyde, with a suffocating smell. Used in medicine as a hypnotic and a sedative.

161.2 [92]: *slosh*: the word may here mean "mush" rather than "billiards" [see #168.4].

161.3 [93]: *Two large buildings*: there were separate sleeping quarters at the Bethlem Royal Hospital for female and male nurses. The Nurses' Home was immediately inside the main gate, to the left, while the male quarters were further down Monks Orchard Road, at some remove from both the main block and the female quarters [Patricia Allderidge to CA].

161.4 [93]: *Cleopatra*: Queen of Egypt, celebrated for her beauty. At her father's death in 51 BC she became joint sovereign with her brother Ptolemy. Dethroned by his guardians, she was restored by Julius Caesar, who, less fussy than Murphy, gave her a son, Caesarion; thereafter, the oft-told tale of barges and burnished thrones, Antony, Actium, and the asp.

161.5 [93]: *the first cyanosis of youth*: i.e., when he was "green," not so much in his salad days as afflicted by a blue jaundice, the effect of insufficient aeration of the blood, an outward and visible sign of the irregular heart.

162.1 [93]: *a garret in Hanover*: explained by Janvier [27] as an image of the Leibniz monad, on the basis of the French translation which adds: "dans la belle maison renaissance de la Schmeidestrasse où avait vécu, mais surtout en était mort, Gottfried Wilhelm Leibnitz" [Fr. "the beautiful Renaissance house on the Schmeidestrasse, where Gottfried Wilhelm Leibniz had lived, and above all had died"]. Beckett's speculation arose only after his visit to the house in 1937. He may be drawing on personal memories of his little room "like a *chambre de bonne* at the top of the Trianon Palace Hôtel" [Knowlson, 145], where he wrote *Dream* in 1932; or the garret of his father's offices at 6 Clare Street, Dublin, which had a skylight and was heated by gas, and in which much of *Murphy* was written [O'Brien, 131, 361]. Swift's narrator claims to be writing *A Tale of a Tub* in a garret [169]. There was no such attic in the Nurses' Homes at the Bethlem Royal, where the sleeping quarters were heated from the boilerhouse.

162.2 [93]: *a mansarde*: a garret differs from a mansarde in having walls, however short, beneath a sloping roof; whereas a mansarde, as devised by François Mansarde (1588-1666), French architect, has a curb roof, the rafters of which, instead of forming an inverted 'V,' are broken on each side into an elbow to give added height.

162.3 [93]: *a strict non-reader*: this comes well from the ex-theological student who rests on Campanella and Bishop Bouvier, and has absorbed the pre-Socratic philosophers through the posterns of his withered soul. It reflects the advice of Thomas à Kempis, Beckett's model for the fundamental unheroic, to restrain oneself from an inordinate desire for knowledge, for therein lurks great distraction and delusion [*De Imitatione Christi*, I.ii.2].

163.1 [93]: *I must have fire*: not so much a desperate ploy to an ending, as what Ruby Cohn terms "a cogent Cartesian reminder" [*Comic Gamut*, 50]; Descartes's predilection during the years in Holland for warmth and solitude, as expressed by Baillet [33]: "il demeurait tout le jour enfermé seul dans un poêle, où il avait tout le loisir de s'entretenir de ses pensées" [Fr. "he would spend all day shut inside a stove (i.e., a small heated room), where he had the leisure to entertain his thoughts"]. The outcome of this *enchauffage*, or mental microwaving, was the celebrated triad of dreams of November 1619 [see #140.1]. From the outset fire was elemental in the protagonist's fate, 'X' and 'H' clarified together until finally consumed: "fire *oder was*" [see #23.2]. Beckett returned to this theme, discussing Murphy's journey to the self in terms of his freedom of choice "when the fire comes" [German Diary 4, January 18, 1937; see #4.2].

163.2 [94]: *aery*: a paronamasia has been attempted, the French translation ignoring the eagle's nest, or aerie, to accentuate the "aire vertigineuse."

163.3 [94]: *the point . . . extension*: a Euclidean jest, a point having position but not magnitude (that which is left when the two lines of an angle are removed); and a line having extension, in the sense of existing geometrically in space.

164.1 [94]: *an aposiopesis*: in rhetoric, a sudden breaking off in mid-sentence, in passion or anger, as if from a reluctance to proceed. As Quintilian notes [IX.ii.54], it indicates

164.2 [94]: *a small Valor Perfection*: a brand of kerosine-burning stove, the name at odds with the fundamental unheroic.

165.1 [94]: *a bijou edifice*: a jewel-like building of elegant workmanship. The Bethlem Royal mortuary is indeed brick, but tucked away more discreetly than this suggests. Patricia Allderidge, Archivist at the Hospital, has suggested that Beckett here blends the features of the real mortuary with those of the lovely brick Gate-house [letters to James Knowlson and CA]. My suspicion, which she does not favor (since 'bijou' no longer applies), is that the "real" model for the fictional mortuary is the equally lovely brick chapel close by, which has a forecourt of lawn and flowers, although not those specified here.

165.2 [95]: *traveller's joy . . . self-clinging ampelopsis . . . a bay of clipped yews*: the mortuary is surrounded by a bay of rhododendrons, rather than yews (there is a yew hedge in front), but 'bay' anticipates the later "hopeless harbour-mouth look" [see #259.5]. The profusion of traveller's joy (*Clematis vitabla*), a climbing plant with white flowers, intimates the "bourne from which no traveller returns" [*Hamlet*, III.1.79-80], and the "self-clinging" of the ampelopsis (or Boston Ivy) is a subtle sweet.

165.3 [95]: *a double obelisk*: the model for Skinner's appears to have been Tyson House, which had a double obelisk shape, and was one of the two wards (Whitley House the other) to combine male and female patients, men in the East Wing and women in the West. The two "convalescent houses" were Fitzmary House for women and Gresham House for men. All four were built of red brick with stone facings, rather than Norwegian gray.

165.4 [95]: *the battle . . . between the psychotic and psychiatric points of view*: the distinction mirrors that between *psychosis* and *neurosis*, the former a pathalogical condition but the latter associated with abnormalities such as anxiety, depression, phobias and obsession—products of repression which are treatable [see #175.5]. The battle (likened to cock-fighting) is between those who consider the patients mad and those who see them as disfunctional.

165.5 [95]: *exit . . . chronic*: a reminder, from p. 160, that if the treatment rendered the prognosis hopeless then out went the patient.

166.1 [95]: *ex hypothesi*: according to what is supposed or assumed.

166.2 [95]: *a by-blow*: a child born out of wedlock. For the Clinch clan, see #156.5.

166.3 [95]: *a decapitated potence*: a tau cross, the neck and extremities cropped to resemble a crutch. Patricia Allderidge confirms the accuracy of this with respect to Tyson East and West.

166.4 [95]: *the sublimatoria*: where "wrecks" might express their unacceptable impulses in a socially acceptable form.

167.1 [96]: *the terms and orientation of church architecture*: the description is true of Tyson East, the male wing at the Bethlem Royal, which faces due east [Patricia Allderidge to CA]. The 'nave' (L. *navis*, "a ship") is the central part of the church, so named for the Ark of Noah which delivered mankind; the 'transepts' (L. *trans*, "across," and *septum*, "an enclosure") of a cruciform church are the arms of the cross cutting across the nave before the chancel-screen.

167.2 [96]: *mansions*: the "mansions of Bedlam" designate the cells of Bethlehem, visited by Boswell and Johnson [*Life*, May 8, 1775, 445], Johnson having earlier gone in the company of Mr. Murphy. Beckett wrote in his *Human Wishes* Notebook [BIF *3461/1*]: "He calls the cell in Bedlam the 'mansions' & the corridors the galleries" [this is not Boswell, but Croker's footnote, 1846]. He would use this in *Watt* and *Malone Dies*. Boswell's wit, an 18th century commonplace, derives from John 14:2: "In my Father's house are many mansions." For Augustine, 'mansio' [L. "a place of abode"] is designated the highest of the seven grades of being, a vision of truth which is not a stage but a goal, the final place of abiding [Brett, 346]; this may be implicit in Murphy's sense of asylum as sanctuary.

167.3 [96]: *in a notable clip, "pads"*: padded cells, intended to dissuade or prevent the patient from banging his head against the walls. The *OED* Supplement cites this as a first instance, but it is less an anticipation of the Hippies than a postmonition of Swift's *Tub*, where padded carriages are called *pads*. There are affinities with the digression on madness in Swift's *Tale*, Beckett's patients posed like Bedlamites, but the echoes are situational rather than sustained. Implicit is Swift's questioning of the right of any human to trust he is sane, and his contention that happiness is the perpetual possession of being well-deceived [see #170.1].

167.4 [96]: *heads or bellies according to type*: the distinction draws on Burton's *Anatomy* [I.1.3.iv, 113]: 'Of the species or kinds of Melancholy,' where it is said that the "species" (symptoms arising from the humors) are infinite, but may be reduced to three kinds:

> The first proceeds from the sole fault of the brain, and is called head-melancholy; the second sympathetically proceeds from the whole body when the whole temperature is melancholy: the third ariseth from the bowels, liver, spleen, or membrane, called mesenterium, named hypochondrial or windy melancholy . . .

167.5 [96]: *paranoids*: 'paranoia' is a general term for various mental disorders characterized by persistent delusions or hallucinations, e.g., grandeur or persecution. Beckett's interest in mental illness and psychoanalytic response was intensified by his therapy under Wilfred Bion and visits to the Bethlem Royal, and by his reading of Surrealists such as André Breton and Paul Éluard, whose poetry imitated the processes of mental disorder. For a special number of *This Quarter* (September 1932), edited by André Breton, Beckett translated several essays with titles such as 'Simulation of mental debility essayed,' 'Simulation of general paralysis essayed,' and 'Simulation of the delirium of interpretation essayed.' He also translated for Nancy Cunard's *Negro Anthology* (1934) a number of surrealist pieces.

167.6 [96]: *feverishly covering sheets of paper*: paranoia which manifests classic symptoms of Juvenal's *scribendi cacoethes*, or incurable itch for writing [*Satire* VII.52], which (in the Loeb translation) "becomes inveterate in your distempered brain." Beckett had recorded Juvenal's phrase in his Dream Notebook [#1018].

168.1 [96]: *their inner voices*: Beckett's fascination with this aspect of inner consciousness would form his greatest theme in the years to come: "the voice ... my voice" [*The Unnamable*, 393]. In the third Tavistock Lecture [72], Jung had argued that unity of consciousness was an illusion, because complexes could emancipate themselves from conscious control and become visible and audible, appearing as visions and speaking in voices. For Beckett, determination of his authentic voice would henceforth be both compelling and problematic.

168.2 [96]: *a hebephrenic*: from Gk. ἥβη, "youth," and φρήν, "mind"; a common form of schizophrenia or dementia praecox, associated with puberty and characterized by hallucination, in which the the subject, becoming more and more detached from reality, exhibits foolish behavior and becomes increasingly careless of personal appearance.

168.3 [96]: *a hypomanic*: one suffering from mild mania, or behavior characterized by elation and over-excitability; as opposed to a *hypermanic*, one with partial or complete disorientation, accompanied by violent behavior; both conditions may form part of the one depressive cycle.

168.4 [96]: *slosh*: i.e., billiards, as played in *Watt* [12-15], the night Larry was born. The typescript reads at this point 'snooker.' The pool table, for Beckett an image of the Newtonian universe, here degenerates to an incongruous fiasco.

168.5 [96]: *a Korsakow's syndrome*: "A form of toxic insanity, with neuritis and peculiar memory changes, most often due to alcoholism" [Jones, *Psycho-Analysis*, 707].

168.6 [96]: *an emaciated schizoid*: Knowlson reports [209] Beckett's recollection during a visit to the Bethlem Royal of standing five or six feet away from a schizophrenic who was "like a hunk of meat. There was no one there. He was absent."

168.7 [96]: *tableau vivant*: Fr. "living picture"; representations of scenes from literature or life depicted by motionless living individuals; a staple of the Victorian drawing-room. Joyce had used both the phrase and the technique in the 'Nausicaa' episode of *Ulysses*, and certain scenes of stasis in *Murphy* (Mr. Willoughby Kelly and Celia in chapter 2, or the ending of chapter 7) are composed in like manner.

168.8 [96]: *plutolaters*: idolatrous worshippers of Mammon. "One who worships wealth" is the definition given in the Supplement to the *OED*, this being the unique citation.

168.9 [96]: *self-immersed indifference to the contingencies of the contingent world*: the *reductio* of Occasionalism, in terms of Murphy's desire to immerse his self entirely in the mind, so that all demands of the macrocosm may be ignored. A complex philosophical tradition sustains this jest. As Windelband notes [398], Leibniz, like Galileo and Descartes, distinguished between truths that are self-evident (the opposite unthinkable), and facts of experience (the opposite possible). In the former, intuitive certainty rests on the *Principle of Contradiction*; with the latter, on the *Principle of Sufficient Reasoning*, which asserts a conditional necessity, or contingency. This distinction, which underlies Kant's analytic vs. synthetic reasoning, is fundamental to Schopenhauer, who explains (*WWI*, II.I.xvi, 354) why possessions and pleasures, which are goods, are nevertheless matters of indifference in a world independent of our will. This is followed [*WWI*, II.1.xvii, 374] with an explanation of why the world is contingent. The view of Spinoza, that would see it as a necessary existence, is false, since the consciousness of the non-existence of this world is just as possible as of its existence (he is criticising Kant's contention that everything contingent has a cause): "Even simple Theism, since in its cosmological proof it tacitly starts by inferring the previous non-existence of the world from its existence, thereby assumes beforehand that the world is something contingent." A pessimistic comment follows: "Nay, what is more, we very soon apprehend the world as something the non-existence of which is not only conceivable, but indeed preferable to its existence." For Schopenhauer contingencies are mere phenomena [*Fourfold Root*, §52, 188], and hence those of a world itself contingent even more so. Beckett recorded in the Dream Notebook [#184, less a quotation from than a summary of book X of Augustine's *Confessions*]: "Contingency—not to trust in the happiness of the world . . . Sustenancy, not to give way to the unhappiness of the world."

169.1 [97]: *the race of people*: an echo which presages that Murphy may find himself alien from the world he wishes to enter: in *Gulliver's Travels* [II.1] the hero is in Brobdingnag, where he compares the coarse skins of the inhabitants with the fair complexions of the Lilliputians, reflecting, however, that it was all a matter of proportion, and that (viewed from some sixty feet) the giants appeared "a comely race of people."

170.1 [97]: *the fool in league with the knave*: echoing Swift's *A Tale of a Tub* [174], and the definition of happiness: "This is the sublime and refined Point of Felicity called *the Possession of being well deceived*; The Serene Peaceful State of being a Fool among Knaves."

170.2 [97]: *Pilate's hands*: Pontius Pilate's act of washing his hands after delivering Christ to His accusers; the following sentence likens Ticklepenny to Barrabas, and Murphy to Christ.

170.3 [97]: *Wood's halfpenny*: since Charles II, the right to mint and circulate copper coins in Ireland had been a privilege farmed out to private individuals. In need of a legal coinage, as in England and Scotland, the Irish government in 1720 petitioned Parliament to introduce coins of guaranteed value. The petition was ignored, and a patent to issue the coins was granted by George I to William Wood, a hardware merchant (Swift calls him an Ironmonger), July 12, 1722, in return for handsome bribes paid to the king's mistress, the Duchess of Kendal. Irish indignation flared high, and was fanned by four letters from Swift, published pseudonomously under the name of M. B. Drapier, and full of vicious invective. The effect was to unite all Irish parties against Wood and Walpole, and to make Swift the hero of the hour, particularly when on October 27, 1724 a reward of £300 was offered for the apprehension of the anonymous writer, and Swift claimed the honor. Beckett studied the *Drapier Letters* at Trinity, in 1926.

171.1 [98]: *a spark-pistol*: a special flint for lighting gas stoves and heaters, activated by a small trigger which flicks a steel across the flint to create a spark.

171.2 [98]: *from the furtherest-fetched of visions to a reality*: from the universal to the particular, and thence the deficiencies of an Idealism accommodating forms to reality.

172.1 [98]: *tubes eked out with caesurae of glass*: Harrington [94-96] sees this as a "quite explicit" reference to Yeats's 'Vacillation' with its sense of life between extremities ending with a flaming breath, and argues the centrality of Yeats within the entire novel. This is dubious; recent attempts to reclaim Beckett for the Irish are chronic [Gael. *cronin*, "full of errors"].

174.1 [99]: *for the convenience of dwarfs*: the unusual plural (British spelling is typically 'dwarves') is presumably unintentional; not so (perhaps) the privy pun. No explanation is forthcoming of why the tap (which works rather like a chess clock) is turned off and the warning is not heeded.

174.2 [99]: *a little bird*: picking up Ticklepenny's 'little b—'; echoing the familiar "a little bird told me," but ignoring the popular superstition about death. Belacqua in 'Echo's Bones' [7] does what Lord Gall says, because a little bird has told him that his hour had come.

174.3 [100]: *the Club*: the Bethlem Royal had a social room for the use of the staff.

175.1 [100]: *Sleep son of Erebus and Night*: Murphy's version of the Orphic Theogony, or genealogy of the Gods, details of which vary. Some begin with Chronos, or Time, begetting Aether, Chaos and Erebus ['Darkness'], Aether in turn generating Phanes ['Light'] and Nux ['Night']; others affirm Night as first principle, begetting Chaos and Necessity. Aristophanes in *The Clouds* states that dark-winged night in the infinite hollows of Erebus bore a wind-egg, from which Eros or Phanes sprang. This parodies

Hesiod's *Theogony* [127], which states that from Chaos Erebus and Black Night were born, and that Night "lay in love" with Erebus to conceive Aether and Hemera ['Day']; Hesiod tells how Night brought forth by herself, "not loved by any God," Death and Sleep and the brood of Dreams. Milton's first *Prolusion*, 'Utrum Dies an Nox praestantior sit?' [L. "Whether Day is more Excellent than Night"], tells how Night was wanted as wife by the shepherd Phanes, but shrank into the incestuous embraces of her brother Erebus; Sleep is listed among the off-spring of that union.

175.2 [100]: *Sleep half-brother to the Furies*: the Furies were generated, according to Hesiod [*Theogony*, 185], by Gaia, or Earth, springing from the bloody drops which fell upon her when Uranus castrated himself; they are denizens of Hades [see #27.3]. The *Britannica* states that in Aeschylus [*Eumenides*, 321] they are the daughters of Night, and in Sophocles [*Oedipus at Colonus*, 40] those of Darkness (Erebus) and Earth.

175.3 [100]: *the etymology of gas*: the Dutch chemist J. B. Van Helmont (1577-1644) first isolated Gas by heating coal without air, and named it for the chaos of the ancients. As Kennedy notes [188], it was commonly supposed that the etymology was Du. *Geest*, "spirit." Burnet's discussion [*Early Greek Philosophy*, 7] of Hesiod's *Theogony* depicts Chaos as an attempt to picture the beginning of things: "as its etymology indicates, the yawning gulf or gap where nothing is as yet." This is footnoted: "The word χάος certainly means the 'gape' or 'yawn'"; this reflects its kinship to Gk. χάσμα, a gaping abyss.

175.4 [100]: *cretin was Christian*: another true etymology, from the Gk. χριστός, "anointed"; whence the French *chrétien*, which was applied in the dialects of Vallois and Savoy, first in pity and then contempt, to the congenital idiots of the Alpine valleys. Jung states that 'cretin': "comes from the saying 'il est bon chrétien.' You could not say anything else of them, but at least they were good Christians" ['Tavistock Lectures' II, 35].

175.5 [100]: *a neurotic into a psychotic?*: Otto Rank's *The Trauma of Birth* [72] notes the difference: *psychosis* is the disturbance of the relation to the outer world; *neurosis*, of the relation to the inner. This derives from Freud: "neurosis is the result of a conflict between the ego and its id, whereas psychosis is the analogous outcome of a similar disturbance in the relations between the ego and the external world" ['Neurosis and Psychosis,' 149]. Karin Stephen, in *The Wish to Fall Ill* (which Beckett had read), makes a similar claim [3]: neuroses are associated with mental abnormalities such as morbid anxiety, depression, phobias and obsession, as the products of repression (and thus treatable); whereas psychoses lead to insanity (presumably incurable). Beckett implies this distinction, which was accentuated by Jung in his fifth Tavistock lecture [167], when he defined a neurosis as a dissociation of personality due to the existence of complexes, which all possess. Jung then argued that if the split reaches the organic structure the dissociation becomes a psychosis, a schizophrenic condition wherein the complex lives an existence of its own.

176.1 [100]: *Let there be Heaven*: alluding to Genesis 1:6: "And God said, Let there be a firmament in the midst of the waters, and let it divide the waters from the waters." Beckett may have in mind St. Augustine's great meditation upon the theme, and his argument that the earth was not created out of nothing but that rather Chaos was created from nothing, and out of that (matter, without form) all things were made [*Confessions*, XII.viii, 298ff].

176.2 [100]: *Chaos and Waters Facilities Act . . . Chaos, Light and Coke Co.*: pedantically, The Gas and Waters Facilities Act, as passed by Parliament in 1934 to regulate domestic and industrial usage. The Gas Light and Coke Company, a London public utility company, had been granted a royal charter in 1812 and was responsible for the supply of gas for light and heating throughout the capital.

176.3 [100]: *Hell. Heaven. Helen. Celia*: by simple association (the only time in the novel that the reader has access to Murphy's interior), Murphy's mind moves from Hell to Heaven by way of Helen (Gk. ἑλένη, "a torch") and Celia (L. *caelum*, "heaven"): in the beginning was the pun. As O'Hara notes [*Hidden Drives*, 51], in a cosmos made up of Love and Strife, chaos lovingly mingles the elements. This is a crucial dream, for it suggests that Murphy in his mind cannot be fully committed to the little world because he is still drawn towards the big.

176.4 [100]: *a postmonition*: an intimation of past disaster, such as the aboriginal calamity of creation. The word, Beckett's variant of 'premonition,' has not yet reached the *OED*. Otto Rank, in *The Trauma of Birth* [18], quotes a curious sentiment from Wilhelm Stekel's *The Language of Dream*: "The water-closet appears in dreams as a typical representation for the womb." The postmonition thus acts as an oblique warning.

176.5 [100]: *turn the blind eye*: the association between Lord Nelson's disobedience at the Battle of Copenhagen and the proverbial ostrich with its head in the sand is perhaps explained by the vulgar meaning of 'blind eye,' that displayed by the ostrich with its head down.

176.6 [100]: *he needed a brotherhood*: given the Proustian sentiment, "we are alone" [*Proust*, 66], this assumes huge irony. Murphy's error is to believe the psychotic has achieved the true sanity of an autonomous self equally at home in both the inner and outer reality [Miller, 14].

177.1 [101]: *The nature of outer reality*: perhaps, Schopenhauer's refusal to admit the findings of empirical science [McQueeny, 163]. In particular, the statement at the beginning of the essay [*WWI*, I.i §5, 16] concerning "the foolish controversy about the reality of the outer world"; foolish because it assumes (perception arising through knowledge of causality) that the relation of subject and object is that of cause and effect, a split that Schopenhauer sees as central to Cartesian realism. In Karin Stephen's *The Wish to Fall Ill*, the "relation to reality" as the index of well-being is assumed, and neurosis defined as a lack of contact with such reality [222]. Treatment involves "the transference of the patient's microcosmic fantasies on to the analytic relationship to enable him to free himself from his unconscious delusions and gain contact with the real world" [238]; a successful outcome consists in the patient being released from the need to make such "transfer reactions," and enabled instead to react to present-day reality [228].

177.2 [101]: *illuminati*: a name [translation of Gk. φωτιζόμενοι] given to the baptized in the early Church, and subsequently assumed by two sects of enthusiasts—the *Alumbrados* in Spain, and the *Guérinets* in France—as well as the Rosicrucians. A note in the Oxford edition of Swift's *A Tale of a Tub* [186] may be Beckett's source of the irony: for Swift, the Writings of the *Illuminati* are fruitful in the Proportion that they are *dark*.

177.3 [101]: *the gulf*: an echo of the great gulf that separates Lazarus and Dives for all eternity [see #5.7]. Murphy might heed Schopenhauer [*WWI*, II.2.xix, 450] on the "impassable gulf" that lies between a man of great mind and a fool. Also, the *deep gulf between the ideal and the real*, between object and subject [II.1.xviii, 400]. He contends that "between the phenomenon and that which manifests itself within it, the thing in itself, there is a deep gulf, a radical difference, which can only be cleared up by the knowledge and accurate delimitation of the subjective element of the phenomenon, and the insight that the ultimate and most important conclusions concerning the nature of things can only be drawn from self-consciousness" [II.1.xvii, 382]. Compare Baudelaire's "gouffre interdit à nos sondes" [Fr. "gulf forbidden to our sounding"] from 'Le Balcon,' as invoked in Beckett's *Proust* [31].

178.1 [101]: *what the psychiatrists called exile*: a recurrent distinction [see #73.6], apparently intimating "a longing to return home," i.e., back to the womb.

178.2 [101]: *a colossal fiasco*: an antonym of the Biblical *fiat*, and used as a synonym of the visible universe, but in reality deriving from It. *fiasco*, "bottle" or "flask".

178.3 [101]: *as a place*: this notion is discussed by Harvey [235-36], in terms of Beckett's later tendency to think of the mind in spatial terms, as in the poem 'bon bon il est un pays' [Fr. "good, good, it is a country"]; one not unlike Dante's dark wood, but isolated, an island, where voices die before reaching its shores, and egress is difficult.

178.4 [101]: *gyves*: shackles, usually for the legs.

178.5 [101]: *the big world and the little world*: the age-old distinction between the Macrocosm and microcosm, the latter reflecting by laws of perfect proportion the wider workings of the greater whole. 'A little world' is used for the microcosm throughout Burton's *Anatomy* and Swift's *A Tale of a Tub*, but the phrase 'the big world' for the Macrocosm may be Beckett's formulation. Compare Donne's *Holy Sonnets* (1610) [V.1-2]:

> I am a little world made cunningly
> Of elements, and an angel sprite.

Schopenhauer uses the phrase [*WWI*, 2.xxii, 18]: "While to one man his consciousness only presents his own existence, together with the motives which must be apprehended for the purpose of sustaining and enlivening it, in a bare comprehension of the external world, it is to another a *camera obscura* in which the macrocosm exhibits itself:

> He feels that he holds a little world
> Brooding in his brain,
> That it begins to work and to live,
> That he fain would give it forth."

Compare Goethe's *Werther* [1774], which Beckett had been reading: "Ich kehre in mich selbst zurück und finde eine Welte!" [Ger. "I turn back into myself and find a world" (22 Mai)]; with the implication that such a world may be unsustainable: "Wenn wir uns selbst fehlen, fehlt uns doch alles" [Ger. "When we fail our selves, then everything fails us" (22 August)].

178.6 [101]: *the occasions of fiasco*: the disasters of the Big World, with an Occasionalist twist [see #178.9].

178.7 [101]: *the beatific idols of his cave*: the cave and its idols are not Plato's [*Republic* 520.c.1], but those of Bacon from the *Novum Organum*, Aphorism #39: "There are four classes of Idols which beset men's minds. To those for distinction's sake I have assigned names—calling the first class, Idols of the Tribe, the second, Idols of the Cave, the third, Idols of the Market-Place, the fourth, Idols of the Theatre." These are the illusions that lead men into error, category (2) *idola specus*, or idols of the cave, being those attributable to individual formation and character, as opposed to (1) *idola tribus*, those attributable to social organization, (3) *idola fari*, to the inadequacy of language, or (4) *idola theatri*, fallacious intellectual constructs like closed philosophical systems [Harvey, 44 n.19]. Beckett's precise source is Windelband [383]. He had earlier observed the idols in *Whoroscope*: "In the name of Bacon will you chicken me up that egg. / Shall I swallow cave-phantoms?" That image is drawn directly from Mahaffy [92].

178.8 [101]: *the beautiful Belgo-Latin of Arnold Geulincx*: Arnold Geulincx (1624-69) was a Flemish philosopher and metaphysician whose works, particularly the *Ethica*, were of lasting fascination to Beckett. Born in Antwerp, Geulincx studied philosophy and theology at Louvain, where he became Professor in 1646. In 1656, following charges prompted by his attacks on scholasticism and accepted religion (he would later forsake Catholicism for Calvinism), he was deprived of his position and left for Leiden. After a period of poverty, he was appointed Professor of Philosophy, and remained there to his death. Deeply influenced by the Cartesians, his works have their roots firmly in the rationalist tradition, and include commentaries on and annotations of Descartes's works. Geulincx published in 1662 and 1663 respectively the *Logica* and *Methodus Invendiendi Argumenta*, which provided the framework for his more significant works, the *Physica, Metaphysica* and *Ethica*, which were not published until after his death, the texts taken from manuscripts used in his classes.

The Occasionalists deeply affected the writing of *Murphy*, which makes the hero's declared lack of interest in the partial congruence of the world of his mind with the world of his body the more ironic [see #109.1]. Beckett had encountered Geulincx earlier, presumably at the *École Normale*, but his sustained reading of the *Opera* was in early 1936, about this point in the writing of *Murphy*. He would travel from Foxrock to Trinity to sit in the Long Room and read the works in Latin, taking some fifty typed pages of notes [Knowlson, 219], mostly from the *Ethica*, to be worked into the fiction. Beckett was fascinated, he told McGreevy, by its saturation in the *sub speciae aeternitatis* vision that is the only excuse for staying alive. Later he would tell scholars interested in his work that the *Ubi nihil vales* [see #178.9] was one place to begin, and that axiom, the central teaching of the *Ethica*, formed the foundation of doubt and self-worthlessness underpinning much of his subsequent work.

The Latin of Geulincx is indeed beautiful, and Beckett was impressed by its range from the clarity of logical dispute to the conceits and polished phrases of ethical persuasion. In his *Quaestiones Quodlibeticae* [L. "Various Questions" (1653-65)], Geulincx discusses a number of knotty points and recurrent topoi of philosophical dispute, among them [*Quaestio XXIV, Opera I*, 130-33]: "*Utra praestantior, Belgica an Latina lingua*" [L. "Whether the Belgian language is superior to Latin"], in which he discusses the Latin language, especially as used in Belguim, lamenting that it is no longer commonly spoken as it should be.

178.9 [101]: *Ubi nihil vales, ibi nihil velis*: L. "where you are worth nothing, there you should want nothing." This is the central axiom of the *Ethica* of Arnold Geulincx, whose very notion of virtue assumes that the true end of Reason is the love of God, this being the first proposition of his *Ethica*: "Virtus est rectae Rationis Amor unicus" [L. "Virtue is uniquely the Love of right Reason"]. As such, it is to be contrasted directly with Philautia, or love of the Self [see #216.6]. As Hesla points out [38], the *ubi nihil* formulation is the strict ethical consequence of the separation of mind and body:

The Being of the I is restricted to the act of thinking, and here it is radically free, for not even God can cause me to think or alter what I think or how I think. But the I does not enter the world of matter and extension, not even into its own body. Indeed, with regard to the body, it is merely the spectator. But since nothing of the I is invested in the realm of *res externa*, and since it can do nothing by itself, the I should set no value on it. The world of things does not affect and is not affected by the I. If the world is worth nothing, it is not worth being desired. *Ubi nihil vales, ibi nihil velis.*

The *Ethica* may be described as a book of the Cardinal Virtues [6], these defined (in a slight departure from tradition) as *Diligentia* (listening to the voice of Reason), *Obedienta* (compliance with the dictates of Reason), *Justitia* (to will no more nor less than Reason dictates), and *Humilitas* (the sense of the lack of one's worth before God). The latter is for Geulincx the core of his ethics (*Radix Ethices est humilitas* [28]), and, as such, of the greatest application to *Murphy*. *Humilitas* has two parts, both of which derive from the *Ipse te nosce* [L. "Know thyself"] of the Greeks [30]: *inspectio sui*, or looking into the self [32]; and *despectio sui*, or contempt of the self [37]. These are discussed specifically in terms of the ethical axiom, *Ubi nihil vales*, for by looking into oneself one realizes an essential lack of worth, *ibi nihil velis*, and by so doing one is led to despise and hence not to desire the material world (having inspected, one sets at naught). The axiom is repeated several times in the *Ethica*, the clearest statement being the footnote to the 'Annotata' [222-23]. It recurs in the *Metaphysica* and other writings; by singling it out, Beckett testifies to its centrality in both Geulincx and his own explorations. The remainder of the *Ethica* is concerned with a consideration of the obligations arising from this sense of one's condition. The further consequence [*Ethica*, 225] that, as a result of self-inspection and the discovery that one is worth nothing, one has no value until dead ("*ex Derelectione me*") underlies the value system in Beckett's later writings of the many derelicts who have this precise metaphysical definition of their being [see also #109.1].

179.1 [102]: *it was not enough*: as in the unpublished 'Echo's Bones,' where Belacqua contends: "It is not enough to be continent . . . you must be sustenant also . . . titter affliction out of existence." Lord Gall's asperic rejoinder, "Christian . . . bleeding science," points directly to St. Augustine [DN, #184] and "the first self-supporting steps of thought in the west."

179.2 [102]: *the intellectual love*: Murphy's perversion of that defined by Spinoza, whereby God loves himself [see #107.1].

179.3 [102]: *deplorable susceptibility*: reflecting another "ethical" axiom, that desire subverts indifference. Harvey suggests [267] that to Murphy the body, that part of him which exists in the macrocosm, is of negligible value: "Indeed, it is primarily a source of suffering. And where no value is attached, no desire is possible." Unfortunately for his thesis, this is the very principle subverted by the existence of deplorabilities such as Celia, and ginger biscuits.

179.4 [102]: *a fly . . . in the ointment of Microcosmos*: a variation of Ecclesiastes 10:1: "Dead flies cause the ointment of the apothecary to send forth a stinking savour; so doth a little folly him that is in reputation for wisdom and honour."

179.5 [102]: *Mayfair and Clapham*: the two nations of London: wealthy Mayfair, haunt of the aristocrat; and depressed Clapham, haunted by the poor. In the French translation, Beckett added 'Chelsea' and 'Bloomsbury,' both associated with the artistic canaille [see #224.5].

179.6 [102]: *the gloomy panoply of melancholy*: a 'panoply' is a full suit of armor, and 'melancholy' derives in the medieval theory of humors from an excess of black bile (a notion going back at least to Plato's *Timaeus* 71, with the liver as the mirror of thought); hence, the image is that of the typical black garb of the melancholic lover, e.g. Hamlet. The French translation may not imply the pun: "la panoplie noire de la mélancolie aux foies et aux fiels desdits districts" [Fr. "the black panoply of melancholy in the livers and galls of said districts"]. Compare the old interrogation: "Is life worth living?" . . . "Depends on the liver" [Fr. "La vie, vaut-elle la peine? Question de foie"].

179.7 [102]: *the Eton and Waterloo causes*: homage to that great Irishman, the Duke of Wellington, who encouraged neglect of studies with his contention that the Battle of Waterloo was won on the playing-fields of Eton.

179.8 [102]: *simulacra*: from L. *simulare*, "to feign"; hence, likenesses, or images.

180.1 [102]: *presupposed*: in logic, implying a necessary axiom.

180.2 [102]: *Lazarus*: not Abraham's bosom friend [see #5.7], but the one raised from the dead [John 11:30-44]. Oscar Wilde's variant of the parable called this the greatest story on earth, its climax being Lazarus's cursing of Christ for being brought back to life. In *Dream* [209], the Polar Bear argues that the humilities and renunciations of the Galilean are on a par with the miracles: "The *crytic* abasement before the woman taken red-handed is as great a piece of megalomaniacal impertinence as his interference in the affairs of his friend Lazarus." The typescript reads simply: "gone too far."

180.3 [102]: *even less weighty considerations*: Murphy's belief in microcosmic happiness is explicable in terms of Adler's *The Neurotic Constitution*, with its emphasis upon "the guiding fiction" [34], defined as "a simple infantile scheme which influences the apperception and mechanism of memory," evolving from the craving for security or longing for the maximation of ego-consciousness [60], so that the imaginary has a pronounced symbolic status, and the individual is unable to find the way back to reality. More simply, Murphy is fooling himself.

180.4 [102]: *his own little dungeon in Spain*: Murphy's variation of the proverbial castles in Spain, or in the air. Spain, it was said, had no castles; hence the imputation of improbability. In a letter to McGreevy [December 1931], Beckett referred to Stendhal's obsession with "heights and ladders and Gothic villains and terraces and grottoes in the Juras—the dungeon up in the air at the end." He alludes to the final chapter of *Le Rouge et le noir*.

180.5 [102]: *higher schizoids*: the expected collocation is 'primates.'

181.1 [103]: *bowers of bliss*: the enchanted garden of Acrasia, the figure of Intemperance in Spenser's *Fairie Queene* [II.xii.69ff]; she is captured by Sir Guyon, who destroys the Bower. Beckett had attended Rudmose-Brown's lectures on *The Fairie Queene* [Knowlson, 54].

181.2 [103]: *three dimensions*: lacking that of time, and thus not quite the hermetic monad.

181.3 [103]: *except for the shuttered Judas*: the exception is significant, in that the presence of the spy-hole distinguishes the padded cell from the monad, the micro-cosm of enclosure and emblem of solipsism (Schopenhauer disliked solipsism, and believed that its advocates belonged in the asylum). The cell, in effect, would be the setting of Beckett's later *Film*, in which Buster Keaton strives in vain to escape being perceived by the Eye or I; in both works, apperception (or the impossibility of avoiding it) is a condition of sanity. Austin Clarke's 'Mnemosyne Lay in Dust,' his record of the time spent in St. Patrick's Asylum [see #193.4], recalls the "Circular peephole rimmed with polished / Brass within the door."

181.4 [103]: *His success with the patients*: as Rabinovitz observes [*Development*, 111], this repetition foreshadows Murphy's failure with the only patient he really cares for, Mr. Endon.

182.1 [103]: *a litigious case*: one given to taking out litigation, literally or otherwise.

182.2 [103]: *force-fed . . . highly irregular*: the irregularity is more obvious in the French translation, where the force-feeding is described as alimentation "par l'autre bout"; i.e., by ends and means made infamous in Huysmann's *A rebours*. In that version there is another melancholic, "très embête par un cul en verre de Venise" [Fr. "very irritated by a bum of Venetian glass"]. This suggests Descartes's first *Meditation*, madmen who think that they are clothed in purple when they are naked, that their heads are made of clay, or their body of glass.

183.1 [104]: *they were his stars*: the sensible gloss is offered by Rabinovitz [*Development*, 109], citing Schopenhauer's "To those in whom the will has turned and has denied itself, this our world, which is so real, with all its suns and milky ways—is nothing" [*WWI*, I, 532]. This may underlie the sense in Beckett's *Proust* [19] of the outer world as "a projection of the individual's consciousness (an objectivation of the individual's will, Schopenhauer would say)." This in turn becomes the expression of a dualism that would remain fundamental for Beckett, separating him from that "seedy solipsist," Murphy, even though the solipsism of the latter (unlike that of Mr. Endon) is not finally sustainable [*Exagmination*, 6-7]:

> Thus we have the spectacle of a human progression that depends for its movement on individuals, and which at the same time is independent of indi-viduals in virtue of what appears to be a preordained cyclicism. It follows that History is neither to be considered as a formless structure, due exclusively to the achievements of individual agents, nor as possessing reality apart from and independent of them, accomplished behind their backs in spite of them, the work of some superior force, variously known as Fate, Chance, Fortune, God. Both these views, the materialistic and the transcendental, Vico rejects in favour of the rational. Individuality is the concretation of universality, and every individual action is at the same time superindividual. The individual and the universal cannot be considered as distinct from each other. History, then, is not the result of Fate or Chance—in both cases the individual would be separated from his product—but the result of a Necessity that is not Fate, of a Liberty that is not Chance.

Years later, in the small hours of the night, Watt rises and goes to the window [212], to look at the stars, which he had once known familiarly by name, "when dying in London."

183.2 [104]: *larval*: as in the stage of caterpillar, grub, or maggot, but with hints of Haeckel's metaphor of the embryonic soul [see #66.1].

183.3 [104]: *a fragment of vitagraph*: transparently, the horoscope, with a pun on *vita-glass*, the trade name of a kind of glass which transmits most of the ultra-violet rays of sunlight.

183.4 [104]: *an out-an-out preterist*: one who believes that the prophecies of the Apocalypse have already come to pass; more simply, one passed over.

183.5 [104]: *in situ*: L. "in its original situation"; the irony resides in Murphy's failure to catch the eye of Mr. Endon.

184.1 [104]: *Quod erat extorquendum*: L. "that which was to be twisted out," a variation of Euclid's *Quod erat demonstrandum*, "that which was to be demonstrated" (Quite Easily Done), from his *Axioms* (Book I Proposition 5). Beckett may have picked out 'extorquendum' from Geulincx's *Ethica* ['Annotata,' 228], where it is used in proximity to 'consummatur' [L. "to be consummated"], the point being errors implicit in the assumption of self-sufficiency in matters concerning one's life and death. The original is twisted into a Hamlet-like consummation devoutly (?) to be wished, and 'slap-up' (usually associated with a high tea, rather than a lucky strike) is perhaps not the right word; but the irony is clear: Murphy wants to twist into himself, or himself into, that which is outside himself, and the reasoning he confers upon the situation is accordingly tortured.

184.2 [104]: *tab*: according to the entries Beckett made in the *Whoroscope* Notebook, the term refers to "suicide tabs," or notes given to the night-duty nurses, who were responsible for ensuring that the patients did not commit suicide. The word is used by the disabled of those who walk and talk, the "temporary able-bodied" whose bodily powers will soon fail and for whom the world will be foreclosed.

184.3 [104]: *Mr. Endon*: from the Gk. preposition, ἔνδον, "within." As Mays has noted, Beckett's early poems pursue a complicated dialogue with MacGreevy's, terminating in the portrait of MacGreevy as Mr. Endon ['How Is MacGreevy a Modernist?', 125-26]. There is a touch of Paul Morphy in his make-up, the chess player being small and delicate of feature.

184.4 [104]: *a love of the purest kind*: an ἀγάπη that is entirely Platonic, despite the nasty 'ejaculations' and the echo of the Anglican Confession: "we have sinned against Thee by thought, word and deed." O'Hara says that Murphy's narcissism has as its object Freud's sense of the ego-ideal: "what he himself would like to be"; adding that Beckett's personifying of the ego ideal as "a homunculus in a padded cell" outdoes Freud in terms of topological exemplifying [*Hidden Drives*, 60-61].

184.5 [104]: *Mr. Higgins*: Frederick Robert Higgins (1896-1941), pioneer of the labor movement before he became a literary yeoman, friend of Austin Clarke and Secretary of the Irish Academy of Letters. Beckett thought little of his work, and in 'Recent Irish Poetry' mocked 'Island Blood' (1925) for accumulating a greater number of "By Gods" than all the other antiquarians put together, and 'Arable Holdings' (1933) for its blackthorn stick and "good smell of dung" [*Disjecta*, 73; see #59.1]. Higgins was fond of Japanese poetry (see Clarke's poem, 'Frederick Higgins'), but the reference is more personal: Beckett mentioned him in a letter to McGreevy [April 9, 1936, about the time of this chapter] as "breaking out of the Fire Insurance Co., looking like a fair-isle

Yeats," and as having been "cut" by Higgins twice at the National Gallery. The mode of revenge is thus appropriate. Beckett had already slashed at him in *Dream* [152-54], as Jem Higgins, weight-lifter and rugby man but not a literary cove in any sense of the word, who has fallen for the Alba "like an angel come down from Heaven in the middle of all those little tarts" [153]. In the *Whoroscope* Notebook 'bellycut' is listed, with its synonyms: "Seppuka, Harakiri, Happy despatch."

184.6 [104]: *Mr. O'Connor*: Cork-born Michael Francis O'Donovan, who took the name of Frank O'Connor, then a minor writer closely associated with Daniel Corkery and the rural margins. He left school at fourteen to join the IRA, and fought in the civil war. He was later a teacher of Irish in the rural schools, then a librarian in Sligo, and in 1935 was appointed as a director of the Abbey Theatre. He gets off lightly in Beckett's 'Recent Irish Poetry,' but Beckett confided to McGreevy [May 15, 1935] that he had read O'Connor on Gaelic literature in a recent.*Dublin Magazine*, and had "flinched at every 4th page." Louit's dog in *Watt* is named O'Connor.

185.1 [105]: *apnoea . . . a physiological impossibility*: 'apnoea' is self-suffocation, or willed cessation of breathing, not facilitated by any other agency; for reasons that go deep to the core of the instinct for survival it is indeed a physiological impossibility, since when loss of breath brings loss of consciousness the involuntary nervous system takes over and the body breathes again. Beckett is here mocking one of the pet notions of John Porter-Phillips, physician-superintendent of the Bethlem Royal (Brian Ryder to CA). Schopenhauer was otherwise persuaded. In *WWI* [I.2 §23, 151] he argues that we could voluntarily suffocate if any motive influenced the will strongly enough to overcome the pressing desire for air, suggesting that: "According to some accounts Diogenes actually put an end to his life in this way," and adding: "Certain negroes are said to have done this."

185.2 [105]: *Dr. Killiecrankie*: see also #88.3 and #257.3. In the French translation, at this point, the association between the good Doctor's Outer Hebridean overtures and his experience of the schizoid voice is made clear, in terms of James Macpherson's *Ossian* (1763), a celebrated forgery from the Gaelic past:

> Mais le directeur, Doctor Angus Killiekrankie, conçu aux Shetlands après quinze ans de coït, né aux Orcades après six mois d'utérus, sevré aux Hébrides après une semaine de sein, et en demeurant grand admirateur d'Ossian, croyait s'y connaître en voix schizoides. Elles ne resemblaient guère aux voix hébriennes, ni aux voix orcadiennes, ni aux voix shetlandiennes. Tantôt elles vous disaient ceci et tantôt cela.

[Fr. "But the Director, Doctor Angus Killiekrankie, conceived in the Shetlands after fifteen years of trying, born in the Orkneys after six months in the uterus, weaned in the Hebrides after one week at the breast, and remaining a great admirer of Ossian, believed he knew about schizoid voices. They barely resembled the Hebridean voices, nor the Orkney voices, nor the Shetland voices. Sometimes they said this and sometimes that."] He is a perfect case study of the type described by Jung in the third Tavistock lecture [72]. Jung suggested that complexes may form personalities of their own: because they have "a certain will-power, a sort of ego, we find that in a schizophrenic condition they emancipate themselves from conscious control to such an extent that they become visible and audible. They appear as visions, they speak in voices . . ." 'Ossianic emotions' is a term used by Jung for wild flights of Romanticism.

186.1 [105]: *the Canutian line*: Canute was the Danish King of England, 1017-35, best remembered for the perhaps apocryphal attempt to reveal to his courtiers the vacuity of their flattery by placing his chair upon the strand and ordering the tide not to come in. The lesson was lost on one retainer, who was heard to mutter, "Silly Cnut."

186.2 [105]: *a schizophrenic*: one suffering from a mental disorder characterized by indifference, withdrawal and a dissociation between the intellectual processes and the affective, though often without the obvious impairment of mental ability. This disorganization, or deterioration, was in Beckett's day generally identified with *dementia praecox*, and characterized as one of four varieties: hebephrenia, catatonia, paranoia or paraphrenia.

186.2a [105]: *amiable*: for Horace's *amabilis insania*, his "amiable madness" (*Odes*, III.4), as cited by Schopenhauer, see #186.4.

186.3 [105]: *as Narcissus to his fountain*: Narcissus was the beautiful Greek youth of whom the nymph Echo became enamoured, but finding him insensible to love she pined away in grief and was reduced to a voice. To punish Narcissus, Nemesis caused him to see his own reflection in a fountain, whereof he became so enamoured that he too pined away, until nothing was left of him but a heap of stones (the central metaphor of 'Echo's Bones'), and he was changed into the little flower which bears his name [Ovid, *Metamorphoses*, III.395ff]. O'Hara offers a consideration of *Murphy* in terms of Freud's theory of Narcissism [*Hidden Drives*, 56ff], stressing Murphy's retreat from Celia when her demands threaten his self, towards Mr. Endon, who fails to return Murphy's love through his impenetrable narcissism. O'Hara's approach, at times monomythic, argues that Murphy's to-ing and fro-ing, from Miss Counihan to the chair, the chair to Celia, Celia to Mr. Endon, and Mr. Endon to Celia via the chair, has its unconscious roots in Beckett's detailed knowledge of depth psychology, and that Murphy has been conceived as one who cannot submit to an object of desire outside his self, and whose love of Self impedes his love of any Other.

186.4 [105]: *perfect in every detail*: as with his chess, Mr. Endon exemplifies and parodies Schopenhauer's notion that by aesthetic contemplation might one escape exigencies of the Will. As Rabinovitz says [*Development*, 95], Mr. Endon is mad, but his is a special sort of madness, in terms of his ability to remain truly indifferent. Murphy envies that condition, but cannot attain it: "Schopenhauer, describing how aesthetic contemplation counters the effects of the will, says that complete indifference to volition can be achieved only by geniuses. But these geniuses, he adds, 'may exhibit certain weaknesses which are actually akin to madness'"; i.e., the outward behavior of those who perceive the ultimate nature of reality is what most would label madness. Beckett was acquainted with this passage [*WWI*, I.3 §36, 246], having alluded to it when claiming that the Proustian stasis is contemplative: "a pure act of understanding, will-less, the 'amabilis insania' and the 'holder Wahnsinn'" [*Proust*, 91]. The Latin ["amiable madness"] derives from Horace [*Odes*, iii.4], as noted by Schopenhauer [246], who advances Wieland's "holder Wahnsinn" as the German equivalent. He later suggests that "The kinship of genius and madness, so often observed, depends chiefly upon that separation of the intellect from the will which is essential to genius, but is yet contrary to nature" [*WWI*, III.3.xxxi, 153]. That separation Murphy will not be able to make, for the cost is madness.

186.5 [105]: *byssus*: originally, fine silky Egyptian linen, used for wrapping mummies. In Luke 16:19 (Greek), Dives is dressed in *porphyras* ["purple"] and *byssus* ["fine linen"].

186.6 [105]: *neo-merovingian poulaines of deepest purple*: long pointed shoes as worn at the court of Charlemagne; compare the amaranth (a purple flower which never dies) and "the mystery of Merovingian time" [*Proust*, 62]. In contrast to the drab tonalities of yellow and green throughout the rest of the novel, Mr. Endon is ablaze with color. There is a curious note in Lucretius [*De rerum natura*, 2:830] about scarlet and purple being the brightest colors of all, whereas atoms have none; compare Murphy's rare postnatal treat [246].

187.1 [106]: *an excellent cigar*: which, according to Freud, is sometimes only a cigar. Yet Belacqua at the outset of 'Echo's Bones' puffs on a cigar, in an image of self-absorption.

187.2 [106]: *Mr. Endon's one frivolity*: and a rather curious one, given that the essence of the game is confrontation. Or perhaps not, given that the essence of the game is the expression of the individual will. Melanie Klein's *The Psychoanalysis of Children* (1932), which Bion had recommended, emphasizes games as substitutes for establishing contacts with external realities, based on the principle of intelligibility as governed by rules and the symbolic relationship between what occurs in the game and in the outside world. See also #243.2.

187.3 [106]: *Fabian methods*: the avoidance of direct engagement, the term derived from the name of Quintus Fabius Maximus (d. 203 BC), nicknamed 'Cunctator', or "the Delayer," from his successes in defending Rome against Hannibal by refusing to engage in direct battle. These Fabian methods will be evident in the confrontation to come [243-45]. The Fabian Society, associated with G. B. Shaw and emphasizing social change by gradual means, was still a worrying force in British political life.

188.1 [106]: *Do not come down the ladder*: a music-hall joke of obscure Welsh origin, much loved by Beckett who repeated it in *Watt* [44]. The punch line is, roughly, "Too late, I'm half-way down already." The joke is perfectly stable, which has not deterred scholars from securing its legs in Wittgenstein and Fritz Mauthner. Rabinovitz [*Development*, 144, n.16] suggests Schopenhauer as a source: "to him who studies in order to gain *insight* books and studies are only steps of the ladder by which he climbs to the summit of knowledge. As soon as a round of the ladder has raised him a step, he leaves it behind him" [*WWI*, II.1.vii, 256]. This is supported by its presence in 'Echo's Bones' [14], where Belacqua confuses Lord Gall with the paradox.

188.2 [106]: *the sad truth*: an echo of Murphy's abstinence [see p. 86].

188.3 [106]: *the galactic coal-sack*: clouds of galactic dust, known otherwise as dark nebulae, that obscure the stars beyond them and hence reveal a blurred and dirty aspect to the naked eye. Compare the Dream Notebook [#1052], suggesting Beckett's reading of Sir James Jeans, *The Universe Around Us* (1929).

189.1 [107]: *the vicarious autology*: the study of the self by means of another.

189.2 [107]: *proxies*: substitutes, proximate accessitae, runners up and maddened prizemen, none of whom are in the same class as Mr. Endon. Beckett was later (1962) to describe the sense of living "by proxy," an unreal being replacing a lost self, an abortive or stunted self, an embryonic being that was somehow kept from developing [Harvey, 266 n9].

189.3 [107]: *His books, his pictures, his postcards*: O'Hara points out the similarities to Valéry's Monsieur Teste, like Murphy a denizen of the head and mind: "Il y a vingt ans que je n'ai plus de livres. J'ai brûlé mes papiers aussi." [Fr. "For twenty years I've had no more books. I've burnt my papers too" ('Beckett Backs Down,' 41-42; *Monsieur Teste*, 28)]. O'Hara's identification is supported by Valéry's epigraph [19]: "Vita Cartesii res est simplicissima" [L. "the Cartesian life is the simplest of things"].

190.1 [107]: *the immemorial way*: i.e., involuntary rather than voluntary.

191.1 [108]: *This could not alarm him*: yet for every effect there is a cause [see #263.2], and ironies implicit in "corpse-obedient matter" will be later apparent.

191.2 [108]: *sit before you lie down*: the repetition of Chamfort's maxim [see #79.4].

191.3 [108]: *Griffith*: i.e., D. W. Griffith's early epic of the silent screen, *Intolerance*.

192.1 [108]: *in this kip*: an echo of Villon's "Dans ce bordel où tenons nostre état" [Med. Fr., "In this brothel where we hold our court"], from the *Ballade de la grosse Margot*.

192.2 [108]: *steak and kidney*: one of his own 'kidney,' or temperament, the kidneys once supposed to be the seat of affections.

192.3 [109]: *incipience*: the initial impulse to exist.

193.1 [109]: *the rationalist prurit*: the urge to scratch the spot that itches; technically, that part of its back which an animal cannot reach (hence 'saddling'). Beckett took the word from Garnier's *Onanisme seul et à deux* [DN, #443], but it appears in Geulincx's *Ethica*, where Pythagoras's doctrine of metempsychosis is attributed to vulgar opinion ['Annotata,' 242]. Compare Burton's *Anatomy*: "*ubi dolor, ibi digitus*, one must needs scratch where it itches" ['Democritus to the Reader,' 5].

193.2 [109]: *Les Girls*: genus, not species; not a particular Parisian girlie show, but a categorization of the kind. In a letter to McGreevy [September 8, 1934], Beckett observed: "The Follies Begères was looking unspeakable but the umbrellas lovely."

193.3 [109]: *rare birds*: Juvenal's *"Rara avis in terris nigroque simillima cycno"* [L. "A rare bird upon the earth, and very like a black swan"; *Satire* VI.165], meaning a prodigy, something unique or out of the ordinary, such as that feathered epiphenomenon of philo-sophical dispute before the discovery in Western Australia of the black species. The last Great Auks were clubbed to death by a couple of Icelandic fishermen in the 1870s.

193.4 [109]: *Clarke*: as Mays notes ['Mythologized Presences,' 199], the description of the cells in the MMM and the Judas in the door echoes Austin Clarke's experiences in St. Patrick's asylum; the details of his incarceration were common knowledge. The Calder and Picador editions spell 'katatonic' with a 'c.' Ernest Jones relates *catatonia* to dementia praecox, catalepsy being a prominent symptom [*Psycho-Analysis*, 705].

194.1 [109]: *take a pull on yourself*: what Beckett called in the *Whoroscope* Notebook, citing Aristophanes's *Nuées* II.i, "le rythme par le dactyle" [see #28.1].

194.2 [109]: *conferred that aspect*: the "nice" distinction arises out of Geulincx's *Ethica*, following the *nudus speculator* conclusion [see #1.5], where the role of the eye is discussed and the conclusion reached that it does not so much see as have the capacity for sight conferred upon it: "Ego, inquam, ope illorum video; et tamen, quid opis ad videndum conferant" [L. "I, I contend, see by means of them; but nevertheless they confer that power to the act of seeing"; *Ethica*, I.II.ii §9, 34 and 'Annotata' 27-28, 214]. The passage forms a natural sequitur from the discussion of body as machine, unable to act save with the Occasional intervention of God. Murphy, it might be observed, is once more untied, I beg your pardon, *united* with his machine.

10

195.1 [110]: *Parallel thirds*: 'thirds' represent the interval between any two notes that are two diatonic scale degrees apart, e.g., C-E, formed when a perfect fifth is divided into two consonant intervals. Traditionally these were regarded as imperfect consonances, and did not form chords of final cadences. The difficulty for Pythagorean harmony is that the ratios assumed are not quite true: if a piano is tuned by perfect fifths the major thirds will be too sharp, and if by depressing the fifth the major thirds are made perfect the fifths may be unsuitably flat. A compromise is therefore made, discords minimalized to be inaudible to most ears. Haydn's memorable observation may derive from John Mahaffy, Provost of Trinity, whose book on Descartes Beckett had rifled for *Whoroscope* and who says of Haydn [21-22]: "He was the first to assert that major thirds were not, as the Greeks held, discords but concords." He adds that the Greeks were perfectly right, if we assume tuning by full tones, which make the thirds so sharp as to be unbearable. Beckett used the more usual "consecutive thirds" in *Whoroscope*, having perhaps picked it out (via Mahaffy) from Descartes's letter to Mersenne of May 15, 1634.

Haydn married in 1760 Maria Anna Aloysia Apollonia Keller, daughter of a wig-maker, preferring (it was said) her younger sister Josepha, who entered a convent. The marriage was not a success, Maria Anna having no sympathy for her husband's works, unable or unwilling to have children, and too fond of the clergy for her husband's taste or purse. The couple spent much time apart. During Haydn's London years his wife found a small house in the Viennese suburbs, saying it would suit her as a widow; Haydn lived there after her death. The decaying Haydn's last words were "Long live the Emperor!"; this was not a tribute to Beethoven.

195.2 [110]: *partition*: in context, a play on 'partimenti' [It. "divisions"], a musical term for figured exercises in florid counterpoint. It is Beckett's word for Proust's 'cloison' [*Jeunes filles*, II.95], intimating Marcel's awareness of the thin wall separating him from his grandmother, as used in *Proust* [25] of the inevitable isolation of one being from another. Schopenhauer's discussion of madness [*WWI*, I.iii §36, 247] quotes Dryden's description of Shaftesbury's fiery soul: "Great wits are sure to madness near allied, / And thin partitions do their bounds divide" [*Absalom and Achitophel*, I.164-65]. (Schopenhauer believed he was citing Pope's "Remembrance and reflection how allied! / What thin partitions sense from thought divide" [*Essay on Man*, I.224-25]). This cannot be called allusion (one might equally invoke the political division of Ireland), but the word had for Beckett such attenuated tonalities.

195.3 [110]: *the correct grass Dido cramp*: a grass widow (L. *viduca de gracia*, one divorced or separated by papal dispensation rather than death). The term was later used of an unmarried woman with a child, or a wife parted from her husband, a widow by grace. Dido, Queen of Carthage, fell in love with Aeneas when he was driven by a storm to her shores, but having dallied there he was compelled by Mercury to move on and fulfil his destiny of founding Rome. Dido in her grief burnt herself to death upon a funeral pyre [Virgil, *Aeneid*, I.494 to III.650].

195.4 [110]: *the offices of the Spectator*: in 1935, at 99 Gower Street, near the British Museum. *The Spectator* has been since 1828 a weekly devoted to the arts and politics, with book and theatrical reviews, chess and bridge columns. Writing in the *Spectator* in 1938, Kate O'Brien was one of the few to appreciate *Murphy*'s rare wit: "It truly is magnificent and a treasure—if you like it. Quite useless to you, quite idiotic, if you don't . . . a joke overloaded with the scholarship of great jokes."

195.5 [110]: *in the midst of Indians, Egyptians, Cyprians, Japanese, Chinese, Siamese and clergymen*: the jest arises because the University of London had recently (1927) acquired with the assistance of the Rockefeller Foundation a site of 10.5 acres north of the British Museum, and moved there some of its Colleges and Institutes, including the School of Oriental Studies (later "African and Oriental"). The blessing of clergy is less a tribute to their learning or missionary zeal than a current quip, with reference to Jeremy Bentham and other founders of UCL, as "the godless of Gower Street" [Julie Campbell to CA].

196.1 [110]: *a Hindu polyhistor*: an Indian of encyclopaedic learning, trusting that he will be given sufficient Prana (the sacred life-breath through which the self has existence) to finish his monograph ('prana' is used in Sean O'Casey's *Juno and the Paycock*, Captain Boyle trying to impress the other Mr. Bentham with his polymathy). Beckett may have absorbed 'polyhistor' from Burton's *Anatomy* ['Democritus to the Reader,' 6].

196.2 [110]: *The Pathetic Fallacy from Avercamp to Kampendonck*: in 'Lightning Calculation,' Mr. Quigley arises to a sky like curdled milk in pale blue tea and the sun pouring down the street, then consults his notes on dreams made through the night: "He found them of interest only in so far as then [*sic*] seemed to take colour from the dilemma in which he found himself, namely, how to perachieve his book, *The Pathetic Fallacy from Avercamp to Campendonk* without reneging on his infatuation with Hercules Seger" (the "camp" connection is concealed by the 'K' in *Murphy*). The subject was central to Beckett's thinking at the time, namely, the impulse in landscape painting towards emotions of the human subject, landscape postulated as being concerned with his feelings (the pathetic fallacy). The two painters named, each of whom he admired for different reasons, represent for Beckett extremes of this tradition.

Avercamp: Hendrick Avercamp (1585-1634), Dutch painter of landscapes, born dumb, but whose eloquent brush specialized in winter scenes. Beckett was familiar with his work at the National Galleries of London and Dublin, but, much as he liked it, felt it represented what he called "the itch to animise" or "landscapability" [letter to McGreevy, September 8, 1934].

Kampendonck: more precisely, Heinrich Campendonk (1889-1957), a German artist friendly with Marc, Klee and Kandinsky. He was invited in 1912 to participate in the first Blau Reiter exhibition, the first German artist to exhibit outside his country after WWI. In 1931 he was declared a degenerate by the Nazis and dismissed from his teaching post in Düsseldorf. He moved to Belgium, then Holland, where he accepted a post at the Rijksacadamie in Amsterdam. Much of his art is concerned with pastoral subjects, these given an aura of wonder and fantasy and treated with the exaggerated features and proportions of mosaic and folk art, to emphasis the moment of metaphysical experience.

The letter to McGreevy [above] constitutes the fullest statement of Beckett's aesthetics at this time, the important figure being Cézanne, whose art left a lasting impression on the young writer. Knowlson [196-97] quotes extensively from that letter to contrast Cézanne's treatment of landscape with earlier painters: essentially, the recognition and dislike of the impulse towards "anthropomorphization," landscape promoted to the emotions of the subject, as opposed to Cézanne's sense of it as separate and alien: "Cézanne seems to have been the first to see landscape and state it as material of a strictly peculiar order, incommensurable with all human expressions whatsoever. Atomistic landscape with no velleities of vitalism, landscape with personality à la rigueur, but personality in its own terms." Beckett goes on to discuss and reject a beloved Ruysdael, *Entrance to the Forest* (another instance of that which is loved but will no longer do). He concludes that the problem "of how to state the emotion of of Ruysdael in terms of post-impressionistic painting" disappears when it is understood: "How far Cézanne had moved from the snapshot puerilities of Manet and Cie when he could understand the dynamic intrusion to be himself and so landscape to be something by definition unapproachably alien, unintelligible arrangement of atoms, not so much as ruffled by the kind attentions of the Reliability Joneses." In a further letter [September 16, 1934], he states that what he feels in Cézanne "is precisely the absence of a rapport that was all right for Rosa or Ruysdael for whom the animising mode was valid, but would have been fake for him, because he had the sense of his incommensurability not only with life of such a different order as landscape, but even with life of his own order, even with the life . . . operative within himself." Knowlson concludes [197]: "It was to be a dozen years more before Beckett found his own way of expressing this 'incommensurabilty' of man with himself." The debate in *Murphy*, however lightly sketched, anticipates both the problem and its resolution.

196.3 [110]: *the Norwich School*: the East Anglian school of landscape painters, founded in 1803 and centered about John Crome (1768-1821), whom Beckett refers to as 'Crome Yellow esq.' [letter to McGreevy, September 8, 1934], and whose works such as 'Yarmouth Harbour at Evening' (c. 1817, in the Tate) emulated the 17th century Dutch tradition (Crome's dying words were "Hobbema, Hobbema, how I do love thee"). The School flourished in the first half of the 19th century, and typically took for its subjects the East Anglian heath and woodland, the River Yare and the Norfolk coast. The polyhistor's thesis may have been anticipated: Wilenski's 'Postscript' to his *Dutch Art* [295] suggests extending his present study from Dutch landscape "to the pictures of the Norwich school, to nineteenth-century romantic landscapes, to Impressionist landscapes, and to Landscapes by artists of the Modern Movement."

196.4 [110]: *"My fut . . . 'ave gut smaller*: in a letter to Con Leventhal [July 26, 1934; Knowlson, 743], Beckett tells of the suicide of an insane Chinese man in Gower Street who had made this bizarre claim before killing himself.

196.5 [111]: *down to the muck*: a variant of "down to the ground," setting up the obscenity of "up to the hilt" (compare *Ulysses,* 609), and the following reference to the turf.

197.1 [111]: *Turf is compulsory in the Saorstat*: a labored version of coals to Newcastle, in the idiom of the "Saorstat Éirann" or Irish Free State. Beckett had recently written a scorching article for *The Bookman* (not immediately published) on 'Censorship in the Saorstat' [*Disjecta*, 84-88]. Ruby Cohn comments: "Ireland lurks behind the titular Saorstat, derived from the Old Testament Saor or Zoar, an iniquitous region redolent of drunkenness and sexual indulgence" [*Disjecta*, 174]. The equivalent idiom in Aristophanes is "Owls to Athens."

197.2 [111]: *ruts*: well-worn routines, but with a touch of the sad animal. Compare the proverbial retort of one invited to lie back and think of England: "You mean, Rutland!"

197.3 [111]: *the famous difficulty in serving two employers*: from Luke 16:13: "No man can serve two masters: for either he will hate the one, and love the other; or else he will hold to the one, and despise the other. Ye cannot serve God and mammon." Beckett has spliced the verse with the language of the marriage service, which states that a man must leave father and mother, and cleave to his wife [Matthew 19:5]. 'Cleave' is a Bruno-word, with identified contraries of splitting and holding tight; traces of that dualism are visible in Clov of *Endgame*.

198.1 [111]: *incorruptible*: combining the sense of immortal substance ("raised incorruptible," I Corinthians 15:52), with the mundane meaning of "unbribable"; the word is used thus in Beckett's poem, 'Malacoda.'

198.2 [112]: *coadjutor*: L. *adjutare*, "to help"; hence, one who aids another.

198.3 [112]: *crapulous*: L. *crapula*, "drunken sickness"; hence, debauched by drinking.

198.4 [112]: *the catspaw of a hardened toff*: a catspaw is one made the dupe of another, as in the fable of the monkey who used the paw of his friend the cat to get roasted chestnuts out of the fire. A toff, from the perspective of the canaille, is a nob or a swell; the word deriving from the 'tuft' worn by titled Oxford undergraduates, but in popular etymology associated with 'toffee-nosed,' or stuck-up. Hence "hardened," as caramel in toffee.

199.1 [112]: *Judas*: Judas Iscariot, betrayer of Christ; hence, a traitor.

199.2 [112]: *Jezebel*: a shameless whore, the wife of Ahab [II Kings 9:30].

199.3 [112]: *you shall not find me ungrateful . . . you shall find me not ungrateful*: a subtle distinction which is exploited (to little effect) on p. 221.

199.4 [112] *homeopathy*: a controversial branch of fringe medicine originated by Samuel Hahnemann (1755-1843), a German physician whose motto was *Similia Similibus Curantur* [L. "Like cures like"]. Treatment requires minute quantities of substances that in a healthy person produce symptoms like those induced by the disease; here, small doses of Miss Counihan have brought Wylie relief from the condition engendered by her contagious presence.

200.1 [112]: *The syndrome known as life*: the words of Wylie [57]; again, for Neary, the sense of palliation as relief for terminal sufferers unable to be cured.

200.2 [112]: *voltefesses*: from Fr. *fesses*, "buttocks"; a twirl on *volteface*, a metaphorical turning of the other cheeks.

200.3 [113]: *turned up the tail of his abolla*: an 'abolla' was a military garment, as opposed to the toga, or robe of peace; but came in time to be worn by the lower orders and "affected by the philosophers in the vanity of humility" [Brewer]. As the French translation makes clear, the reference is to Socrates before his judges, observing the call of nature even as his life is most in danger. The detail is given in 'Echo's Bones' [14], yet it is not to be found in Plato's dialogues, Xenophon's *Memorabilia*, the *Lives* of Diogenes Laertius, nor Burton's *Anatomy*. Socrates had treated his accusation with contempt, and after his condemnation had the right under Athenian law to suggest an alternative penalty to the death sentence passed on him. Imprisonment, a substantial fine, or exile would have been accepted, but in the spirit of the gadfly to which he likened himself Socrates argued that since he had served the state without self-interest he should henceforth be given free meals in the Prytaneion [*Apology*, §26 36D, 128-29]. He later modified this to the derisive fine of one mina of silver (100 drachmas), all he could afford [§28 38B, 134-35]. This was raised to 30 minas upon security of his friends, but his response was regarded as an act of contempt, and the death sentence affirmed by a larger majority than had originally voted for it.

200.4 [113]: *Neary's concept of friendship*: the concept is curious because it conflicts with some remarkable statements in Proust [*Guermantes*, II.79-80], leading to Beckett's conclusion [*Proust*, 66] that we cannot know and we cannot be known. The intellectual honesty of this underlies, like Pascal's terror of the infinite abyss, much of Beckett's writings:

> Friendship, according to Proust, is the negation of that irredeemable solitude to which every human being is condemned. Friendship implies an almost piteous acceptance of face values. Friendship is a social expedient, like upholstery or the distribution of garbage buckets. It has no spiritual significance . . . Proust situates friendship somewhere between fatigue and ennui. He does not agree with the Nietzschean conception that friendship must be based on intellectual sympathy, because he does not see friendship as having the least intellectual significance . . . It represents a false movement of the spirit . . .

This is echoed in Windelband [174-75], who sets the Epicurean view of friendship, arising from the atomist assumption that individuals first exist for and by themselves, against the Stoic sense of the world constituted by Nature for society, and thus rational.

201.1 [113]: *The advantage of this view*: as on p. 58, the precise phrasing of Wylie (whose words leave an indelible impression on all who hear them).

201.2 [113]: *yearning*: the anagram is pertinent: *Neary* is trapped upon a wheel of desire, a cycle of yearning defined by Rabinovitz [*Development*, 103]: that willing arises from want, and therefore suffering; that the satisfaction of a wish ends it, but for one wish satisfied ten are denied; that desire lasts long, and demands are infinite; that every satisfied wish makes room for new ones; that attained objects of desire give merely fleeting gratification; that as long as our consciousness is given up to our will we can never have happiness or peace; and that without peace no well-being is possible. In Bryden's words [42]: "desire for the attainable followed by disgust for the attained." The cycle derives partly from Beckett's *Proust*, but key references in Schopenhauer make the point that the causes of pain, as of pleasure, lie for the most part not in the real present as in abstract thoughts [*WWI*, I.iv §55, 386, and I.iii §38, 253-54]. Compare Proust [*Albertine disparue*, I.72-73], to the effect that as soon as we realize our desire cannot be accomplished we become intent upon it once more.

201.3 [113]: *buried his face in the pillow*: as does Belacqua [*Dream*, 123], but in vain: it is impossible to switch off the inward glare. Beckett may have recycled this passage, Belacqua lying in his skin on his belly, and feeling the weight of his inertia; the wings of his "horrible border-creature, a submarine bird" transformed into those of the pillow.

201.4 [113]: *Le pou est mort. Vive le pou*: Fr. "The flea is dead. Long live the flea"; a parody of the words spoken when a monarch dies. Neary is wondering "if there is not some desire that once satisfied would not engender new desires" [Webb, 52]. The 'keyflea' (*causa sui*), like Donne's, may enter the pudenda of the psyche, but dying without issue ends the futile cycle of birth and renewal. The detail thus anticipates the drama of life renewed in *Endgame*.

201.5 [113]: *a Newtonian*: in that he equates Newton's third law of motion, the "principe de l'égalité de l'action et de la réaction," as Beckett had copied from Henri Poincaré into the *Whoroscope* Notebook [see #113.1], with the horse leech's daughter of Proverbs 30:15 [see #57.3], to the effect that for every itch that is satisfied another is created. Murphy's genius, reduced to its simplest terms, is to acknowledge the principles of pessimism.

201.6 [113]: *something of Hugo*: perhaps as suggested in Beckett's *Proust* [80], one receding rather than proceeding, moving away from an elegant skepticism and the marmorean modes back to an outdated romanticism, and thus a solitary and independent figure, but tragic (or pathetic) in attributing lasting value to his sufferings. For example, Hugo's vow of fidelity, in exile on Jersey, to the Republican cause: "Et s'il n'en reste qu'un, je serai celui-là" [Fr. "And if only one remains, I will be that one"]. This line is cited in Proust [*Guermantes*, II.121], soon after the meditation upon friendship [see #200.4]. Stephen Dedalus, Joyce's artist as a young man, places similar value on his own sufferings, but outgrows that in *Ulysses*.

202.1 [113]: *the water from his mouth*: as in Burton's curious tale of the woman complaining of her husband's impatience, who was told an "excellent remedy" for it: "A glass of water, which when he bawled she should hold still in her mouth." The cure worked, the key being not the "fair water" but the woman's silence (*Anatomy*, III.3.4.ii, 658). Compare Swift's *Letter to Stella* VIII [October 31, 1710]: "I have my mouth full of water, and was going to spit it out, because I reasoned with myself, how could I write when my mouth was full. Han't you done things like that, reasoned wrong at first thinking?"

202.2 [113]: *the Friend*: an image of Christ, quite impossible for Beckett [see #200.4]; but to give Neary his due his is not an ideal of Friendship vitiated by such base thoughts. For him, it remains a Platonic ideal, the shadow of which may be seen obscurely in Coleridge's 'The Friend,' which celebrates with Wordsworth the desired anemesis.

202.3 [113] *a surgeon*: compare Murphy's "surgical quality" [#62.3]. Miss Counihan's problem has been diagnosed, by the unmerciful, as the need for a slipodichtomy.

202.4 [114]: *to give their cake to the cat*: presumably, after taking it out of the bag: the miscegenation of two proverbs, a perverb: having one's cake and eating it, first giving one's tongue to the cat. For "are extraordinary" the implied alternative is "take the cake."

203.1 [114]: *kill the thing they think they love*: a sentiment made famous by Oscar Wilde's 'The Ballad of Reading Gaol': "each man kills the thing he loves." The phrase comes from *The Merchant of Venice* [IV.i.65-66], in the exchange between Bassanio and Shylock:

> *Bassanio*: Do all men kill the things they do not love?
> *Shylock*: Hates any man the thing he would not kill?

This follows in Bartlett the reference to men who go mad when they behold "a harmless necessary cat" (IV.i.55). Beckett added by hand the cogito "they think" to the typescript.

203.2 [114]: *the astute comment*: i.e., *chercher la femme*, with the proper Conan Doyle intonation, and Cooper certainly an Irregular (Holme's premises at 22B could be described as more sitting-bedroom than bed-sitter).

203.3 [114]: *What number*: again, Cooper's inability to give the exact number is a curious denial of realism in a novel which ostentatiously flaunts such detail [see, again, #1.3].

204.1 [114]: *a florin*: a two-shilling piece; a sizable vail, given that Ticklepenny works for the sum of 4d (or 5d) an hour [see #157.1]. Her offer is raised 6d to half-a-crown, or 2/6, these being the two largest coins then in common currency.

204.2 [115]: *stepping out of her step-ins*: 'skirt' was changed in manuscript to 'step-ins,' *that* most intimate article of underwear. See also #227.2. This may have been suggested by a detail in Burnet's *Early Greek Philosophy* [81], for the sake of a joke as erudite as it is obscure, Burnet discussing the wild worship of Dionysus associated with Orpheus:

> In this religion the new beliefs were mainly based upon the phenomenon of "ecstasy" (ἔκστασις, "stepping out"). It was supposed that it was only when "out of the body" that the soul revealed its true nature.

204.3 [115]: *more pippin than orange*: "misbegotten" rather than "née," the pun being upon that variety of apple known as "Cox's Orange." For *Ariadne*, see #116.4.

204.4 115]: *the same great group*: as on p. 210: hence, the canine command that follows.

205.1 [115]: *analphabetes*: those lacking a basic mastery of the alphabet, the Mr. Nackybals of life. Yet Cooper, who has known A and B, is now aware of C.

206.1 [116]: *formerly a brunette*: but not from the bottle, i.e., Miss B's hair pulled out by Miss A., as opposed to Miss A's having gone gray: the point less the accuracy of the reading than the way that apparently identical phrases have generated different meanings. Cooper's *amours* are couched in keeping with the notes taken by Beckett in the *Whoroscope* Notebook from Kant's *Kritik*, where 'A' and 'B' are used respectively for analytic and synthetic knowledge, with the question raised, with respect to Hume, "Wie sind synthetische Urteile a-priori möglich?" [Ger. "How are a-priori synthetic judgements possible?"]. Cooper's knowledge of such matters is not *a priori*; rather, his "pains" underlie his synthetic [with reference to the world] response to Wylie's apparently analytic [tautologous] statement: "You know what women are when it comes to women," and his dead-toned analytic response: "That will be all right." Given Cooper's recent experience of Miss Counihan, the unsatisfactory answer to Kant might be: through *a-posteriori* sensory experience.

207.1 [116]: *a desinvolture*: with casual unselfconsciousness; despite Beckett's desultory use of the word, it is French and not yet assimilated to English.

207.2 [116]: *a bank of bluebells*: an echo of Orsino's opening speech in *Twelfth Night*, where he hears music, a dying fall "That breathes upon a bank of violets" [I.i.6]; the point being that for Neary at least, "It is not so sweet now as it was before."

207.3 [116]: *crispated*: from L. *crispare*, "to curl"; the involuntary retraction of small arteries in muscle or skin, to bring about the state more commonly called "goose-flesh."

207.4 [116]: *his smattering of Greek urns*: identified by Rabinovitz [*Development*, 102] as an allusion to Lessing's *Laokoön* [1766] in which [11, n1] he mentions that in antiquity Death and Sleep were represented as twin brothers, often with their feet crossed; or his 'Wie die Alten den Tod Gebildet' [Ger. "How the Ancients Represented Death"], where the point is discussed extensively, and drawings of the figures included. The *Laocoön* traces the notion back to Pausanias, and leaves open the question: "Was sollten die krummen Füsse hier ausdrücken?" [Ger. "What might the crossed feet mean here?"]. This was taken up in the later article [1769], Lessing contending that the ancient figures of Sleep were depicted with crossed feet to indicate the unconsciousness of Dream; then, to intimate that Death is but a dream [15]: "dennoch hatte der Tod ebenso krumme Füsse" [Ger. "therefore death likewise has crossed feet"].

207.5 [116]: *Sleep's young brother*: Death, offspring of Chaos and dreadful Night, the two often considered twins, as by Lessing. Bartlett lists other instances: Homer, *Iliad* [xiv.231, xvi.672]; Virgil, *Aeneid* [VI.278]: "Death's brother, Sleep"; Samuel Daniel's 'Sonnets to Delia'; Shelley's *Queen Mab* [I]: "How wonderful is Death, / Death and his brother Sleep!"; Tennyson's *In Memoriam* [V.lxviii]: "Sleep, Death's twin brother"; and Hesiod's depiction of night as carrying her child Sleep in her arms: "and he is Death's brother" [*Theogony*, 756].

207.6 [116]: *some vague theory about his terminals being thereby connected*: not an exhausted battery but a sparkling joke: Neary's nightmare arises from the fear, logical or otherwise, that in certain kinds of syllogisms should the premises be transposed the conclusion may not be valid, i.e., the "terminals" or terms [L. *termini*] will not be connected. The image arises in Schopenhauer [*WWI*, II.1.x, 304]:

> The voltaic pile may be regarded as the sensible image of the syllogism. Its point of indifference, at the centre, represents the middle, which holds together the two premises, and by virtue of which they have the power of yielding a conclusion. The two different conceptions, on the other hand, which are really what is to be compared, are represented by the two opposite poles of the pile. Only because these are brought together by means of their two conducting wires, which represent the copulas of the two judgements, is the spark emitted on their contact—the new light of the conclusion.

See also André Breton's 1924 *Manifeste* [59]: "La valeur de l'image dépend de la beauté de l'étincelle obtenue; elle est, par conséquent, function de la différence entre les deux conducteurs" [Fr. "The value of the image depends on the spark obtained; it is, consequently, a function of the difference between the two conductors"]. Breton attributes this sentiment to Jules Renard [see #208.2].

208.1 [117]: *hot buttered buttocks*: not entirely a compliment; Neary's version of the once current "buttered bun," or woman taking in quick succession more than one sexual partner.

208.2 [117]: *so that water is oozing*: the source of an elaborate jest [see #213.1]. Beckett had been fascinated by Jules Renard's description in his *Journal* of the indignities of his last illness [Bair, 118; Cronin, 148], and the haunting account of how, unable to leave his bed and get to the chamber pot, he sat on the edge of the bed and watched the urine trickle down his leg:

Je veux me lever, cette nuit. Lourdeur. Une jambe pend dehors. Puis un filet coule le long de ma jambe. Il faut qu'il arrive au talon pour que je me décide. Ça sechera dans les draps, comme quand j'étais Poil de Carotte.

[Fr. "I want to get up, this night. Heaviness. One leg hangs out. Then a trickle runs along my leg. It will have to get to my heel for me to decide. It will dry in the sheets, as when I was a carrot-top"]. This is the last entry [April 6, 1910, 861], Renard dying a few weeks later.

208.3 [117]: *no staple*: compare the Song of Solomon 5:4: "My beloved put in his hand by the hole of the door, and my bowels were moved for him."

209.1 [117]: *belladonna*: It. "beautiful lady"; but also a name for deadly nightshade, since the poisonous plant could be distilled for eye-drops, which, dilating the pupils, create the allure of mysterious dark beauty. Compare Eliot's *The Waste Land* [line 49].

209.2 [117]: *the chamber pot*: the weaker vessel who tends the gentlemen of this unnamed establishment, but whose unflattering comparison to a skotora is an unobtrusive reminder of the water yet oozing towards the center of the floor.

211.1 [118]: *I thank you*: with rising pitch, "*Ay thang youw*," Arthur Askey's signature on *Band-Wagon* in the mid 1930s. The comedian reputedly "borrowed it from the London bus conductors" [Partridge].

211.2 [118]: *your doxy's*: traditionally, a woman of the stews. "Picked up" picks up the metaphor of venery [see #203.2].

211.3 [118]: *feels it in his bones . . . Uric acid*: Neary feels it "in his waters."

212.1 [119]: *he found it forcible*: since it is to him the irrefutable "Credo quia absurdum est" [L. "I believe because it is absurd"], a variant of "Certum est, quia impossibile est" [L. "I believe because it is impossible"], attributed (in Bartlett) to Tertullian [*De Carne Christi*, 5] or Augustine [*Confessions*, VI.v.7]. It is used in *Dream* [39], with reference to the proposition, relevant here, that love demands narcissism.

212.2 [119]: *I shall break my bed*: on the analogy of breaking one's fast. A phrase in the *Whoroscope* Notebook, ticked by Beckett as used but nowhere discernible, may be implicit in Neary's nakedness: "Not a rag of love about me." This derives from John Ford's *The Lover's Melancholy* [III.i], the words of the foolish Cuculus: "Pish! I have not a rag of love about me; 'tis only a foolish humour I am possessed with, to be surnamed the conqueror. I will court anything; be in love with nothing, nor no-thing."

212.3 [119]: *a little finger*: from the genteel custom in polite conversation of extending one's little finger thus in drinking tea; but here the little lacquered finger held out to Dives [see #5.7].

213.1 [119]: *To the absentee*: a sop for the groundlings, who would laff and quaff at a broken chamber pot; but an amber moment for the connoisseur who appreciates the Jacobite toast to the King "over the water": when followers of James II were obligated to make the loyal toast to William they would do so by first passing the glass over a bowl of water.

213.2 [120]: *one thief was saved*: at the crucifixion of Christ, in unorthodox opinion, the repentant thief (Dismas) was saved, while the unrepentant one (Gestas) was consigned to hell. Beckett commented to Harold Hobson in 1956:

> I take no sides. I am interested in the shape of ideas. There is a wonderful sentence in Augustine: "Do not despair, one of the thieves was saved. Do not presume, one of the thieves was damned." That sentence has a wonderful shape. It is the shape that matters.

The phrase in *Murphy* is the earliest citation of Beckett's most celebrated theme, rehearsed in *Waiting for Godot*, where it acts as an image of the uncertainty of salvation ("It's an even chance"). The *Whoroscope* Notebook records: "Never despair (1 thief saved) / nor presume (only 1 saved)." This is from 'The Repentance of Robert Greene,' the Elizabethan writer's recantation of his wicked ways, which includes several phrases and notions echoed in Beckett: a diatribe against his having ever been born; a cry to Dives to "haue one drop of water" for his tongue; admitting his faults to have been "red as skarlet"; but falling like the Dog to his old vomit; despairing that his soul could find favor in the sight of its maker; yet hoping that "as his iudgements are inscrutable, so are his mercies incomprehensible." The essay concludes with the sentiment that so appealed to Beckett that in the years to come he made it his own:

> To this doth that golden sentence of S. *Augustine* allude, which hee speaketh of the theefe, hanging on the Crosse. *There was* (saith hee) *one theef saued and no more, therefore presume not ; and there was one saued, and therefore despaire not.*

213.3 [120]: *Our medians . . . meet in Murphy*: a discrepancy lies at the heart of this exchange: Neary says, truly, that the circumference of some circle must pass through all three vertices of any and every triangle, including those which contain an *obtuse angle*, one greater than 90°, in which instance the center of that circle will lie outside the triangle. However, the *medians* of a triangle, the lines drawn from any angle of a triangle to the mid-point of the side subtending that angle, meet at the *median point*, which forms the center of the circle that may be inscribed *within* the triangle, in such a way as to touch all three sides. Neary is being obtuse, which is ironic given the motto above Plato's Academy: "Let no man ignorant of geometry enter here." Most who discuss this figure [e.g., Cohn, *Comic Gamut*, 46] mis-scribe it, yet the error is axiomatic: is Murphy to be the moving body that touches the figure of their three lives ("Outside us"), then moves on; or is he to be contained within them?

214.1 [120]: *You to play*: later the words of Hamm in *Endgame*, lost of old.

214.2 120]: *to the best of his ability*: the Socialist dictum: "From each according to his ability; to each according to his needs." In some citations, 'means' replaces 'ability.'

215.1 [120]: *snarled*: i.e., caught and held, but also entangled; another Bruno-word, the identified contraries of 'God' and 'Dog.'

215.2 [120]: *Coleridge-Taylor*: Samuel Coleridge-Taylor (1875-1912), an English composer whose father was from Sierra Leone. He is best known for his cantata, *Hiawatha's Wedding Feast* (1897), which led to similar works, collectively termed *The Song of Hiawatha*. These were received enthusiastically by a public intoxicated with the cult of the exotic, but less regarded by musicians, who saw the music as derivative of Dvořák but lacking the latter's harmonic inventiveness. He became a byword for banality. Beckett's French equivalent, rather unfairly, was Gounod. In his first year at Trinity, the University of Dublin Choral Society featured 'The Death of Minnehaha' and 'Hiawatha's Departure' (May 22, 1925). The concert reportedly played to a large and appreciative audience, and the essential qualities of Coleridge-Taylor's work were "exquisitely rendered by the choir" [*TCD: A College Miscellany*, xxi.543 (May 28, 1925), 163-64]. Beckett presumably saved his 2/-.

215.3 [120]: *the horehound*: a bitter aromatic herb with small purple flowers, *Ballota nigra*, known as "Black" or "stynkyng" horehound, or "stinkhound." In Fletcher's *The Faithfull Shepherdesse* [II.ii.13] it is said to be good for "sheepe or shephearde, bitten by a wood / Dogs venomd tooth." Pliny's *Natural History* [XX.xxii.75] says that a liniment made of horehound and old swine's grease cureth all wounds occasioned by the biting of mad dogs.

215.4 [120]: *an insult to human nature*: is Wylie offended (like Oscar Wilde) by Neary's suggestion of speaking the truth; or (like Karl Marx) by the socialist innuendo of its expression ("to the best . . ."); or by the physical impossibility of looking on the dark side of the moon? The midnight sun is literally that of the Arctic summer, but metaphorically implies the moon.

215.5 [121]: *Luke's portrait of Matthew*: in medieval tradition, St. Luke was a skilled painter, and, saith John of Damascus, painted a picture of the Virgin Mary, supposed to be in Rome; however, no such painting of Matthew by Luke is known to exist. *Dream* [138] mentions "the cute little Saint Matthew angel that I swear van Ryn never saw the day he painted"; prompting O'Brien to suggest [147]: "It is possible that Beckett's use of St. Luke as the artist was influenced by the painting in the National Gallery of Ireland, and that the St. Matthew he had in mind, as suggested to me by James Knowlson, was Rembrandt's painting of St. Matthew in the Louvre" (1661). The St. Luke (by Rogier van der Weyden) has the right expression, more or less, but there is no angel or parrot, and Rembrandt's Matthew, with the painter's son Titus as angel, is nothing like that described, saving the seated pose. O'Brien gives other paintings in which an Evangelist is seated with a dove at his ear [363]: Poussin's *Le Paysage avec Saint-Mathieu et l'Ange* and Carel Fabritus's *St. Matthew Writing his Gospel*. The literary portrait is a composite one, formed partly by the works O'Brien notes, but also by Wilenski's *Dutch Art* [72], which discusses another *St. Luke Painting the Holy Virgin and Child* (1532), by Martin Heemskerk for the Haarlem Cathedral; the text is opposite a striking Franz Hals portrait, *Hile Bobbe* (c. 1650), of a crazy old woman with an owl on her shoulder.

216.1 [121]: *its ballcock*: the floating ball, attached to a handle, inside the lavatory cistern, that shuts off the flow of water once the small tank is filled. Wylie and Miss Counihan continue the flow, responding to the Marxist implications of 'means' [see #214.2].

216.2 [121]: *covering his praecordia*: literally, his hand over the thoracic region of the heart; but see #6.5 for suggestions of the precordial, even the heartless.

216.3 [121]: *Old Moore*: an ancient almanac, offering astrological forces and determinants. An early incarnation read: "Vox Stellarum: Being an Almanack (a Loyal Almanack) for 1701. By Francis Moore, licensed Physician and Student in Astrology. Printed for the Stationers' Company, London, 1701." Publisher, title and format have been subject to mutablity over the years, but the *Almanack* has persisted to this day. In 1907 it begat a periodical publication, *Old Moore's Monthly Messenger*, which became the *British Journal of Astrology* [see #93.2].

216.4 [121]: *the Weekly Irish Times*: the Saturday supplement of the *Irish Times*, "Ireland's picture paper," which carried sports and features of the gossipy kind. It was published from June 1875 until November 1941, continuing thereafter as the *Times Pictorial* till June 1955 and the *Irish Pictorial* until March 1958 [John Gibson to CA].

216.5 [121]: *the ausculation, execution and adequation*: in a word, balance, as in "a balanced attitude." The sequence (listening, performing, and making equal) may derive from Geulincx [see #216.6], but I have not located the reference.

216.6 [121]: *Reason and Philautia*: 'Philautia,' from Gk. φίλος, "loving," and αὐτός, "self"; hence, "self-love"; an uncommon word, but picked up by Burton in his *Anatomy* [I.2.3.xiv, 193; DN, #779]. It occurs in Spinoza's *Ethica* [III §55; Brunschvicg, 209], and in the *Ethica* of Geulincx, where it is used in deliberate opposition to 'Ratio' or Reason, Geulincx affirming as an ethical principle listening [L. *ausculare*] to the voice of Reason. The clearest statement of the two is that given in the first note of the 'Annotata' [153]: "nam si nos ipsos curaverimus, non id fecerimus quod Ratio, sed quod Philautia, hoc est, amor sui ipsius jubet." [L. "thus if we stray, we do so not through Reason but through Philautia, that is, love which commands itself of itself"]. For Geulincx, Philautia was the greatest single cause of error, having its roots in the fact that 'Amor' is an amphibology ['Annotata,' 154], which in its wrong reading becomes *Amor Concupiscentiae*, concupiscent love that is a violation of the ethical axiom of Humilitas, or Humility, and thus a betrayal of the opening statement and central proposition of the *Ethica*: *Virtus est rectae Rationis Amor unicus* [L. "Virtue is uniquely the Love of right Reason"].

216.7 [121]: *a bull Io*: Io was a priestess of Juno at Argos; she was loved by Jupiter, but they were discovered by the goddess, even though Jupiter had shrouded himself in clouds and mists (as Neary tends to do). Jupiter changed his mistress into a beautiful heifer, but Juno sent one of the furies in the guise of a gad-fly to torment her, which it did incessantly until she was restored to human form.

216.8 [121]: *the Twenty-six Counties*: those making up the Republic of Eire, as distinct from the six counties of Ulster.

217.1 [121]: *so importunate*: inviting the Gilbertian rhyme, "most unfortunate."

217.2 [121]: *the creepy thing that creepeth*: a variation of Genesis 1:26, in which God gives man dominion over the fish of the sea, the fowl of the air, the cattle and "every creeping thing that creepeth upon the earth." This is St. Augustine's "omnium repentium, quae repunt super terram" [*Confessions*, XIII.xxiii, 432-33], the anticipation of the serpent of Genesis, an abomination in the eye of God and cursed by His Law to crawl upon its belly henceforth. In 'Walking Out' Lucy wonders if her Belacqua, a young man of good family, so spiritual, and a Varsity man too, could be "a creepy-crawly," or voyeur [*MPTK*, 116].

217.3 [122]: *the beaver bites his off*: i.e., his testicles. The reference is to Pliny's account in his *Natural History* [VIII.xlvii.109] of how beavers of the Black Sea region when hunted *castoreum id vocant medici* [L. "for what the doctors call castor-oil"] save their lives by biting off their testicles. The story is repeated by Juvenal [*Sat.* XII, 33-35], Nashe [*The Unfortunate Traveller*, 215], and Burton [*Anatomy*, II.3.6, 413; DN, #819], where it is urged to those with toothache to "pull them quite out." In the Middle Ages it featured in many a bestiary as an allegory of mankind casting aside temptation when pursued by the devil. The legend derives from L. *castor*, "beaver," with its scrotum-tightening suggestion of castration, and is described in *Dream* [63] as "a very persuasive chapter of Natural History." It is also implicit in 'What a Misfortune,' the title of which echoes Voltaire's *Che sciagura*: this ends with Belacqua's babylan vision of impotence, a beaver astride a mule, flogging it with a wooden sword [*MPTK*, 160].

217.4 [122]: *Since Heaven lay around you as a bedwetter.* Wordsworth's sentimental image of childhood in the *Immortality Ode* [line 66]: "Heaven lies about us in our infancy!" There may be a trace of the opening of Joyce's *Portrait*, where the infant Stephen Dedalus recalls an immediate sensation: "When you wet the bed first it is warm then it gets cold."

217.5 [122]: *half on the make*: diverting the diverb, "Half in earnest and half in jest."

218.1 [122]: *There is a mind and there is a body*: Miss Counihan, alas, confuses her self with her body. She has not cast off the cang of Cartesian realism, nor appreciated the force of what Schopenhauer says time and again, paying tribute to Kant for having recognized and articulated so clearly the distinction between the noumenal and the phenomenal, and insisting that our knowledge of the forms of space and time comes from within [*WWI*, II, 6-10, his criticism of Kant]. Schopenhauer's distinction beween Idea and Will must not be confused with the Cartesian or Occasionalist distinction between mind and body, but for him the latter had special significance as that part of the phenomenal world which can come into immediate knowledge. In his words: "The action of the body is nothing but the act of the will objectified, i.e., passed into perception"; and "the body is the knowledge a posteriori of the will" [*WWI*, I.ii §18, 130];. Hence, perhaps, Neary's sense of the part to be kicked.

218.2 [122]: *the one parched palm*: i.e., "on the one hand" (the body).

218.3 [122]: *the little ego and the big id*: Beckett knew the convenient capsulation of Freud's *The Ego and the Id* (1923) in Woodworth [154-55]. Freud revised his earlier consciousness-unconsciousness polarity as he appreciated that the ego, carrying out repression and resistance, was acting unconsciously. It was replaced by the theory of the battle between the two, between what may be called the surface of the mind, in contact with the environment, and the interior (which Neary, rather neatly, calls the pudenda of his psyche [see #47.5]). The id embraces the instinctive driving forces of the individual, reaching out to the environment and the conscious life, to be repressed by the ego, which makes it comply with the world's demands. Woodworth continues [155]:

> The id strives blindly for gratification in accordance with the pleasure principle; but it has to work through the ego which has learned the reality principle. The ego at first is weak and only slightly developed; consequently, it meets with many rebuffs in carrying out the behests of the id. It goes after many objects that the environment denies it. When the ego has to give up a love-object, it retains an image of that object and hugs the image to its heart, identifying itself with the object; and thus the ego grows by appropriating the character of the objects which it has had to renounce. If the ego develops successfully, it becomes coherent and well-organised, and adjusted to its environment. The id remains primitive and unorganized.

In Wylie's view of the matter, which seems to hold good for most of the group, this drama of the id and the ego seems to have been resolved in favor of the former.

218.4 [122]: *Infinite riches in a w.c.*: the mind within the body. The phrase anticipates the necessary house of the Abbey Theatre [see #269.2] where Murphy's happiest hours have been spent. The direct allusion is to Marlowe's *The Jew of Malta* [I.i.37]: "Infinite riches in a little room," the play opening with Barrabas discovered in his counting house. Beckett cited this in the *Whoroscope* Notebook, and ticked it as included. It became a commonplace, Shakespeare echoing it in *As You Like It* [III.iii.11-12]: "a great reckoning in a little room," 'reckoning' intimating the death of Marlowe; and Jonson borrowing it as a visual metaphor for the opening of Volpone.

218.5 [122]: *ineffable*: a favorite word to describe the incapacity to comprehend the workings of God; hence Arsene's attempt in *Watt* [62] to eff the ineffable. Malone contemplates conating and ineffing [218]. Geulincx uses 'ineffabile' in his *Ethica* [I.II.ii §6.3, 46] to describe the conjunction of mind and body; then, in the 'Annotata' [§17 and §18, 242-43] glosses the word by reference to the hypostasis, or dual nature of God in Christ: this may be the "sole redeeming feature" which Miss Counihan cannot remember (the pun on 'soul' very much the point).

218.6 [122]: *Darwin's caterpillar*: from Charles Darwin's *Origin of Species* [VII, 208], on the topic of Instinct, which is likened to habit and repetition:

> As in repeating a well-known song, so in instincts, one action follows another by a sort of rhythm; if a person can be interrupted in a song, or in repeating anything by rote, he is generally forced to go back to recover the habitual train of thought: so P. Huber found it was with a caterpillar, which makes a very complicated hammock; or if he took a caterpillar which had completed its hammock up to, say, the sixth stage of construction, and put it into a hammock completed only up to the third stage, the caterpillar simply re-performed the fourth, fifth, and sixth stages of reconstruction. If, however, a caterpillar were taken out of a hammock made up, for instance, to the third stage, and were put into one finished up to the sixth stage, so that much of its work was already done for it, far from feeling the benefit of this, it was much embarrassed, and, in order to complete its hammock, seemed forced to start from the third stage, where it had left off, and thus tried to complete the already finished work.

Belacqua tells the story in 'Echo's Bones' [23], but Doyle, the gardener, does not smoke the reference, so is taken further: "'He was working away at his hammock' said Belacqua, 'and not doing a damn bit of harm to man or beast, when up comes old Monkeybrand bursting with labour-saving devices. The caterpillar was far from feeling any benefit.'" Mr. Magershon begins to spin the same yarn, but, appropriately, is disturbed as he does [*Watt*, 194]. Beckett picked up a copy of the *Origin* in London in 1932 for 6d, but was disappointed ("badly written catlap"), preferring *Moby Dick*, which he got at the same time for the same price [Knowlson, 161]. The image is anticipated in Schopenhauer: "the caterpillar spins itself in leaves without knowing the end; but if we destroy the web it skillfully repairs it" [*WWI* III.2.xxvii, 101].

218.7 122]: *the cart-tail of the body*: malefactors might be tied to a cart-tail, and whipped as they were driven through the streets. Miss Counihan typically puts Descartes before discourse: the reversal of cart and horse is a commonplace for the confusion of cause with effect. The unnamed would include Kant and Schopenhauer, who expressed their dissatisfaction with the simple Cartesian dualism.

219.1 [122]: *psychosomatic fistulas*: from L. *fistulas*, "a pipe"; medically, an abnormal passage or communication between two internal organs, or from one to the surface of the body, the word usually designating the organs so linked ('aortoentric': linking the aorta to the intestine). 'Psychosomatic,' itself a semantic fistula, is nowhere listed, Miss Counihan using the word in its etymological sense of Gk. ψυχή, "mind," with σῶμα, "body." 'Fistula' appears in Swift's *A Tale of a Tub* [166], where, in a parody of Scholasticism, the "Vapours" of a mighty king (Louis XIV) are gathered in a tumor: "The same Spirits which in their superior Progress would conquer a Kingdom, descending upon the *Anus*, conclude in a *Fistula*."

219.2 [122]: *puerile grossness . . . senile agility*: an instance of chiasmus, the rhetorical changing of cart and horse.

219.3 [123]: *some colossal pitch of pure smut*: compare Keats's 'Ode on a Grecian Urn':

> Hear melodies are sweet, but those unheard
> Are sweeter, therefore, ye soft pipes, play on:
> Not to the sensual ear, but, more endear'd,
> Pipe to the spirit ditties of no tone.

Neary's response may critique Wordsworth's "The still, sad music of humanity" [*Tintern Abbey*, l.91], in terms of the Democritean sense of "tunes our ears cannot hear" [Beare, 207]. This is the consequence of his theory of sounds, according to which particles thrown off the sonic body as a stream of atoms make their way to their destination, where they try to enter all parts of the body, with only the ears shaped to receive them; in effect, the recognition of the small realm of auditory sense against the spectrum of possible sound, acoustical figures standing out against the ground of noise and the inaudible, as the rational against the absurd. This is another sense of Baudelaire's "gouffre interdit à nos sondes" [Fr. "the gulf forbidden to our sounding"; *Proust*, 31], or perhaps George Eliot's "roar which is the other side of silence" [*Middlemarch*, chapter 22]. Similar notions may lie behind Beckett's first published short story, 'Assumption,' with its paradox of silence and "the great storm of sound" [*Complete Short Prose*, 7], elsewhere termed the "incoherent continuum" [*Dream*, 102].

220.1 [123]: *the cat out of the bag . . . the pig out of the poke*: the first is to reveal something best kept back; the second, "to buy a pig in a poke," is to buy without seeing, 'poke' being a diminutive of "poche" or "pocket." The two are usually distinct, but Brewer (which Beckett owned) describes each in terms of the other:

> It was formerly a trick among country folk to substitute a cat for a sucking-pig, and bring it in a bag to market. If any greenhorn chose to buy a "pig in a poke" without examination, all very well; but if he opened the sack, "he let the cat out of the bag," and the trick was disclosed.

220.2 [123]: *the Goddess of Gout . . . brooding over a Doan's Pill*: there is, as Beckett had gleaned from Burton [*Anatomy*, II.1.3, 298], such a goddess: "Lucian makes Podagra (the gout) a goddess, and assigns her priests and ministers." The reference, not given by Burton, is to the Alexandrian satirist's PODAGRA, or 'Gout,' a 334-line dramaticule which celebrates the triumph of the gouty (ποδάγρος) over the doughty (πόδαργος), as the Goddess Podagra calls upon her retinue of Pains (Πόνοι) to assail every joint. Her opponents venture against her an ointment, which proves about as effective as a Doan's Pill, a patent remedy for back-ache.

220.3 [123]: *a true-born jackeen*: a variation of the stock phrase, "a true-born Englishman," best known from Shakespeare's *Richard II* (I.iii.308); echoed in Boswell's description of Dr. Johnson as "A stern, true-born Englishman" [1791]; but made infamous by Defoe [1701], who used it as the title of a satire. Beckett's source was probably Bartlett, where these three references are listed; but among his personal papers, Knowlson reveals [723], were notes he made for Joyce, probably in 1929, including "manuscript and typescript pages of notes on the *Trueborn Jackeen*." These are mostly on Irish history. Wylie enacts the phrase by his next comment, a Wilde-like quip about his "superiority to nothing."

220.4 [123]: *If the cock does not crow*: perhaps a reworking of Swift's mockery of platitudes in *A Tale of a Tub* [66]: "*Wisdom* is a *Hen*, whose *Cackling* we most value and consider, because it is attended with an *Egg*."

221.1 [123]: *met*: echoing Murphy's magnificent rejoinder to Celia [36]; and hereafter assuming various rags of love, as in Miss Counihan's use of Marlowe's *Hero and Leander*, (1598)]: "Who ever lov'd that lov'd not at first sight?" [line 176]. This is cited by Schopenhauer [*WWI*, III.4.xliv, 363], where it is attributed to *As You Like It* [III.v.82], the Bard having stolen Marlowe's mighty line. For indications that this usage had become a bauble compare the opening salvo of Swift's *Polite Conversation*, where the elegance of Marlowe and Shakespeare has degenerated into twaddle too tedious to recite. There may be a sense of things hobbling to their end, as in "they were all met together" of 'Fingal': "Surely it is in such little adjustments that the benevolence of the First Cause appears beyond dispute" [*MPTK*, 33].

221.2 [124]: *have a little conduction*: i.e., behave more convectionally. Beckett noted to Barney Rossett (20 November, 1958): "as my West Meath Nanny used to tell me—I have no conduction."

222.1 [124]: *these eyes of flesh*: from Job 10:4: "Hast thou eyes of flesh? Or seest thou as man seeth?"

222.2 [124]: *An obole*: in Ancient Greece, an insignificant coin, the sixth part of a drachma. In Plato's Academy, a struggling student asked what practical end mathematics served and was given an obole that he might feel he had gained something, then expelled. Hence the Biblical allusion that follows [I Corinthians 8:1]: "Knowledge puffeth up, but charity edifieth."

222.3 [124]: *this celebrated act of love*: i.e., charity, from L. *caritas*, a translation of the Gk. ἀγάπη, love, as in "Now abideth faith, hope, charity, these three; but the greatest of these is charity" [I Corinthians 13:13]. Neary's points three, one and two (an un-Hegelian sequence) may be based upon this teaching, with 'charity' interpreted in the tradition of the marketplace.

222.4 [124]: *on the way in . . . on the way out*: Thomas à Kempis's glad going out in the morning and sad coming in at night [*De Imitatione Christi*, I.xx.7; see also #103.3]; with his next sentiment, that a gay evening maketh a rueful morning: "Sic omne carnale gaudium blande intrat, sed in fine mordet et perimit" [L. "So every carnal joy enters pleasantly, but in the end it bites and stings to death"].

222.5 [124]: *the repudiation of the known*: the rejection of his "friends" in accordance with Hegel's dialectical process, whereby negation achieves the sublation [see #4.6].

223.1 [125]: *There He blows*: Leviathan, denizen of the Abyss, or darkness. ˌ

223.2 [125]: *crackling with sins*: the language is that of the unshriven penitent, and the situation more or less parallel with that in *Hamlet* [III.iii.37ff], where Claudius kneels in prayer, his sins heavy upon him and he unable to be absolved.

223.3 [125]: *an old flicker*: the typescript reads 'old admirer,' but Beckett recorded from Burton's *Anatomy* [III.2.1.ii, 500; DN, #969]: "An old Priapus flickering after a young wench"; the change (echoing 'crackling' and 'heat') was made accordingly.

223.4 [125]: *idle*: as in 'Tears, idle tears,' the opening words of the song of that title, in Tennyson's *The Princess*, and as echoed in *Dream* [149], a tale told at twilight.

224.1 [125]: *a curious feeling*: Neary begins to experience the irrational heart [see #3.9].

224.2 [125]: *The number of seconds in one dark night*: Sunday October the 20th, with sunset at 16:57 and the following sunrise at 6:34 (figures from Whitaker, 118); this gives 13 hours and 37 minutes of dark night, or 49,020 seconds. My pleasure.

224.3 [125]: *Neary's hair was white as snow*: a medical condition known as *leukotrichia*, the whiteness of the hair in a circumscribed area; admittedly, Neary's is somewhat excessive.

224.4 [125]: *a Junior Fellow*: Fellows of Trinity College were elected young after passing the difficult Fellowship examinations and providing evidence of distinguished scholarship; as such, they were a class apart from the teaching staff [Knowlson, 48]. There were two categories of Fellow, Junior and Senior, the distinction having little to do with age. The Madden Prize, in later works a recurrent motif, was a cash sum awarded to the runner-up in the Fellowship examination, provided he were of sufficient caliber.

224.5 [125]: *the canaille*: the word is not unusual (Beckett uses it in 'Serena I'), but when Schopenhauer discusses the aristocracy of the intellect, he contends that the multitude of men is "mere populace, mob, rabble, *canaille*." [*WWI*, 2.1.xv, 342]; a sentiment with which Bloomsbury would not disagree, saving its application. Beckett intensely disliked the precious literary clique, even before *Murphy* was rejected by the "Hogarth Private Lunatic Asylum," or Hogarth Press, run by Leonard and Virginia Woolf, who had also turned off *Ulysses*. When Leonard Woolf failed to return the typescript, Beckett wondered if it was his turn in the bin.

225.1 [126]: *I thank you*: like a London bus conductor [see #211.1].

225.2 [126]: *Millbank*: to the Tate Gallery, presumably to check out the Norwich School [see #196.3], the discovery of which may drive him to the gas-oven. Why Miss Counihan is "handing it out" remains a mystery, as she had earlier sucked up to him [196]. The Gallery, dedicated primarily to British art, opened in 1897 on the site of the Millbank Gaol, the £80,000 cost of erection borne by Sir Henry Tate, who contributed the nucleus of the later collection.

225.3 [126]: *Lassata*: from Juvenal's *Satire* VI.130 the infamous diatribe against women: "et lassata viris necdum satiata recessit" [L. "then exhausted by men but unsatisfied she went back"]. This refers to Messalina, wife of the emperor Claudius, who by night would take on all comers in a reeking brothel, remaining till the last and going away with passion still raging. Beckett had used the allusion in *Dream* [50], and wrote the phrase "lassata sed" on a card to Con Leventhal postmarked May 2, 1934 [Pilling, 'Losing One's Classics,' 13].

226.1 [126]: *a Bible in one hand and a poker in the other*: the Christian Soldier, imitating Pallas Athena, and traditionally depicted with lance and book as emblem of the soldierly life tempered by wisdom. Jeremy Taylor in *Holy Living* [68] is critical of the image: "St. Jerome very wittily reproves the Gentile superstition, who pictured the virgin-deities armed with a shield and lance, as if chastity could not be defended without war and direct contention."

226.2 [126]: *the groves of Blarney*: the Pythagorean Grove [see #54.2], blessed with the gift of cajolery. Blarney Castle, and its famous stone, is a few miles north of Cork, overlooking a glorious 18th century demesne on the banks of the Shournagh River, known as 'The Groves of Blarney' [O'Brien, 291]. These were celebrated by Father Prout [see #50.6] in 'A Plea for Pilgrimage,' written to recall Sir Walter Scott's visit to Blarney; and in a popular song, by Richard Alfred Milliken, as sung by Uncle Charles in Joyce's *A Portrait of the Artist* [60].

226.3 [126]: *the ruins of the ruins of the broth of a boy*: cited in the *Whoroscope* Notebook as "the ruins of the ruins of a fine man," attributed to Ford, and ticked as interpolated. From *The Broken Heart* [II.iii], the words of Penthea to Orgilus, whose suit she has rejected: "Alas, poor gentleman! / He looked not like the ruins of his youth, / But like the ruins of those ruins."

226.4 [126]: *East End*: Miss Counihan rather gives herself away: her vision of Murphy in the City comes across instead in terms of a Cockney's barrow.

227.1 [127]: *silk handkerchief*: the most outrageous touch in an outrageous chapter.

227.2 [127]: *if you care to step in*: this brings Miss Counihan out of her ecstasy [see #204.2].

227.3 [127]: *It was at this moment*: note the identity of phrasing with p. 213.

227.4 [127]: *hobble together for the only possible*: a maxim to be interpreted in accordance with Classical, Biblical and philosophical precepts. It reflects the sole surviving words of Leucippus, Master of Democritus, from his chapter 'On Mind': "Nothing happens at random, all happens out of reason (ἐκ λόγου) or by necessity" [Freeman, 289; Bailey, 85]. To the later ancients it seemed as if the Atomists assigned everything to chance, whereas their point was that "necessity" orders all things, that indeed by necessity the whole cause of things is ordained for all eternity: "the whole history of the universe is but the inevitable outcome, step by step, of its original and eternal constitution" [Bailey, 121]; the eternal atomic movement being the cause of all. Beckett may have taken the notion of hobbling from Bailey's "step by step." The Biblical text is unequivocal: "And we know that all things work together for good to them that love God, to them that are the called according to his purpose" [Romans 8:28]. Or, in Molloy's paraphrase [41]: "For all things hang together, by the operation of the Holy

Ghost, as the saying is." This is oft cited in support of predestination, and Murphy, for better or worse, is one of the elect [63]. Compare the writing on the wall at the Temple of the Holy Bottle [Rabelais, IV.xxxvii, 398]: "All things tend to their end." This is the doctrine of pre-established harmony, *harmonia praestablia*, maintained most famously by Leibniz, according to which there exists a harmony established before creation, whereby monads correspond though there is no communication between them each so prearranged that all its changes are accompanied by corresponding changes in others [*Monadology*, 41]. The notion is parodied in Swift's *A Tale of a Tub* [193], where Jack consoles himself for bouncing his Head against a Post: "*It was ordained*, said he, *some few Days before the Creation, that my Nose and this very Post should have a Rencounter; and therefore, Nature thought fit to send us both into the world in the same Age.*" Proust might call this the psychopathic universe [*Albertine disparue*, I.68]. Beckett's characters, their body-mind harmony dis-established and Occasionalist clocks disfunctional, would cautiously assent.

228.1 [127]: *Vermeer's*: the reference is to Vermeer's 'View of Delft' and to the passage in *A la recherche* where the dying writer Bergotte drags himself from his deathbed to see once more the rare beauty of the "petit pan de mur jaune" [Fr. "little patch of yellow wall"; *La Prisonnière*, I.255]. The "grand old yaller wall" outside the hospital is one of the last things Belacqua sees in 'Yellow' [*MPTK*, 180].

228.2 [127]: *the Balzac chairs*: see #63.4: there, the chairs threatened to collapse.

228.3 [127]: *Claude's Narcissus in Trafalgar Square*: a *paysage moralisé* by Claude Gellée, "called Le Lorrain" (1600-82), who started his career as a pastry-cook and ended in Rome as a popular landscape artist. The subject of the painting is Narcissus seeing himself, although with more pleasing opinion than the high-class whores, their new faces more art than nature. As O'Hara neatly describes the subject [*Hidden Drives*, 59]: "in love with himself, he has no need of a woman. Beautiful here in a work of art, he is untouched by the ravages of time that require face-lifting . . . Inclined to see his face in the water, he need not negotiate with it in the quid pro quo world that the whores inhabit." Claude might not have been impressed by Freud's critique of Narcissism, or creativity as disease or neurosis: the contention that artists are by definition narcissistic, given the rather crass notion that art is the product of self-absorption, and the artist too immature to face the pressures of outer reality.

228.4 [127]: *At the best nothing*: Neary's despairing realization, in Proustian terms [*Albertine disparue*, I.59], that while we cannot change things to our desire, our desire keeps changing: oblivion alone brings its extinction [57]. In Plato's *Apology* [40], Socrates concludes that either death is a state of nothingness and utter unconsciousness, or there is a change and migration of the soul from this world to another; either way, to die is to gain.

228.5 [127]: *The considered verdict*: Wylie, quick as a zebra, picks up Neary's allusion, and runs with his version of the Socratean judgement that the unexamined life is not worth living [Plato, *Apology*, 38]. The two citations follow consecutively in Bartlett.

228.6 [127]: *the Engels sisters*: the complex symbiosis of Marx and Engels, as manifested in their political lives and writings, transferred to the private realm. Although Friedrich Engels came to England in 1848 he did not marry until 1864; this suggests the better-known daughters (Jenny, Laura and Eleanor) of Karl Marx (1818-83), who shared their father's exile. There is a hint of the Elsner sisters, German-born and naturalized neighbors of Moran and of Beckett [Knowlson, 24-25]. The rhythm is used in *Watt* [70]: "We are the Galls, father and son."

229.1 [128]: *footfalls*: Beckett would use this image in the 1976 play of that name.

229.2 [128]: *green and yellow*: Neary blends his picture of the unseen Celia with that of Miss Counihan and the literary image of Duke Orsino's question in *Twelfth Night* [II.iv.112-18]:

> *Duke*: And what's her history?
> *Viola*: A blank, my lord. She never told her love,
> But let concealment, like a worm i'the bud,
> Feed on her damask cheek: she pin'd in thought,
> And with a green and yellow melancholy,
> She sat like Patience on a monument,
> Smiling at grief.

The various references to green and yellow, of the decay of nature, so conspicuous throughout the text, are drawn together at this moment. Beckett would pick up the contrast again in *Mercier and Camier* [109]: "Then there are the pretty colours, expiring greens and yellows vaguely speaking; they pale to paler still but only the better to pierce you, will they die, yes, they will."

229.3 [128]: *my swan crossword*: deliberately cryptic, but with echoes meant to be half-heard even as they fail to fall into a pattern. The most obvious, despite the extraneous swan-song, is Keats's panting rhyme to 'breath' ['Ode to a Nightingale']:

> Darkling I listen; and, for many a time
> I have been half in love with easeful Death,
> Call'd him soft names in many a mused rhyme,
> To take into the air my quiet breath;
> Now more than ever it seems rich to die...

The swan enters courtesy of Lord Gall's lines in 'Echo's Bones' [11], citing Burton [*Anatomy* III.3.1.i, 629; DN, #926], who is in turn citing Chaucer's 'The Parlement of Foules' [lines 342-43]:

> The jealous swan against his death that singeth,
> And eke the owl that of death bode bringeth.

The myth of the swan that sings before it dies, familiar from Coleridge and Mallarmé ("Un cynge d'autrefois . . ."), goes back to Plato's *Phaedo* [35 §84E-85B, 294-95]: "But men, because of their own fear of death, misrepresent the swans and say that they sing for sorrow, in mourning for their own death." Rather, he contends, they rejoice in their foreknowledge of the blessings in the world to come. This is not Celia's position, but the image implies that she has been contemplating suicide. Her distress is reflected in her rejection of the voices of the street, the myriad voices, which earlier sought to detain Murphy in the Big World.

230.1 [128]: *Do not give way to despair*: Miss Carriage's various words of *corajo* form a curiously bland panoply of classical and biblical exhorta: "Nil desperandum" [Horace, *Odes* I.vii]; "Be sober, be vigilant" [I Peter 5:8]; "Hope to the end" [I Peter 1:13]; and

"God shall wipe away all tears from their eyes; and there shall be no more death, neither sorrow, nor crying" [Revelation 21.4]. Each is to be found in Bartlett.

230.2 [129]: *But everything to gain*: to which Celia replies in kind [Matthew 16:26]: "For what is a man profited, if he shall gain the whole world, and lose his own soul?"

231.1 [129]: *bonam fidem*: a sign of good faith, but in the accusative singular, as seems proper to the fan rather than the letters which comprise it. Murphy, a declared non-reader, was once (it seems) a beau-lettrist.

232.1 [129]: *the post-golgothan kitty*: the pun is on 'redeemers,' in both the economical and ecumenical senses, as in Yeats's "For men were born to pray and save" ['September 1913']. Yet behind this lies Beckett's personal memory, dating from 1926 and invoking the insoluble problem of suffering and faith, as described by Knowlson [67]:

> One evening, he went with his father to All Saints Church at Blackrock to hear his father's friend, Canon Dobbs, deliver a sermon about his pastoral visits to the sick, the suffering, the dying and the bereaved. 'What gets me down,' said the minister, 'is pain. The only thing I can tell them is that the crucifixion was only the beginning. You must contribute to the kitty.' Beckett was horrifed by the logic of the cleric's position: not merely an open admission of total failure to cope with the problem of apparently undeserved suffering and an overt acceptance of the fact that it is the human lot to suffer, but a grisly justification for it. 'When it's morning, wish for evening,' Dobbs went on. 'When it's evening, wish for morning.' His sad litany of human suffering was close enough to Beckett's own feelings at the time to strike a vibrant, if chilling chord in the young scholar who had recently read Voltaire's story *Candide* with its remorseless, if ironic, piling up of human misfortunes and natural disasters.

As Knowlson concludes, the "kitty" for Beckett was a senseless accumulation of pain; thus pain and suffering could not have any moral value, and the argument that evil, pain and suffering are somehow part of a divine plan that we cannot hope to understand became an appalling affront to the suffering of the individual. Beckett used the notion in his poem 'Ooftisch' ("Auf dem Tisch," or put your money down, make your contribution):

> Golgotha was only the potegg
> bring along your misery
> the whole misery diagnosed undiagnosed misdiagnosed
> we'll put it in the pot with the rest.

One index of Moran's insensitivity is his relaxed disposition towards the Sabbath, "so long as you go to mass and contribute to the collection" [*Molloy*, 92]. Despite Miss Counihan's sneer, Celia's suffering has an intense immediacy and its lack of moral value renders it the more acute.

232.2 [130]: *the mental belch*: the repetition (Murphy is well brought-up).

233.1 [130]: *a soft perturbation*: mild confusion, unlike Burton's "great perturbation" [*Preface*, 12], as recorded in the Dream Notebook [#733].

233.2 [130]: *Errors and omissions excepted*: 'E. & O.E.,' a quasi-legal formula used by the insurance industry to cover inadvertent omissions. Beckett would later use the French version of the formula ('eooe', "erreur ou omission exceptée") to conclude his acrostical poem to Joyce, 'Home Olga.'

234.1 [130]:*the widow woman's cruse*: the account of Elijah in the desert, when the brook Cherith dried up, and he was told by the Lord to visit a widow woman who would sustain him [I Kings 17:16]: "And the barrel of meal wasted not, neither did the cruse of oil fail, according to the word of the Lord, which he spake by Elijah."

234.2 [130]: *resumed its fall*: to Wylie's ears, as to Duke Orsino at the beginning of *Twelfth Night*: "That strain again! It had a dying fall." The allusion hints at the end of T. S. Eliot's 'Portrait of a Lady': "Now that we talk of dying . . ."

234.3 [130]: *the little temporary gent and pure of heart*: difficult syntax, 'temporary' being adjectival and post-modifying 'little'; the geminate 'gent and pure in heart' chiefly used in poetical phrases, 'gent' having the sense of "elegant" or "slender."

234.4 [131]: *the last exile*: traditionally, Babylon before the return of the Jews to Zion. There may be a suggestion of 'Fingal' [*MPTK*, 34], and the tragedy of Vanessa (Swift's "motte"): "A land of sanctuary, he had said, where much had been suffered secretly. Yes, the last ditch." Celia's suffering is like that of Vanessa, abandoned by Swift, with only death before her.

234.5 [131]: *prostasis*: a proposition couched in the conditional clause, as in this sentence.

235.1 [131]: *Weep not, my wanton*: from Robert Greene's *Menephon* (1589), his "pastoral historie, conteyning the manifold injuries of fortune," the song of Sephestia to her babe when shipwrecked upon the Arcadian shore. Menaphon, the melancholy shepherd, hears her and declares his love, but proves unworthy; after many complexities, the baby seized by pirates and Menaphon outsung by one Melicertus (lost husband of Sephestia), the lady and child (now grown) are restored to their own, and Menaphon, having betrayed the shepherds' code, must recognize that his passions were too aspiring, and leave "such lettice as were too fine for his lips," marrying instead his old love, Pesana. The song is often anthologized, as an attractive, melancholy piece that forms a touching image of distant childhood and a sign of grief to come. Beckett had read widely in Greene [see #46.3, #79.3 and #213.2]. Best known as a dramatist, Greene wrote a variety of verse and prose, which exemplified his learning as a University wit and his dissipated life in the London stews. He was reviled for his attacks on his fellow dramatists, accusing Marlowe of "wind-puff'd wrath and drunkenness" and decrying Shakespeare as "an upstart crow wearing our bright feathers"; the scorn heaped on him in consequence ("hypercritical white-liver'd Greene") has contributed unfairly to the negligible opinion of his works.

235.2 [131]: *Love is a prick*: from 'What Thing is Love,' a song in *The Hunting of Cupid* (1591) by George Peele (1558-97). The verse begins:

What thing is love? for, well I wot, love is a thing.
It is a prick, it is a sting,
It is a pretty pretty thing;
It is a fire, it is a coal,
Whose flame creeps in at every hole;

And as my wit doth best devise,
Love's dwelling is in Ladies' eyes:

Peele was known less as a dramatist than as a lyricist. Educated at Pembroke and Christ Church, he achieved some success upon the stage, but led a dissolute life and died in distress. Leslie Daiken's notes from Trinity reflect the dismissive attitude to him prevalent in the 1920s: "a master of song-sense, Lyle's earliest follower. Popular pastoralian. Rhyming pentameters. His style must have produced MND. *Poor old pastoral Peele pegged out from pox.*"

Neither song was originally part of the text, as the Austin typescript reveals; the sense ran originally from Neary's "Call the woman" to Wylie's "She is at hand." Both passages are in the *Whoroscope* Notebook, marked for interpolation, and ticked as having been included. The effect is of a touching flashback to Celia's earliest years, beautifully integrated so as to leave the chapter with the focus on Celia, and on a poignant melancholy note. Which is then brutally undercut . . .

235.3 [131]: *a real goat*: as things now limp to their promised end, one is perhaps reminded of the ending of *Watt*, and Frank Doherty's comment about a metaphysical farce of cruelty taking place in the midst of a self-satisfied world [Doherty, 20]:

Riley's puckaun again, said Mr Nolan, I can smell him from here.
And they say there is no God, said Mr Case.
All three laughed heartily at this extravagance.

11

236.1 [132]: *Late that afternoon*: October 19, 1935, Murphy's moon in its last Quarter [Whitaker, 118].

236.2 [132]: *music, MUSIC, MUSIC*: the crescendo, or typographical "scream" (the echo of Edvard Munch may be audible), is present in the *Whoroscope* Notebook [§30], and survived the attentions of the gentle compositors, even in the Picador edition. The next words, whatever their musical overtones, derive from the art of typesetting:

brilliant: a size of type about $3^1/2$ point; so-called for its clarity.
brevier: about 8 point; so-called from its use in printing breviaries.
canon: from Gk. κανών, "belonging to a rule"; a 48 point type.

236.3 [132]: *instruments of recreation*: the expected collocation might be "instruments of torture," as shown ritually to victims of that fourth Fury, the Inquisition. That they are "at the foot of the cross" and "shrouded" authorizes the pun on *re-creation*, while Murphy's walking round suggests the Stations of the Cross, with his death an ironic Imitation of Christ. Compare Estragon in *Waiting for Godot* [34]: "All my life I've compared myself to him."

236.4 [132]: *the gulf . . . to cross it . . . dreaded*: a teasing intimation of two familiar sentiments: Tennyson's 'Crossing the Bar' (in popular belief, his last work), and Hamlet's dread of something after death. This kind of "allusion" (one cannot even call it echoing) is more a *petite perception* than an *apperception*, yet the quiet insinuation of poetic effect is part of Beckett's staffage: thus, "crossing the gulf" invokes other staurolitic "wrecks" [see pp. 166 and 239]. For aspects of the gulf between the ideal and the real, object and subject, see #5.7 and #177.3.

237.1 [133]: *man proposed, but God disposed*: proverbial, but deriving for Beckett from Thomas à Kempis's "homo proponet sed Deus disponit" [*De Imitatione Christi*, I.xix.2]:

> Neverthless in divers ways we may fail in our purpose; and even though our falling off be slight, the omission of our exercises causes hindrance to our souls. The resolution of righteous men depends not on their own wisdom but upon the grace of God, in Whom, in whatsoever they do, they put their trust. For man proposeth, but God disposeth; neither is any man sufficient unto himself.

With similar resignation, Burton notes several times in the *Anatomy* that the stars incline, but do not compel (yet he died to fulfil his prediction of the day of his own death). In his 1924 *Manifeste* [30], André Breton challenged this commonplace ("L'homme propose et dispose") by affirming poetry as a compensation for the miseries we must endure; one advantage of surrealism being its farewell of such romantic extravagances as "les rêves de gouffres" [Fr. "the dream of gulfs"].

238.1 [133]: *The indicator was most ingenious*: there was such a system at the Bethlem Royal Hospital, in effect a model of a neurological stimulus-response system, but one that (Beckett noted) could be (and was) subverted by tired or indolent nurses. He entered the procedure in the *Whoroscope* Notebook:

> Night round. Must visit wards every 15 or 20 minutes, stop at every cell, switch on light from outside & look through judas. As he does each cell he must press switch that records on main switchboard so that his round can be calculated by authority in morning.

238.2 [133]: *"uncooperative"*: the phrases in quotation marks, concerning the treatment of patients objecting to being bullied, are recorded in the Notebook and derive directly from Beckett's visits to the Bethlem Royal.

238.3 [133]: *the therapeutic voodoo*: the likening of psychiatric procedure to the rites and rituals, mumbo-jumbo and sorcery, of creole cults; an interesting comment in the light of Beckett's experiences of therapy. Beckett had translated for Nancy Cunard's *Negro, an Anthology* (1934) a number of pieces, including Jenner Bastien's 'Summary of the History of Hayti' [459-64] and Ludovic Lacombe's 'A Note on Haytian Culture' [470-71].

238.4 [133]: *the Phidias and Scopas of Fatigue*: as Vivien Mercier points out [93], Beckett ranges over the history of sculpture from Periclean Athens to his day: "Phidias and his school of the fifth century BC are of course famous for the restraint and repose of their work, whereas that of Scopas and his school of the following century is notorious for violence and emotionalism." Neary's contrast of the two in terms of Sleep and Insomnia, whatever academy inspired it, shapes the next two paragraphs.

Phidias: son of Charmidas and creator of the statue of Athena, a 39' work of ivory and gold commissioned by Pericles for the Parthenon. He may have carved the Elgin marbles. Phidias was admired for his taste and learning, but was accused of arrogance and banished from Athens to Elis, where he created a statue of Zeus, some 60' high, that passed for one of the wonders of the world. Robert Greene comments in 'Penelope's Web' [V.144]: "I sleep content like Phidias in myne own follies, thinking all is well, till proofe tells me the contrarie."

Scopas: architect and sculptor of Ephesus, c. 430 BC. was employed in making the mausoleum which Artemisia raised to her husband; this too was reckoned one of the wonders of the world. His statue of Aphrodite (Venus) was much admired by the Romans.

239.1 [134]: *the Pergamene Barlach*: this reference is not in the typescript of *Murphy*, and represents one of the few changes made to the text between submission (1936) and publication (1938). Beckett was familiar with the Pergamene school of Hellenistic sculpture, and one reason for visiting Berlin (December 1936) was to see its greatest surviving monument, the Altar of Zeus from Pergamon. During that visit he became familiar with the work of the sculptor Ernst Barlach (1870-1938), whose huddled figures in stone and teak, as Mercier says [94], are irresistibly suggestive of his own. One of the books he sent home from Germany (as listed in the *Whoroscope* Notebook) was Barlach's *Zeichner des Volkes* [Ger. "Artist of the People"].

239.2 [134]: *Puget's caryatids of Strength and Weariness*: Beckett had visited Toulon with his brother Frank in summer of 1931 [Knowlson, 132], and Murphy's experience was no doubt his own, as a glance at the caryatids on the *Hôtel de Ville* will confirm. Pierre Puget (1620-94), native of Marseilles, was a sculptor, naval decorator and marine artist. In 1656 the Toulon authorities decided to embellish the Town Hall, and Puget, who had made his mark with a series of carvings for the naval base and arsenal, submitted his design for the facade. The crowning piece was to be two *Atlantes* in the style of Michelangelo supporting the balcony above them, the one representing *Force* and the other *Fatigue*. The commission was granted enthusiastically. It was completed by 1657, and the caryatids have been the glory of the Town Hall since. The Inventory of *Monuments civils de Toulon* describes them as follows [details courtesy of M. Louis Soccoja, *Adjoint au Maire, Ville de Toulon*, to CA]:

> Ces deux figures d'hommes, dont tous les muscles sont contractés, semblent succomber sous le poids du balcon; elles font un effort suprême pour ne pas être écrasseés par ce lourd fardeau. L'une, celle du gauche, soutient son torse, pour l'empêcher de fléchir, en appuyant sa main droite sur la hanche, tandis qu'elle port son avant-bras gauche contre son front, pour ne pas être aveuglée par les rayons solaires. La seconde figure, à droite, supporte de la main gauche le balcon et arc-boute de l'autre sa tête qui semble céder sous le faix.

[Fr. "These two male figures, whose every muscle is contracted, seem to succumb beneath the weight of the balcony; they make a supreme effort not to be crushed beneath this heavy burden. One, to the left, holds its body, to stop it giving way, by leaning its right hand on the hip, while it brings its left fore-arm against its forehead, so as not to be blinded by the rays of the sun. The second figure, to the right, supports the balcony and buttress with its left hand, and with the other its head, which seems to give way beneath the burden."] The columns are about three meters high. The model for the left figure was one Bertrand Marquet, a legendary strong-man of the region, who once lifted a large bell onto his shoulders and hoisted it up to the campanella. He represents Strength, and even though nobody seems anxious to claim Weariness the similarity of the two makes Murphy's perplexity understandable. Murphy's experience at Toulon is not unlike that of Proust's Marcel at Combray [*Swann*, I.121, as marked in Beckett's copy], where faced with the "Vertues et Vices de Padour" he first registers his dislike of their apparent rapport with their allegorical subjects, then later understands:

. . . que l'étrangeté saisissante, la beauté spéciale de ces fresques tenait à la grande place que le symbole y occupait, et que le fait qu'il fut représenté non comme un symbole puisque la pensée symbolisée n'était pas exprimée, mais comme réel, comme effectivement subi ou matériellement manié, donnait à la signification de l'oeuvre quelque chose de plus littéral et de plus précis, à son enseignement quelque chose de plus concret et de plus frappant.

[Fr. "that the arresting strangeness, the special beauty of these frescos, arises from the great part played in each of them by its symbols, while the fact that these were represented, not as symbols since the symbolized thought was not expressed, but as real, as actually felt or materially handled, gave something more literal and more precise to their meaning, something more concrete and striking to the lesson they imparted."]

239.3 [134]: *the frozen attitudes of Herculaneum*: the great eruption of Vesuvius in AD 79 destroyed Pompeii and devastated the neighboring city of Herculaneum, which was covered by a sudden shower of ashes and cinders and drenched with water, so that the effluvia hardened into a kind of tufa, in places 65 foot deep. The deluge was so sudden that it acted like clay or plaster of Paris, which made it possible in later years to take molds of artifacts and dead bodies "frozen" in the precise positions and postures as when the calamity occurred. Compare Proust [*Jeunes filles* II.198]: "La nature, comme la catastrophe de Pompeii, comme une métamorphose de nymphe, nous a immobilée dans le mouvement accutomé" ["Nature, like the catastrophe of Pompeii, like a metamorphosis of a nymph, has frozen us in habitual movement"].

239.4 [134]: *an act of God*: the usual euphemism for disasters such as the destruction of Herculaneum or the Lisbon earthquake, for which no human or insurance agency can bear responsibility.

239.5 [134]: *nature's soft nurse*: the Phidias of Fatigue, as apostrophized in *2 Henry IV*.i.4-8:

O sleep! O gentle sleep!
Nature's soft nurse, how I have frighted thee,
That though no more wilt weigh my eyelids down
And steep my senses in forgetfulness.

239.6 [134]: *knit up the sleave*: the Scopas of Fatigue, as endured in *Macbeth* II.ii.36-41:

Methought I heard a voice cry, "Sleep no more!
Macbeth does murder sleep!" The innocent sleep,
Sleep that knits up the ravel'd sleave of care,
The death of each day's life, sore labour's bath,
Balm of hurt minds, great nature's second course,
Chief nourisher in life's feast.

240.1 [134]: *adminicles*: from L. *adminiculum*, "a prop or support." Beckett took the word from Geulincx's *Ethica*, where it combines exhortation, admonition, and advice. It is associated with the ethical obligations discussed in the first Tractatus, and which embody the principle teaching of the book. Geulincx concludes his discussion of these by summarizing the previous argument ['Annotata,' 268], listing the adminicles which constitute his ethical system, and reiterating the *adminiculum humilitatis*, of which the *Nihil vales* [see #178.9] is the core.

240.2 [134]: *the adjacent female wards*: confirming the earlier speculation [see #165.3] that the model for Skinner's Ward was Tyson's, which contained, partitioned from one another, both male and female patients. The touch of Cleopatra in the "infinite variety" of sound is not, one assumes, a compliment to those within.

240.3 [134]: *The cackle of a nightingale*: less Keats than Shelley, and probably neither; but in the latter's 'Defence of Poetry' the poet is likened to a nightingale "who sits in darkness and sings to cheer its own solitude with sweet sounds."

240.4 [134]: *all. All. ALL*: the pattern of brilliant, brevier and canon [see #236.2] anticipates not only Murphy's wish to scream, but his other need, as yet unacknowledged, to face the music by recognizing that the gulf between him and the microcosmopolitans must remain "unintelligible"—a word with all the weighting of the Greek ἄλογος [see #77.2].

240.5 [134]: *the most biddable little gaga*: the most compliant of the insane, one who does as he is bid. 'Gaga' means in argot "a senile old man," such as Proust's Baron de Charlus: "une impayable bobine de gaga de la plus haut ligne" [Fr. "a priceless spool of a gaga, of the highest lineage"; *Jeunes filles*, III.20]. In English the word is used attributively, as in "he was quite gaga"; the *OED* Supplement cites this as its first recorded use as a substantive.

241.1 [134]: *the thousand candles*: a kilowatt light bulb, or, more reasonably, the switch turning on a smaller bulb or bulbs to flood the cell with light of hyperbolic ferocity.

241.2 [135]: *tailor fashion*: cross-legged, a position characteristically assumed by the Buddha (seeking the light), or prisoners sewing mailbags (dwellers in cells).

241.3 [135]: *in fifty-six other directions*: not compass directions, which would necessitate a further sixty for the requisite power of two; but the temporal displacement of extension (as is appropriate in Mr. Endon's world), with reference to the face of a clock or watch. Beckett's fascination with the incommensurability of the co-ordinates of space and time emerge later in *Ill Seen Ill Heard*, with its structure of sixty-one paragraphs, the last a desperate coda, a surplus minute or hour [Piette, 238], and its central image of the stop-watch with "Sixty black dots," each set to a compass point.

241.4 [135]: *smooth and taut as a groaning wife's belly*: listed among the Elizabethan and Jacobean citations marked for interpolation in the *Whoroscope* Notebook. It is drawn from Thomas Nashe's *The Unfortunate Traveller* [255], where Jack Wilton arrives at the house of Tabitha the Temptress: "On her beds there was not a wrinkle of any wallowing to be found, her pillows bare out as smooth as a groning wiues belly, & yet she was a Turk and an infidel, & had more dooings then all her neighbours besides."

241.5 [135]: *winsome fiat*: happy sanction, or compliant authority; in the circumstances the suggestion of *fiat lux* [L. "Let there be light"; Genesis 1:3] suggests less fiat than fiasco.

242.1 [135]: *Murphy's eye . . . the chessy eye*: a distant vista of Wordsworth's 'Daffodils': "That inward eye / Which is the bliss of solitude"; more nearly, "Morphy's eye," that of the great American (1837-84) who could play for hours without fatigue, barely acknowledging the existence of his opponent; closer still, Ernest Jones's 'The Problem of Paul Morphy' (1931), which examined his problems in finding a job, his difficulties in maintaining relations with women, and the depression which led to a reclusive and sedentary existence, mental illness, and an ambiguous death. The problem is discussed in Ian Fleming's *Moonraker* [56]:

> Morphy, the great chess player, had a terrible habit. He would never raise his eyes from the game until he knew his opponent could not escape defeat. Then he would slowly lift his great head and gaze curiously at the man across the board. His opponent would feel the gaze and would slowly, humbly, raise his eyes to meet Morphy's. At that moment he would know it was no good continuing the game. The eyes of Morphy said so. There was nothing left but surrender.

Looking into Mr. Endon's eyes [249], Murphy will experience that knowledge of defeat.

242.2 [135]: *the hypomanic*: the hypomanic has become a hypermanic [see #168.2].

243.1 [136]: *an Endon affence*: the word 'affence' derives not from Ger. 'Affe,' "ape," tempting though that might seem in light of Beckett's fondness for the chimps playing chess, but from the rather obscure chess term, 'affidatus,' meaning "immune from capture."

243.2 [136]: *Zweispringerspott*: Ger. "Two Knights Mockery"; this variation of the conventional 'Two Knights Defence' begins with Black's first move, which should also have been P-K4. Beckett's lasting fascination with chess is well known. He learned as a child, played all his life, and the Chess Club at Trinity College was perhaps the only society in which he ever took office, acting as Treasurer in his final year. The attraction needs little comment. Gerald Abrahams in *The Chess Mind* [ix] makes the unassailable claim that chess is the closest the human mind has come to creating a game which is purely an act of pure contemplation: "If it be clear, in any context, that a mind can succeed in completely controlling its subject matter, and in advancing far beyond its earliest restrictions, then there is a principle of activity in being which cannot be explained away as a mere epiphenomenon of material forces in collision." Yet it is also a confrontation in which one will meets another, with rational laws agreed to by both parties (the world reduced to a set of intelligible rules), these points qualifying any hint of the free or solipsistic imagination. See also #187.2.

243.3 [136]: *1. P-K4*: indeed, the primary cause of all White's subsequent difficulties, as it initiates a movement towards increasing disorder that cannot be reversed. The ultimate consequences of this attrition may be seen, many years later, in *Endgame*. Mr. Endon is not unaffected by the course of events, for, to move his Bishops about, he is forced at moves 9 and 13 to make the smallest concessions to entropy compatible with the laws of chess. By then, of course, Murphy's men are in irreversible disarray. P-K4, the royal opening, might be regarded as predictable, Kingside openings generally less adventurous than the Queenside ones; the Voice of 'Assumption' [5] accordingly scorns P-K4.

243.4 [136]: *2. Kt-KR3*: the first attempt to create symmetry, but to little avail since Murphy, despite playing white, is a tempo behind. His next two moves keep the faith, but when at move 4 Black takes his Knight to K4 Murphy is confounded because his opening move has occupied that key square. Hence the annotation (a parody of chess analysis): "Apparently nothing better, bad as this is."

243.5 [136]: *7. Kt-QB3*: symmetry apparently restored. Not for long. After White's ninth move Black is perfectly composed, his Fabian outing completed without loss [see #187.3], but White still has his pawn on K4 poorly placed. Black (P-K3) makes a necessary compromise, and Murphy (P-KKt3) makes a move indeed ill-judged: there can be no going back.

243.6 [136]: *12. P-KKt4*: again, White was unable to mirror the previous move because the square is occupied. For a while he manages to follow Black's lead—but he is now two moves behind. On move 16, Black places his Queen on K1, reversing the looking-glass polarities of his own forces. White struggles on; then, apparently giving up ("The flag of distress"), at move 18 brings out his Queen's Knight. After this loss of tempo there is no catching up.

243.7 [136]: *20. Kt-QR4*: curiously, the first opportunity to take a piece without significant loss; Black may choose to win the Knight with either his Knight or his Queen. Instead, he moves his Bishop to Q2, and is now attacking the piece three times.

244.1 [136]: *22. K-QB1*: Black's move earns the approbation "Exquisitely played" because White cannot duplicate it. He tries! But by the end of move 23 Black has retained perfect symmetry, and White's position is a disgrace.

244.2 [136]: *27. Q-KR6*: more despair than ingenuity: a Queen sacrifice with no return, simply to force Black to react. Mr. Endon calmly completes yet another perfectly symmetrical pattern (his irresistible game); and White can violate that integrity only by taking a piece. His attenuated efforts to force Black to do so, however, meet with no success.

244.3 [136]: *30. Kt-QB5*: White now has three pieces *en prise*. His next move, of the Knight back to KR1, and described as a *coup de repos*, however one might translate that, less asylum than exile perhaps, is surely the most futile in the history of Chess; it is not even bad. Mr. Endon continues relentlessly, beginning his wandering to find home.

244.4 [136]: *34. Q-K1*: as the note points out, Murphy is in check. This is adventitious, rather than advantageous; nevertheless, White moves out of check.

244.5 [136]: *38. Kt-QR6*: the offensive is "abject" because it threatens to force Mr. Endon to move his Rook back to its corner in precipitate haste. But Black is immune to such threats.

244.6 [136]: *41. Q-QB6*: a moment of truth. Both sides may temporize for a move or two, Black completing the return of the minor pieces and White marking time with his King; but this move creates the crisis, for when Black at move 44 returns the King to its home square this will constitute an illegal move, into check. Murphy has the options of doing nothing, removing his Queen, or moving into K8, to force Mr. Endon to take note of him; the latter could not be ignored. Bair says [225] "one more square," i.e., to Q7, which resolves nothing. Henning suggests ['Guffaw,' 14] that Murphy resigns because the move (to K8) would indicate once and for all whether Mr. Endon perceives him, that is, whether he exists for Mr. Endon or not. Murphy knows the answer, but does not put it to the test, as he will a little later. His surrender therefore recognizes that Mr. Endon's next move will complete a pattern, to the fearful symmetry of which he has no other response; but it is a surrender that makes inevitable another to come. To be sure, Murphy could force the issue by moving to K8 or insisting on the check; but to little avail, as Mr. Endon, without the least trace of annoyance, would simply fade away. It has been an exquisitely comical game, but the joke is on Murphy.

244.7 [136]: *42. . . . K-K2*: as Declan Kiely first noted [135], in many editions of *Murphy* Mr. Endon's move 42 is incorrect, being printed as K-Q2, an illegal move into check. The Routledge original, the Grove Press printing and the French translation are correct; the error crept in when the novel was reset for the 1963 Jupiter edition, and was replicated in the Picador version where it went unnoticed even by those (Taylor and Loughery, 1989; myself, 1998) writing specifically on the game.

244.8 [137]: *the Café de la Régence*: in Paris, "the Mecca of chess players from all over the world" [Jones, 'Paul Morphy,' 6], particularly in the late 18th and early 19th centuries, when it was frequented by players such as Philidor, Rousseau, Deschapelles and Bourdonnais, and amateurs such as Voltaire, Franklin and Napoleon. Morphy played there in the 1850s, in the Café's last days of glory.

244.9 [137]: *Simpson's Divan*: in 1828 Samuel Reis opened in the Strand a "Home of Chess," known also as "The Grand Cigar Divan"; the daily charge was 6d with coffee, and the original chess pieces may be seen in the hall. In 1848, John Simpson, a noted caterer, joined Mr. Reis; they enlarged the building and renamed it "Simpson's Grand Divan and Tavern" [details from the menu]. Mr. Simpson became known for his excellent meals, and under his direction the habit of wheeling in hot joints on silver carving wagons became a celebrated feature. The leading English chess player, Harold Staunton, dined there often, and from 1857 Charles Dickens was a regular guest, enjoying the boiled fish. Simpson's in the Strand has been thereafter one of the more popular and expensive London restaurants.

245.1 [137]: *j'adoube*: Fr. "I adjust"; said by a player who wishes to adjust a pawn or piece that he would be otherwise obliged to move. Mr. Endon's inversion of his two rooks, or castles, promotes them undeservedly to Queens.

245.2 [137]: *A coup de repos*: untranslatable [see #244.3], but implying the need for rest, if not grace.

245.3 [137]: *Law 18*: an historical curiosity: the Laws of Chess, as established by FIDE (the *Fédération Internationale des Échecs*), currently state [Article 9.3] that "Declaring a check is not obligatory." This would have been so when this game took place; one is not absolved from attending to an undeclared check. The rules and their numbering have undergone extensive revisions over the years. Before 1924 there was no international authority, and tournaments were plagued by different interpretations of minor points. Howard Staunton, the 19th century giant of English chess (Beckett owned a Staunton chess set, inherited from his father and later stolen from Ussy), in his various promotions published the Rules; these were generally accepted in the English-speaking world, and Ireland. Beckett is probably citing one such early guideline in which it would not be improbable to find the condition specified here.

245.4 [137]: *vis-à-vis*: Fr. "face to face"; i.e., not an opponent, since that implies a sense of engagement, but the one sitting opposite; the epiphenomenal salute is described conditionally as 'adventitious,' or accidental, to emphasize the point.

245.5 [138]: *solitaire*: not a chess term, but rather a variety of "fox and geese," as invented by a French nobleman in solitary confinement in the Bastille, and played by an individual on a cross-shaped board with 32 pegs and 33 holes, the object being to jump over pegs and remove them, in such a way as to end with one peg in the middle hole.

245.6 [138]: *fool's mate*: metaphorical, rather than literal: this is the quickest form of Mate, sometimes called the Irish Gambit, which results in White being checkmated at Black's second move. Eight Watt-like permutations bring about the promised end:

	1. P-KB3	P-K3	2. P-KKt4	Q-R5++
or:	1. P-KB3	P-K4	2. P-KKt4	Q-R5++
or:	1. P-KKt4	P-K3	2. P-KB3	Q-R5++
or:	1. P-KKt4	P-K3	2. P-KB4	Q-R5++
or:	1. P-KB4	P-K3	2. P-KKt4	Q-R5++
or:	1. P-KB4	P-K4	2. P-KKt4	Q-R5++
or:	1. P-KKt4	P-K4	2. P-KB3	Q-R5++
or:	1. P-KKt4	P-K4	2. P-KB4	Q-R5++

Flann O'Brien uses variant #5 in *At Swim-Two-Birds*, in mock-celebration of the ancient Irish legends that feature chess, the Pooka winning Granya from Dermot by that strategy.

245.7 [138]: *laying his Shah on his side*: an act of resignation, conceding defeat by placing the King on its side. Technicalities apart (time, infringement of the rules), victory in chess arises only from checkmate (derived from two Persian words, *Shah*, or "king," and *mat*, "helpless" or "defeated"; in popular parlance "the King is dead"); however, a player may choose to resign, even from a winning position.

246.1 [138]: *an after-image*: more strictly, an *after-sensation*, the image formed by the continuance of the process in the sense receptor after the external stimulus has ceased. Such images are often marked by complementary color-contrast; hence, perhaps, the emphasis upon Mr. Endon's finery and the colorless treat that follows.

246.2 [138]: *a rare postnatal treat*: the absence of *percipere* in terms of the return to the womb. With respect to Plato's account of sensation, and invoking his distinction between *percipiens* and *percipiendum* [perceiving and being perceived], Beare comments [214]:

> The eye does not see when not affected by colour; the object is without colour when not seen by an eye. Nothing therefore is or becomes what it is or becomes for itself and in itself, but only in relation to the subject perceiving.

Thus, to see nothing is to see that which has no color, and that which has no color is, by reciprocation, Nothing. The "colourlessness" of Mr. Endon's irises supports this conjecture.

246.3 [138]: *the absence . . . not of percipere but of percipi*: the distinction so nicely (i.e., precisely) abused, though pertinent to pre-Socratic thought, derives from Jules Gaultier's *De Kant à Nietzsche*, as recorded in the Dream Notebook [#1150]. However, in *Murphy* it reflects the celebrated assertion of George Berkeley [1685-1753], Anglo-Irish philosopher and Bishop of Cloyne, who lectured at Trinity before his ordination into the Church of Ireland [see #58.2]. His main argument is summarized in what he admitted to be the keystone to his work, *esse est percipere*, "to be is to be perceived," or, in the extension to which Beckett alludes, *esse est aut percipi aut percipere*, "to be is either to be perceived or to perceive." These assert that the objects of sense perception (his famous instance was the tree in the quad of TCD) have no knowable existence outside the mind that perceives them; from this premise he reasoned that all reality ultimately consists in the mind of God. In response to this Boswell observed to Johnson (1763) that Berkeley's doctrine, however unlikely it might seem, did not admit of refutation; to which the Great Man replied with his celebrated *coup de pied*, "I refute it thus" [Boswell, *Life*, August 6, 1763, 160]. Berkeley's paradox remained central to Beckett's perception hereafter, as witness the tree in *Waiting for Godot*, or Buster Keaton's difficulties in *Film* (which arises directly out of *Murphy*), trying to evade the all-seeing Eye/I. There are also the celebrated Limerick twins, the first fathered by Monsignor Ronald Knox and the second appropriately anonymous:

> There was a young man who thought, "God
> Must find it eternally odd
> If He thinks that this tree
> Will continue to be,
> When there's no-one about in the Quad."

> "Dear sir, your astonishment's odd;
> I am *always* about in the Quad,
> And that's why this tree
> Will continue to be,
> Since observed by, yours faithfully, God."

Compare, too, the distinction made by Democritus between "true knowledge" and that which is not genuine, between the existence of atoms and the void, on the one hand, and t   ctive characterisitics of perception on the other [Baldwin, II, 336]. Protaç   jarded perception as the only source of knowledge, and so denied any knowl   vhat IS; yet he asserted its value as a transient and relative reality; and theret   elband indicates [104-06], distinguished between two kinds of knowl- edge,   erception to a changing actuality (phenomena), and that of thought to a reality   e and abiding. Beckett would not have accepted the consequence that ration   it gives things as they are in truth, but he appreciated in Democritus the startling pre-Kantian assertion that perception yields phenomena essentially distinct from things in themselves. The rationalistic basis of the Platonic doctrine of knowledge and its allegiance to an immaterial reality, Windelbrand argues [116-18], is rooted explicitly in this theory of perception. Beckett, having read this passage, was intrigued by its implications for Democritus and himself.

246.4 [138]: *at peace*: Democritus's quiet, to which the philosophical mind aspires; and Schopenhauer's contemplation, when the Will is at abeyance: the experience of the *Nichts*, or Nothing, a peace beyond all reason, calm of spirit, deep rest and the confidence of serenity [*WWI*, I, 531]. This is Malone's region of great calm and indifference beyond the tumult and commotion of the mind [198; see #113.1]; itself a precise echo of the realm described by Thomas à Kempis [*De Imitatione Christi*, III.vii.5] as "post tempestatum, magna serenitas" [L. "after the storm, a great calm"].

246.5 [138]: *the Nothing than which . . . naught is more real*: the usual phrasing is "nothing is more real than nothing," cited later by Beckett as being (with the *Ubi nihil* of Geulincx) a point of departure for the study of his work. Thus the terror of Malone [192]:

> I know those little phrases that seem so innocuous and, once you let them in, pollute the whole of speech. *Nothing is more real than nothing.* They rise up out of the pit and know no rest until they drag you down into its dark. But I am on my guard now.

Although the sentiment is attributed directedly to Democritus [see #246.6], it does not appear in this form either by or of him; the closest thing to it is one of his opinions as listed by Diels [#156]: "Das Nichts existiert ebenso sehr wie das Ichts" [Ger. "Naught

e
tl

τ

from that which is not nor pass away into that which is not"]. This was quite compatible with the opinion of the younger Eleatics (Zeno, Melissos) who argued for the existence of the One by means of such propositions as: "What is nothing cannot be" [Burnet, *Early Greek Philosophy*, 323]. Democritus argued against such reasoning by asserting that not-Being (the vacuum, the void) had an equal right with Being to be considered existent. He distinguished (in a curiously pre-Kantian way) between "true" and "bastard" knowledge, the latter of the senses (hence phenomenal), but the former of the atom and the void (hence real); and it was his conviction that the void (that which Is Not) is as real as the atom which Is. As Bailey notes [118-19], the concept is also tricky in Greek, there being a substantial distinction between οὐκ ὄν, "unreal," οὐδέν, "nothing," and μὴ ὄν, "not real". Sextus Empiricus sums up the issue [II.i.135] by stating that Democritus affirmed that sensible objects do not truly exist, but only the atoms and the void; and [II.ii.329] by citing Epicurus who argued that if motion exists, the void exists: motion exists, *ergo*, the void exists. Centuries later, Robert Burton at the beginning of the *Anatomy* summed up the paradox of motion: "*in infinito vacuo, ex fortuitâ atomorum collisione*, in an infinite waste, so caused by an accidental collision of motes in the sun, all of which Democritus held, Epicurus and their master Lucippus of old maintained, and are lately revived by Copernicus, Brunus, and some others" ['Democritus to the Reader,' 1]. These "others" did not include Descartes, who nevertheless attempted to redefine the celebrated problem: "de démontrer l'impossibilité du mouvement sans admettre le vide" [Fr. "of showing the impossibility of movement without admitting the void" (Baillet, 247)].

Beckett's phrase seems a distillation of Diels and Diogenes Laertius, arising from two passages in Burnet. The first, in *Greek Philosophy* [120], concerns his discussion of Gorgias, who maintained there was no truth at all: "he sought to prove (1) that there is nothing, (2) that even if there is anything, we cannot know it, and (3) that, even if we could know it, we could not communicate our knowledge to anyone else." Gorgias, says Burnet, first contended that "What is not" *is* not, that is to say, it *is* just as much as "what is." The second, from *Early Greek Philosphy* [333] is Burnet's assertion of Leukippos of Mileta, master of Demokritos: "He held, further, that *what is* is no more real than *what is not*, and that both are alike causes of things that come into being: for he laid down that the substance of the atoms was compact and full, and he called them *what is*, while they moved in the void which he called *what is not*, but affirmed to be just as real as *what is*." Beckett's rendition, with its capitalized 'Nothing' set against an antithetical 'naught,' is a remarkable image of the impossible paradox.

246.6 [138]: *the guffaw of the Abderite*: the laugh of Democritus of Abdera, called by Horace the laughing philosopher, in contrast with Heraclitus, the weeping one. Little is known about his life: he is reputed to have been born about 460 BC, to have lived until 90 or 100, to have traveled much, then to have founded a school in Abdera where he wrote much, most of which has not survived, perhaps because he later came to share in the discredit that attached itself to the Epicureans [Burnet, *Greek Philosophy*, 201]. Burton's Preface to the *Anatomy* [1] describes him as "a little wearish old man, very melancholy by nature, averse from company in his later days, and much given to solitariness" (this figure appears in 'Sanies II'). Democritus inherited his theory of atoms and the void from Leucippus, of whom, as Beare notes [24] with an unintentional pun, "so little is known separately that we can neglect him or merge him in his pupil." As Windelband indicates [43], the Atomism of Leucippus develops from the Eleatic conception of Being by asserting that that which is Non-Being must have a metaphysical reality ascribed to it, and thereby "shatters in pieces the world body of Parmenides, and scatters its parts through infinite space." The laugh of Democritus was based on indifference (εὐθυμία), and directed finally at the doctrine of the immortality of the soul,

Democritus contending instead that the elements of things are homogeneous atoms, infinitely numerous, moving eternally in the void, and that the combination of atoms which makes up the individual (body and soul) is broken up and dispersed at death [see #275.2]. The guffaw of Democritus is thus progenitor of that mirthless laugh, the dianoetic laugh of Arsene's "short statement": the *risus purus*, the laugh that laughs at that which is unhappy [*Watt*, 48].

246.7 [138]: *posterns of his withered soul*: Burnet [*Greek Philosophy*, 196]: "As the soul is composed of atoms like everything else, sensation must consist in the impact of atoms from without on the atoms of the soul, and the organs of sense must simply be 'passages' (πόροι) through which these atoms are introduced." In 'Yellow' [*MPTK*, 173], Belacqua defines the eyes as "The posterns of the mind," and as such safer closed.

246.8 [138]: *the accidentless One-and-Only*: τὸ ἄπειρον, the "Unlimited" or "Boundless," that essential substrate (i.e., without "accidents" or attributes) from which all that Is is formed. According to Democritus, since only atoms and space (Nothing) have unchanging existence, then only the knowledge which is of them can be real [see also #246.5 and #246.6]. Murphy, alas, is about to have an accident.

246.9 [138]: *stenches, asperities, ear-splitters and eye-openers*: the world of the senses, from which touch is missing, that being (his enemies said) the one sense to which Democritus's theory of sensation reduced itself, and the underlying condition of all the others.

247.1 [138]: *ringing the changes*: a brief prelude to the more exhaustive changes rung up in *Watt*; here, the options do not form a complete set of permutations, as did the biscuits in the park, since there is missing, from the off position, the option of *indicated, extinguished, lit*.

247.2 [139]: *at regular intervals of ten minutes*: a slip in the English text, but corrected in the French which reads: "à des intervalles régulières de vingt minutes" [Fr. "at regular intervals of twenty minutes"].

248.1 [139]: *his colours nailed to the mast*: the inappropriate cliché comes from Sir Walter Scott's *Marmion*: "Stood for his country's glory fast, / And nail'd her colours to the mast."

248.2 [139]: *the famous ant*: the consequence of Democritus's theory of vision, as outlined by Beare [27]: if there were pure vacuum, and not air, around us, the images from visible objects would reach the eye unblurred, and we would report the exact form of an object, no matter how great the distance from which its image might come; as it is, however, the air takes the first copy of the object and the eye receives it only at second hand (the object "molding" the air into visible forms), and hence the likeness of the copy to the original becomes more imperfect in proportion to the distance it has to travel. Aristotle [*De Anima*, 419.a.15] disagreed with this theory of vision, and in his disagreement the striking image from Democritus is recorded: "For it was a mistake in Democritus to assume that if the intervening space became a void, even an ant would be distinctly seen, supposing there were one in the sky. That is impossible." The issue is summed up by Burnet [*Greek Philosophy*, 196]:

> It follows that the objects of vision are not strictly the things we suppose ourselves to see, but the "images" (δείκελα, εἴδωλα) that bodies are constantly

shedding. The image in the pupil of the eye was regarded as the essential thing in vision. It is not, however, an exact likeness of the body from which it comes; for it is subject to distortion by the intervening air. That is why we see things in a blurred and indistinct way at a distance, and why, if the distance is very great, we cannot see them at all. If there were no air, but only the void, between us and the objects of vision, this would not be so; "we could see an ant crawling on the sky."

248.3 [139]: *across a narrow gulf of air*: as ever, 'gulf' signifies the impassible [see #5.7 and #177.3], but the phrasing alludes to Democritus's theory of vision [above]. In *The Pre-Socratic Philosophers*, her Companion to *Diels*, Freeman states: "Vision, like the reflections in mirrors, is due to the reception of the emanation by a subject capable of retaining it: in the case of vision, by the pupil of the eye" [288]. In the act of seeing, objects constantly give off material images of themselves, which are impressed upon the air between the object and the eye, as in wax. This impression is then reflected back to the eye, into which it enters, and is communicated to the rest of the body [311]. Objections were raised by Theophrastus and Aristotle: if the image is stamped on the air in front of the object, why do we not see it in reverse? What happens when several things are seen in the one place? How do we see past one another, or past the surrounding images? And, in a point most pertinent to Murphy's experience, why do we not see ourselves? For Murphy, the perception is painful: if he is unseen by Mr. Endon and can see himself only as mirrored in the other's unseeing, then for Mr. Endon he, Mr. Murphy, cannot exist.

248.4 [139]: *one of Nature's jokes*: otherwise, a *lusus naturae*, such as the five-legged sheep of which Flaubert was so fond. Beckett may be playing with Aristotle's perception, as cited by Beare [81]: "Creatures with protruding eyes are short-sighted; those with deep-set eyes are long-sighted, the sockets serving as a tube to combine and direct the movement of the visual ray." It is difficult to reconcile both deficiencies.

249.1 [140]: *prodigiously dilated*: a medical curiosity, as excessive light should lead to *contraction* of the pupils [Stan Gontarski to CA]. Beckett was probably casual, but the error could be construed as a critique of Murphy's certainty.

249.2 [140]: *glaucous*: here, displaying the merest touch of grayish-green-blue, the word also suggesting the Greek for "owl," which half-explains the dilation.

249.3 [140]: *a ballrace*: the outer conduit of a roulette wheel, the point being that the ball is thrown in the direction opposite to the rotation of the wheel. The word is not in the *OED*, but a small pedantic point may be gleaned there, in that the 'ball' of the eye once referred specifically to the pupil, as distinct from the iris or the eye-ball itself.

249.4 140]: *everted in an ectropion*: literally, "turned away in a turned-out manner"; i.e., with an abnormal display of the inner eyelids. Celia's eye [137] was described as "everted"; here, the word is more correctly used of the lids.

249.5 [140]: *suppuration*: the discharging of pus.

249.6 [140]: *the filigree of veins*: a delicate intertwined lacework effect. Democritus claimed that eyes which see better possess veins that are "straight and free from moisture, so as to conform in shape to the images moulded by, and thrown off from, the object" [Beare, 26].

249.7 [140]: *like the Lord's Prayer on a toenail*: a phenomenon rendered insignificant by the micrographics of the computer age, but an intricate act of devotion in past ages, whereby the pious would endeavor to inscribe devotional texts, even the entire Bible, onto the smallest surfaces, in such minute perfection as to be invisible to the naked eye until magnified.

249.8 [140]: *his own image*: while anyone staring into the eye of another may see a reflected image of himself (a "baby"), this moment is phrased in terms of Democritus's sense of vision, wherein it is contended that images similar in shape to the things they come from impinge upon the eye of those who see them [see #248.3], in proof of which he adduces the fact that in the pupil of the eye of those who see there is invariably the likeness of the object seen [Mooney, 227]. Despite this, Murphy perceives that he is himself unseen by Mr. Endon.

249.9 [140]: *a butterfly kiss*: a light brushing of the lips, a fleeting touch. It is still the correct expression. O'Hara comments [*Hidden Drives*, 60]: "This is the pose of Narcissus, bent over the stream to see himself. The butterfly is a traditional image of the psyche." Chaos theory has propounded the "butterfly effect," the triggering of catastrophe by the tiniest final impulse, just as for Neary that Red Branch bum marked the limit of Cork endurance.

249.10 [140]: *stigmatised*: here, a distorted optical image (compare #27.1), but the recent hint of the Lord's Prayer suggests the Christian connotations. Harvey comments [268]: "one more among many examples of a recurrent figure that associates a suffering Christ with the protagonist. Being is being perceived, and being perceived is painful. We are crucified by others or by ourselves." Begam suggests [50] that underlying the entire encounter is 1 Corinthians 13:12: "For now we see through a glass, darkly; but then face to face: now I know in part; but then shall I know even as also I am known."

250.1 [140]: *the last at last seen of him*: as Mays points out, there is an identification between Mr. Endon and Thomas McGreevy, not "on the gross level of the penny-a-line vulgarity of a literature of notations," but through echoes of the kind of poetry which McGreevy wrote, with its "hypnotic narcissistic attraction" ['Mythologized Presences,' 209]. Mays discusses Beckett's 'Humanistic Quietism,' a 1934 review of McGreevy's *Poems* [*Disjecta*, 68-69], and uses its language to make the excellent point [210], that what Mr. Endon means to Murphy is set out as in the syntax of a McGreevy poem, originating from the same nucleus of "endopsychic clarity." Murphy's words thus illustrate what Beckett meant by considering poetry as prayer.

250.2 [140]: *A rest . . . A rest . . . A long rest*: the identical pattern of pause as on p. 234, when Celia takes stock of her situation (she has one more breve). Rabinovitz suggests that the effect of the repetition is to show how Celia and Murphy are each hurt and bewildered by rejection [*Development*, 78]. It would seem logical, were this a romance, that each should turn back to the other to find the love that has never quite been lost.

250.2a [140]: *immunity*: in *Film*, SB returned to the monad, to the problem of perception explored in *Murphy*. The convention determining the action is that O is unperceived by E until he enters the "anguish of perceivedness," when the angle of 45° is exceeded. E is at pains, therefore, to keep within the "angle of immunity."

250.3 [140]: *Mr. Murphy is a speck in Mr. Endon's unseen*: a muted climax, but of extreme significance, for this is the moment, an ironic dénouement that only Beckett could perfect, when Murphy realizes, more in sorrow than in anger, that his destiny is not to be that of the microcosmopolitans—because, unlike Mr. Endon, HE IS ESSENTIAL-LY SANE. In the words of Deirdre Bair [330], having tried to perfect the hermeticism of his mind he realizes that he is doomed to sanity and cannot surrender to his inner being. O'Hara sums it up differently [69]: Beckett, he suggests, "shows that the narcissist is victimized by a psychic drama that has no solution." The philosophical position advanced in chapter 6 cannot be translated into actuality. Or, to look at it in another way, Mr. Endon's tragedy is not so much that he fails to "see" Murphy, but rather that (Murphy sees) Mr. Endon *sees* but does not *perceive* his own existence. There is a basic incommensurability here, an absurdity that (like the existence of *pi*) cannot be reasoned away: the desire to attain the freedom of the mind is a valid impulse, but its cost is the abnegation of awareness. And the loss of apperception is a price, Murphy now understands, that he is not prepared to pay. From this revelation rational conclusions follow: he is part of the Big Word; he needs Celia; he must face the Music. After giving it one more try. With the consequences that we know of, but he (presumably) does not.

250.4 [140]: *the little afflatulence*: a farty afflatus, as if to dismiss the consequences of the above revelation for what they and it are worth, in a world where one is worth nothing: a Geulincxean critique of the Proustian moment, which redeems nothing.

250.5 [140]: *incandescent*: Rachel Dobbin offers a critique ['Interview,' 15]: "Between the incandescent body and the damp body, says Proust. No real tangency between the subject and the object." The reference is to Marcel's awareness of the screen between his consciousness and the object it perceives [*Swann*, I.124], and his phrase "comme un corps incandescent" [Fr. "like an incandescent body"] forms the precise image of Murphy's state of mind.

250.6 [140]: *the moon had been obliged to set*: Murphy's death takes place during the waning of the moon, in the last quarter. According to Rabinovitz ['Unreliable Narrative,' 64, 69], this statement is determined by symmetry, not fact: both Whitaker and the laws of astronomy affirm that the moon was visible before dawn on October 21, 1935, and that it set long after sunrise. Beckett probably wanted the "starless inscrutable night" of *Whoroscope*, where he imagines Descartes mounting the *perron*, or bitter steps, to his death.

251.1 [141]: *He took off his clothes*: the French translation adds a nice touch: "Même le papillon citron, il le jetu" [Fr. "He even threw away the lemon bow-tie"], his squeeze of lucky lemon gone. Given the comment [*Dream*, 199]: "Nicolette in the dew," this scene forms an ironic parallel to the medieval *Aucassin et Nicolette* [xii], where Nicolette steals out before dawn to see her imprisoned lover, raising her silk dress on account of the dew.

251.2 [141]: *tried to get a picture*: Murphy's prosopagnosia is anticipated in Beckett's *Proust* [14]: "Voluntary memory (Proust repeats it ad nauseam) is of no value as an instrument of evocation, and provides an image as far removed from the real as the myth of our imagination or the caricature furnished by direct perception." Rabaté sees Murphy's terror as a response to the abyss of nothingness that has opened before him, the failure of ghosts of his unconscious to return as images ['Fluxions,' 27-28]. In like manner, Watt is not always successful in his attempts to elicit the image of his father [77]. Many years later Beckett would return to Murphy's experience, with the terms transposed: the narrator of 'Old Earth,' standing at gaze, recalls memories seen on the screen of the sky, and fails differently: "For an instant I see the sky, the different skies, then they turn to faces."

251.3 [141]: *the Child in a Giovanni Bellini Circumcision*: a painting in the National Galley, London, by Giovanni Bellini (1428-1516), showing a group of elders and rabbis gathered about the pudgy babe. The ritual signifies Christ's acceptance of the Law, affirming His descent through the flesh from Abraham. The Feast of the Circumcision is January 1, the eighth day [Luke 2:21]. There is a circumlocution, *amplissimum fortitudini testimonium*, for the male organ of Christ, since the greatest testimony of fortitude is the Circumcision: Murphy, however, responds to the understandable terror shown by Bellini's infant, poor little prick, in the face of what he does not comprehend.

252.1 [141]: *reeled upward off a spool*: the primary image of corporeal dissolution is the kite, reeling string off its spool as it climbs "out of sight." Yet there is a secondary sense which Beckett in his revisions chose to obscure: in 'Lightning Calculation,' Quigley notes: "Item: He could not forget his father's death, the entire process of which, from the falling ill to the internment, had become a talkie in his brain of almost continuous performance featuring himself, in postures that impressed him as ignoble." With this montage in mind, the logic of transition in Murphy's mind from the "pictures" to the kite becomes more compelling.

252.2 [141]: *lit the dip*: a mistake: better the vision without the dip. 'Sconce' refers to a candlestick, or tube into which the candle is inserted.

252.3 [141]: *to face the music*: to own up to wrong-doing, but also to regain the delights of serenade, nocturne, and alba [see #74.9]. O'Hara points out [*Hidden Drives*, 61] that this return completes a pattern, for when Murphy's love cannot penetrate Mr. Endon's impenetrable narcissism [see #186.3], he turns back to Celia, first turning to his chair to recharge his depleted ego with self-love.

252.4 [141]: *Herschel in Aquarius*: a warning: having avoided accidents of strangury and the stone, Murphy has not guarded against an act as necessary as the flushing of a toilet.

253.1 [142]: *Soon his body would be quiet*: repeated thrice, situation and phrasing duplicating the first chapter, and the venture terminated equally abruptly. This time, however, there is no second chance: the ironies mount (*free*, *quiet*), and Murphy goes out not with a whimper but a bang. There are curious similarities between Murphy's death and Wilenski's description [255] of that of Carel Fabritus, killed in the explosion of a powder magazine in Delft, October 12, 1654, aged about thirty. For further considerations of the Democritean dimensions of this superfine guffaw at the expense of Murphy's body, mind, and soul, see #269.1 and #275.2.

12

254.1 [143]: *Not a cloud*: according to Whitaker [1937, 151], October 23, 1935 was fine, with light wind and 9.1 hours of sunshine [see, however, #276.1]. The moon was at apogee, 252,160 miles from the earth; Murphy now is far away. The "happy days" feeling is belied by the year moving into Scorpio, and, in a novel so intensely aware of religious detail, the very absence of even a little cloud implies no relief [c.f. I Kings 18:44, and Joyce's 'A Little Cloud'].

254.2 [143]: *Cooper sat*: the repetition accentuates the theory of the two buckets, Murphy's loss equaling Cooper's gain. Mays asserts the parallel between Cooper's new lease of life and that of Hairy 'Capper' Quinn, after the death of Belacqua in 'Draff' ['Mythologized Presences,' 215; *MPTK*, 200]. Beckett had commented in his lectures on Racine: "Comic resolution is establishment of equilibrium. Tragic resolution is the abolition of any need for equilibrium" [Rachel Dobbin, 'Interview,' 8]. Thus, Neary, despite his perilous position, finds in Celia's face a figure to replace his need for Murphy, who will revert to being part of the ground.

254.3 [143]: *Wylie considered himself better off than Neary*: a pin-prick taking its point from two carriage rides in Joyce's *Ulysses*: the first, the funeral procession in 'Hades,' over the cobbled stones ("Only a pauper, Nobody owns"); the second, in 'Wandering Rocks,' Lenehan's return from the Lord Mayor's dinner at Glencree, lost in the Milky Way.

255.1 [143]: *sexpit*: compare the use of 'cockpit' [165].

255.2 [143]: *affective mechanisms*: semi-automatic reaction patterns, that issue from and respond to repressed emotional stimuli. The "old endless chain" is the concatenation of habit, the dog chained to its vomit, to which Beckett returns throughout his essay on *Proust*.

256.1 [144]: *a shakedown*: a make-shift bed, rather than a threat of extortion; Cooper "to cap all" going to bed in his hat, although enough of a gentleman to take off his boots.

256.2 [144]: *an assurance*: to the rational reader, "evidence" that Murphy must have registered his address while working at the MMM [see #262.3].

257.1 [144]: *beyond recall*: as befits 'Love's Old Sweet Song,' with its dear dark days.

257.2 [145]: *that frail partition*: the hymenal metaphor again [see #195.2]; the usual proverb claims "ill-concealed is half revealed."

257.3 [145]: *Dr. Angus Killiekrankie*: see #88.3 for the good Doctor's name, and #185.2 for his troubled upbringing and voices. The Pass of Killicrankie, near Pitlochry in Tayside, was the scene of a bloody victory by the Jacobite Highlanders over the English, 1689. The defeat was recalled in Wordsworth's 1803 sonnet, 'In the Pass of Killicranky,' with sentiments more akin to MacGonagall than Ossian: "the slaughter spread like flame . . . 'Twas a day of shame." Haydn did better with his song 'Killiecrankie' (1801).
   The original of Dr. Killiecrankie, Brian Ryder suggests, was the senior assistant physician at the Bethlem Royal Hospital, one Murdo McKenzie, originally from Inverness, Beckett presumably finding the pun on "murder" ("Killie") irresistible. Murdo McKenzie, who had resigned shortly before Beckett visited the hospital, did not get on with his superior, John Porter-Phillips [see 259.1].

257.4 [145]: *eminescent*: not yet eminent, but in the process of becoming so; a quasi-Latin formulation yet to be recorded in the *OED*. The "home counties" are those near London, viz. Middlesex, Kent, Essex and Surrey (perhaps Hertford and Sussex).

257.5 [145]: *devout Mottist*: a follower of F. W. Mott (1853-1926), who was instrumental in building up the Maudsley and a pioneer in the study of GPI [Phil Baker to CA]. The word is misleading, suggesting either a trace of the infamous poisoner, Madame de la Motte (Jeanne de Saint-Rémy de Valois, comtesse, 1756-91), mentioned with a shiver in 'Sanies II'; or the tower near the Portrane Asylum in which Dean Swift "kept his motte" ['Fingal,' *MPTK*, 34].

258.1 [145]: *cowl whiskers*: shaped like a monk's hood, or cowl.

258.2 [145]: *lanugo*: indicative of a regression to the infantile: a covering of delicate downy hairs, usually associated with the foetus or the newly-born infant. Belacqua celebrated the signing of the Armistice with a pubic lanugo [*Dream*, 66].

258.3 [145]: *degenerative changes*: from L. *degenerare*, "to become unlike one's race"; Dr. Killiekrankie has been seeking signs of sub-normal mentality or behavior.

258.4 [145]: *a singed envelope*: singed, rather than signed. There is a mystery about this letter [see #269.5], given that nobody at the MMM knew of a Mrs. Murphy (Murphy would never call Celia this, although Miss Carriage uses the phrase [227]), or the address in Brewery Road, and the laborious capitals were certainly not formed by Murphy. Who has been monkeying around? The rational reader might suppose that Murphy when registering for work gave some of these details ("Mrs. Murrphy" remains a problem), but who has made use of them? Could Ticklepenny have been prying? See #262.3 for answers to these and other questions. Curiously, the word 'will' is never mentioned. Democritus noted among his *Fragments* [Diels, 1.a, 131]: "On making a will: those who cannot endure to do so are compelled to endure a double lot" (to die twice); Freeman glosses this as the foolishness of evading the thought of death by postponing the making of a will [295]. Murphy might have heeded the advice to those reading the Will in Swift's *A Tale of a Tub* [87]: "to take care of *Fire*, and put out their *Candles* before they went to sleep." Among the bad puns besetting this chapter there is the simple frustration of the Schopenhaurean Will.

259.1 [145]: *the county coroner*: the original of this figure, in his pin-stripe suit, Brian Ryder has suggested, was Dr. John Porter-Phillips, Physician-Superintendent of the Bethlem Royal Hospital, who was insistent that suicide could be achieved by apnoea [see 185.1], dressed in a dapper manner, and was at odds with his senior assistant physician, Murdo McKenzie [see 257.3]. His outside interests, which included golf, meant that his attendance at the Bethlem Royal was irregular [Brian Ryder to CA].

259.2 [146]: *wreathed together*: the words "wreathed together" and "twined together" are cited in the *Whoroscope* Notebook with the enigmatic line: "Dumb solitary path best knitteth woe," the latter ticked as if included. Any relevance remains obscure, but the crowded doorway is a set piece of the silent screen, in the Marx Brothers, the Keystone Cops and Laurel and Hardy. In a letter of July 7, 1936, Beckett responded to what McGreevy saw as a problem, the post-mortem burlesque. He had given much thought to the ending, he said, but rather than have Murphy's death as a frank climax he had chosen to keep it subdued because it accorded better with "the mixture of compassion, patience, mockery and 'tat twam asi' that I seemed to have directed on him throughout, with the sympathy going so far and no further." A rapturous recapitulation of Murphy's experience was the kind of promotion he wished to avoid; an ironic one, he hoped, superfluous. He concluded by saying that this section should have been more rapid and that the dialogue had got out of hand; but perhaps it was saved from anti-climax "by the presence of M. throughout"; the reader might feel, as he did, the grotesque presence of Murphy "until he was literally one with the dust." The tone is polite, but Beckett was obviously aware precisely how the farce accentuates the absurdly tragic effect.

259.3 [146]: *the post-mortem room*: the "real" mortuary at the Bethlem Royal consisted of three rooms, all about the same size and on a clover-leaf plan: a body-store with three slabs, a viewing room (which was a chapel of sorts), and a post-mortem room

[Patricia Allderidge to CA]. There was no unbroken bay of glass, frosted or otherwise; and only one refrigerator.

259.4 [146]: *lancination*: from L. *lancinare*, "to tear"; hence, an act of tearing, or piercing. The word is usually used figuratively, as of painful feeling.

259.5 [146]: *the hopeless harbour-mouth look*: picking up the pun of 'bay,' as in window, and relating it to Kingston Pier, in chapter 2 of *Ulysses* described as "a disappointed bridge": the West and East piers of Kingston Harbour, or Dún Laoghaire, turn towards one another in the manner prescribed, but fail to touch. A similar image is evoked in 'Serena II.'

260.1 [146]: *ruin marble*: marble showing irregular marking like ruins. Beckett could have taken this from the *Britannica* [1893, XVI.397/2], or the *OED*, which cites that example.

260.2 [146]: *in the key of the bay*: i.e, the central strategic location.

260.3 [146]: *the graded swoon*: calibrated in degrees. Compare Schopenhauer's 'On Death': "as sleep is the brother of death, so the swoon is its twin-brother" [*WWI*, III.4.xli, 256].

260.4 [146]: *rather more abundant*: perhaps in compensation for the triorchous affliction which is presumably responsible for the trichocephalic condition.

260.5 [146]: *in his nancy soprano*: i.e., in a high effeminate voice.

260.6 [146]: *Another long putt*: a few feet further and Murphy would have died in another county, and the Coroner could be playing golf.

261.1 [146]: *spouted . . . bubbled and was still*: sounding like an image from *Moby Dick*, which Beckett had bought for 6d, and enjoyed: "the real stuff, white whales and natural piety" [letter to McGreevy, August 4, 1932]. Dr. Killikrankie's Freudian theories might explain the coroner's phallic and balleinic images, which seem otherwise a mystery of the deep.

261.2 [146]: *irrrefragible*: that which cannot be rrefuted.

261.3 [147]: *Burns always shocks*: the apology is to Robert Burns (1759-96), the Scots skald renowned for his impiety. Henning [*Complicity*, 211] finds an allusion to Carlyle's opinion of Burns: he found the passion shocking. Much of the desperately inane dialogue, before and after, is as recorded in the *Whoroscope* Notebook, the cross-outs and rewrites offering a rare glimpse of Beckett's compositional mode. The word 'burner' (can a noun be passive?) here designates the one burnt. The byplay is considerably toned down in the French translation.

261.4 [147]: *Sepsis does not arise*: the coroner's query about the possibility of sepsis mocks the notion that Bethlem under Porter-Phillips was one of the last bastions of the doctrine of focal sepsis, a school of thought arising from the discovery that syphilis and GPI were caused by the same infection, and seeking to discover seats and strains of sepsis that might cause other diseases [Brian Ryder to CA].

262.1 [147]: *the modus morendi*: L. "the mode of dying," in contradiction to the legal terms *modus vivendi*, the mode of living, or *modus operandi*, the way things should be done.

262.2 [147]: *an accident*: perhaps the only time that Neary has used this word in the tradition of the market-place rather than in its metaphysical sense, and hence the greater irony of the coroner's stupefication. Mahaffy [101] tells of the furor provoked when a Cartesian proposed that "man, as being composed of two heterogeneous elements, thinking and extension, was not a substance *per se*, but a substance *per accidens*"; Neary upsets the psychopathological wholehogs [98] in much the same way.

262.3 [147]: *A classical case of misadventure*: the verdict, not dissimilar to the Scottish "non-proven," given by a Coroner in circumstances not quite satisfactory, but to which blame cannot be unequivocally attributed; especially suicides (here assumed), should there be pressure from relatives to bury the body in consecrated ground (not an issue). The question remains: was Murphy's death suicide, an accident or otherwise? In the words of *Dream* [184]: "The official finding was very fine. But it was erroneous." The survival of the will suggests suicide, but on reflection (and despite the coroner's opinion) this may be ruled out as at odds with all we know of Murphy (admittedly, not much), and his clear decision [252] to return to Celia and face the music. Moreover, in Schopenhauerean terms, felo-de-se is contrary to the Will (the matter is discussed in *Dream*, 123 and 184). Accident? Then what about the will, that most un-Murphy-like relict of a non-reader? Here I venture an interpretation that is quite unconscionable, and must be seen in terms of the ironic qualification that follows, or not at all: that Murphy has been murdered. This is suggested by Rabinovitz [*Development*, 113-18], in an account which is unsatisfactory for several reasons: to advance it seriously, as he does, is preposterous; to construct a scenario whereby Cooper is the murderer (his hypothesis) is risible; and to argue it in a chapter entitled 'Unreliable Narrative' is like judging the action of *Ulysses* by weighing the evidence of 'Eumaeus.' And yet—the idea will not quite go away, and the evidence Rabinovitz cites, ranging from this verdict, the anxiety of the Mercyseat officials to get away to golf or avoid scandal, and, above all, the mystery of the Will, is weighty. Beckett was enough of an admirer of Conan Doyle to know Holmes's axiom, that when the impossible has been eliminated then what remains, however improbable, must be the truth. Rabinovitz's hypothesis is impossible, because Cooper could not have known where Murphy was, nor the intimate details of his garret and heating arrangements; and Cooper, Lord preserve us, could not walk in the vicinity of the Mercyseat without being put inside. The only person intimately acquainted with Murphy's ways, and who might have pulled the chain is—Ticklepenny. It takes little imagination to conceive a Ticklepenny goaded by Murphy into exacting his revenge, a Ticklepenny who knows how the gas works, a Ticklepenny who has been and is close enough to be, well, privy to Murphy's moves [191], a Ticklepenny who knows the Abbey, and a Ticklepenny foolish enough to write the will (the letters on the envelope and the 'Mrs Murphy' error are exactly the pot-poet's style). The more one ratioincinerates the matter, the more it greyens; there is thus immense authorial irony in the earlier statement [85], that Ticklepenny is "the merest pawn in the game." I suggest, gentlefolk of the jury, that when you weigh this matter *rationally*, THIS is the only account, however improbable, consistent with the facts: Ticklepenny pulled the plug, I beg your pardon, *the chain*, on Murphy. [*Long silence*]. Now for the qualification: the key word is 'rationally,' for the scenario proposed is absurd. Yet enough has been given to invite a rational reconstruction; and the real question is, in the end, whether one believes in a cosmos, physical or literary, in which everything is explicable by causality, and hence harmonious and reasonable; or one essentially irregular and absurd, in which the irrrefragable presence of *pi* must be acknowledged. G. K. Chesterton once observed that the problem with the universe is that it is almost reasonable, but not quite; the jury, we assume, is still out on that one as well.

263.1 [147-48]: *a Brymay safety . . . a wax vesta*: i.e., a Bryant and May wooden safety match, as opposed to a Swan Vesta, or wax match with phosphorescent head that might be struck on any rough surface. Beckett, aged about ten, dropped one of the latter into a discarded petrol can, burning his skin and singeing his eyebrows [Knowlson, 19].

263.2 [148]: *Neary attended to his nose*: a variation of digital emunction, otherwise *eutrapelia*, or cultivated insolence.

263.3 [148]: *Never the rose without the thorn*: not Burns's rosy love, but the *rosa sine spina*, emblem of the Virgin Mary's freedom from the taint of sin, the rose that grew in Eden before the fall, as in Robert Herrick's 'The Rose':

> Before Man's fall, the Rose was born,
> (S. Ambrose says) without the Thorn:
> But, for Man's fault, then was the Thorn,
> Without the fragrant Rose-bud, born;
> But ne're the Rose without the Thorn.

264.1 [148]: *converted it deftly into octavo*: Bim receives the sheet, now folded once, as if it were a folio sheet of paper; then he folds it twice more, to convert it into eighths.

265.1 [149]: *split pins*: in golf, the pin is the distant flag which marks the hole on the green; to split the pin is to drive or pitch directly in a line towards it.

266.1 [149]: *an extensive capillary angioma*: Murphy's *naevus*, correctly described as a large superficial tumor constituted by a network of capillaries, i.e., tiny terminal arteries and veins; but with an additional pun on its unusual "situation." Such a disfiguration was commonly called a port-winer, in popular superstition said to afflict one conceived during menstruation. Shortly after Dr. Johnson's birth a similar inflammation was discovered upon his buttock.

267.1 [150]: *No man is without blemish*: with the possible exception of Christ, who (to adopt the phrasing of Watt) is often described as a man, which, to be sure, in a way, he was.

267.2 [150]: *Dear old indelible Dublin*: Beckett's variation of Joyce's "dear dirty Dublin" [*Ulysses*, 139], the dirt having deepened.

267.3 [150]: *the Coombe*: a slum area of Dublin, celebrated for its "characters" [O'Brien, 163], such as the blind paralytic, a power in the Coombe, whom Belacqua regularly observes [*Dream*, 200, and 'Ding-Dong,' *MPTK*, 42]. It was previously known for its maternity wards, the Coombe Lying-In Hospital; however, the coroner's only female link is a rather ancient connection ("so remote as to be scarcely credible"), George II having passed away in 1760.

267.4 [150]: *Clonmachnois . . . Connaught*: in an apparent parody of Gabriel Conroy's vision at the end of 'The Dead,' Neary's vision journeys westward until it comes to rest beside Lough Corrib, in the province of Connaught. The passage follows Beckett's trip to Galway with his brother Frank in 1936, with only three chapters of *Murphy* to write. In a letter to McGreevy [March 25, 1936], Beckett described the profound effect that the trip had upon him:

> Frank . . . had to go down to Galway so I went with him, just two nights & a day there, a pick day, the Corrib shining & foaming and the light coming through the Connaught walls like filigree. On the way back we stopped at Clonmacnoise, which is indescribably beautiful, as site & monument.

Beckett would not have appreciated the comparison, but Neary's vision closely echoes that of Austin Clarke, whose 'Pilgrimage' invokes the nearby waters of the Shannon: "O Clonmachnoise was crossed / with light."

Clonmachnois: in Leinster, some eight miles from Athlone, the name 'cluain-mac-nois' signifying in Irish "the Retreat of the Sons of the Noble." The abbey dates from 548, attracting to it a castle, a nunnery and a cathedral. In 1199 it was attacked by William de Burge; in 1200 plundered by the English under Miles Fitz-Henry, and in 1201 and 1204 it was sacked by both the above. A castle was erected by the English in 1214 but in 1227 this was set alight by the . . .

O'Melaghins: descendants of the princes of Meath, and led by the son of Donnell Bregagh O'Melaghin. The castle is celebrated as a place of burial, the mounds of many mighty chieftains rising there amidst the . . .

eskers: long, continuous steep ridges of sands and gravel, deposited as the moraine of retreating glaciers; then, beyond Galway and the white cottages of the west . . .

the wide bright water: of Lough Corrib, north of Galway, the largest body of fresh water in the ancient province of . . .

Connaught: or Connacht, one of the four fields of ancient Ireland and comprising the counties of Sligo, Leitrum, Mayo, Roscommon, and Galway.

268.1 [150]: *unbaptised*: not, apparently, a disqualification for this ex-student of theology.

269.1 [151]: *body, mind and soul*: anticipating the huge Democritean joke of the chapter's end [see #275.2]. Aristotle said, disparagingly, that for Democritus: "ψυχήν μὲν γὰρ εἶναι ταὐτὸ καὶ νοῦν" [Gk. "soul and mind are the same" (*De Anima*, 405.a.9; Bailey, 160)].

269.2 [151]: *the Abbey Theatre*: Murphy's last will and testament takes its point from the fact that the theater, previously the Mechanics' Institute, had earlier been a morgue. By 1904, the stone-brick building in Abbey Street (a block up from Wynn's Hotel and Mooney's) was unoccupied. With the aid of Miss Annie Horniman, an Englishwoman and admirer of Yeats, it was purchased and named the Abbey, becoming a home for the Irish National Theatre Society, recently formed to promote Irish drama. From the outset it was associated with the Irish literary revival, the first productions being the one-act plays, Yeats's *On Baile's Strand* and *Cathleen ni Houlihan*, and Lady Gregory's *Spreading the News*. For the next twenty-four years it stood at the fore of the literary movement, occasionally engulfed in the conflict between art and propaganda as most notoriously with the riots at the opening of Synge's *The Playboy of the Western World* (1907) and O'Casey's *The Plough and the Stars* (1928), both of which touched sensitive raw nerves of the Irish psyche. Beckett saw productions of both, but by his time at Trinity the Abbey was less innovative (there was a curious boast that no new scenery was ever required), and was being challenged by the European-conscious Gate [see #86.1].

269.3 [151]: *Lord Chesterfield*: Lord Philip (1694-1773), fourth earl, statesman and writer. In a letter of December 11, 1747, Chesterfield describes a man who managed his time so well "that he would not even lose that small portion of it which the calls of nature obliged him to pass in the necessary-house, but gradually went through all the Latin poets in those moments" [Rabinovitz, *Development*, 123, n39]. The posthumous *Letters to His Son* (1774) caused an outcry because of their alleged cynicism and heartless morality; in Johnson's words, inculcating "the morals of a whore, and the manners of a dancing master." In Johnson's opinion, Chesterfield was not so much "great and good" as deserving of rebuke for his long neglect and belated offer of patronage for the *Dictionary*: "Is not a patron, my lord, one who looks with unconcern on a man struggling for life in the water, and when he has reached the ground, encumbers him with help?" [Boswell, *Life*, February 7, 1755, 86].

269.4 [151]: *the necessary house*: whatever the grammar, it is a moot point whether Murphy's happiest hours were spent at the Abbey or in its littlest room (by the stairs to the right at the front of the auditorium). He would not often have been permitted such ease, since the Abbey had strict injunctions against the use of the "famously noisy convenience" during productions, the noise being amplified into the audience [Mays, 'Mythologized Presences,' 208].

269.5 [151]: *When is it dated?*: the question ensures that the mystery of the will is finally irresolvable: if Murphy's death is an accident, there is no rational way of accounting for its existence; if suicide, it contradicts his entire experience with Mr. Endon, and the decision to return to Celia and face the music. Hence, the desperate attempt to resolve the irresolvable [see #262.3]. The only other option is to assume Beckett was casual, or willing to sacrifice narrative coherence for local effect; in a novel otherwise so meticulous this would seem unlikely.

271.1 [152]: *the reverberatory type*: designating a furnace or kiln of the type whereby the flame is deflected downwards from the roof, to intensify the heat.

271.2 [152]: *the negligible sum of thirty shillings*: despite the suggestion of pieces of silver, still a good deal cheaper than membership of The Cremation Society (Telegrams: 'Incinerate, Wesdo, London'), as advertised in Whitaker [22], where Life Membership was offered for six annual subscriptions of £1.1s or one payment of £5.5s; in the event of death abroad, cremation or refund of £5 (how the refund is to be claimed is not clear).

271.3 [152]: *Life is all rather irregular*: a revealing admission from a sadder but wiser Pythagorean scholar and Newtonian man.

271.4 [152]: *the Fifty Shilling lapels*: a speciality of the Fifty Shilling tailors, an early off-the-peg company with a number of London branches, known for cutting corners as well as prices [Vada Hart to CA].

272.1 [152]: *the dear land of our birth*: the sentiment is Thomas Moore's, but the words are curiously akin to J. M. Synge's 'Prelude':

> I knew the stars, the flowers, and the birds,
> The gray and wintry sides of many glens,
> And did but half remember human words,
> In converse with the mountains, moors and fens.

272.2 [153]: *110 aspirins*: an echo of *Ulysses* [146], where Bloom misreads the writing on the wall: "POST NO BILLS. POST 110 PILLS."

272.3 [153]: *Mr. Sacha Few*: the Anti-Vivisectionist movement was strong in the 1930s, there being several societies dedicated to the "abolition of scientific torture of animals," opposing their use in medical and psychological experiments. An Anti-Vivisection Hospital was attached to the Battersea General Hospital, with the touching solicitation, "Accidents free at all hours" [Whitaker, 471]. This part of the sub-plot seems to have suffered most from compression when Beckett began in June 1936 to reduce the 800 manuscript pages in six notebooks to the final form [Knowlson, 743]; what remains is enigmatic. The novel may have been entitled in its manuscript form *Sasha Murphy* [Knowlson, 203]. 'Sacha Few' cannot be identified: the only such entry in *Who's Who* is one Colonel Robert Few, retired Army officer, who listed his hobbies as golf and hunting. A final footnote: Descartes had no qualms about performing experiments on animals, since he regarded them as soulless machines; Beckett, who probably thought this true of even the exceptional anthropoids, could nevertheless feel pity for a lobster.

273.1 [153]: *his ancient bowler*: the first of a line leading directly to *Waiting for Godot*. While Cooper's treatment of his headpiece has affinities to Marcel's response to Baron Charlus [*Guermantes*, II.219], it is also an anticipation of that other "tinker," Lucky.

274.1 [154]: *the station*: the station nearest the Bethlem Royal is Eden Park, ten minutes' walk from the Hospital, and half an hour from Charing Cross, Waterloo or London Bridge, via the Hayes line. There is an ordinary-looking pub just up the road.

274.2 [154]: *the evening session*: British pubs of the time were required by law to close between 3.30 and 5.30, this being considered not so much two holy hours as one way of mitigating public drunkenness. Mercier notes [122-23] the false rhetorical effect of "the radio struck up," as if it were a band. MURPHY was a popular brand of radiogram at the time.

274.3 [154]: *a slow cascando*: diminishing in volume and decreasing in tempo, the pun on the first part of that definition. Beckett had recently published a poem by that title in the *Dublin Magazine* (1936); in a manner suggestive of Cooper's new life, it invokes the quietism of acceptance as one mode of being moves into another: "the past is dead beyond recall" [Harvey, 174].

275.1 [154]: *the gentleman's code*: rugby rather than soccer, the parcel passed rather than kicked or headed (rugby associated with public schools rather than the canaille). The French translation considers those "dont le préférence allait au ballon ovale" [Fr. "those whose preference went to the oval ball"].

275.2 [154]: *the body, mind and soul of Murphy*: the joke is profoundly Democritean, the loudest guffaw of the Abderite, asserting that nothing is more real than Nothing [see #246.5]. The mainstream of Greek thought affirmed the immortality of the soul after death, perhaps the best-known expression of this being Plato's *Phaedra*, with Socrates's contention that death is but the release and separation of the soul from the body [12 §67D, 234-35], and that hence: "A soul which has been nutured in this way . . . is not likely to fear that it will be torn asunder at its departure from the body and will vanish into nothingness, blown apart by the winds, and be no longer anywhere" [34 §84B, 292-93]. Such was the belief of many pre-Socratic thinkers, Parmenides for instance, who asserted that death is not the end of sensibility for matter but only the cessation of the individual's sensations [Brett, 31]. Democritus, while not rejecting the soul, argued that since it was composed of atoms, albeit exceedingly fine ones, and distributed throughout the body [Bailey, 384], it must follow that upon death, when the particular atoms which make up the individual are dispersed, the soul must share the dissolution of the body. The Atomists were thus the first directly to deny the immortality of the soul.

There are other dimensions to this, besides the infinite jest of one of my ex-students, who thought Murphy was cremoted [*sic*; see my 'Preface to the Second Edition']. Kennedy [270-71] recounts George Moore's last joke, recorded in Gogarty's *Intimations* [25-40]: when he died in 1932, Moore left a will instructing that his remains be reduced to ashes in the ancient mode and spread over Hampstead Heath where the donkeys graze, knowing that his family would never permit the enormity: "Ashes to asses would never do." There may be a suggestion of the final triplet of Swift's 'Description of a City Shower' (1710), when the kennels of London swell and join in confluence:

Sweepings from butchers' stalls, dung, guts and blood,
Drown'd puppies, stinking sprats, all drench'd in mud,
Dead cats, and turnip tops, come tumbling down the flood.

Note, too, the implied contrast [as in *Watt*, 38] of 'greyened' with "il Zodïacal rubecchio" of *Purgatorio* IV.64 [see #78.6]; the link is the archaic word 'dayspring.' Finally, a Gestalt configuration: in Neary's conceit, the body, mind and soul of Murphy are now literally at one with the ground against which he had previously figured so prettily.

13

276.1 [155]: *October the 26th*: twice the fateful 13, Beckett determined that his novel should have precisely that many chapters. A speculative note: the meteorological records for October 26, 1935 are given in Whitaker 1937 (the printer's deadline was October 1, so details October to December relate to two years earlier): the day warm, 1.3 hours of sunshine, no rainfall, barometer 30.015 high and rising, temperature 54.3°F, and a light wind west-southwest of 1.2 pressure lbs per foot. This does not match the book, but the conditions cited in Whitaker 1935 are almost exact: not so warm (46.6°F), but more sun (3.4 hours), and a northwest wind of 9 pressure lbs per foot—which would allow Mr. Kelly's kite to fly towards the Dell. Beckett seems to have written this chapter with Whitaker 1935 to hand, taking the conditions from it, although they refer strictly to 1933.

276.2 [155]: *a pine of smoke*: innocent, yet reverbatory. It derives in part from *Dream* [23], a column of quiet, "pinus puella quondam fuit" [L. "the pine was once a girl"], as cited by Beckett in the Dream Notebook [#928] from the *Anatomy* [III.3.1.i, 630]: this, saith Burton, is the account by Constantine, who "in the eleventh book of his Husbandry, *cap.* 11, hath a pleasant tale of a pine-tree; she was once a fair maid, whom Phineus and Boreas, two co-rivals, dearly sought; but jealous Boreas broke her neck." Beckett's pine is "toppled" by the northerly wind [278] ("Alas fuit"). This metamorphosis is blended with Beckett's recollection of Paris from his window at the École Normale, with the bare tree, dripping, and smoke from the janitor's pot "rising stiff like a pine of ashes" [*Dream*, 52; DN, #238, from Renard's *Journal*, January 27, 1905]; the hint of smoke (an ancient image of the soul) investing the landscape here with the almost imperceptible presence of Murphy's absence.

276.3 [155]: *the Broad Walk*: the wide path tangential to the Round Pond [see #153.1]; just before the Pond a gentle incline allows Mr. Kelly to build up his reckless speed.

276.4 [155]: *a glistening slicker*: a light oilskin. Beckett picked up the unfamiliar word from his American friend, Charles Clarke [Knowlson, 166], and cinched it into 'Sanies I.' The outfit would reflect little credit on the *The House for Men*, prop. W. J. Kelly, 87 Grafton Street, which in the 1920s advertised itself in *TCD: A College Miscellany* as "Ireland's Best Service."

277.1 [155]: *the statue of Queen Victoria*: just off the Broad Walk, on Mr. Kelly's right, H. M. facing the Round Pond with her back to Kensington Palace where she was born and resided until her accession. The work was conceived by Princess Louise, who cultivated such arts, and erected by her loyal Kensington subjects to commemorate fifty years of her reign.

277.2 [156]: *nainsook*: from Hindi *nain*, "the eye," and *sukh*, "pleasure"; a fine Indian muslin or cotton cloth. Knowlson [207] tells how Beckett overcame his natural reticence to ask a stranger what the kite [the text says the tassels] was made of, and how he relished the reply. Gerty MacDowell in *Ulysses* [350] wears nainsook knickers, most pleasing to Bloom's eye.

278.1 [156]: *the Long Water*: the northwards continuation of the Serpentine [see #150.4]. There may be a muted suggestion of Ecclesiastes 12:5: "man goeth to his long home."

278.2 [156]: *his sacrum*: a triangular bone of fused vertebrae at the lower end of the spinal column. The ugly detail removes any sentimentality from what remains an elegaic final scene.

279.1 [157]: *the historical process of the hardened optimists*: according to Henning [80], this is the path marked by Hegel in his lectures on the philosophy of history, but known in the British post-Hegelian tradition as meliorism, as associated with George Eliot, for whom Beckett had (otherwise) considerable respect. Compare André Breton's *Deuxième manifeste* (1930), which critiques the theory and seems to underlie other things in the chapter [see #279.3 and #280.3].

279.2 [157]: *the Dell*: mild hyperbole, or, rather, fragmented perspective: the Dell is a lovely little wooded glen, but far in the distance, at the SE corner of Hyde Park; a natural spring there once formed the head of the Serpentine.

279.3 [157]: *prehensile*: having the capability of grasping, as the tails of certain monkeys. The phrasing may be drawn from Breton's *Deuxième manifeste* [803], where surrealism is defined as the prehensile tail of a fading Romanticism (not a bad description of Beckett's coda).

279.4 [157]: *A kid and a drunk*: "A bad business doing bad business" [Doherty, 34].

280.1 [157]: *the end of its tether*: all out: literally and figuratively for Celia the end of the line.

280.2 [157]: *hypermetropic*: farsighted, as a consequence of *hypermetropia*, the rays of light focussing behind the retina so that distant objects are seen more clearly than close ones.

280.3 [157]: *the point at which seen and unseen met*: the metaphysical conarium, couched in the terms of analytical geometry, and glossed by Henning [*Complicity*, 211] with a citation from Hölderlin: "Neither our knowledge nor our action, in any period whatever of existence, attains that point at which all conflict ceases and all is one: the determinate line unites with the indeterminate one only in infinite approximation." More simply, the sky images the void of Democritus, the speck of the kite as an atom or ant moving therein [see #248.2]. Compare Breton's *Deuxième manifeste* [781], as cited by Kennedy [22]:

> Tout porte à croire qu'il existe un certain point de l'esprit d'où la vie et la mort, le réel et l'imaginaire, le passé et le futur, la communicable et l'incommunicable, le haut et le bas cessent d'être perçus contradictoirement. Or, c'est en vain qu'on chercherait à l'activité surréaliste un autre mobile que l'espoir et détermination de ce point.

[Fr. "Everything leads to the belief that there exists a certain point of the spirit where life and death, the real and the imaginary, the past and the future, the communicable and the incommunicable, cease to appear as contradictions. Now, it is in vain to seek in the activity of surrealism any other motivation than the hope and determination of this point."]

280.4 [157]: *his beautiful deduction of Neptune from Uranus*: by 1821, astronomers had noted that the orbit of Uranus did not conform to Newton's laws, and an English cleric, the Rev. Hussey, suggested that this might be due to a farther body perturbing its movement. He wrote to the Astronomer Royal, Biddell Airy, but was ignored. In 1845, a student named John Couch Adams (1812-92) calculated where the planet must be; he turned up at the Aerie, but the great man was dining and would not be disturbed. Adams left a letter, but Airy insolently demanded more information, and Adams, infuriated, did not reply. Meanwhile, in France, Urbain le Verrier of the Paris Observatory had reached the same conclusions, and published his findings on August 30, 1846. On the night of September 23, in Berlin, Johann Galle verified the discovery, which was relayed to a startled world. Airy belatedly claimed to have seen it in early August, but had not (he said) published his findings; the planet, he declared, was British, and should be named *George*. The French disagreed, and cartoons of the time showed English astronomers with telescopes trained across the Channel finding it in the papers of French scientists. Le Verrier tried to persuade the Academy of Science to name it after him to affirm the Gallic claim; Airy countered with *Oceanus*; and the Academy compromised with *Neptune*.

Beckett had written in the Dream Notebook [#1048]: "Neptune calculated (not observed) from observed vagaries of orbit of Uranus (Greatest triumph of human thought)!!" The discovery is anticipated in *Dream* [221] and 'A Wet Night' [*MPTK*, 72], at the Frica's party, when the Ovoidologist booms that to his mind "the greatest triumph of human thought was the calculation of Neptune from the observed vagaries of the orbit of Uranus." "And yours," replies the Polar Bear. Beckett switched loyalties in the French translation, paying tribute to Le Verrier "dans les dix milles pages de calculs dont sortit Neptune" [Fr. "in the ten thousand pages of calculations from which Neptune emerged"].

280.5 [157]: *conferred*: the word assumes the optical precision given to it earlier [see #194.2].

280.6 [157]: *eagle eyes*: those of Balboa in Keats's sonnet, 'On First Looking into Chapman's Homer':

Then felt I like some watcher of the skies
When a new planet swims into his ken;
Or like stout Cortez when with eagle eyes
He star'd at the Pacific—and all his men
Looked at each other with a wild surmise—
Silent, upon a peak in Darien.

280.7 [157]: *unction*: from L. *ungere*, "to anoint"; hence, the sense of a blessing. Beckett reminded himself in the *Whoroscope* Notebook of the need to include this echo of Celia's Irish childhood. Compare the end of chapter 3.

281.1 [158]: *the ludicrous fever of toys*: the unusual coupling is explained by the Cartesian conceit of the body as a toy [112]. Celia's dreams are equally in ruins [see 152-53].

282.1 [158]: *the ravaged face*: the typescript originally read: "the bones of his ravaged face stood out like a Spagnoletto hermit's". The reference is to one of the religious figures of José Ribera (1590-1652), Spanish baroque painter at the court of the Viceroy at Naples, where he was known as 'Spagnoletto,' or "the Little Spaniard," and praised for his somber tones and dramatic effects of light. The deletion renders the description more immediate, but conceals its artistic affinities.

282.2 [158]: *All out*: the cry of the park rangers blends with Celia's grief and Mr. Kelly's collapse (the kite of his mind about to leave the hand of his body) to form an image of total ("all out") exhaustion. The final effect is comparable to what Beckett called "perhaps the greatest passage Proust ever wrote" [*Proust*, 39]; his reference being to *Les Intermittences du coeur* [Fr. "the irregularities of the heart"], in terms of Proust's uncanny ability to invoke the presence of one who is not there, and without a single involuntary memory, in a manner poignant and elegiac yet free of sentimentality. The heart, as Neary has acknowledged and Murphy and Celia have in their own ways proven, is all rather irregular.

Bibliography

This bibliography is in three sections: texts by Beckett used in this study; critical studies relating to *Murphy*; background works and sources. Where possible, details are cited from editions that Beckett is known or was likely to have used (Freud is an exception). The criterion for inclusion is direct reference or primary significance. Classical authors not listed are cited from texts that are (Bartlett, Burton, Lemprière), or from John Pilling's edition of *Beckett's* Dream *Notebook* ("DN" in the notes). "BIF" indicates material held at the Beckett International Foundation, University of Reading; and "JOBS" designates *The Journal of Beckett Studies*. Casual quotations are from standard editions. Biblical references are to the King James Version unless otherwise stated. '*Proust*' indicates Beckett's monograph; '*A la recherche*' Proust's original, in the *NRF* edition that Beckett found so abominable. Texts are cited in the notes by author or short title, as seems most appropriate.

A. By Beckett

'Assumption.' *transition* 16-17 (spring-summer 1929): 268-71. Rpt. in *Samuel Beckett: The Complete Short Prose*, ed. S. E. Gontarski, 3-7.

Beckett's Dream *Notebook*, ed. John Pilling. Reading: Beckett International Foundation, 1999.

'A Case in a Thousand.' *Bookman* LXXXVI (Aug. 1934): 241-42. Rpt. in *Samuel Beckett: The Complete Short Prose*, ed. S. E. Gontarski, 18-24.

'Che Sciagura.' *TCD: A College Miscellany* XXXVI (Nov. 14 1929): 42.

Collected Poems in English and French. London: John Calder, 1977.

Collected Shorter Plays. London: Faber and Faber, 1984.

Company. London: John Calder, 1980.

'Dante ... Bruno . Vico .. Joyce.' *transition* 16-17 (Spring-Summer 1929): 242-53. Rpt. in *Our Exagmination round his Factification for Incamination of Work in Progress*. London: Faber and Faber, 1929, 3-22.

Disjecta: Miscellaneous Writings and a Dramatic Fragment by Samuel Beckett, ed. Ruby Cohn. London: John Calder, 1983.

Dream of Fair to middling Women, ed. Eoin O'Brien and Edith Fournier. Dublin: Black Cat Press, 1992.

'Echo's Bones' [unpublished typescript]. Baker Library, Dartmouth College [copy at the BIF].

Echo's Bones and Other Precipitates. Paris: Europa Press, 1935.

Endgame: A Play in One Act Followed by Act Without Words: A Mime for One Player. 1957; New York: Grove Press, 1958.

Film: New York: Grove Press, 1969.

German Diaries [four notebooks]. BIF, University of Reading.

Happy Days. New York: Grove Press, 1961.

How It Is. 1961; rpt. New York: Grove Press, 1964.

Human Wishes [three Notebooks]. BIF, University of Reading [RUL MS 3461/1-3].

Letters to Mary Hope Manning [Mary Manning Howe]. Harry Ransom Center, University of Texas at Austin.

Letters to Thomas McGreevy. Samuel Beckett Archives, Trinity College, Dublin.

'Lightning Calculation' [unpublished typescript]. BIF, University of Reading [RUL MS 2902].

Malone Dies. 1951 and 1956; rpt. in *Three Novels*, 177-288.

Mercier and Camier. 1970; London: Calder and Boyars, 1974.

Molloy. 1951 and 1955; rpt. in *Three Novels,* 7-176.

More Pricks Than Kicks. 1934; rpt. London: Calder and Boyars, 1970.

Murphy. London: Routledge, 1938.

---. 1938; rpt. New York: Grove Press, 1957..

---. 1938 [Jupiter Books]; rpt. London: John Calder, 1963.

Murphy [French translation]. Paris: Bordas, 1947.

Murphy [German translation], trans. Elmar Tophoven. Hamburg: Rowoht Taschenbuch Verlag GmbH, 1959.

'Murphy' [carbon copy of the typescript]. Harry Ransom Humanities Research Center, University of Texas at Austin [Samuel Beckett Collection, #75].

Negro: An Anthology, ed. Nancy Cunard. London: Wishart and Co., 1934. [Includes several translations by Beckett; see Davis et al, *Calepins de bibliographie*, 1934].

Proust and 3 Dialogues with Georges Duthuit. 1931 and 1949; rpt. New York: Grove Press, 1970.

'Recent Irish Poetry' [pseud. "Andrew Belis"]. *Bookman* LXXXVI (Aug. 1934): 235-44. Rpt. in *Disjecta*, ed. Ruby Cohn, 70-76.

Samuel Beckett: The Complete Short Prose, 1929-1989, ed. S. E. Gontarski. New York: Grove Press, 1995.

'Sedendo et Quiesc[i]endo.' *transition* 21 (March 1932): 13-20.

This Quarter (Sept. 1932), edité par André Breton. [Includes several translations by Beckett; see Davis et al, *Calepins de bibliographie*, 1932].

Three Novels by Samuel Beckett: Molloy; Malone Dies: The Unnamable. 1955, 1956, 1958; rpt. New York: Grove Weidenfeld, 1991.

The Unnamable. 1953 and 1958; rpt. in *Three Novels*, 289-414.

Waiting for Godot. 1952; New York: Grove Press, 1954.

Watt. 1953; rpt. New York: Grove Press, 1959.

Whoroscope. Paris: The Hours Press, 1930.

Whoroscope Notebook. BIF, University of Reading [RUL MS 4000/1].

B. Critical Studies Relevant to *Murphy*

Acheson, James. 'Beckett, Proust, and Schopenhauer.' *Contemporary Literature* 19 (1978): 165-79.

---. 'A Note on the Ladder Joke in *Watt.*' *JOBS* n.s. 2.1 (1992): 115-16.

---. 'Murphy's Metaphysics.' *JOBS* 5 (autumn 1979): 9-24.

---. *Samuel Beckett's Artistic Theory and Practice: Criticism, Drama and Early Fiction.* London: Macmillan, 1997.

Ackerley, C. J. '"In the Beginning Was the Pun": Samuel Beckett's *Murphy.*' *AUMLA* 55 (1981): 15-22.

---. '"Do Not Despair": Samuel Beckett and Robert Greene.' *JOBS* n.s. 6.1 (fall 1996): 119-24.

---. 'Beckett's *Murphy.*' *The Explicator* 55.4 (summer 1997): 226-27.

---. 'Samuel Beckett and the Bible: A Guide.' *JOBS* n.s. 9.1 (autumn 1999): 53-125.

---. 'Samuel Beckett and Thomas à Kempis: The Roots of Quietism.' *Samuel Beckett Today / Aujourd'hui* 9 (2000): 81-92.

---, and S. E. Gontarski. *The Grove Companion to Samuel Beckett.* New York: Grove Press, 2004.

Admussen, Richard. *The Samuel Beckett Manuscripts: A Study.* Boston: G. K. Hall, 1979.

Anon [Austin Clarke]. '*Murphy*. By Samuel Beckett.' *Dublin Magazine* XIV, n.s. 2 (April-June 1939): 98.

Anon. *The Samuel Beckett Collection: A Catalogue*. BIF, University of Reading, 1978, with typescript supplements, various dates.

Armstrong, Gordon S. *Samuel Beckett, W. B. Yeats, and Jack Yeats*. Lewisburg: Bucknell University Press, 1990.

Bair, Deirdre. *Samuel Beckett: A Biography*. London: Jonathan Cape, 1978.

Baker, Phil. *Beckett and the Mythology of Psychoanalysis*. Basingstoke: Macmillan, 1997.

Barale, Michèle Aina, and Rubin Rabinovitz. *A KWIC Concordance to Samuel Beckett's Murphy*. 2 vols.; New York and London: Garland, 1990.

Begam, Richard. *Samuel Beckett and the End of Modernity*. Stanford: Stanford University Press, 1996.

Ben-Zvi, Linda. *Samuel Beckett*. Boston: Twayne, 1986.

Bryden, Mary. *Women in Samuel Beckett's Prose and Drama: Her Own Other*. Basingstoke and London: Macmillan, 1993.

---. *Beckett and the Idea of God*. Basingstoke: Macmillan, 1998.

---, Julian Garforth and Peter Mills. *Beckett at Reading: Catalogue of the Beckett Manuscript Collection at The University of Reading*. Reading: Whiteknights Press and the Beckett International Foundation, 1998.

Calder, John, ed. *Beckett at 60: A Festscrift*. London: Calder and Boyars, 1967.

Caselli, Daniela. 'Looking it up in My Big Dante: A Note on "Sedendo et Quiesc[i]endo".' *JOBS* n.s. 6.2 (spring 1997): 85-93.

Coe, Richard N. *Samuel Beckett*. New York. Grove Press, 1964.

---. 'Beckett's English.' In *Samuel Beckett: Humanistic Perspectives*, ed. Morris Beja, S. E. Gontarski and Pierre Astier. Colombus: Ohio State University Press, 1983, 36-57.

Coetzee, J. M. 'The English Fiction of Samuel Beckett: An Essay in Style and Analysis.' Ph.D. diss., University of Texas at Austin, 1969.

Cohen, David. '"For This Relief Much Thanks": Leopold Bloom and Beckett's Use of Allusion.' In Carey, Phyllis and Ed Jewinski, eds. *Re: Joyce'n Beckett*. New York: Fordham University Press, 1992, 43-49.

Cohn, Ruby. 'Philosophical Fragments in Works of Samuel Beckett.' *Criticism* 6.1 (winter 1964): 33-43.

---. *Samuel Beckett: The Comic Gamut*. New Brunswick, N.J.: Rutgers University Press, 1962.

---. *Just Play: Beckett's Theater*. Princeton: Princeton University Press, 1980.

---. *A Beckett Canon*. Ann Arbor: University of Michigan Press, 2001.

Cronin, Anthony. *Samuel Beckett: The Last Modernist*. London: HarperCollins, 1997.

Culik, Hugh. 'Mindful of the Body: Medical Allusions in Beckett's *Murphy*.' *Eire-Ireland* 14.1 (spring 1979): 84-91.

---. 'Entropic Order. Beckett's *Mercier and Camier*.' *Eire-Ireland* 17.1 (spring 1982): 91-106.

Davis, R. J., J. R. Bryer, M. J. Friedman, and P. C. Hoy, eds. *Samuel Beckett: calepins de bibliographie*, No.2. Paris: Lettres modernes Minard, 1972.

Dobbin, Rachel. Notes from Beckett's lectures [unpublished ms]. Trinity College, Dublin [MIC 60].

Dobbin, Rachel [Burrows]. 'Interview with Rachel Burrows, Dublin, Bloomsday, 1982.' Interviewers: S. E. Gontarski, Martha Fehsenfeld and Dougald McMillan. *JOBS* 11 & 12 (1989): 6-15.

Doherty, Francis. *Samuel Beckett*. London: Hutchinson, 1971.

---. 'Mahaffy's Whoroscope.' *JOBS* n.s. 2.1 (autumn 1992): 27-46.

Dowd, Garin. 'Reading the Beckettian Baroque.' *JOBS* 8.1 (autumn 1998): 15-49.

Driver, Tom. 'Beckett by the Madeleine.' *Columbia University Forum* IV (summer 1961): 21-25.

Duckworth, Colin, ed. 'Introduction' to *En attendant Godot*. London: George Harrap, 1966, xvii-cxxxv.

Eade, J. C. 'The Seventh Scarf: A Note on *Murphy*.' *JOBS* 7 (spring 1982): 115-17.

Ellis, Rueben J. '"Matrix of Surds": Heisenberg's Algebra in Beckett's *Murphy*.' *Papers on Language and Literature* (Winter 1989), 120-23. Rpt. in Butler, Lance St. John, ed., *Critical Essays on Samuel Beckett*. Aldershot, Hants.: Scolar Press, 1993, 362-65.

Farrow, Anthony. *Early Beckett: Art and Illusion in More Pricks than Kicks and Murphy*. Troy, N.Y.: Whitston, 1991.

Federman, Raymond. *Journey to Chaos: Samuel Beckett's Early Fiction*. Berkeley and Los Angeles: University of California Press, 1965.

---, and John Fletcher, eds. *Samuel Beckett: His Works and His Critics: An Essay in Biography*. Berkeley and Los Angeles: University of California Press, 1970.

Fletcher, John. *The Novels of Samuel Beckett*. London: Chatto and Windus, 1964.

Friedman, Alan, ed. *Beckett in Black and Red: The Translations for Nancy Cunard's Negro (1934)*. Lexington: University Press of Kentucky, 1998.

Gluck, Barbara Reich. *Beckett and Joyce: Friendship and Fiction*. Lewisburg: Bucknell University Press, 1979.

Gontarski, S. E., ed. *The Beckett Studies Reader*. Gainesville: University Press of Florida, 1993.

Graver, Lawrence, and Raymond Federman. *Samuel Beckett: The Critical Heritage*. London: Routledge and Kegan Paul, 1979.

Harrington, John. *The Irish Beckett*. Syracuse, New York: Syracuse University Press, 1991.

Harrison, Robert. *Samuel Beckett's Murphy: A Critical Excursion*. Athens, Ga.: University of Georgia Press, 1968.

Harvey, Lawrence. *Samuel Beckett, Poet and Critic*. Princeton: Princeton University Press, 1970.

Henning, Sylvie Debevic. *Beckett's Critical Complicity: Carnival, Contestation, and Tradition*. Lexington: University Press of Kentucky, 1988.

---. 'The Guffaw of the Abderite: *Murphy* and the Democritean Universe.' *JOBS* 10 (1985): 5-20.

Hesla, David. *The Shape of Chaos: An Interpretation of the Art of Samuel Beckett*. Minneapolis: University of Minnesota Press, 1971.

---. "Being, Thinking, Telling and Loving." In *Samuel Beckett: The Art of Rhetoric*, ed. Edouard Morot-Sir, 11-23.

Hill, Leslie. *Beckett's Fiction: In Different Words*. Cambridge: Cambridge University Press, 1990.

Janvier, Ludovic. *Pour Samuel Beckett*. Paris: Minuit, 1966.

Jones, Anthony. 'The French *Murphy*: From "Rare Bird" to "Cancre".' *JOBS* 6 (autumn 1980): 37-50.

Keller, John Robert. *Samuel Beckett and the Primacy of Love*. Manchester and New York: Manchester University Press, 2002.

Kennedy, Sighle. *Murphy's Bed: A Study of Real Sources and Sur-Real Associations in Samuel Beckett's First Novel*. Lewisburg: Bucknell University Press, 1971.

---. '"The Devil and Holy Water": Samuel Beckett's *Murphy* and Flann O'Brien's *At Swim-Two-Birds*.' In *Modern Irish Literature: Essays in Honor of William York Tindall*, ed. R. J. Porter and J. D. Brophy. New Rochelle, N.Y.: Iona College Press, 1972, 251-60.

Kenner, Hugh. *Samuel Beckett: A Critical Study*. New York: Grove Press, 1961.

Kiely, Declan D. '"The Termination of This Solitaire": A Textual Error in *Murphy*.' *JOBS* n.s. 6.1 (autumn 1996): 135-36.

Knowlson, James. *Damned to Fame: The Life of Samuel Beckett.* London: Bloomsbury, 1996.

Lake, Carlton, ed. *No Symbols Where None Intended: A Catalogue of Books, Manuscripts, and Other Materials Relating to Samuel Beckett in the Collections of the Humanities Research Center.* Austin: Harry Ransom Humanities Research Center (University of Texas), 1984.

Lees, Heath. '*Watt*: Music Tuning and Tonality.' *JOBS* 9 (1984): 5-24. Rpt. in *The Beckett Studies Reader*, ed. S. E. Gontarski, 167-85.

Leventhal, A. J. 'The Thirties.' In *Beckett at Sixty*, ed. John Calder, 7-13.

Marculescu, Ileana. 'Beckett and the Temptation of Solipsism: "Esse est aut percipere aut percipi."' *JOBS* 11 & 12 (1989): 53-64.

Mays, J. C. C. 'Mythologized Presences: *Murphy* in its Time.' In *Myth and Reality in Irish Literature*, ed. Joseph Ronsley. Waterloo, Ont.: Wilfrid Laurier University Press, 1977, 197-218.

---. 'Young Beckett's Irish Roots.' *Irish University Review* 14.1 (spring 1984): 18-33.

---. 'How is MacGreevy a Modernist?' In *Modernism and Ireland: The Poetry of the 1930s*, ed. Patricia Coughlan and Alex Davis. Cork: Cork University Press, 1995, 125-26.

McCarthy, Patrick A., ed. *Critical Essays on Samuel Beckett.* Boston: G. K. Hall, 1986.

McQueeny, Terence. 'Beckett as a Critic of Joyce and Proust.' Ph.D. diss., University of North Carolina, 1977 [copy at BIF, University of Reading].

Mercier, Vivien. *Beckett/Beckett.* New York: Oxford University Press, 1977.

Mintz, Samuel. 'Beckett's *Murphy*: A Cartesian Novel.' *Perspective* 11.3 (autumn 1959): 156-65.

Mooney, Michael. 'Presocratic Skepticism: Samuel Beckett's *Murphy* Reconsidered.' *EHL* 49.1 (spring 1982): 214-34.

Moorjani, Angela. *Abysmal Games in the Novels of Samuel Beckett.* Chapel Hill: University of North Carolina Press, 1982.

Morot-Sir, Edouard. 'Samuel Beckett and Cartesian Emblems.' In *Samuel Beckett: The Art of Rhetoric*, ed. Edouard Morot-Sir, Howard Harper and Dougald McMillan III [North Carolina Studies in the Romance languages and Literature, #5]. Chapel Hill: University of North Carolina Press, 1976, 25-103.

Murphy, P. J. 'Beckett and the Philosophers.' In *The Cambridge Companion to Beckett,* ed. John Pilling, 222-40.

---, Werner Huber, Rolf Breuer and Konrad Schoell. *Critique of Beckett Criticism.* Columbia, S.C.: Camden House, 1994.

O'Brien, Eoin. *The Beckett Country: Samuel Beckett's Ireland.* Dublin: Black Cat Press, 1986.

O'Brien, Kate. 'Fiction.' *The Spectator* (March 25, 1938): 546.

O'Hara, J. D. 'Beckett Backs Down: From Home to Murphy via Valéry.' *JOBS* n.s. 3.2 (spring 1994): 37-55.

---. *Samuel Beckett's Hidden Drives: Structural Uses of Depth Psychology.* Gainesville: University Press of Florida, 1997.

Piette, Adam. *Remembering and the Sound of Words: Mallarmé, Proust, Joyce, Beckett.* Oxford: Clarendon Press, 1996.

Pilling, John. *Samuel Beckett.* London: Routledge and Kegan Paul, 1976.

---. 'Beckett's Proust.' *JOBS* 1 (winter 1976): 8-29.

---. 'From a (W)horoscope to Murphy.' In *'The Ideal Core of the Onion.' Reading Beckett Archives,* ed. John Pilling and Mary Bryden. Reading: Beckett International Foundation, 1992, 1-20.

---, ed. *The Cambridge Companion to Beckett.* Cambridge: Cambridge University Press, 1994.

---. 'Losing One's Classics: Beckett's Small Latin, and Less Greek.' *JOBS* n.s. 4.2 (spring 1995): 5-14.

---. *Beckett before Godot.* Cambridge: Cambridge University Press, 1998.

Rabaté, Jean-Michel, ed. *Beckett avant Beckett: Essais sur le jeune Beckett.* Paris: Presses de l'École Normale Supérieure, 1984.

---. 'Beckett's Ghosts and Fluxions.' In *Beckett & la Psychoanalyse / & Psychoanalysis,* ed. Sjef Houppermanns. Amsterdam: Rodopi, 1996, 23-42.

---. *The Ghosts of Modernity.* Gainesville, Fla.: University Press of Florida, 1996.

Rabinovitz, Rubin. 'Unreliable Narrative in Murphy.' In *Samuel Beckett: Humanistic Perspectives,* ed. Morris Beja, S. E. Gontarski and Pierre Astier. Columbus: Ohio State University Press, 1983, 58-70.

---. *The Development of Samuel Beckett's Fiction.* Urbana: University of Illinois Press, 1984.

---. *Innovation in Samuel Beckett's Fiction.* Urbana: University of Illinois Press, 1992.

Robinson, Michael. *The Long Sonata of the Dead: A Study of Samuel Beckett.* London: Rupert Hart-Davis, 1969.

Smith, Frederik N. '"A Land of Sanctuary": Allusions to the Pastoral in Beckett's Fiction.' In *Beckett Translating / Translating Beckett,* ed. Alan Warren Friedman,

Charles Rossman and Dina Sherzer. University Park and London: Pennsylvania State University Press, 1987, 128-39.

---. 'Dating the *Whoroscope* Notebook.' *JOBS* n.s. 3.1 (autumn 1993): 65-70.

---. *Beckett's Eighteenth Century.* New York: St. Martin's Press, 2002.

Taylor, Neil, and Bryan Loughery. 'Murphy's Surrender to Symmetry.' *JOBS* 11 & 12 (1989): 79-90.

Thomas, Dylan. 'Recent Novels.' *New English Weekly* (March 17, 1938): 454-55.

Warger, Thomas A. 'Going Mad Systematically in Beckett's *Murphy.' Modern Language Studies* 16.2 (1986): 13-18.

Webb, Eugene. *Samuel Beckett: A Study of His Novels.* Seattle and London: University of Washington Press, 1971.

Wood, Rupert. '*Murphy*, Beckett, *Geulincx*, God.' *JOBS*, n.s. 2.2 (spring 1993): 27-51.

Zurbrugg, Nicholas. 'Beckett, Proust, and Dream of Fair to Middling Women.' *JOBS* 9 (1984): 25-41.

---. *Beckett and Proust.* Gerrards Cross: Colin Smythe, 1988.

C. General studies used in this work

Abrahams, Gerald. *The Chess Mind.* London: Hodder and Stoughton, 1951.

Adam, Charles, et Paul Tannery, éditeurs. *Oeuvres de Descartes.* 12 tomes; Paris: Léopold Cerf, 1897-1913.

Adler, Alfred. *The Neurotic Constitution: Outlines of a Comparative Individualistic Psychology and Psychotherap*y, trans. Bernard Gleuck and John E. Lind. London: Kegan Paul, 1921.

'A. E.' [George Russell]. *The Candle of Vision.* London: Macmillan, 1918.

Aldington, Richard. *The Colonel's Daughter.* London: Chatto and Windus, 1931.

Aristophanes. *The Clouds*, ed. W. J. M. Starkie. London: Macmillan, 1911.

Aristotle. *De Anima*, ed. and trans. R. D. Hicks. Cambridge: Cambridge University Press, 1907.

---. *Aristotle, the Poetics; "Longinus," On the Sublime; Demetrius, On Style*, trans. W. Hamilton Fyfe [Loeb Classical Library]. London: Heinemann, 1927.

Aucassin et Nicolette: chantefable du XIII siècle, éditée par Mario Roques. Paris: Librairie de la société des anciens textes français, 1954.

Augustine, St. *Confessions*, trans. William Watts [Loeb Classical Library]. 2 vols; London: Heinemann, 1922.

---. *Confessions*, trans. E. B. Pusey [Everyman]. London: Dent, 1907.

Bacon, Sir Francis. *Novum Organum*, ed.Thomas Fowler. 2nd ed., cor. and rev.; Oxford: Clarendon Press, 1889.

Bailey, Cyril. *The Greek Atomists and Epicurus*. Oxford: Clarendon Press, 1928.

Baillet, Adrien. *La Vie de Monsieur Des-Cartes*. 2 tomes; Paris: Daniel Horthemels, 1691.

Baker, Alan. 'Pentonville Prison.' Unpublished brochure, n.d. [1995].

Baldwin, James M. *Dictionary of Philosophy and Psychology*. 2 vols.; New York: Macmillan, 1928.

Bartlett's Familiar Quotations. 10th edition; Boston: Little, Brown and Co., 1914.

Baudelaire, Charles. *Les Fleurs du mal, 1857-1861*, préface de Paul Valéry. Paris: Payot, 1928.

Beare, John I. *Greek Theories of Elementary Cognition*. Oxford: Clarendon Press, 1906.

Beaumont, Francis, and John Fletcher. *Plays*, ed. J. St. Loe Strachey [Mermaid]. 2 vols.; London: Vizetelly and Co., 1887.

Bendedetta, Mary. *The Street Markets of London*. London: John Miles, 1936.

Berkeley, George. *Berkeley's Commonplace Book*, ed. G. A. Johnston. London: Faber and Faber, 1930.

---. *A New Theory of Vision, and Other Writings*, ed. A. D. Lindsay [Everyman]. 1910; rpt. London: Dent, 1926.

---. *Siris: A Chain of Philosophical Reflexions and Inquiries Concerning the Virtues of Tar-Water, and divers other subjects connected together and arising from one another* [1744]. In *The Works of George Berkeley*, vol. 2, ed. A. C. Fraser. Oxford: Clarendon Press, 1871, 357-508.

The Book of Common Prayer. London: William Clowes and Sons, n.d.

Boswell, James. *Life of Johnson, Including Their Tour to the Hebrides,* ed. J. W. Croker. London: John Murray, 1847.

Breton, André. *Oeuvres complètes*. 2 tomes; Paris: Gallimard, 1988. In particular: *Manifeste de surréalisme: Poisson soluble* [1924]; and *Deuxième manifeste de surréalisme* [1930], 1, 775-828.

Brett, George Sidney. *A History of Psychology, Ancient and Patristic*. London: Allan and Unwin, 1912.

Brewer, E. Cobham. *The Dictionary of Phrase and Fable.* 2nd ed., rev.; London: Cassell, Petter and Galpin, 1894.

British Journal of Astrology, ed. E. H. Bailey. Vols. XXVII.1 (Oct. 1934) to XXIX.12 (Sept. 1936).

Browne, Sir Thomas. *The Works of Sir Thomas Browne,* ed. Charles Sayle. 3 vols.; Edinburgh: John Grant, 1927.

Brunschvicg, Léon. *Spinoza et ses contemporains* [1894]. 3 ième édition, révue et augmentée; Paris: Félix Alcan, 1923.

Burnet, John. *Early Greek Philosophy.* 1892; 3rd ed., rev., London: A. and C. Black, 1920.

---. *Greek Philosophy: Thales to Plato.* 1914; rpt. London: Macmillan, 1950.

Burton, Robert. *The Anatomy of Melancholy, what it is, with all the kinds, course, symptoms, prognostics, and several cures of it. In three partitions; with their several sections, members and subsections, philosophically, medically, historically opened and cut up. By Democritus Junior [Robert Burton], with a satyrical preface, conducing to the following discourse* [1562]. A new edition. London: Chatto and Windus, 1881.

Campanella, Thomae. *Astrologicum Libri VII, in quibis astrologia & physiologiae tracatur, secundum S. Scripturas et doctrinum theologicum.* Francofurti, 1630.

Campanella, Thommaso. *La Città del sole: A Poetical Dialogue* [1602]; trans. and ed. Daniel J. Donno [Biblioteca Italiana]. Berkeley, Los Angeles and London: University of California Press, 1981.

Chamfort [Sébastien Roch Nicolas]. *Oeuvres principales, comprenant de nombreux textes réprimés pour la première fois.* Paris: Pauvert, 1960.

Chaucer, Geoffrey. *The Works of Geoffrey Chaucer,* ed. W. W. Skeat. Oxford: Clarendon Press, 1894.

Chesterfield, Lord. *Letters of Philip Dorner, Fourth Earl of Chesterfield, to his Godson and Successor* [1776], ed. Carnavon, Henry Howard Molyneaux Herbert, 4th Earl of. Oxford: Clarendon Press, 1890.

Clarke, Austin. *Collected Poems,* ed. Liam Miller. Dublin: Dolmen Press, 1974.

Clunn, Harold P. *The Face of London: The Record of a Century's Change and Development.* London: Simpkin and Marshall, 1932.

Conan Doyle, Sir Arthur. *The Annotated Sherlock Holmes,* ed. William S. Baring-Gould. 1967; rpt. Avenel, N.J.: Wings Books, 1992.

Cooper, the Rev. William M. [pseud. of James Glass Bertram]. *Flagellation and the Flagellants: A History of the Rod in all Countries from the Earliest Period to the Present Time.* London: John Camden Hotten, 1869.

Cunard, Nancy. *Negro: an Anthology*. London: Wishart, 1934.

---. *These Were the Hours: Memories of My Hours Press*, ed. Hugh D. Ford. Carbondale: Southern Illinois University Press, 1969.

Daiken, Leslie. Unpublished notes from courses at Trinity College, Dublin, 1928-31. BIF, University of Reading [RUL number unassigned at time of writing].

Damon, S. Foster. *A Blake Dictionary*. London: Thames and Hudson, 1965.

Dandieu, Arnaud. *Marcel Proust: sa révélation psychologique*. Paris: Firmin-Didot, 1930.

Dante Alighieri. *Tutte le opere di Dante Alighieri*, nuovamente rivedute nel testo dal Dr. E. Moore, con indice dei nomi propri e delle cose notabili compilato dal Dr. Paget Toynbee. Terza edizione, riveduta; Oxford: nella stamperia dell'università, 1904.

---. *The Divine Comedy*, trans., with a commentary, by Charles S. Singleton [Bollingen Series LXXX]. 6 vols, 1970; rpt. Princeton: Princeton University Press, 1977.

Darwin, Charles. *On the Origin of Species*. London: John Murray, 1859.

Dekker, Thomas. *Thomas Dekker*, ed. Ernest Rhys [Mermaid]. London: Fisher-Unwin, n.d.

Descartes, René. *Oeuvres choisis de Descartes*. Nouvelle édition, Paris: Garnier Frères, n.d.

---. *A Discourse on Method, Meditations and Principles*, trans. John Veitch and intr. A. D. Lindsay [Everyman]. London: Dent, 1912.

Diderot, Denis. *Oeuvres philosophiques*, textes établis avec introduction, bibliographies et notes par Paul Vernière. Paris: Garnier Frères, 1964.

Diels, Hermann. *Die Fragmente der Vorsokratiker, Grieschisch und Deutsch*. 3 Bände; Berlin: Weidman, 1912.

Diogenes Laertius. *Lives of the Eminent Philosophers*, trans. R. D. Hick [Loeb Classical Library]. 2 vols.; London: Heinemann, 1925.

Donne, John. *Complete Poetry and Selected Prose*, ed. John Hayward. London: The Nonesuch Press, 1929.

Edwards, Paul, et al. *The Encyclopedia of Philosophy*. 8 vols.; London and New York: Collier-Macmillan, 1967.

Eliot, George. *Middlemarch*. Edinburgh and London: Blackwood, 1875.

Éluard, Paul. *Oeuvres complètes*. 2 tomes; Paris: Gallimard, 1968.

Encyclopaedia Britannica. 11th ed., 28 vols.; Cambridge: Cambridge University Press, 1911. Also consulted: editions of 1926 and 1954.

Epicurus. *Epicurus: The Extant Remains*, ed. Cyril Bailey. Oxford: Clarendon Press, 1926.

Fielding, Henry. *The History of the Adventures of Joseph Andrews and his Friend Mr Abraham Adams*. London: George Bell, 1906.

---. *The History of Amelia*. 2 vols.; London: Hutchison, 1905.

---. *The Journal of a Voyage to Lisbon*. In *The Works of Henry Fielding*, vol. 6, *Miscellanies*, ed. G. H. Maynadier. Philadelphia: John D. Morris and Co., 1902, 181-337.

---. *Tom Jones*, or the History of a Foundling. In *The Works of Henry Fielding,* vols. 1-2, ed. Leslie Stephen. London: Smith, Elder and Co., 1882.

Fleming, Ian. *Moonraker*. London: Pan, 1959.

Fletcher, John. *The Faithful Shepherdess*, ed. F. W. Moorman [Temple]. London: Dent, 1922.

Ford, John. *Plays*, ed. Havelock Ellis [Mermaid]. London: Vizetelly and Co., 1888.

Freeman, Kathleen. *Ancilla to the Pre-Socratic Philosophers: A Complete Translation of the Fragments in Diels, 'Fragmente der Vorsokratiker.'* Oxford: Blackwell, 1948.

---. *The Pre-Socratic Philosophers: A Companion to Diels, 'Fragmente der Vorsokratiker.'* 1946; 2nd ed., Cambridge, Mass.: Harvard University Press, 1959.

Freud, Sigmund. *The Standard Edition of the Complete Psychological Works of Sigmund Freud*, ed. James Strachey, in collaboration with Anna Freud. 24 vols.; London: Hogarth Press and the Institute of Psychoanalysis, 1953-74. In particular: 'Heredity and the Aetiology of the Neurosis' [1896], III, 141-56; *The Psychopathology of Everyday Life* [1901], VI; *Jokes and the Relation to the Unconscious* [1905], VIII; 'Five Lectures on Psycho-Analysis' [1909], XI, 1-55; 'On Narcissism: An Introduction' [1914], XVI, 73-102; 'The Unconscious' [1915], XVI, 166-215; *General Theory of the Neuroses* [1917], XIV; 'The Ego and the Id' [1923], XIX, 1-59; and 'Neurosis and Psychosis' [1922], XIX, 149-53.

Garnier, Pierre. *Onanisme seul et à deux*. Paris: Garnier Frères, n.d.

Gearrfhoclóir Gaeilge-Béarle. Baile Átha Cliath: Richview Browne and Nolan, 1981.

Geulincx, Arnoldus. *Opera Philosophica*, recongnivit J. P. N. Land. 3 vols.; Hague Comitum: Martinum Nijhoff, 1891-93.

Gifford, Don, and Robert J. Seidman. *Ulysses Annotated: Notes for James Joyce's Ulysses*. 1974; 2nd ed., rev., Berkeley, Los Angeles and London: University of California Press, 1988.

Giles, H. A. *The Civilization of China*. London: Williams and Norgate, [1911].

Goethe, Johann Wolfgang von. *Die Leiden des jungen Werthers* [1774]. In *Frühe Prosa*, hrsg. von Peter Boerner. Munchen: Deutscher Taschenbuch Verlag, 1962, 42-150.

Gogarty, St. John. *Intimations*. New York: Abelard Press, 1950.

Greene, Robert. *The Life and Complete Works of Robert Greene*, ed. Alexander Grosart. 15 vols.; London and Aylesbury: Printed for Private Circulation, 1881-86. Rpt. London: John Lane, the Bodley Head, 1923.

---. *Groats-worth of Witte and The Repentance of Robert Greene* [1592]. Rpt. London: John Lane, the Bodley Head, 1923.

---. 'A Notable Discovery of Coosnage. 1591.' Rpt. in *The Art of Conny-Catching*, ed. G. B. Hamson. London: John Lane, the Bodley Head, 1923.

Grove's Dictionary of Music and Musicians, ed. Eric Blom. 9 vols.; New York: St. Martin's Press, 1954.

Haeckel, Ernst. *The Riddle of the Universe*, trans. Joseph McCabe. London: Watts and Co., 1900.

Headlam, Cecil. *The Story of Oxford*. London: Dent, 1907.

Herrick, Robert. *The Poems of Robert Herrick*. London: Grant Richards, 1902.

Hesiod. *Hesiode: Théolgonie—Les Travaux et les jours—Le Bouclier*, texte établi et traduit par Paul Mazon. Paris: Société d'édition 'Les Belles Lettres,' 1928.

Hiscock, W. G. *A Christ Church Miscellany*. Oxford: Printed for the Author, 1946.

Hooper, David, and Kenneth Whyld, eds. *The Oxford Companion to Chess*. 1984; rev. and rpt. Oxford: Oxford University Press, 1988.

Horace. *Satires. Epistles. Ars Poetica*, trans. H. Rushton Fairclough [Loeb Classical Library]. London: Heinemann, 1926.

Jeans, Sir James. *The Universe around Us*. Cambridge: Cambridge University Press, 1929.

Johnson, Samuel. *A Dictionary of the English Language, in which words are deduced from their originals and illustrated in their different significations by examples from the best writers*. 10th ed., 2 vols; London, 1810.

---. *Johnsonian Miscellanies*, ed. George Birbeck Hill. 2 vols; London: Constable, 1897.

Jones, Ernest. *Papers on Psycho-Analysis*. London: Ballière, Tindall and Cox, 1920.

---. 'The Problem with Paul Morphy.' *International Journal of Psychoanalysis* 12.1 (Jan. 1931): 1-23.

Jonson, Ben. *Plays*, ed. Brinsley Bicholson and C. H. Herford [Mermaid]. London: T. Fisher-Unwin, n.d. [1935].

Joyce, James. *Dubliners.* 1914; rpt. as *Dubliners: Text, Criticism, Notes*, ed. Robert Scholes and A. Walton Litz. New York: Viking, 1969.

---. *A Portrait of the Artist as a Young Man.* 1916; rpt. Harmondsworth: Penguin, 1960.

---. *Ulysses.* 1922; ed. Jeri Johnson [the 1922 text]; Oxford: Oxford University Press, 1993.

Jung, Carl. 'The Tavistock Lectures' [1935]. In *The Collected Works*, XVIII, *The Symbolic Life: Miscellaneous Writings,* trans. R. F. C. Hull. London and Henley: Routledge and Kegan Paul, 1977, 5-182.

Juvenal. *Juvenal and Persius*, trans. G. G. Ramsay [Loeb Classical Library]. London: Heinemann, 1918.

Kant, Immanuel. *Immanuel Kant's Critique of Pure Reason* [1781], trans. Norman Kemp Smith. 1929; rpt. London: Macmillan, 1933.

Keats, John. *The Poems*, ed. E. de Selincourt. 3rd ed., London: Methuen, 1912.

Kirk, G. S., and J. E. Raven. *The Presocratic Philosophers.* Cambridge: Cambridge University Press, 1969.

Klein, Melanie. *The Psychoanalysis of Children.* London: Hogarth Press, 1932.

Koffka, Kurt. *The Growth of the Mind*, trans. R. M. Ogden. 1924; 2nd ed., rev., London: Kegan Paul, Trench, Trubner and Co., 1931.

---. *Principles of Gestalt Psychology.* New York.: Harcourt, Brace and World, 1935.

Köhler, Wolfgang. *The Mentality of Apes*, trans. Ella Winter. 1917; 2nd ed., rev., London: Kegan Paul, Trench, Trubner and Co., 1925.

Laloy, Louis. *La Musique chinoise.* Paris: Librairie Renouard (Henri Laurens), n.d. [1900?].

Leibnitz, Gottfried. *The Monadology and Other Philosopical Writings*, trans. and ed. Robert Latta. London: Oxford University Press, 1898.

Lemprière's Classical Dictionary. 1865; rpt. London: Bracken Books, 1984.

Lessing, Gotthold. 'Laocöon' [1766]. In *Samtliches Schriften* 9, hrsg. von Karl Lachmann und Franz Muckner. Stuttgart: G. D. Göschen'sche Verlagshandlung, 1893, 1-77.

---. 'Wie die Alten den Tod gebildet' [1769]. In *Samtliches Schriften* 11, hrsg. von Karl Lachmann und Franz Muckner. Stuttgart: G. D. Göschen'sche Verlagshandlung, 1893, 1-55.

Lewis, Samuel. *A Topographical Dictionary of Ireland.* 1837; 2 vols.; rpt. Baltimore: Genealogical Publishing Co., Ltd., 1984.

Lucien. 'Gout' [ΠΟΔΑΓΡΑ]. In *Lucian* VIII, trans. and ed. M. D. MacLeod [Loeb Classical Library]. London: Heinemann, 1967, 324-55.

Lucretius. *De la nature* [*De rerum natura*], 2 tomes, texte établi et traduit par Alfred Ernout. 2ième édition, revue et corrigée, Paris: Société d'édition 'Les Belles Lettres,' 1924.

MacGreevy, Thomas. *The Collected Poems of Thomas MacGreevy*, ed. Susan Schreibman. Dublin: Anna Livia Press, 1991.

Mahaffy, J. P. *Descartes*. Edinburgh and London: William Blackwood, 1880.

Malraux, André. *La Condition humaine*. Paris: Gallimard, 1933.

Marlowe, Christopher. *Plays,* ed. Havelock Ellis [Mermaid]. London: Vizetelly and Co., 1887.

Marston, John. *The Works of John Marston*. 3 vols., ed. A. H. Bullen; London: John C. Nimmer, 1887.

Mauthner, Fritz. *Beiträge zu einer Kritik der Sprache*. 3 Bände; Leipzig: F. Meiner, 1923.

McIntyre, J. Lewis. *Giordano Bruno*. London: Macmillan, 1903.

Melville, Herman. *Moby Dick, or, the Whale*. New York: Modern Library, 1930.

Meredith, George. *The Egoist*. London: Constable, 1928.

Miller, Joe. *Joe Miller's Jest-Book, or the Wit's Vade Mecum, being, A Collection of the most Brilliant Jests; the Politest Repartees; the most Elegant Bons Mots, and most pleasant Short Stories in the English Language*, ed. Elijah Jenkins Esq. London, 1739.

Milligan, Spike. *Puckoon*. London: Anthony Blond, 1963.

Milton, John. *Paradise Lost* [Temple Classics]. London: Dent, 1904.

---. *The Prolusions of John Milton*, ed. Donald L. Clark, with a translation by Brandy Smith. In *The Works of John Milton* XII. New York: Columbia University Press, 1935, 118-285.

Molière [Jean Baptiste Poquellin]. *Théâtre complet*. Paris: Hachette, 1926.

Murphy, George. *Historical Introduction to Modern Psychology*. London: Routledge and Kegan Paul, 1928.

Nashe, Thomas. *The Unfortunate Traveller*. In *The Works of Thomas Nashe*, Vol. 2, ed. Ronald B. McKerrow. London: Sigwick and Jackson, 1910, 187-328.

Oxford Classical Dictionary, ed. N. S. L. Hammond et al. 2nd ed., rev., Oxford: Clarendon Press, 1970.

Oxford English Dictionary [Compact Edition, complete text reduced micrographically]. 2 vols.; Oxford: Oxford University Press, 1971. With *A Supplement to the Oxford English Dictionary* [*Compact Edition*, Vol. 3], ed. R. W. Burchfield. Oxford: Clarendon Press, 1987.

Partridge, Eric. *A Dictionary of Catch Phrases*. London: Routledge and Kegan Paul, 1977.

Pascal, Blaise. *Pensées*. Paris: Flammarion, n.d.

Peele, George. *The Dramatic Works of Robert Greene and George Peele*, with memoirs of the authors and notes by the Rev. Alexander Dyce. London: Routledge, 1874.

A Pictorial and Descriptive Guide to London. 52nd ed., rev., London: Ward, Lock and Co., n.d. [1936].

Plato. *Euthyphro. Apology. Crito. Phaedo. Phaedrus*, trans. Harold North Fowler [Loeb Classical Library]. London: Heinemann, 1914.

---. *The Collected Dialogues, Including the Letters*, ed. Edith Hamilton and Huntington Cairns [Bollingen Series LXXI]. Princeton: Princeton University Press, 1961.

Pliny the Elder. *Natural History*, 10 vols., trans. H. Rackham [Loeb Classical Library]. London: Heinemann, 1938-63.

Pope, Alexander. *The Poetical Works of Alexander Pope*. Edinburgh: Gall and Inglis, 1881.

Post Office London Directory [1935]. London: Kelly's Directories [1935].

Proust, Marcel. *A la recherche du temps perdu* [Édition de la *Nouvelle revue française*]. 16 vols.; Paris: Gallimard, 1919-27 [Beckett's copy, annotated, at the BIF]. Individual texts cited by short title: *Swann; Jeunes filles*; *Guermantes*; *Sodome et Gomorrhe*; *La Prisonnière*; *Albertine disparue*; *Le Temps retrouvé*.

---. *A la recherche du temps perdu*, ed. Pierre Clarac et André Ferré. 3 vols; Paris: Gallimard [Bibliothèque de la Pléiade], 1968-69.

---. *Remembrance of Things Past*, trans. C. K. Scott Moncrieff [Books 1-6] and Frederick A. Blossom [Book 7]. 2 vols., 1924 and 1927; rpt. New York: Random House, 1934.

Quintilian. *The Institutio Oratoria of Quintilian*, trans. H. E. Butler [Loeb Classical Library]. 4 vols.; London: Heinemann, 1920-22.

Rabelais, Francis. *François Rabelais: tout ce qui existe de ses oeuvres: Gargantua— Pantagruel*, édité par Louis Moland. Paris: Garnier Frères, n.d.

---. *The Works of Mr. Francis Rabelais, Doctor in Physick. Containing Five Books of the Lives, Heroic Deeds and Sayings of Gargantua and His Sonne Pantagruel*, trans. Sir Thomas Urquhart [Books 1-3] and Peter Motteux [Books 4-5]; illustrated by W. Heath Robinson. London: The Navarre Society, 1931.

Racine, Jean. *Théâtre complet*, édité par Félix Lemaistre. Paris: Garnier, n.d.

Rank, Otto. *The Trauma of Birth* [1924]. London: Kegan Paul, Trench, Trubner and Co., 1929.

Renard, Jules. *Journal*. Paris: Gallimard, 1935.

Redshaw, Thomas Dillon. *Thomas McGreevy: Collected Poems*. Dublin: New Writers Press, 1971.

Rimbaud, Arthur. *Oeuvres de Arthur Rimbaud, vers et proses*, préface de Paul Claudel. Paris: Mercure de France, n.d.

Rousseau, Jean Jacques. *Émile, ou, de l'éducation* [1762]. Paris: Garnier, 1919.

---. *Les Rêveries du promeneur solitaire* [1782]. Genève: Librairie Droz, 1948.

Schopenhauer, Arthur. *On the Fourfold Root of the Principle of Sufficient Reason* and *On the Will in Nature*, trans. Mme. Karl Hillebrand. 1887; rev. ed., London: George Bell, 1915.

---. *Parega and Paralipomena: Short Philosophical Essays*, trans. E. F. J. Payne. 2 vols.; Oxford: Clarendon Press, 1974.

---. *The World as Will and Idea*, trans. R. B. Haldane and J. Kemp. 1883; 3 vols.; rpt. London: Kegan Paul, Trench, Trübner and Co., 1896.

Sextus Empiricus, trans. R. G. Bury [Loeb Classical Library]. 4 vols.; London: Heinemann, 1949-61.

Shakespeare, William. *Complete Works*, ed. Peter Alexander. 1951; rpt. London and Glasgow: Collins, 1978.

Shelley, Percy Bysshe. *The Poetical Works of Percy Bysshe Shelly*, ed. with a critical memoir by William Michael Rossetti. London: Ward, Lock and Co., n.d.

Sheridan, Richard Brinsley. *The Dramatic Works of the Right Honourable Richard Brinsley Sheridan, with a Memoir of his Life*, ed. "G. G. S." London: Bell and Daldy, 1872.

Stekel, Wilhelm. *Psychoanalysis and Suggestion Therapy: Their Technique, Applications, Results, Limits, Dangers*. London: Kegan Paul, Trench, Trubner and Co., 1923.

Spinoza, Baruch. *Ethica*. In *The Chief Works of Benedict de Spinoza*, Vol. 2, trans. and ed. R. H. M. Elwes. London: George Bell, 1909.

Stendhal [Henri Beyle]. *Le Rouge et le noir*. Paris: Garnier, n.d.

Stephen, Karin. *Psychoanalysis and Medicine: A Study of the Wish to Fall Ill*. Cambridge: Cambridge University Press, 1933.

Swift, Jonathan. *The Works of the Rev. Jonathan Swift, D.D.*, ed. D. Laing Purves. Edinburgh: William P. Nimmo and Co., 1880. In particular: *Gulliver's Travels*, 110-216; *Journal to Stella*, 226-403; 'A Letter of Advice to a Young Poet,' 498-505.

---. *The Poems of Jonathan Swift, D.D.* 2 vols; ed. William Ernst Browning. London: George Bell, 1910.

---. *Polite Conversation, in Three Dialogs*, ed. George Sainstbury. London: Charles Whittingham and Co. at the Chiswick Press, 1892.

---. *A Tale of a Tub, to which is added The Battle of the Books and The Mechanical Operation of the Spirit* [1704], ed. A. C. Guthkelch and D. Nicol Smith. Oxford: Clarendon Press, 1920.

Synge, John Millington. *J. M. Synge's Plays, Poems, and Prose*, ed. Mícheál Mac Liammóir. London: Dent, 1941.

Taylor, Jeremy. *Holy Living and Dying, together with Prayers Containing the Whole Duty of a Christian and the Parts of Devotion Fitted to All Occasions, and Furnished for All Necessities.* New edition, carefully revised; London: Henry G. Bohn, 1851.

TCD: A College Miscellany. Dublin: Trinity College, 1923-30 [various issues].

Thackeray, William. *Vanity Fair: A Novel without a Hero.* London: Bradbury and Evans, 1848.

Thomas à Kempis. *De Imitatione Christi: Libri Quatuor.* Paris: Librairie Tross, 1868.

---. *The Earliest English Translation of De Imitatio Christi, Now First Printed from a Ms. in the Library of Trinity College, Dublin, with various Readings from a Ms. in the University Library, Cambridge*, ed. John K. Ingram [Early English Text Society]. London: Kegan Paul, Trench, Trubner and Co, 1893.

Titus, Edward W., ed. *This Quarter* V.1 (Sept. 1932); rpt. New York: Arno and the New York Times, 1969.

Toynbee, Paget. *Concise Dictionary of Proper Names and Notable Matters in the Works of Dante.* Oxford: Clarendon Press, 1914.

Tuke, D. A., ed. *A Dictionary of Psychological Medicine.* 2 vols.; London: J. and A. Churchill, 1892.

Valéry, Paul. *Monsieur Teste.* Paris: Gallimard, 1929.

Virgil. *Virgil: Eclogues, Georgics, Aeneid, Minor Poems*, trans. H. Rushton Fairclough [Loeb Classical Library]. London: Heinemann, 1916.

Voltaire. *Candide, ou l'optimisme* [1758]. In *Voltaire: romans et contes*, texte établi par Henri Bénac. Paris: Classiques Garnier, n.d., 137-221.

Weinreb, Ben, and Christopher Hibbert. *The London Encyclopedia.* London: Macmillan, 1983.

Whitaker, Joseph. *An Almanack for the Year of Our Lord 1935.* London: Whitaker, 1934. Also consulted: volumes for the years 1931 to 1937.

Wilenski, R.H. *An Introduction to Dutch Art.* London: Faber and Faber, 1929.

Windelband, Dr. Wilhelm. *A History of Philosophy, with special reference to the formation and development of its problems and conceptions*, trans. James H. Tufts. 2nd ed., rev. and enlarged, London: Macmillan, 1914.

Woodworth, Robert. *Contemporary Schools of Psychology.* New York: The Ronald Press, 1931.

Wordsworth, William. *The Poetical Works of Wordsworth*, ed. Thomas Hutchinson. London: Oxford University Press, 1904.

Yeats, W. B. *Collected Poems*. London: Macmillan, 1933.

Young, Edward. *The Poetical Works of Edward Young* [Aldine Edition]. 2 vols.; London: Bell and Daldy, n.d.

Index

This is a thematic listing, so that scholars interested in (e.g.) 'narcissism' may follow up not only the explicit references but the various notes that touch upon the theme (e.g., references to 'Echo's Bones'), even if the key word is only hinted at. The Index is keyed to the Annotations and reflects the Grove Press pagination. Important entries are italicized. 'T' signifies 'Title.' Names and places are included if (a) the reference is a primary one (explicitly cited in *Murphy*), or (b) a secondary one that is thematically significant. Included are scholars and other persons cited in the notes, and places and particulars pertinent to Beckett, especially those that anticipate developments in his later work.

Begam, Richard: 249.10.
behaviorism: 4.1, 79.5, 80.3, 81.1, 81.2, 84.2, 159.2, 238.1.
Belacqua: 2.5, 3.10, 6.3, 6.6, 7.4, 9.2, 12.2, 16.1, 20.1, 27.3, 28.1, 36.3, 37.2, 38.1, 42.5, 42.6, 44.2, 50.4, 71.1, 71.4, 73.2, 74.2, *78.1*, 78.2, 78.4, 78.6, 78.8, 78.9, 84.3, 87.5, 99.2, 100.2, 103.4, 110.1, 111.3, *111.7*, 112.3, 112.10, 113.1, 117.4, 140.3, 145.3, 148.2, 149.3, 174.2, 179.1, 187.1, 188.1, 201.3, 217.2, 217.3, 218.6, 228.1, 246.7, 254.2, 258.2, 267.3.
Bellini, Giovanni: 251.3.
Belloc, Hilaire: 7.3.
Bérard, Victor: 134.4.
Berkeley, Bishop: 58.1, *58.2*, 108.1, 108.2, *246.3*.
Berwick Market: 23.1.
Bethlem Royal Hospital: 87.1, *156.2*, 156.3, 156.5, 158.1, 159.1, 160.1, 160.2, 161.3, 162.1, 165.1, 165.3, 166.3, 167.1, 167.2, 167.5, 168.6, 174.3, 185.1, 238.1, 238.2, 240.2, *257.3*, 259.1, 259.3, 261.4, 274.1.
Bible: 1.1, 3.5, 3.9, *5.7*, 7.3, 8.1, 14.5, 22.2, 22.3, 22.4, 23.3, 23.5, 28.3, 37.2, 39.1, 40.2, 46.3, 46.6, 47.3, 57.3, 65.4, 71.2, 72.3, 76.1, 83.1, 99.2, 104.3, 104.4, 109.3, 119.1, 120.1, 132.1, 137.3, 138.2, 156.2, 176.1, 178.2, 179.4, 180.2, 183.4, 186.5, 197.1, 197.3, 198.1, 199.1, 199.2, 201.5, 208.3, 217.2, 222.1, 222.2, 222.3, 226.1, 227.4, 230.1, 230.2, 234.1, 241.5, 249.7, 249.10, 251.3, 254.1, 278.1.
bicycle: 14.9, 55.2.
Big World [Macrocosm]: 1.1, 1.2, 1.5, 2.1, 2.5, 6.4, 7.2, 14.5, 17.1, 17.5, 21.2, 25.1, *32.2*, 63.3, 76.2, 113.10, 168.9, 175.5, *176.3*, 176.6, *177.1*, *178.5*, 178.6, 179.3, 188.3, 229.3, 250.3.
Bim and Bom [clowns]: *156.5*, 157.1, 227.1, 264.1.
Bildad the Shuhite: 70.5, 70.6.
billiards: 161.2, 168.4.
Bion, Wilfred: 3.2, 32.2, 83.3, 111.3, 167.5, 187.2.
birds: 1.4, 2.4, 7.2, 10.1, 11.6, 38.1, 41.1, 54.6, 84.5, 88.6, 94.2, 96.2, 97.3, 103.5, 140.2, 163.2, 174.2, 193.3, 201.3, 217.2, 220.4, *229.3*, 240.3, 263.1.
birth: 12.8, 24.1, 32.7, 32.8, 32.10, 33.2, 33.4, *44.3*, *46.3*, 54.8, 57.2, 64.4, 66.1, 67.1, 71.2, *71.4*, 71.7, 73.2, *111.3*, 112.10, 149.3, 166.2, 201.4, 201.5, 207.5, 213.2, 241.4, 258.2.
Blake, William: 13.2, 15.1, 65.1, 67.3, 70.3, 70.4, 70.5, 70.6, 71.8, 73.11, 74.8, 79.1, 120.1.
Blarney: 50.6, 226.2.
Bloom, Leopold: T, 4.2, 24.3, 26.2, 62.3, 63.1, 92.2, 131.5, 143.1, 277.2.
Bloomsbury: 179.5, 224.5.
body: 1.4, 2.3, 2.9, 3.3, 3.8, 6.4, 6.6, *6.7*, 8.1, *10.1*, 11.2, 11.6, 12.2, 14.4, 18.3, 19.1, 20.2, 22.4, 22.5, 24.2, 25.1, 28.1, 28.3, 32.2, 32.14, 39.2, 40.5, 42.4, 43.2, 49.3, 56.4, 60.3, 62.3, 71.3, 72.5, 74.9, 85.3, 90.3, 92.2, 99.1, 105.3, 105.5, 107.1, 108.1, 108.2, 108.5, *109.1*, 109.4, 109.7, 110.1, 113.3, 115.1, 117.5, 117.6, 119.2, 119.4, 126.3, 134.5, 152.3, 178.4, 178.8, 178.9, 179.3, 184.2, 185.1, 191.1, 192.2, 193.1, 194.2, 200.2, 204.2, 207.3, 211.3, 212.3, 218.1, 218.2, 218.4, 218.5, 218.7, 219.1, 219.3, 227.4, 239.2, 239.3, 246.6, 248.2, 248.4, 249.1, 249.2, 249.3, 249.4, 249.5, 249.6, 249.7, 250.5, 251.3, 252.1, 253.1, 258.2, 263.3, 266.1, 275.2, 281.1, 282.2.
Bonaventura, Saint: 60.3.
Book of Common Prayer: 67.6, 184.4, 197.3.
Boswell, James: 17.4, 167.2, 220.3, 246.3.
Bouvier, Bishop: 72.1, 162.3.
Boydell, Brian: 71.6.
Braque, Georges: 2.5, 63.5, *63.6*, 106.4.

Breton, André: 5.6, 21.2, 167.5, 207.6, 237.1, 279.1, 279.3, 280.3.
Brett, George: 2.9, 5.3, 9.1, 21.1, 49.3, 110.5, 111.4, 275.2.
Brewer [*Phrase and Fable*]: 17.2, 31.3, 116.1, 145.2, 200.3, 220.1,
Brewery Road: 63.1, 63.5, 73.9, 73.10, 74.3, 74.5, 74.6, 74.7, 74.8, 135.1, 258.4.
Bright, Dr. Richard: 33.7.
Britannica: 21.4, 31.3, 32.3, 33.1, 33.4, 148.1, 175.2, 260.1.
British Museum: 84.3, 84.4, 84.5, 195.4, 195.5.
Broad Walk: 153.1, 276.3.
Browne, Sir Thomas: 58.5, 138.1.
Bruno [identified contraries]: 1.4, 9.1, 17.1, 65.2, 73.6, 107.4, 111.3, 197.3, 198.1, 215.1, *246.5.*
Brunschvicg, Léon: 2.3, 107.1, 111.3, 216.6.
Bryden, Mary: 10.1, 201.2.
Buddha: 3.4, 241.2.
Bühle, Karl: 80.3, 81.1.
Burnet, John: 1.1, 3.7, *3.8,* 5.4, 6.3, 15.4, 44.1, 47.8, 47.9, 49.3, 50.5, 71.2, 90.1, 102.5, 108.1, 108.7, 130.2, 175.3, 204.2, 246.5, 246.6, 246.7, 248.2.
Burns, Robbie: 261.3, 263.3.
Burton, Robert [*Anatomy of Melancholy*]: 1.4, 3.9, 11.5, 14.4, 17.1, 29.4, 31.1, 32.2, 44.3, 58.5, 60.2, 84.2, 86.3, 87.2, 97.4, 99.2, 107.3, 108.2, 110.2, 117.4, 140.5, 167.4, 178.5, 193.1, 196.1, 200.3, 202.1, 216.6, 217.3, 220.2, 223.3, 229.3, 233.1, 237.1, 246.5, 246.6, 276.2.
Busby, Sir Richard: *97.5.*

Café de la Régence: 244.8.
Calderón: 46.3, 78.5.
Campanella, Tommaso: *17.1,* 17.2, 23.3, 162.3.
Campbell, Julie: 195.5.
candle: 102.6, 155.2, 252.2.
cang: 131.4, 218.1.
Cantle, Kenneth: 156.5.
Canute: 185.2, 186.1.
Capricorn: 32.7, 33.2, 33.4, 33.6.
Caroline, Queen: 99.8, 150.2, 150.6.
carpe te ipsum: 4.2, 19.1, 84.4.
Carriage, Miss: 64.3, 64.4, 68.1, 74.6, 102.6, 132.2, 132.3, 134.2, 144.1, 155.2, 226.1, 258.4.
'A Case in a Thousand': 3.9.
cat: 36.3, 198.4, 202.4, 203.1, 220.1, 275.2.
Cathleen ni Houlihan: 4.4, 46.5, 62.1.
Cattle Market [Caledonian Market]: 62.3, *63.3,* 73.8, 73.10, 74.3.
Cattley, William [cattleyas]: 50.7.
Catullus: 10.1.
causality: 22.5, 90.6, 107.1, 168.9, 107.4, 109.1, 113.3, 177.1, 191.1, 201.4, 218.7, 262.3.
Celia: 7.5, *7.6,* 8.2, 8.3, *10.1,* 11.5, 11.7, 12.3, 12.5, 12.6, 12.7, 12.8, 14.1, 16.1, 16.2, 16.5, 17.3, 18.3, 20.1, 22.3, 22.4, 23.5, 29.5, 36.2, 40.4, 63.3, 63.5, 66.1, 66.3, 68.1, 90.6, 109.7, 114.1, 122.5, 130.1, 137.1, 139.1, 142.2, 145.3, 150.1, 152.2, 153.2, 155.1, 155.2, 168.7, 176.3, 179.3, 186.3, 221.1, 229.2, 229.3, 230.2, 232.1, 235.2, 249.4, 250.2, 250.3, 252.3, 254.2, 258.4, 262.3, 269.5, 280.1, 280.7, 281.1, 282.2.
Celtic Twilight: 3.1, 3.5, 42.3, 46.7, 71.3, 84.6, 88.5, 89.2, 89.3, 117.5, 184.5, 184.6, 245.6, 257.3, 267.4, 269.2.
Cézanne, Paul: *196.2.*

Chamfort: 57.2, *79.4*, 191.2.
chaos [gas]: 13.2, 32.2, 48.2, 62.2, 65.4, 162.1, 168.4, 175.1, *175.3*, 176.1, 176.2, 176.3, 207.5, 249.9.
Charles II: 12.9, 14.8, 97.5, 127.3, 170.3.
Chaucer, Geoffrey: 5.5, 229.3.
Chelsea [embankment]: 1.3, 12.8, 12.9, 14.6, 14.7, 14.8, 14.9, 14.10, 15.1, 15.3, 16.4, 120.1, 127.2, 179.5.
'Che Sciagura': 129.3, 217.3.
chess: 8.4, 17.5, 23.3, 85.1, 174.1, 184.3, 186.4, 187.2, 195.4, 214.1, *242.1*, 243.1, *243.2*, 243.3, 243.4, 243.5, 243.6, 243.7, 244.1, 244.2, 244.3, 244.4, 244.5, *244.6*, *244.7*, 244.8, 244.9, 245.1, 245.3, 245.4, 245.5, 245.6, 245.7, 262.3.
Chesterfield, Lord: 269.3.
Christ: 2.1, 3.10, 5.7, 23.5, 27.1, 28.1, 28.3, *32.7*, 32.13, 39.1, 48.1, 64.1, 66.3, 72.3, 73.1, 73.4, 83.1, 92.2, 99.5, 104.3, 107.2, 109.3, 119.1, 170.2, 175.4, 180.2, 199.1, 202.2, 213.2, 218.5, 236.3, 249.10, 251.3, 267.1.
church: 15.3, 31.2, 77.4, 154.1, 167.1, 177.2.
circle [closed]: 3.8, 4.1, *5.3*, *5.5*, 5.6, 6.2, 47.9, 53.2, *57.4*, *60.3*, 108.7, 109.2, 117.1, 150.2, 168.3, 183.1, 201.2, 201.4, 213.3.
Clarke, Austin: 84.6, 86.1, 86.4, 88.5, 88.6, 94.1, *117.5*, 181.3, 184.5, 193.4, 267.4.
Claude: *228.3*.
Cleopatra [*Antony and Cleopatra*]: 106.3, 161.4, 240.2.
clocks: 16.5, 18.3, 74.1, 74.3, 76.2, *109.1*, 109.6, 114.6, *178.9*, 227.4, 241.3.
Clonmachnois: 267.4.
clothes: 1.5, 2.2, 37.3, 72.4, *72.5*, 73.1, 85.6, 129.1, 138.1, 138.4, 142.2, 186.5, 186.6, 200.3, 204.2, 212.2, *251.1*, 256.1, 257.5, 259.1, 271.4, 276.4.
Clunn, Harold: 63.2, 70.1.
Cockpit: 50.3, 84.3, 96.1, 165.4.
Coe, Richard: 14.9.
Cohn, Ruby: 4.2, 11.5, 138.1, 156.5, 163.1, 197.1, 213.3.
coincidence: T, 3.2, 12.5, 16.5, 23.3, 26.1, *26.2*, 114.4, 121.1.
Coleridge, S. T.: 5.2, 202.2, 229.3.
Coleridge-Taylor, Samuel: 215.2.
Collected Poems: 57.2, 79.4.
colors: 1.5, 2.5, 4.3, 6.1, 7.3, 26.7, 31.3, 33.9, 63.6, 71.8, 78.7, 108.2, 155.2, 161.5, 186.6, 206.1, 213.2, 224.3, 229.2, 246.1, *246.2*, 251.1, 275.2.
comedy: 3.9, 7.6, 86.6, 115.1, 141.2, 235.3, 254.2, 259.2.
Company [**Mrs. Coote**]: 64.3.
Conan Doyle, Sir Arthur: 26.7, 144.1, 203.2, *262.3*.
conarium: 6.6, *6.7*, 12.1, 72.5, *109.1*, 280.3.
Coney Island: 59.1.
consciousness: 2.10, 3.4, 3.8, 5.1, 5.6, 9.2, 19.1, 21.1, *21.2*, 64.7, 65.4, 67.4, 71.2, 77.2, 79.2, 81.1, 89.6, 90.6, 107.2, 107.4, *107.6*, 108.2, 109.1, *110.5*, *111.3*, 111.4, 111.5, 112.1, 112.2, *112.3*, *112.7*, 112.10, *113.3*, 159.2, 168.1, 176.3, 178.5, 180.3, 183.1, 185.1, 201.2, 201.3, *218.3*, 228.4, 250.3, 251.2.
contingency: 1.1, 1.2, 9.1, 36.2, 40.3, 74.9, 107.1, *168.9*, 183.1.
the Coombe: 267.3.
Cooper: 26.7, 43.2, *54.5*, 54.6, 54.8, 57.4, 118.2, 119.2, 121.3, 122.2, 123.1, 150.1, 203.2, 203.3, 204.2, 205.1, 206.1, 254.2, 256.1, 206.1, 262.3, 274.3.
Cooper, Becky: 6.6, 54.5.
Cooper, William: 54.5, 97.5.
Cork: T, 3.1, 5.5, 6.5, 47.2, 50.6, 53.2, 54.3, 74.8, 89.3, 122.3, 184.6, 226.2, 249.9.
Corkery, Daniel: 3.1, 184.6.

'Ding-Dong': 27.3, 33.9, 70.1, 71.8, 103.3, 267.3.
Diogenes of Apollonia: 49.3, 49.5.
Diogenes Laertius: 49.3, 102.5, 200.3, 246.5.
disease [deformity]: 3.8, 3.9, 12.1, 29.1, 33.7, 33.8, 34.3, 36.3, 43.2, 49.4, 54.5, 54.6, 54.7, 59.4, 63.7, 97.3, 97.4, 99.2, 99.3, 113.4, 138.5, 158.2, 175.5, 177.1, 184.2, 199.4, 200.1, 208.2, 219.1, *228.3*.
Disjecta: 3.5, 5.7, 21.1, 59.1, 83.2, 88.5, 88.6, 102.6, 111.3, 117.5, 155.2, 156.3, 184.5, 197.1, 250.1.
Dobbin, Rachel: 5.5, 122.5, 250.5, 254.2.
dodecahedron: 47.8, *47.9*, 143.1.
dog: 21.4, 32.16, 76.5, 79.5, 97.3, 98.3, 101.1, 102.1, *103.5*, 104.5, 105.5, 184.6, 204.3, 213.2, 215.1, 215.3, 255.2, 275.2.
Doherty, Frank: 51.2, 149.1, 235.3, 279.4.
Donne, John: 103.1, 178.5, 201.4.
Don Quixote [Cervantes]: 99.10, 142.2.
Dowd, Garin: 107.6, 109.1.
Dowden, Hester: 104.5.
'Draff': 134.4, 254.2.
The Drapier Letters: 170.3.
Dream of Fair to Middling Women: 1.4, 4.6, 5.7, 6.3, 6.6, 10.2, 12.2, 13.1, 14.5, 31.1, 33.9, 39.2, 42.5, 42.6, 43.2, 44.2, 46.5, 60.2, 63.4, 74.2, 78.2, 78.4, 93.1, 96.2, 97.3, 110.1, 110.2, 110.3, 111.3, 113.1, 117.4, 131.1, 134.4, 156.5, 162.1, 180.2, 184.5, 201.3, 212.1, 215.5, 217.3, 219.3, 223.4, 225.3, 251.1, 258.2, 262.3, 267.3, 276.2, 280.4.
dreams: 14.9, 46.3, 78.5, 84.3, 100.1, 111.5, 111.7, *140.1*, 149.3, 175.1, *176.3*, 176.4, 207.4, 237.1.
Dream Notebook: 1.4, 3.9, 12.3, 23.3, 28.1, 29.4, 31.1, 38.1, 42.6, 49.3, 60.2, 60.3, 65.2, 74.2, 78.1, 78.4, 94.2a, 93.2, 95.2, 97.5, 103.3, 106.3, 107.3, 117.2, 117.4, 134.4, 138.5, 141.1, 167.6, 168.9, 188.3, 216.6, 223.3, 229.3, 233.1, 276.2, 280.4.
drink: T, 3.1, 3.2, 11.2, 16.1, 20.2, 26.7, 33.9, 45.3, 46.1, 46.5, 54.1, 54.5, 56.3, 62.3, 67.5, 68.2, 80.2, 83.3, 84.1, 84.7, 85.5, 86.3, 86.5, 87.5, 88.6, 118.3, 119.5, 120.1, *120.4*, 121.2, 139.5, 139.6, 140.3, 156.3, 188.2, 198.2, 212.3, 213.1, 213.2, 274.2, 279.4.
Drinker, Philip: 49.6.
Driver, Tom: 51.2.
dualism: 1.2, 1.5, 2.3, 2.9, *2.10*, *6.7*, 8.1, 9.2, 11.6, 14.9, 20.1, 25.1, 32.2, 32.7, 32.14, 40.1, 105.5, 107.1, 108.2, 108.5, *109.1*, 109.4, 111.3, 156.7, 178.8, 183.1, 218.2, 218.5, 218.7, 229.3, 262.2.
Dublin: T, 3.2, 33.8, 42.2, 42.4, 42.5, 43.1, 45.1, 46.1, 46.2, 46.4, 47.1, 54.1, 55.1, 55.3, 56.1, 56.3, 70.1, 84.6, 86.1, 71.6, 97.3, 119.3, 129.3, 131.5, 162.1, 184.5, 184.6, 267.2, 267.3, 269.2, 276.4.
Dublin Magazine: 84.6, 184.6, 274.3.
Dubliners: 56.3, 129.3, 254.1, 267.4.
Dun Laoghaire [Kingston]: 119.3, 165.2, 259.5,
Dwyer, Miss: 5.3, 5.5, 6.2, 48.1, 49.8.

Earl's Court: 1.3, 22.1.
Easter 1916: *42.2*, 42.3, 42.4, 45.2, 54.1, 57.1.
Eckhardt, Meister: 60.3.
'Echo's Bones': 12.3, 16.1, 18.1, 33.9, 38.1, 71.4, 87.5, *99.2*, 99.3, 99.6, 99.7, 103.4, 140.3, 174.2, 179.1, 187.1, *186.3*, 188.1, 200.3, 218.6, 229.3.
École Normale: 4.6, 43.2, 178.8, 276.2.
Edith Grove [Cremorne Road, Stadium Street]: 12.8, 15.4, 95.2.
Eliot, George: 219.3, 279.1.

'First Love': 6.6, 28.1.
Fitt [Father and Miss]: 5.5.
Flaubert, Gustave: 105.3, 248.3.
flea: 99.2, 201.4.
Fleming, Ian: 242.1.
Fletcher, John: 49.8, 215.3.
food: 11.2, 14.9, 20.2, 37.1, 43.2, 49.7, 50.4, 58.5, 73.8, 74.7, 81.3, 83.1, *96.3*, 115.3, 116.2, 127.4, 138.4, 182.2, 212.2, 234.1, 239.6, 244.9.
football: 11.3, 120.3, 143.1, 275.1.
Footfalls: 229.1.
Ford, John: 4.2, 47.5, 212.2, 226.3.
forms: 90.6, 107.4, 107.6, 108.4, 108.5, 108.7, 109.4, 110.5, 111.4, 111.5, 112.3, 112.6.
Foxrock: T, 3.9, 5.5, 43.1, 61.1, 119.3, 178.8.
freedom: 1.2, 1.4, 2.9, *2.10*, 4.2, 5.3, *9.1*, 9.2, 40.3, 85.1, 105.1, 107.4, *109.1*, 110.2, 111.3, 111.4, *112.1*, 112.8, 113.1, *113.3*, 122.5, 243.2, 250.3.
Freeman, Kathleen: 47.9, 60.3, 116.2, 227.4, 246.5, 248.3, 258.4.
friendship: 11.7, 12.2, 15.2, 54.4, 116.2, 124.1, *200.4,* 201.6, *202.2*, 222.5.
Freud, Sigmund: 2.2, 37.1, 44.3, 65.4, 98.1, 107.2, 111.5, 112.3, 125.1, 126.3, 175.5, 184.4, 186.3, 187.1, 218.1, *218.3*, 228.3, 261.1.
the Frica: 280.4.
'From an Abandoned Work': 120.3.
Frost, Mrs.: 1.3, 63.5, 67.5, 69.2, 134.5.
fundamental unheroic: 3.9, *4.2*, 32.13, 33.10, 38.1, 38.2, 42.3, 42.4, 46.7, 79.1, *156.1*, 162.3, 164.2.
furies: *27.3*, 175.2, 216.7, 236.3.

Galileo: 168.9.
Gall, Lord [wormwood]: 18.1, *99.2*, 99.5, 104.1, 140.3, 174.2, 179.1, 188.1, 229.3.
Galls, father and son: 228.6.
Garnier, Pierre: 138.5, 193.1.
garret [mansarde]: 63.4, 162.1, 162.2, 163.2.
Gate Theatre: 86.1, 86.2, 269.2.
Gaultier, Jules: 246.3.
General Post Office: *42.2*, 42.3, 42.4, 57.1.
geometry: 5.3, 5.4, 5.5, *47.7*, *47.8*, *47.9*, 50.5, 53.2, 60.3, 63.5, 63.6, 65.4, 78.7, 92.2, 107.1, 112.9, 140.1, 150.2, 163.3, 184.1, *213.3*, 222.2, 241.3, 280.3.
George [I and II]: 150.6, 170.3, 267.3.
German Diaries: 4.2, 13.2, 19.1, 50.6, 163.1.
Germany: 138.5, 162.1, 196.2, 228.6, 239.1.
Gertrude Street: 12.8, 67.5, 69.2, 96.3, 134.5.
Gestalt Psychology: 2.11, *4.1*, *4.2*, *4.3*, 4.6, *5.3*, 6.1, 6.2, 29.3, 42.6, *48.1*, 48.2, *56.4*, 275.2.
'Getting One's Money's Worth': 80.1a.
Geulincx, Arnold: *1.5*, 2.3, 2.10, 6.5, 6.7, 16.1, 17.3, 20.2, 30.1, 36.4, 44.3, 72.5, 105.1, 105.5, 107.1, 108.5, *109.1*, *110.2*, 110.6, 156.1, *178.8*, *178.9*, 184.1, 193.1, 194.2, 216.5, 216.6, *218.5*, 240.1, 246.5, 250.4.
Gibson, John: 216.4.
Giles, H. A.: 117.2.
ginger biscuits: *96.3*, 97.2, 109.7, 179.3.
Glasshouse Street: 115.3.
goats: 23.3, *32.2*, *32.7*, 32.12, 47.7, 72.2, 134.1, 137.2, 235.3.
God: 6.6, 6.7, 7.1, 7.5, 14.5, 17.1, 17.3, 17.5, 21.5, 25.1, 32.2, 37.2, 39.1, 50.6, 58.2,

Hesla, David: 48.1, 77.2, 107.4, 109.1, 137.1, 178.9, 246.5.
Higgins, Frederick: 59.1, 88.5, *184.5.*
Higgins, Jem: 184.5.
Hill, Leslie: 73.6.
Hindu: 23.2, 32.4, 33.1, 34.1, 196.1.
Hippasos: *47.7,* 47.8, 47.9, 77.2.
Hobbema, Meindert: 96.3, 196.3.
Hobson, Harold: 213.2.
Hölderlin, Gottfried: 131.1, 280.3.
Holland: 17.5, 19.3, 53.3, 163.1, 175.3, 196.2, 196.3.
'Home Olga': 233.2.
Homer: 134.4, 207.5, 280.6.
Hopkins, Gerard Manley: 132.2.
Horace: 17.5, 85.5, 98.2, 134.1, 186.2, 186.4, 230.1, 246.6.
horoscope: 1.5, 23.2, 23.3, 23.4, *32.2,* 32.3, 32.5, 32.7, 33.4, 33.5, 33.10, 39.3, 93.2, 107.6, 183.3.
horse leech's daughter: *57.3.*
How It Is: 5.7, 156.5.
Hudson, W. H. [Rima]: 94.2, *96.2.*
Hugo, Victor: 201.6.
Human Wishes: T, 11.5, 167.2.
humility: 38.1, 87.4, 110.6, *178.9,* 180.2, *216.6,* 240.1.
Huysmanns, J. K. [*A rebours*]: 182.2.
Hyde Park: 11.4, 11.7, 50.3, 77.3, 84.3, *94.2,* 95.1, 96.1, 96.2, 99.8, 99.9, 99.10, 103.4, 103.5, 105.4, 150.4, 150.5, 150.6, 150.7, 151.1, 151.2, 276.1, 279.2.

Id [ego]: 11.5, 48.1, 184.4, 218.1, *218.3.*
Idealism: 2.10, 21.2, 40.4, 82.2, 90.6, 107.1, *107.6, 108.1, 108.3,* 108.4, *109.1,* 111.3, *113.3,* 171.2, 177.3, 202.2, 218.1, 236.4, *246.3.*
Ill Seen Ill Heard: 241.3.
India: 3.2, 3.4, 3.6, 61.3, 79.4.
indifference: 1.1, 2.4, 9.1, 105.1, 106.5, *168.9, 113.1,* 179.3, 186.2, 186.4, 207.6, 246.6.
Inferno: 14.9, 14.10, 73.3, 78.10.
Inge, W. R.: 60.3.
Io: 216.7.
Ireland: T, 3.1, 11.4, 11.5, 17.2, 24.3, 42.2, 42.3, 42.5, 46.2, 46.7, 57.1, 59.1, 61.1, 84.6, 89.2, 106.1, 118.3, 156.3, 170.3, 172.1, 184.5, 184.6, 195.2, 197.1, 216.4, 216.8, 220.3, 245.5, 246.3, 267.4, 280.7.
iridescence: 1.5, 2.5, 63.5, 152.4.
irrationality: 2.2, *3.8, 3.9,* 5.4, 6.6, 9.2, *13.2,* 40.3, *47.8, 65.4,* 65.5, 77.2, 81.3, 82.2, 83.3, 84.1, 84.6, 88.3, 90.3, 90.6, 92.2, 93.1, 109.1, *112.10,* 113.4, 119.2, 123.1, 177.4, 187.2, 193.1, 195.1, 224.1, 240.4, 240.5, 250.3, *262.3,* 271.3, 280.3.
isonomy: *3.8.*
Ixion: 21.4.

Jacob and Esau: 23.3, 33.3, 76.1.
James [I and II]: 94.2, 213.1, 257.3.
James, William: *4.3.*
Janvier, Ludovic: 5.5, 162.1.
Jeans, Sir James: 188.3.
Jerome, Saint: 101.1, *104.3,* 226.1.

14.2, 15.1, 17.5, 19.3, 21.4, 21.5, 27.2, 27.5, 32.1, 34.1, 37.1, *39.2*, 40.4, 47.1, 55.1, 56.3, 56.4, 59.1, 59.2, 62.3, 64.5, *65.4*, 66.2, 71.1, 71.4, 71.7, 72.2, 73.6, 73.10, 75.2, 77.1, *77.2*, *79.3*, 85.3, 86.4, 87.3, 89.2, 90.4, 92.2, *97.3*, 102.2, 102.5, 105.2, 105.5, 106.1, *108.2*, 108.6, 112.7, 116.1, 117.4, 117.5, 119.1, 119.2, 119.5, 120.3, 122.3, 126.1, 128.1, 131.1, 131.4, 134.5, 136.1, 145.1, 145.3, 149.1, 152.3, 152.4, 156.4, 161.2, 161.5, 167.1, *167.2*, 167.3, 168.7, 168.8, 174.1, *175.3*, 175.4, 175.5, *176.3*, 176.4, 178.7, *178.8*, 180.5, 184.1, 184.2, 184.5, 189.1, 189.2, 193.1, 194.2, 196.4, 197.1, 198.1, 198.3, 198.4, 204.2, 205.1, 206.1, 207.1, 211.1, 211.2, 216.5, 216.6, 218.5, 219.1, *219.3*, 220.1, 220.4, 224.5, 225.1, 226.2, 234.2, 234.3, 242.2, 246.5, 250.1, 262.2, 269.4, 276.4, 277.2, 280.5, 281.1.

Arabic: 32.4, 64.2.

Dutch: 175.3, 178.8.

French: 1.3, 2.3, 2.4, 3.7, 5.6, 5.7, 5.8, 6.7, 8.3, 8.4, 14.6, 43.2, 48.3, 50.7, 54.4, 54.7, 56.2, 57.2, 58.4, 61.3, 71.1, 72.1, 74.4, 80.1a, 88.2, 99.6, 102.3, 107.6, 108.3, 109.5, 110.4, 112.8, 113.1, *115.1*, 116.5, 117.3, 122.5, 140.1, *156.1*, 163.2, 175.4, 177.3, 178.3, 179.5, 179.6, 182.2, 185.2, 189.3, 192.1, 194.1, 195.2, 200.2, 201.5, 201.6, 207.1, 224.5, 239.2, 240.5, 244.3, 245.1, 245.2, 245.4, 247.2, 251.1, 275.1, 280.4, 282.2.

Gaelic: 3.1, 5.8, 11.2, 89.2, *117.5*, 172.1, 184.5, 184.6, 185.2, 267.4.

German: 4.2, 48.1, 60.2, 88.1, 88.3, 97.4, 105.3, 178.5, 207.4, 243.1, 243.2.

Greek: T, 2.10, 3.3, *3.8*, 5.8, 6.3, 14.4, 21.3, 23.3, 24.1, 32.5, 47.7, 47.9, 49.3, 50.4, 50.5, 54.6, 65.4, 71.5, 75.2, 77.2, 81.3, 85.3, 89.6, 97.3, 102.5, 107.4, *108.7*, 111.4, 120.4, 131.1, 134.1, 138.5, 148.1, 154.1, 168.2, *175.3*, 175.4, 176.3, 177.2, 184.3, 184.4, 186.5, 194.1, 204.2, 216.6, 219.1, 220.2, 222.3, 227.4, 240.4, 246.5, 246.6, 246.7, 246.8, 269.1.

Italian: 5.7, 10.2, 12.2, 14.2, 21.5, 50.4, 64.1, *71.1*, 73.3, 78.1, 78.2, 78.3, 78.6, 78.7, 78.8, 85.6, 99.3, 111.4, 116.3, 178.2, 195.2, 209.1.

Latin: 1.5, 2.3, 2.7, 2.10, 6.5, 12.3, 14.9, 17.2, 17.3, 17.5, 19.1, 21.3, 22.5, 23.3, 28.1, 32.2, 34.3, 38.1, 44.3, 44.4, 48.1, 58.3, 60.2, 65.2, 65.4, 66.2, 72.1, 72.2, 72.3 74.2, 74.7, 77.2, 78.4 85.4, 86.4, 87.2, 90.5, 97.5, 98.2, 102.2, 102.5, 103.3, 105.3, 105.5, *107.1*, 107.3, 108.2, *109.1*, 110.2, 110.6, 112.10, 114.2, 132.2, 137.3, 145.3, 156.1, 166.1, 167.2, 175.1, 176.3, 178.7, *178.8*, 178.9, 183.5, 184.1, 189.3, 193.1, 194.2, 195.3, 199.4, 207.6, 212.1, 216.6, 217.2, 217.3, 222.4, 225.3, 230.1, 231.1, 237.1, 240.1, 241.5, 246.3, 248.4, 251.3, 262.1, 263.3, 276.2.

Persian: 245.7.

Sanskrit [Hindi]: 3.6, 32.2, 34.1, 37.2, 196.1, 259.2, 277.2.

Spanish: 46.3, 78.5, 85.6, 282.1.

cliché: 5.2, 23.5, 24.3, 28.3, 29.4, 49.2, 51.1, 51.2, 67.5, 67.6, 83.2, 88.6, 104.4, 106.3, 106.5, 111.6, 116.6, 122.4, 127.1, 138.2, 150.1, 158.2, 159.1, 179.7, 188.2, 190.1, 192.2, 193.3, 194.1, 196.5, 203.2, 214.2, *218.1*, 218.4, 221.1, 230.1, 230.2, 233.2, 248.1, 252.3, 254.1, 267.1, 272.1, 280.1.

jest: 2.2, 3.5, 6.2, 6.5, 7.3, 10.1, 11.2, 11.3, 14.6, 18.3, 21.2, *32.2*, *32.7*, 32.12, 33.9, 39.2, 43.2, 44.1, 44.3, 50.3, 60.1, 64.4, *65.3*, *65.4*, 68.1, 72.4, 76.5, 83.3, 87.4, 92.2, *97.3*, 100.1, 102.1, 108.4, 112.2, 113.4, 114.3, 114.4, 117.3, 117.4, 119.2, 134.2, 139.2, 139.5, *139.6*, 163.3, 165.2, 180.5, 186.1, *188.1*, 195.4, 204.2, 207.6, *208.2*, 213.1, 217.1, 220.3, 248.4, 261.3, 269.1, *275.2*.

names: *T*, 3.2, 4.4, 5.5, *7.6*, *10.1*, 11.4, 11.5, 17.5, 32.4, 33.3, 33.7, 33.8, 46.5, 49.6, 54.2, *54.5*, 59.4, 61.1, 61.2, 61.2, 80.2, *84.6*, 96.2, 99.1, *99.2*, 99.3, 115.1, 116.4, *156.5*, 184.3, 184.5, 184.6, 185.2, 193.4, 257.5.

proverb: 17.2, 18.2, 52.1, 57.2, *57.3*, 71.2, *79.4*, 102.5, 114.5, 116.1, 129.2, 132.1, 152.3, 174.2, 176.5, 179.4, 180.4, 186.1, 191.2, 193.1, 197.1, 198.4, 202.4,

217.5, 220.1, 220.3, 220.4, 228.5, 237.1, 257.2.

     pun: *1.5*, 2.1, *2.7*, *3.8*, 4.4, 5.4, 5.5, 5.8, 6.2, 6.4, 7.3, 7.5, 7.6, 8.2, 10.2, 14.10, 15.5, 17.4, 22.5, 24.1, 24.3, 27.3, 31.2, 32.1, 32.4, 32.6, 32.12, 36.3, 44.3, 49.1, 50.4, 54.4, 56.3, 57.1, 59.1, 60.3, *64.4*, *65.4*, 66.2, 69.1, *70.3*, 71.1, 71.2, 71.3, 71.7, 72.3, *72.5*, 73.8, 73.11, 74.8, 84.4, 84.6, 84.7, 86.5, 88.1, *88.3*, 88.6, 89.1, 89.6, *90.3*, 90.6, *97.5*, 99.1, *99.2*, 99.3, 102.1, 103.4, 104.6, 107.3, 109.3, 110.6, 114.3, *115.1*, 118.3, 121.2, 126.1, 126.3, 131.1, 138.1, 139.1, 139.3, 139.5, *139.6*, *140.3*, *156.5*, 163.2, 164.2, 166.4, 168.4, 174.1, *176.3*, 179.6, 183.3, 184.3, 186.1, 195.2, 197.2, 198.1, 204.3, *207.6*, 208.1, 209.1, 209.2, 211.3, 212.2, 217.3, 217.4, *218.5*, 220.2, 221.2, 227.2, *232.1*, 232.2, 236.3, 246.6, 250.4, 255.1, 256.1, 259.5, 261.3, 262.1, 266.1, 267.2, 274.3.

     rhetoric: 12.3, *17.3*, 22.4, 26.2, 28.4, 55.2, 57.5, 65.4, 71.2, 76.3, 77.1, 90.1, 90.3, 92.2, 102.5, 103.1, 105.5, 106.4, 115.1, 118.2, *131.3*, 164.1, 166.1, 184.1, 199.3, 211.1, *213.2*, 218.2, 219.2, 234.5, 253.1.

larval stage: *66.1*, 111.3, 134.3, 183.2.

Laurel and Hardy: 44.5, 259.2.

Lazarus [Dives]: *5.7*, 25.1, 48.4, 107.6, 177.3, 180.2, 212.3, 213.2.

Leibniz, Gottfried: 21.1, 60.3, *107.4*, 107.5, *107.6*, 108.2, *109.1*, 110.2, 111.3, 162.1, 168.9.

Lemprière: 21.4.

Lessing, Gotthold: *207.4*, 207.5.

Leucippus: 227.4, 246.5, 246.6.

Leventhal, Con: 42.4, 196.4, 225.3.

Leviathan: 223.1.

Le Verrier, Urbain: 280.4.

Libra: 33.6, 114.3.

light and dark: 4.1, 9.1, 12.6, 13.1, 46.6, 50.5, 66.3, 102.6, 104.2, *107.2*, *110.5*, *111.3*, 111.5, 112.2, 112.6 112.7, 134.3, 134.4, 140.4, 153.4, 155.2, 175.1, 176.2, 177.2, 207.5, 207.6, 241.1, 241.2, 241.5, 280.2, 282.1.

'Lightning Calculation': 1.3, 3.9, 17.5, 37.2, 80.2, 96.3, *196.2*, 252.1.

Limit [doctrine of]: 3.7, *50.5*, 72.5, *246.8*.

Lincoln's Inn Fields: 79.3, 84.3.

little world [microcosm]: *1.1*, 2.10, 3.8, 5.7, 25.1, 62.2, 63.1, 63.2, *72.5*, *107.4*, 112.1, 113.1, 138.1, 175.5, 177.1, *176.3*, 176.6, *178.5*, *179.4*, 180.3, 181.3, 218.4, 240.4, 250.3.

Liverpool: 129.3, 139.4.

Locke, John: 58.2, 108.2.

logic: 2.2, 6.5, 12.4, *16.1*, 17.3, 17.5, 19.3, 20.1, 21.1, 21.5, 22.3, 22.4, 24.2, 35.1, 37.2, 41.1, 77.2, 105.5, 107.1, 107.2, 110.1, 112.7, 113.4, 134.5, 138.4, 144.1, 178.8, 180.1, 184.1, 206.1, *207.6*, 232.1, 246.5, 250.2, 250.3, 252.1.

London: 1.3, 3.2, 3.11, 11.2, 11.4, 12.6, 12.8, 12.9, 14.3, 14.6, 14.7, 14.8, 14.9, 15.3, 15.4, 22.1, 23.1, 26.5, 26.6, 47.1, 50.3, 50.6, 55.1, 59.4, 63.1, 63.2, 63.3, 70.1, 73.4, 73.7, 73.8, 73.9, 73.10, 74.3, 76.4, 79.3, 80.2, 84.3, 94.2, 95.1, 95.2, 96.2, 103.4, 103.5, 104.5, 115.3, 119.3, 120.1, 120.3, 121.5, 127.2, 127.3, 127.4, 139.4, 150.3, 151.3, 153.2, 156.2, 176.2, 179.5, 183.1, 195.1, 195.4, 195.5, 211.1, 216.3, 225.1, 225.2, 226.4, 235.1, 244.9, 257.4, 271.2, 271.4, 274.1, 275.2.

Long Water: 96.1, 99.8, 150.4, 150.5, 150.6, 151.2, 278.1.

love: 5.3, 5.4, *5.5*, *5.7*, 5.8, 6.3, 6.5, *6.6*, 7.1, 10.1, 10.2, 11.1, 14.1, 20.1, 27.7, 29.4, 29.5, 32.7, 36.1, 36.2, 40.3, 41.1, 42.3, 44.1, 48.3, 49.8, 50.7, 57.3, 64.7, 72.1, 99.9, 100.2, 103.2, *107.1*, 111.3, 112.2, 112.6, 115.2, 116.4, 122.4, 122.5, *131.2*, 157.1, 176.3, 179.2, 184.4, 186.3, 197.3, 206.1, 207.2, 212.1, 212.2, *216.6*, 222.3, 229.2, *235.1*, 235.2, 251.1, 252.3, 257.1.

Mercier and Camier: 123.1, 229.2.
Mercier, Vivien: 5.5, 16.1, 238.4, 239.1, 274.2.
Mercury: 31.3, 32.1, 32.10, 33.1, 33.6, 42.2, 195.3.
Meredith, George: *11.5*.
metaphysics: 22.5, 40.4, 57.4, 72.5, *109.1*, 112.9, 178.8, 178.9, 196.2, 198.1, 235.3, *280.3*.
mew [cage, cell]: *1.4*, 7.2, 8.3, 63.1, 63.2, 84.6, 181.3, 238.1.
midsummer [*A Midsummer Night's Dream*]: 12.6, 12.7, 12.8, 36.1, 49.7, 51.1, 235.2.
Miller, Lawrence: 176.6.
Milligan, Spike [*Puckoon*]: 156.3
Milton, John [Milton House]: 40.2, 73.7, 73.9, 120.1, 175.1.
mind: 1.1, 1.2, 2.9, 2.10, 2.11, 5.3, 6.7, 10.1, 11.6, 12.3, 14.5, 18.3, *21.1*, 21.2, 22.4, 25.1, 32.14, 39.2, 57.4, 58.2, 63.1, 74.9, 78.9, 80.3, 87.1, 105.5, 107.1, *107.2*, 107.4, 107.5, *107.6*, 108.2, 108.3, 108.5, *109.1*, 109.4, 109.6, 109.7, *110.1*, *111.3*, *111.4*, *111.5*, 112.1, 112.6, 112.7, *112.10*, *113.1*, 113.3, 114.4, 115.1, 120.3, 149.1, 167.4, 167.5, 167.6, 168.1, 168.2, 168.3, 168.5, 168.6, 168.9, 176.3, 177.3, 178.3, 178.8, 178.9, 186.2, 189.3, *218.1*, 218.3, 218.4, 218.5, 219.1, 227.4, 232.2, *243.2*, 246.3, 246.4, 246.7, 250.3, 253.1, 269.1, 275.2, 282.2.
Mintz, Samuel: 1.5.
MMM: 74.5, 82.2, 88.4, *156.2*, 156.3, 193.4, 256.2, 258.4, 262.3.
Molière: 88.2.
Molloy: 5.1, 5.8, 6.6, 7.4, 46.2, 60.1, 105.3, 112.5, 134.4, 138.3, 140.4, 227.4, 228.6, 232.1.
monad: 5.7, 7.2, 48.2, 50.5, 60.3, 69.1, *72.5*, *107.4*, 107.5, *107.6*, 109.7, 112.7, 144.1, *162.1*, 181.2, *181.3*, *227.4*, 250.2a.
moon: 1.1, 9.2, 16.3, 17.2, 26.1, *26.3*, 26.5, 32.10, 33.2, 33.6, 50.2, 106.4, 114.1, 114.4, 121.1, 121.2, 126.2, 130.2, 138.1, 155.1, 215.4, 236.1, *250.6*, 254.1.
Mooney, Michael: 112.6, 249.8.
Mooney's [the Abbey]: 46.1, 54.1, 56.1, 269.2.
Moore, George: 275.2.
More Pricks than Kicks: 3.10, 7.4, 27.3, 28.1, 33.9, 42.5, 44.2, 70.1, 71.1, 71.8, 73.2, 93.1, 99.2, 100.2, 103.3, 134.4, 145.3, 217.2, 217.3, 221.1, 228.1, 234.4, 246.7, 254.2, 257.5, 267.3, 280.4.
Morot-Sir, Edward: 104.2.
Morphy, Paul: T, 184.3, *242.1*, 244.8.
Morro Castle: 12.5.
motion: 2.9, 2.5, *4.2*, 6.7, 9.1, 9.2, 12.1. *22.5*, 27.3, 28.2, 53.3, 57.5, 58.1, 64.2, 69.1, 71.1, *72.5*, 79.3, 105.5, 107.4, 108.7, *109.1*, *110.2*, 111.1, 112.6, 112.7, 112.11, *113.1*, 113.2, 122.5, 195.3, 201.5, 222.4, 229.1, 246.5, 246.6.
Mott, F. W.: 257.5.
Motte, Madame de la: 257.5.
Munch, Edvard: 236.2.
murder: 4.2, 26.7, 27.3, 124.1, *262.3*.
Murphy [French translation]: 1.3, 2.9, 5.8, 6.7, 8.3, 8.4, 16.1, 17.2, 26.3, 37.1, 54.7, 58.4, 61.2, 74.4, 80.1a, 87.5, 117.3, 119.3, 129.2, 140.3, 155.2, 179.5, 179.6, 182.2, 185.2, 200.3, 215.2, 244.7, 247.2, 251.1, 261.3, 275.1.
Murphy, Arthur: T, 167.2.
muses: 7.4, 86.6.
music [song]: 2.6, 2.8, 3.7, *3.8*, 3.11, 4.2, 14.5, 20.1, *40.4*, 47.8, *71.5*, 71.6, *74.9*, 77.2, 78.1, 92.1, 113.1, 116.3, 117.5, 117.6, 122.4, 141.3, 156.7, *195.1*, 195.2, 207.2, 215.2, 216.5, 218.6, 219.3, 226.2, *229.3*, 235.1, *236.2*, 240.3, 240.4, 250.2, 250.3, 252.3, 257.1, 262.3, 269.5.

mysticism: 3.4, 5.4, 40.4, 47.7, 47.8, 47.9, 107.2, *110.5*, 111.7.

Napoleon: 51.2, 244.8.
Narcissus [narcissism]: 6.6, 14.5, 36.4, 74.2, 81.1, 107.1, 111.3, 184.4, *186.3*, 187.1, 212.1, *228.3*, 249.9, 250.1, 250.3, 252.3.
National Gallery [Dublin]: 184.5, 196.2, *215.5*.
National Gallery [London]: 101.1, 140.4, 196.2, 228.3, 251.3.
Nashe, Thomas: 217.3, 241.4.
Neary: T, *3.2*, 3.3, 3.4, 3.8, 4.3, 4.5, 4.6, 5.2, 5.3, 5.4, 5.5, 6.2, *6.3*, 6.6, 11.2, 11.5, 16.2, 24.2, 44.3, 44.5, 46.2, 46.6, 46.7, 47.8, 47.9, 48.1, 49.2, *50.4*, 50.5, 50.7, 54.3, 56.2, 57.2, 57.3, 58.2, 58.4, 59.3, 61.3, 62.1, 62.2, 71.3, 77.2, 79.4, 114.7, 116.2, 116.4, 116.6, 117.1, 123.1, 131.2, 200.1, *200.4*, *201.2*, 202.4, 202.3, 207.2, 207.6, 208.1, 211.3, 212.2, 213.3, 215.4, 216.7, 218.1, 218.3, 219.3, 222.1, 222.3, 224.1, 224.3, 228.4, 228.5, 229.2, 235.2, 238.4, 249.9, 254.2, 254.3, 263.2, 267.4, 275.2.
necessity [determinism, fate]: T, 1.1, 1.2, 2.1, *2.10*, 27.7, 32.2, 32.3, 33.10, 87.6, 112.8, 122.5, *156.1*, 168.9, 175.1, 183.1, 186.1, 221.1, *227.4*, 228.4, 252.4.
Nelson, Lord [Nelson's Pillar]: 45.1, *46.2*, 176.5.
Neptune: 33.5, 280.4.
neurosis [neurology]: 2.3, 20.1, 29.1, 49.4, 57.3, 65.5, 75.1, 79.5, 98.1, 98.2, 110.4, 119.2, 160.2, 165.4, 168.1, 168.2, 168.3, 168.5, 168.6, 175.5, 177.1, 180.3, 185.1, 238.1, 255.2.
Newton, Sir Isaac: 57.4, 58.1, 72.5, 102.4, 107.2, 109.2, 109.7, 112.10, *113.1*, 113.2, 117.1, 168.4, 201.5, 271.3.
Nietzsche: 44.3, 49.3, 200.4.
Niobe: 21.4, 139.2.
Nominalism: *13.2*.
Norwich School: 196.3, 225.2.
nothing [Void]: 2.5, *6.3*, 21.2, *25.1*, 36.4, 48.2, 64.7, 65.1, 65.2, 65.4, 90.2, 94.2a, 112.3, 113.1 127.1, 137.2, 148.1, 175.1, *176.1*, *178.9*, 183.1, 212.2, 220.3, 227.4, *228.4*, 246.2, 246.3, *246.4*, *246.5*, *246.6*, *246.8*, 248.3, 250.4, 251.2, 275.2.

O'Brien, Eoin: 4.4, 42.2, 45.1, 46.2, 47.1, 50.6, 64.3, 162.1, 215.5, 226.2, 267.3.
O'Brien, Flann: 42.5, 45.1, 245.6.
O'Brien, Kate: 195.4.
O'Casey, Sean: 42.4, 196.1, 269.2.
Occasionalism: *1.5*, 2.10, 12.2, 72.5, 74.3, 76.2, 105.5, 108.5, 108.6, *109.1*, 109.6, 112.1, 113.1, 168.9, 178.6, *178.8*, 178.9, 194.2, 218.1, 227.4.
O'Connor, Frank: 3.1, *184.6*.
OED: 5.7, 6.5, 49.4, 59.4, 86.3, 86.4, 97.3, 107.3, 117.4, 119.2, 126.1, 134.3, 152.3, 152.4, 167.3, 168.8, 176.4, 240.5, 249.3, 257.5, 260.1.
O'Hara, J. D.: T, 2.2, 3.8, 4.2, 14.5, 40.3, 79.2, 98.2, 105.4, 113.4, 122.5, 156.2, 176.3, 184.4, 186.3, 189.3, 228.3, 249.9, 250.3, 252.3.
Old Boy: 24.3, 25.1, *69.2*, 134.5, 137.1, 144.1, 145.2.
Oldfield, Thomas: 76.4.
'Old Earth': 251.2.
Old Moore: 32.2, 93.2, *216.3*.
'Ooftisch': 232.1.
orchids: 50.4, 54.6.
Ossian: 3.5, *185.2*, 257.3.
ostrich: 176.5.
Ovid: 74.2, 186.3.
the Ovoidologist: 280.4.

Porter-Phillips, Dr. John: 160.2, 185.1, 257.3, 259.1, 261.4.
A Portrait of the Artist: 2.8, 14.1, 51.2, 87.3, 105.2, 217.4, 226.2.
Pound, Ezra: 4.3, 156.3.
Poussin, Nicholas: 215.5.
pre-established harmony: *107.4*, 107.6, 109.1, 221.1, *227.4*, 235.3.
pre-Socratics: *3.8*, *6.3*, 44.1, 47.7, 47.8, 47.9, 50.5, *107.2*, 111.5, 112.6, 246.3, *246.5*, 246.6, 246.7, 246.8, 248.2, *248.3*, 249.8, 275.2.
prison [Pentonville]: *63.2*, 74.3, 122.2, 142.1, 149.1, 149.2, 241.2.
Protagoras: 246.3.
Proust, Marcel: 2.4, 2.6, 5.3, 6.6, 36.2, 38.2, 40.4, *50.7*, 56.2, *57.3*, 107.4, 108.3, 110.1, 110.4, 111.4, 112.8, 153.4, 182.2, 186.4, 195.2, 200.4, 201.6, 227.4, *228.1*, 228.4, 239.2, 239.3, 240.5, 250.4, 250.5, 273.1, 282.2.
Proust [Beckett's monograph]: 2.6, 5.3, 5.5, 6.6, 21.4, 36.2, 40.4, 46.3, 47.5, 48.1, 50.4, 74.9, 105.3, 108.3, 137.1, 176.6, 177.3, 183.1, 186.2a, 186.4, 186.6, 195.2, 251.2, 200.4, 201.2, 201.6, 219.3, 255.2, 282.2.
Prout, Father [F. S. Mahony]: *50.6*, 54.3, 226.2.
Psyche [psyche]: 47.5, 66.1, 67.4, 98.2, 103.3, 104.5, 109.1, 113.4, 201.4, 218.3, 219.1, 250.1.
psychiatry [psychosis, psycho-analysis]: 67.3, 89.6, 98.2, 111.3, 111.5, 119.2, 139.5, 158.1, 160.1, 165.4, 165.5, 166.4, 167.5, 167.6, 168.1, 168.2, 168.3, 168.5, 168.6, 175.5, 176.6, 178.1, 180.3, 185.2, 187.2, 218.7, 227.4, 228.3, 238.3, 242.2, 262.2.
psychology: 2.11, 3.8, 3.9, *4.1*, 4.2, 4.3, 5.3, 6.1, 6.2, 40.3, 48.1, 79.5, *80.3*, *81.1*, 81.2, 83.3, 84.2, 107.2, 133.4, 165.4, 168.5, 175.5, 185.2, 186.3, 218.7, 246.1, 250.3, 258.4, 272.2.
Puget, Pierre: *239.2*.
puppet: 3.11, *122.5*.
Purgatorio: 10.2, 14.7, 77.4, 78.1, 78.2, 78.3, 78.6, 78.7, 78.8, 78.10, 149.3, 155.1, 275.2.
Pythagoras: 3.1, 3.4, *3.7*, *3.9*, *5.4*, 6.3, 24.1, 47.7, *47.8*, *47.9*, *50.5*, 54.2, 77.2, 90.1, 102.5, 107.2, 130.2, 193.1, *195.1*, 271.3.

quanta: 57.4, 57.5, *112.3*, 112.10, *113.1*, 219.3.
quid pro quo [money]: *1.5*, 2.6, *2.7*, 6.4, 17.5, 40.2, 44.4, 63.3, 67.2, 70.1, 70.3, 76.1, 76.4, 82.1, 83.2, 89.4, 94.3, 103.2, 106.5, 108.4, 118.3, 132.1, 157.1, 168.8, 170.3, 178.7, 204.1, 222.2, 222.3, 228.3, 230.2, *232.1*, 271.2.
quietism: 28.3, 67.3, 78.1, *78.4*, 103.3, 107.3, 110.1, 113.3, 162.3, 194.2, 196.2, 201.5, 237.1, *246.4*, 250.1, 274.3.
Quigley: 1.3, 3.9, 17.5, 19.3, 37.2, 53.3, 80.2, 96.3, 196.2, 252.1.
Quin: 17.3, 17.5.
Quintilian: 12.4, *17.3*, 164.1.

Rabaté, J-M.: 3.2, 4.6, 83.3, 251.2.
Rabelais, François [Pantagruel]: 58.3, 60.3, 78.4, 85.6, 97.5, 120.4, 227.4.
Rabinovitz, Rubin: 11.5, 26.1, 26.3, 26.4, 32.7, 32.13, 33.5, 60.1, 102.5, 113.3, 114.1, 157.1, 181.4, 183.1, 186.4, 188.1, 201.2, 207.4, 250.2, 250.6, 262.3, 269.3.
Racine: *5.5*, 49.8, 122.5, 254.2.
Rank, Otto [*The Trauma of Birth*]: 44.3, 67.3, 67.4, 73.2, *112.10*, 175.5, 176.4.
rats: 4.1, 110.3, 134.4, 159.2.
realism [literary]: 1.3, 2.11, 10.1, 11.2, 11.4, 13.2, 14.8, 26.1, 26.3, 26.5, 42.4, 45.1, 46.1, 46.2, 54.6, 63.1, 63.2, 63.3, 63.4, 74.3, 74.6, 74.7, 74.8, 75.3, 76.4, 77.3, 79.3, 80.2, 94.2, 95.1, 95.2, 96.1, 96.2, 99.8, 103.4, 103.5, 114.1, 114.2, 114.4, 114.6, 135.1, 150.2, 150.3, 150.4, 150.5, 150.6, 150.7, 151.1, 151.2, 151.3, 152.1, 153.2,

156.3, 159.2, 161.3, 165.1, 165.2, 165.3, 166.3, 167.1, 195.4, 195.5, 203.3, 224.5, 225.2, 227.1, 228.3, 235.3, 239.2, 240.2, 248.4, 249.1, 249.2, 249.8, 250.6, 254.1, *258.4*, 262.3, 267.3, 267.4, 269.2, 269.4, 272.2, 276.1, 276.3, 276.5, 277.2, 282.1.
realism [philosophical]: 2.9, 6.3, 13.2, 40.4, 58.2, 72.5, 81.3, 90.6, 95.2, 107.1, 107.4, *107.6*, 108.1, 108.3, 108.4, 109.4, 113.1, 113.4, 148.1, 171.2, *177.1*, 177.3, 186.4, 187.2, 218.1, 218.3, 228.3, 236.4, 239.2, *246.3*, *246.5*, 246.8, 275.2.
reason [rationalism]: 5.4, *6.7*, 17.1, 17.3, 17.5, 19.3, *21.1*, 21.2, 62.2, 64.7, *65.4*, *77.2*, 85.3, 90.6, 107.1, 107.2, *109.1*, *110.5*, 111.5, 112.2, 113.4, 178.8, *178.9*, 187.2, *193.1*, 200.4, 202.1, *216.6*, 227.4, 243.2, 246.3, 250.3, 256.2, 258.4, *262.3*, 269.5.
'Recent Irish Poetry': 3.5, 21.1, 59.1, 84.6, 88.5, 88.6, 102.6, 117.5, 155.2, 184.5, 184.6.
Regent Street: 14.3, 115.3.
religion: 31.2, 42.2, 42.3, 46.1, 50.6, 51.2, 65.4, 66.1, 67.6, 70.5, 71.1, 72.1, 72.3, 72.4, 78.8, 103.3, 104.2, 104.3, 110.1, 114.2, 114.6, 130.1, 143.2, 167.1, 167.2, 168.9, 183.4, 195.5, 196.1, *213.2*, 223.2, 226.1, 227.4, *232.1*, 249.7, 250.1, 254.1, 258.1, 267.1, 268.1.
Rembrandt: 215.5.
Renard, Jules: 42.6, 48.3, 207.6, *208.2*, 276.2.
Richard II: 58.5, 220.3.
Rimbaud, Arthur: *90.3*.
rocking-chair: 1.5, 2.2, 2.3, 2.7, 4.2, 9.1.
romanticism: 100.1, 100.2, 106.3, 106.4, 180.4, 185.2, 201.6, 217.4, 237.1, 250.2, 279.3.
Romeo and Juliet: 27.7, *32.6*, 33.10, 50.4, 86.2.
Roscellinus: 13.2.
Round Pond: 25.1, *150.2*, 276.3, 277.1.
Rousseau, Jean-Jacques: *109.5*.
Roussel dummy: 14.3.
Royal Free Hospital: 76.4, *77.3*.
Rudmose-Brown, Thomas: 122.5, 181.1.
Russell, Bertrand: 107.5.
Russell, George: 88.5, 102.6, 155.2.
Ruysdael, Jacob: *196.2*.
Ryder, Brian: 156.5, 185.1, 257.3, 259.1, 261.4.

St. Martin's in the Fields: 95.2, 127.4.
'Sanies I': 28.1, 276.4, 73.2.
'Sanies II': 246.6, 257.5.
Saturn: 32.7, 33.4, 33.6.
scarlet: 7.3, 26.7, 186.6, 213.2.
schizophrenia: 49.4, 168.1, 168.2, 168.6, 185.2, 186.2, 204.3.
Schopenhauer, Arthur: 2.7, 2.9, 2.10, 4.2, *21.1*, 21.2, 21.3, 22.5, 32.11, 37.2, 40.1, *40.4*, 46.3, 47.5, 57.2, 59.3, 64.7, 65.1, 65.2, 65.4, 67.2, 74.9, 78.5, 79.2, 82.2, 90.6, 103.2, 105.1, 105.3, 107.2, 107.4, 111.3, 112.1, 112.3, 113.2, *113.3*, 115.2, 122.5, 142.2, *168.9*, 177.1, 177.3, 178.5, 181.3, 183.1, 185.1, 186.2a, 186.4, 188.1, 195.2, 207.6, 218.1, 218.6, 218.7, 224.5, 246.4, 258.4, 260.3, 262.3.
Scorpio [scorpion]: 32.2, 32.10, 33.2, 33.6, 83.1, 84.2, 114.3, 254.1.
Scotland: 17.4, 185.2, 257.3.
Scott, Sir Walter: 226.2, 248.1.
self: 2.10, *4.2*, 4.3, 20.1, 21.1, 21.2, 37.2, 65.2, 66.1, 67.3, 82.2, *107.1*, 107.2, 107.4, 107.6, 109.1, *110.5*, *111.3*, 112.10, 113.3, 145.3, 156.1, 168.9, 178.5, 179.2, 183.1, 184.1, 186.3, 189.1, 189.2, 194.1, *194.2*.
senses: 4.1, 6.2, 19.1, 21.1, 49.3, 72.5, 90.6, *108.2*, 111.4, 112.4, 206.1, 217.4, 222.1,

239.5, 246.3, 246.5, 246.7, 246.9, 275.2.
'Serena I': 15.1, 224.5.
'Serena II': 259.5.
seriality: *96.3*, 247.1, 247.2.
serpent [python]: 8.1, 21.2, 24.1, 32.10, 83.1, 85.2, 99.2, 161.4, 217.2.
Serpentine: 94.2, 96.1, *99.8*, *99.9*, 150.4, 150.5, 150.6, 151.1, 278.1, 279.2.
sex: 1.5, 2.2, 4.4, 5.5, 6.2, 6.3, 6.4, 6.6, 7.3, 8.1, 14.6, 16.2, 20.1, 29.5, 36.2, 37.1, 47.1, 47.5, 49.8, 50.4, 50.7, 57.3, 65.2, 66.2, 70.2, 72.3, 74.4, 74.9, 76.1, 86.4, 104.3, 114.5, 117.2, 117.4, 122.3, 126.3, 180.2, 184.4, 192.1, 193.2, 194.1, 197.1, 197.2, 199.2, 201.4, 202.3, 204.2, 208.1, 209.1, 211.2, 217.3, 218.3, 223.3, 228.3, 241.4, 255.1, 263.3.
Sextus Empiricus: 246.5.
Shakespeare: T, 12.6, 58.5, 218.4, 220.3, 221.1, 235.1.
sheep: 22.2, 23.3, 32.7, 76.1, 99.10, 100.1, 100.2, 100.3, 106.1, 138.2, 215.3.
Shelley, P. B.: 49.2, *99.9*, 207.5, 240.3.
Shelley, Mary and Harriet [*Frankenstein*]: *99.9*, 124.1.
Sheridan, Richard Brinsley: 18.1, 84.6.
Sherlock Holmes [Conan Doyle]: 26.7, 144.1, 203.2, *262.3*.
short circuit: *5.5*, 5.6, 16.1, 24.3, 28.2, 29.5, 40.3, 74.9, *207.6*.
Sidney, Sir Philip: 117.5, 155.1.
Simpson's in the Strand: 95.2, 244.9.
Sinclair, Peggy: 50.6, 93.1.
Skinner, B. F.: 80.2, 156.5, *159.2*, 165.3, 240.2.
sleep: T, 2.6, 14.7, 14.9, 20,2, 33.7, 55.3, 57.2, *100.1*, 110.1, 175.1, 175.2, 175.3, 207.4, *207.5*, *238.4*, 239.3, 239.5, 239.6, 260.3.
Smeraldina: 10.2, 39.2, 96.2, 117.4.
Smith, Frederik: 99.1, 100.1.
Soccoja, Louis: 239.2.
Socrates: 3.8, 15.4, 17.3, 71.2, 90.2, *200.3*, 228.4, 228.5, 275.2.
solipsism: *82.2*, 108.1, 181.3, 183.1, 243.2.
solitude: 2.9, 7.2, 11.7, 21.2, 66.2, *67.3*, 69.2, 72.5, 82.2, 105.1, 107.1, 107.4, 107.5, *109.5*, 109.7, 111.3, 112.2, *112.10*, 113.1, 113.3, 116.1, 149.1, *156.1*, 163.1, *176.6*, *200.4*, 201.6, 240.3, 244.5.
soul: 2.9, 3.4, 3.7, 3.8, 4.5, 5.3, *6.7*, 8.1, 19.1, 22.3, 38.1, *66.1*, 67.1, 67.3, 67.4, 70.6, 71.2, 78.4, 79.3, 84.5, 90.1, 99.9, 99.10, 104.5, 104.6, 107.2, *109.1*, 110.2, 110.5, 111.3, 117.5, 124.1, 137.2, 149.3, 155.2, 162.3, 183.2, 204.2, 213.2, 218.5, 227.4, *228.4*, 230.2, 237.1, 246.6, 246.7, 253.1, 269.1, 272.2, 275.2, 276.2.
space [extension]: 4.2, 6.6, 6.7, 8.3, 12.8, 40.4, 64.7, 65.1, 72.5, 90.6, 109.1, 109.2, 112.9, 112.11, 113.3, 163.3, 178.3, 218.1, 241.3.
Spagnoletto [José Ribera]: 282.1.
spectator: *1.5*, 12.2, *109.1*, *178.9*, 183.1, 193.2, 194.2, 195.4.
Spenser, Edmund: 181.1.
sphere: *47.9*, 54.6, 60.3, 78.10, 107.4.
Spinoza: 2.2, 2.9, 110.2, *107.1*, 107.4, 110.2, 111.3, 168.9, 179.2, 216.6.
spiritualism: 98.4, 99.5, 99.6, 102.3, 104.2, 104.5, 104.6, 111.1,
stars: 11.7, 12.5, 12.8, 14.5, 21.2, 23.3, 27.7, 32.2, 32.3, *32.6*, 32.13, 33.4, 33.10, 86.2, 87.6, 93.1, 97.1, 113.1, *183.1*, 188.3, 216.3, 237.1, 250.6, 254.3.
statues: 42.2, 96.2, *142.2*, 152.1, 168.7, *238.4*, *239.1*, 239.2, 277.1.
Steiss's nosonomy: 97.4.
Stekel, Wilhelm: 75.1, 119.2, 176.4.
Stella ['Letter to Stella']: 34.3, 50.6, 72.4, 118.3, 202.1, 234.4, 257.5.
Stendhal: 180.4.
Stephen, Karin: 175.5, 177.1.

'Still': 109.1.
Stillorgan: 43.1, 44.3.
stout porter: T, 3.1, 56.3, 89.3, 139.3, 140.3, 139.5.
strife of opposites: *3.8*, 44.1, 104.2, 111.5, 112.6, 176.3.
subject and object: 21.2, 40.1, 48.1, 57.3, 79.2, 90.6, 101.2, 102.6, 113.3, 155.2, *177.1*, 177.3, 186.3, 189.1, *196.2*, 236.4, 250.5.
suffering: 2.9, 3.9, 14.1, 28.3, 33.7, 33.8, 34.3, 36.3, *40.4*, 44.3, 46.3, 54.7, 56.2, *57.2*, 58.4, *70.3*, 70.5, 73.3, 73.4, 75.2, 78.4, 78.8, 79.4, 89.6, 90.3, 103.2, *105.3*, 113.2, 113.3, 115.2, 116.2, 125.1, 155.1, 168.9, 179.3, 200.1, 201.2, 201.6, 220.2, 229.3, 230.1, *232.1*, 234.4, 235.1, 235.2, 237.1, 238.2, 246.6, 259.4.
suicide: 24.3, *134.5*, 136.1, 139.1, 139.3, 144.1, 145.3, 184.2, 184.5, *185.1*, 196.4, 229.3, 259.1, *262.3*, *269.5*.
Suk, Pandit: 32.2, 32.4, 34.1, 93.2.
sun: *1.1*, 2.1, 10.1, 12.7, 16.3, 16.4, *17.1*, 17.2, 21.2, 32.2, 32.7, 33.2, 33.6, 78.3, 78.6, 86.2, 106.4, 114.3, 183.1, 183.3, 215.4, 224.2, 246.5, 276.1.
surrealism: 12.1, 54.6, 63.4, 167.5, 237.1, 280.3.
Swift, Jonathan: 10.1, 32.12, 34.3, 36.1, 46.3, 50.6, 70.2, 72.4, 72.5, 89.1, 90.6, 105.4, 110.3, 116.1, 117.5, 118.3, 131.3, 138.1,, 139.6, 156.5, 162.1, 167, 169.1, 170.1, 170.3, 177.2, 178.5, 202.1, 219.1, 220.4, 221.1, 227.4, 234.4, 257.5, 275.2.
syllogism: 16.1, 22.3, 207.6.
Synge, John Millington: 47.4, 106.1, 269.2, 272.1.
syzygy: 15.2, 54.8, *93.1*, 152.2.

A Tale of a Tub: 70.2, 72.5, 89.1, 90.6, 105.4, 118.3, 131.3, 138.1, 162.1, 167.3, 170.1, 170.3, 177.2, 178.5, 219.1, 220.4, 227.4.
Tantalus: 21.4, 121.2, 139.2.
Tate Gallery: 15.1, 73.11, 120.1, 196.3, 225.2.
Taylor, Jeremy: 41.1, 226.1.
TCD: a College Miscellany: 129.3, 215.2, 276.4.
Tenerife: *5.1*.
Tennyson, Alfred: 110.3, 153.4, 207.5, 223.4, 236.4.
Thackeray, William: *122.5*.
Thales: 6.3, 114.5.
Thames River: 12.9, 14.6, 14.7, 14.8, 15.1, 15.2, 16.4, 26.5, 26.6, 127.2.
thieves: 3.5, 5.7, 64.6, *213.2*.
thirteen: T, 276.1.
Thomas à Kempis: 8.1, 48.1, 78.4, *103.3*, 107.3, 162.3, 222.4, 236.3, 237.1, *246.4*.
Thompson, Geoffrey: 97.3, 158.1,
three: 9.1, 70.5, 90.1, 93.1, *111.3*, 112.3, 113.3, 181.2, 213.3, 222.3, 253.1.
Ticklepenny, Austin: *84.6*, 85.1, 86.2, 87.5, 156.5, 157.1, 170.2, 174.2, 204.1, 258.4, 262.3.
time: 1.1, 2.1, 4.5, 6.6, 6.7, 8.3, 9.2, 10.1, 12.6, 12.7, 12.8, 16.3, 16.5, 21.3, 24.3, 26.1, 26.3, 26.4, 26.5, 28.4, 34.2, 38.1, 40.4, 42.1, 46.1, 50.2, 64.7, 65.1, 65.6, 69.3, 74.1, 74.3, 75.3, 76.2, 78.4, 90.6, 107.4, 108.3, *109.1*, 111.6, 113.3, 114.1, 114.2, 114.3, 114.4, 114.5, 114.6, 114.7, 116.3, 122.4, 129.1, 137.1, 175.1, 181.2, 183.4, 216.3, 218.1, 224.2, 236.1, 241.3, 247.2, 250.6, 254.1.
Tintoretto: 140.4.
Tough, Ruby: 93.1.
Toynbee, Paget: 77.4, 78.4, 78.10.
tragedy: 86.6, 89.6, 109.5, 134.1, 201.6, 234.4, 254.2, 259.2.
The Trilogy: 109.1, 113.3, 116.1.
Trinity College: 3.2, 5.5, 16.1, 54.7, 58.1, 58.2, 84.6, 170.3, 178.8, 181.1, 195.1,

215.2, 224.4, 235.2, 243.2, 246.3.
Turner, Mairi: 142.1.
Turner, William: 120.1.
Twelfth Night: 207.2, 229.2, 234.2.
twins: *23.3*, 32.2, 61.2, 123.1, 156.5, 207.4, 207.5, 259.2, 260.3.
Tyburn: *11.4*, 18.2, 94.2.
Tynan, Kenneth: 61.3.

Ubi nihil vales: 20.2, 36.4, *109.1*, 156.1, 178.8, *178.9*, 240.1, 246.5.
Ulysses: T, 4.2, 21.2, 24.3, 26.2, 45.1, 46.2, 46.5, 54.1, 55.3, 62.3, 63.1, 65.1, 66.1, 92.2, 98.2, 100.2, 104.5, 131.5, 143.1, 168.7, 196.5, 201.6, 224.5, 254.3, 259.5, 262.3, 267.2, 277.2.
The Unnamable: 5.5, 90.3, 105.3, 105.5, 106.2, 109.1, 110.2, 113.1, 115.1, 168.1.
unreliable narration: 1.3, 2.2, 3.9, 10.1, 11.2, 11.3, 11.4, 63.1, 17.5, 26.1, 26.2, 26.3, 26.4, 26.7, 32.7, 32.13, 37.3, 42.1, 53.4, 62.1, 63.1, 65.6, 74.3, 78.2, 103.1, 106.6, 114.1, 114.3, 117.4, 120.2, 121.3, 123.1, 129.1, 139.1, 144.1, 153.3, 157.1, 163.1, 172.1, 203.3, 213.3, 227.1, 231.1, 244.7, 247.2, 249.1, 250.6, *262.3*, 267.3, *269.5*, 276.1.
Uranus: 33.3, 33.5, 175.2, 280.4.

vagitus: *71.4*.
Valéry, Paul [*Monsieur Teste*]: 79.2, 122.5, 189.3.
Vanity Fair: 63.3, 122.5.
Venus: 11.7, 33.5, 33.6, 37.1, 97.3, 238.4.
Vermeer: *228.1*.
Verne, Jules: 54.4.
Vico, Gianbattista: 21.5, 183.1.
Victoria Gate: 103.4, 103.5, 150.7.
Victoria, Queen: 95.2, 151.3, 277.1.
Villon, François: 192.1.
Virgil: 32.13, 87.2, 195.3, 207.5.
Virgil [Dante]: 78.1, 78.2, 78.3, 78.6.
Virgo [virgin]: *2.1*, 33.6, 114.3, 134.2, 215.5, 226.1, 263.3.
vision: 90.3, 102.6, 113.3, 155.2, 167.2, 252.2.
Vis Vitae Bread Co.: 74.7.
voice: 85.3, 92.1, 98.4, 101.3, *168.1*, 141.1, 149.1, 178.3, *185.2*, *229.3*, 234.2, 243.3.
Voltaire [*Candide*]: 4.4, 217.3, 232.1, 239.4, 244.8.
voyeurism: 60.2, 74.2, *90.3*, 217.2.

Waiting for Godot: 17.3, 28.4, 42.5, 123.1, 127.1, 156.5, *213.2*, 236.3, 246.3, 273.1.
'Walking Out': 7.4, 28.1, 217.2.
Walham Green: 95.2.
Wapping: 121.5.
war: 74.1, 128.1, 131.1, 151.1, 184.6, 187.3, 226.1, 258.2.
Watt: 2.8, 4.1, 5.3, 12.2, 17.3, 17.5, 24.3, 49.6, 58.5, 61.1, 66.1, 71.5, 103.3, 106.3, 110.3, 131.3, 140.3, 155.2, 167.2, 168.4, 183.1, 188.1, 184.6, 205.1, 218.5, 218.6, 228.6, 235.3, 246.6, 247.1, 251.2, 267.1, 275.2.
Watt, Henry: 80.3, 81.1.
Watts, G. F.: 152.1.
Webb, Eugene: 1.4, 62.3, 201.4.
Wellington, Duke of: 95.2, 179.7.
West Brompton: *1.3*, 22.1, 95.2, 120.3.
West, Mrs.: 5.5.

Printed and bound by CPI Group (UK) Ltd, Croydon, CR0 4YY

29/01/2025

01828169-0008